Knowledge, Options, and Institutions

Knowledge, Options, and Institutions

Bruce Kogut

OXFORD
UNIVERSITY PRESS

OXFORD
UNIVERSITY PRESS

Great Clarendon Street, Oxford OX2 6DP

Oxford University Press is a department of the University of Oxford.
It furthers the University's objective of excellence in research, scholarship,
and education by publishing worldwide in

Oxford New York

Auckland Cape Town Dar es Salaam Hong Kong Karachi
Kuala Lumpur Madrid Melbourne Mexico City Nairobi
New Delhi Shanghai Taipei Toronto

With offices in

Argentina Austria Brazil Chile Czech Republic France Greece
Guatemala Hungary Italy Japan Poland Portugal Singapore
South Korea Switzerland Thailand Turkey Ukraine Vietnam

Oxford is a registered trade mark of Oxford University Press
in the UK and in certain other countries

Published in the United States
by Oxford University Press Inc., New York

British Library Cataloguing in Publication Data
Data available

Library of Congress Cataloging in Publication Data
Data available

Typeset by SPI Publisher Services, Pondicherry, India
Printed in Great Britain
on acid-free paper by
Biddles Ltd., King's Lynn, Norfolk

ISBN 978–0–19–928252–4 (hb)
ISBN 978–0–19–928253–1 (pb)

10 9 8 7 6 5 4 3 2 1

To my mother, Kathleen Deutsch Kogut, who always provided a home and universe where love, warmth, intelligence, and uncommon common sense are the givens, and the rest, simply the logical consequence.

⬜ CONTENTS

PART IV **LOOKING FORWARD**

⬚ LIST OF FIGURES

⧉ LIST OF TABLES

☐ ACKNOWLEDGMENTS

I was very honoured when David Musson at Oxford University Press asked me to assemble a selection of articles for publication in a book. Somewhat characteristically, I was too engaged in all the many things I was currently doing, or would be doing, or I should be doing, that the project drifted. David patiently prodded me along. A proposed table of contents and explanation were sent to reviewers, who provided the very kind and useful advice to focus on a set of related themes. They told me what the title should be and their suggestion is pretty much the title of this collection. If you have been a reviewer of a book and if you have despaired that your time has not been rewarded by simple acknowledgement by the authors, no less by tangible evidence of having influenced the eventual product, despair no more. I assure you there is nothing so valuable as critique. Hopefully pleasant, but even when not, critique is a godsend, an anonymous gift, and, I would add, a prized example of how identity and participation in community swamps the motives to say, the heck with it, I am an island unto myself.

I have been fortunate in my career in participating in great institutions of learning. As I have always been fascinated by history, I recall finding it odd to read how far people travelled across the Western world by primitive means in order to take part in medieval universities. How mesmerizing, enticing is knowledge, how Faustian is the young heart's desire to know. I have learned in my own career that there is common sense, if the desire should be there, for the making of the journey. For time and place are not constants, institutions have their great yet transitory moments, like fire before its fundament is extinguished. At every institution where I have spent time, I can still see the faces of a few remarkable people who made a difference, not just as individuals, but as motors of a collective energy.

Editors, publishers, universities, institutions are more than the setting behind theatrical action. They are the silent partners to the text. I would like sincerely to thank David and Oxford University Press for their invitation to assemble the contents of this book, and Stephanie Paille for her patience and assistance. I would like to thank my colleagues and friends along my institutional journey for their support and for their tolerance of a mutual regret that journeys do not allow for multiple worlds of residence.

1 Introduction: Knowledge, Options, and Institutions

Bruce Kogut

An introduction to a collection of articles is a postscript disguised as a preface. Greek dramatists used a device to put the spectators immediately into the action, thus engaging them emotionally and rendering them empathically as actors in the performance. Since empathy is a behavioral cornerstone to the argument that follows, it is consistent to follow this device and to plunge right in. Across four levels of analysis (cognitive, micro, meso, and macro), we will traverse a discussion of neuroscience and behavioral studies on sociality as a dominant human motivation. The goal of this journey is to arrive at a critical review of current topics in management and strategy (e.g. resources, organizational economics) and an introduction to the subsequent chapters.

This book is a collection of articles published in the period of 1988 to 2005. It is my hope that together that they provide unification to otherwise disparate articles around one common insight: economic value is built on coordinated action among people with specialized and personal knowledge and who are members of a social community. It is the inherent sociality of people that provides the basis for sustained coordination. We some times have names for the *organizing principles* that coordinate this action, such as Taylorism or Kanban systems, but in most cases we do not. Because we often don't have names for these principles, we take them for granted and ignore them. It is my claim in these essays that the great advances in material and social wealth are built upon the principles that coordinate and organize action of people and other actors, including machines that are becoming ever more intelligent and purposeful.

The vision I hold of the workings of groups, firms, and larger entities such as countries and world systems is rooted in the cognitive foundation that people are social. This sociality is expressed not only in their awareness of the 'other,' but in the learning of social knowledge that informs beliefs and coordinates behavior. In the parlance of current economics, these beliefs are called equivalently norms and institutions. I prefer to hold the equivalence of norms and institutions in abeyance and to start with an eye on the intermediation of beliefs and institutions via social categories.

Categories are observable and correspond to important social and economic facts, such as profession or religion. The acquisition of social knowledge is the category formation of what is normal and abnormal, what is good and bad, who is like us and who is not like us, what works and what does not work. The fundamental link of the individual and the social is that categories are anchored in multiple and contradictory but shared identities: family, ethnic, class, status. Individuals are skilled navigators across these lexicographic orderings and are tolerant of contradictory claims, such as the moral behavior required by religious beliefs and the moral behavior as conducted in secular spheres. Individual behaviors become comprehensible in relation to our understanding of social identities and their associated learned repertoires.

I flag the concept of social identity at the outset in order to emphasize that sociality represents a fundamental re-orientation that is percolating in the social sciences and economics. The well-deserved fame of the essay by Mark Granovetter on economic action and social structure rests on his analysis of the under- and over-socialized view of individuals. The conventional sociological view is the description of a stage and the actors but there is no action because there is no individual choice; the conventional economic view is the isolated utility maximizer for whom well-ordered preferences, a budget constraint, and prices constitute sufficient data for decisions. The position to which I hold is that people's choices are influenced by 'relevant' others in their neighbourhood or social locality. Relevance pertains to those 'others' that people categorize as salient, with positive or negative attribution influenced by social identity and learning. Classifying triggers primed responses that are drawn from a repertoire of routines. These routines are the interdependent atoms that constitute the organizing principles (e.g. kanban systems) by which work is designed and coordinated among people in defined communities.

As most writers desire, I would like the message of these articles to be broadly understood. The above phrasing is relatively abstract, and yet it has the simple meaning that people care, for example, about status and fairness and love and hate. People react differently to the same stimuli not because they have a priori and given preferences. They react differently, as so many classic experiments in social psychology have shown, depending upon the cues in their social context. Since, for example, status requires that people classify others as higher and lower along a dimension, we employ categories that say, people who graduate from my school are better than some other school. It is a common place understanding that humans assign considerable meaning to these rather arbitrary distinctions, such as skin color, social rank, religion, and occupation.

In the following pages, I propose to establish first why sociality is an appropriate framing for human motivation that excludes neither altruistic, nor selfish motivations. The section argues that behavioral economics drove the social from a previous tradition of 'social pyschology' and has only belatedly, by the impoverishment of many of its results, backed into a creeping acceptance that society is present. The subsequent section presents the neuroscience evidence for sociality and against a narrow supposition of either altruism or selfishness. The next four sections trace the implications of sociality across four levels discussed in the chapters in this book. In doing so, I explain why there are currently two contending theoretical domains in the study of organizations and knowledge: organizational economics and organizational sociology. Both of these domains should be founded on a common psychology.

As I have learned much from the field of evolutionary economics and in particular from Richard Nelson and Sid Winter, I would like to acknowledge that this tradition provides a useful arena to meld economics and sociology through an appropriate emphasis on dynamics and change; my interpretation of this dialogue, however, may not be shared by many in this field. Particular bodies of work, such as the resource-based view of strategy, are theoretically incomplete and if they were to be complete, they would align along one of these two theoretical domains. I propose that such areas as cognition and templates are promising areas of investigation that are fruitfully absorbed into a sociological treatment of knowledge. In short, my argument is to condense the theoretical basis of organizational and strategy studies along the two axes of economics and sociology, while attending carefully to historical and case context. In my view, we cannot achieve this parsimony until we agree upon the innate and learned motivations of people. There is sufficient scientific evidence on which we should be able to agree, and it is this evidence that I would like to review first.

Behavioral Experiments and Society

Armed with extensive studies, social science research consistently finds evidence for the power of social context and for categories. Some of these studies are remarkable in their findings, even if by today's standards, ethically challenged.

Consider two classic social psychology studies, chosen because they indicate, one, that people understand themselves socially and, two, interpretations are influenced by categorization of the situation.

1. In a famous study of the construal processes underlying emotional experience, Stanley Schachter and Jerome Singer (1962) showed that people who are aroused by an injection of adrenaline can be influenced to

experience anger, euphoria, or fear, depending on the situation in which they are placed, even though the chemical stimulus is the same. It is the construal of situations aided by cues from other people that determines precisely which emotion will be experienced.

2. Based on a series of experiments at Yale University between 1961 and 1962, Stanley Milgram (1974) found that 65 percent of the subjects, residents of New Haven, were willing to apply electric shocks-up to 450 volts-to a protesting victim, because a scientific authority commanded them to do this, and despite that the victim clearly did not deserve such punishment. A construal of the social context *categorized* as hierarchical authority lead to acted-upon behaviors that treated the victim inhumanly.

Why are these experiments still meaningful? Many experiments show that arbitrary and artificial groups assigned in experimental conditions instill identities, categories, and perceptions of 'in' and 'out.' The assumption in economics and in many social sciences is that preferences or cognition determines choice. People are racist, hence they segregate. But these experiments suggest a reciprocal causality. People are segregated, hence they are racist. Segregation is associated, by definition, with a category of type 'A' as opposed to 'B.' Segregation only makes sense in reference to a category. Consequently categorization and self-categorization are prior to the problem of racism.

Categorization reveal when people make negative attributions about 'outsiders.' The tendency of firms to reject 'not invented here' ideas implies that evaluations of economic merit is influenced by social categories. After all, the boundary of a firm requires a category that distinguishes 'here' and 'there.' By the same functional mechanism, people inside a firm attribute bad intentions to behaviors of outsiders that would be justified if done by insiders. The boundaries of the firm lead to the perception of higher transactions costs of the market compared to those inside the firm, regardless of whether in fact people act better or worse as insiders or as outsiders. Transactions costs do not determine boundaries; boundaries determine the perception of transaction costs.

These two experiments are legendary in social psychology and in undergraduate college courses. But for whatever reasons, their powerful and pathological demonstrations of sociality as a principle mechanism in choice and in action were ignored in economics and inadequately codified in sociology. Instead, in economics and increasingly so in political science and, to a lesser extent, in sociology, the principal psychological mechanism in the dominant theory of rational choice has been the individual's pursuit of self-gratification. The individual precedes choice.

This belief in individual choice has many reasonable justifications. To name two, it leads to mathematically tractable analysis and it is consistent with the political philosophy of liberalism and hence of capitalism and democracy. Economics is largely the study of exchange and production in capitalist economies. These are good reasons to defend the theoretical importance of assuming exclusively self-interest. However, the assumption comes at great cost.

Economics has been highly cognizant of the limitations of its definition of rationality as pursuit of self-interest and complete information. Early fixes, such as the proposition of Gary Becker regarding altruism, is to add in a concern for others as part of an individual's utility function. This fix still treats choice as rational in reference to a priori preferences. Others have not sought fixes and have taken pleasure in measuring the size of the holes in the Swiss cheese of economic rationality. Anomalies in the classic sense of Thomas Kuhn's description of scientific revolutions are bountiful. A Nobel Prize has been awarded to psychologists and economists who have meticulously uncovered the *behavioral* contradictions of observed choices with decision theory. Most of this work is psychological, not social psychological. The adjectival qualification of *behavioral* has the meaning of empirical observations from structured laboratory experiments on individuals, which despite their yield of insights, are designed to minimize the social influence among participants. Their results have not adequately accounted for society and social interactions.

The limitations to laboratory experiments that make social science claims are revealed in the many experiments testing game theoretic ideas. In the very first experiments of the so-called prison dilemma, the two Rand economists John Williams and Armen Alchian failed to optimize jointly because the differences between their pay-offs caused one to demand compensation in order to make the winnings equals; their pay-offs were asymmetrical. As Udo Zander and I note (Chapter 4), sociality struggles to emerge even in these most arid and socially deprived contexts. It is this deprivation of sociality and the human insistence to express it that is often the most startling untold story of laboratory experiments.

Of course, the world also seeps into the laboratory in other ways. Even in purely individual cognitive experiments, such as asking people to guess sizes of cities, we know people seek cues from the names, e.g. assuming that capital cities are larger (Ortmann and Gigerenzer 1997). There are vanity experiments that rely upon relatively sophisticated mathematic skills involved in calculating what should I do knowing that you know what I know that you know, etc. (Ho et al. 2004). Very often, intelligent people fail these tests. But we also find people failing to get the right answer to arithmetic problems and then performing the same calculations in purchasing groceries. There is plenty of reason to suspect people, often undergraduate students, don't behave the same way in a laboratory than they do buying a used car.

Recent efforts to isolate the social influences in experiments are a promising development. Economics has been rightly fascinated by a particular anomaly, called the ultimatum bargaining game, which touches upon our 'unsocial sociality' and the norms of fairness. This experiment, due to Gueth et al. (1982), has generated a large literature and many variations. The simple idea is the following. An individual is given €10. He can offer a portion of the sum to a second individual. If the second individual refuses the offer, the entire sum is lost. If it is accepted, the first individual keeps the residual. The exchange is conducted only once, and both individuals know this is a one-shot trans-action. (Variations on this experiment can include a sequence of exchanges.) The rational decision by the second individual is to accept whatever is offered, for even one centime is more than nothing. Thus, the first person should make a small offer; even a few centimes should be sufficient. And yet, the observed behaviors are that either the first person offers close to a 50/50 split or the second person tends to reject any offer which is viewed as 'unfair.'

Samuel Bowles and colleagues (2003) collaborated to test the universality of these results. The study consisted of running a few experimental games, principally the ultimatum game, in field settings in 15 locations populated by small-scale societies. The experiments replicated the design of identical experiments conducted on university students in developed countries. The offers and responses are made anonymously. Many of these societies were located in remote regions. In all, they represented a variety of social, economic, and cultural conditions. The study is more impressive for its ambition than for its design. The primary finding is that the subjects in these different cultures perform quite differently than university students used in prior experiments. Thus, behaviors that could be classified as 'selfish' or as 'fair' vary by societies. Individual predictors (e.g. wealth, income, age) of the average mean offer were not important. Two variables appeared to matter: whether the society was based on cooperation in its economic activities and whether it engaged often in market exchange. Society mattered to the results.

If the ever present effect of society is the central learning in this experiment, then we have to ask in how many other experiments has society crept in through the cracks under the doors and through the window frame to inform the responses of the 'subjects.' Do these findings not say that if you want to understand social responses of people even in controlled settings, you need to have a theory of society?

It is not my claim that laboratory experiments cannot contribute to our knowledge; to the contrary, their results are often fascinating and illuminating. I make rather the following claim: as our laboratory lens moves from trying to link individual choice and individual cognition to individual choice and social interaction, society and sociality must be taken into account. An example of the former (individual choice and individual cognition) is an experiment that wishes to understand if risk aversion is symmetrical, that is whether people make the same cost/benefit tradeoff when they are in a winning versus losing context can focus on individual choice. If however the claim is that people make choices in reference to 'sociality' and the experiment isolates the individual, then there is something peculiar in this research design. And its possible to capture social influences by appropriately designed field experiments (see, e.g. Shang and Croson 2006).

The fascination of research communities is that progress is sometimes made by false starts. By putting the laboratory into the field, we find that social laboratories are not sealed experiments in a frictionless and zero gravity environment. Social context matters, because people are members of communities and society engaged in fairly predictable patterns of interaction and behavior that may have, curiously, unpredictable collective outcomes. This conclusion, however simple, is the foundation to the social sciences.

Return of Sociality: Social Neuroscience and Cognitive Foundations

The logical inference from the above discussion is that the better research design for understanding sociality is to observe interactions among people. This argument between the isolated individual and the social individual is an old saw and you know by now my view on this argument. Let's therefore put it aside and turn surprisingly not to society but to the brain as the level of analysis to support the importance of sociality as a dominant human motive. By the brain, I mean the explosion of studies in the neurosciences that have been enabled in recent years through the invention of imaging technologies.

I prefer to call these studies social neuroscience. Others have proposed neuroeconomics, or social cognition neuroscience (see Ochsner and Lieberman 2001; Camerer et al. 2005). It is a non-trivial proposal that the broader social science appellation be used instead of any particular disciplinary label. After all, if it is true that there is a neural hardwiring to emotions and cognitions, we will have established a foundation that must apply to all social sciences.

I acknowledge a caveat. The studies of the brain now being used in the social sciences rely on an assumed correlation of brain activity location and function. This assumption implies a 'modular' theory of the brain, or what Marvin Minsky called 'the society of mind.' A rival to modularity theory is connectionism. Both theories admit aspects of the other as being valid, but differ in the weight they attach to modular/local functionalities or to connectionist/distributed processing. There is considerable debate over the relative merits of these two theories of brain versus mind, with conflicting evidence pointing to functional impairment due to localized damage of brain tissues and also pointing to the ability of the brain to compensate for some kinds of damage. I will sensibly not comment on this debate, even if it has obvious parallels to competing theories of organizations. Rather my interest here is to exploit the recent literature that links particular parts of the brain to concepts such as fairness, empathy, and sociality.

The brain reveals many levels of modularized activity. At the most general level, the brain topography consists of two systems.[1] The first is the sub-cortical region that includes the brain stem and striatum; the stem releases neurotransmitters such as dopamines which the striatum receives. The basal ganglia ('the reptilian brain') is located near the core, where neural circuits of long-standing habit are formed and held. This part of the brain supports those 'routine' or 'skilled' activities, such as bicycle riding, that is an important component of tacit and implicit knowledge. The amygdala is part of this cortical structure and is critically involved in gauging the emotional significance of events and perceptions, or what constitutes 'social intelligence.' Through its connections with those brain regions that process sensory experiences, it permits perception to trigger automatic emotional responses despite inattention.

A second major system of the brain is the neocortex that consists of the higher order functions of reasoning and judgment. One-third of the neocortex is the prefrontal cortex located toward the front of the brain and responsible for 'executive decisions,' consisting of short-term (working) memory, decision-making, and judgments. These parts of the brain are also connected to emotion-related areas of the brain. However, for simplicity, neuroeconomic studies ignore these connections and focus on the reasoning abilities and the capacity for cognitive control—that is, the ability to guide thought and action in association with abstract goals or intentions and to counter emotional reflexes.

An important limitation should be kept in mind: these studies do not measure directly the brain function but brain activity.[2] For example, functional magnetic resonance imaging (fMRI) measures blood flow. Thus, the observations identify regions of the brain that correlate with the manifest experimental observations, namely the behavior or expressed attitude of the subjects. In many of the studies, attitudes and behaviors (such as racist attitudes as opposed to racist behaviors) do not activate the same part of the brain. The technology of imaging favors looking at neural activity related to transactions or beliefs among people as opposed to their on-going procedural coordination. As organizational knowledge emphasizes the procedural relative to the transactional, this technological bias should be kept in mind.

IMITATION AND TECHNOLOGY TRANSFER

What then would be important examples of neuroscience studies that support a view of social knowledge as founded on human sociality with implications for learned behaviors and identities? Consider imitation and technology transfer which are discussed in the chapters that follow. By the above description, and by considerable evidence, information that is not familiar activates the prefrontal cortex. Thus, successful technology transfer could be seen as the gradual passage of new knowledge that necessitates a lot of hard cerebral work to encoding in learned responses stored in long-term and automatic memory.

This transfer is effected through the imitation of observed behaviors. As many studies show (and cited in the essays below), technology transfer often involves the movement of people who have these skills to teach others. This particular type of learning poses the question of what is the cognitive process triggered by the presence of another individual.

We know that humans have an exceptional ability to empathize with the other. One reasonable mechanism is that people can mentally simulate the other person's reasoning. A popular but controversial claim is that this simulation implies a 'theory of the mind' or 'mentalizing.' This theory claims that an evolved capability consists of the ability to simulate and hence to 'mind read' the other person's thoughts, emotions, or intentions. By this 'theory of mind' model, I watch you ride a bike and attempt to develop a mental map that indicates a theory of riding a bicycle: maintain dynamic equilibrium by peddling sufficiently fast.

However, the cognitivist's theory of mind bumps against the familiar objections. The controversy is multiple, but what I find interesting is that it echoes the Gilbert Ryle debate regarding if an individual acts upon a theory or upon a codebook. In his concept of mind—discussed in Kogut and Zander, Chapter 4, Ryle dismissed the 'category error' of Descartes in thinking there are separate physical and mental processes. Instead, Ryle proposed that cognition is a mental act. The cognitive problem is that when we observe someone doing an act that we want to learn, this visual perception still must be translated into a series of motor commands. This mind/body problem has a purely neural analogue.

Recent evidence claims that imitation does not rely upon a mental model of the other's actions but is neurally hardwired and hence involves automatic responses.[3] An Italian research team discovered serendipitously that monkeys (macaques) observing another monkey evidenced similar neural activity to the observed individual (monkey or human). Subsequent research confirmed similar evidence for 'mirror neurons' in humans. In an article summarizing these results, the Italian researchers Rizzolatti, Fogassi, and Gallese (2006: 367–88), write that

much as circuits of neurons are believed to store specific memories within the brain, sets of mirror neurons appear to encode templates for specific actions. This property may allow an individual not only to perform basic motor procedures without thinking about them but also to comprehend those acts when they are observed, without any need for explicit reasoning about them.

These conclusions are of particular interest to the empirical study in this book (Chapter 3) which shows the impediment to transfer when technology cannot be well articulated in written materials. A dozen studies indicate that technology transfer is very rarely produced by the sharing of documentation. 'Codifiability' of experience in manuals is accompanied by other means of leaning, such as apprenticeship, perhaps because our neural circuitry is keyed to imitate visual images. There is much more work to be done here, and it is exciting to look forward to a greater understanding of the media of transfer (e.g. written, verbal, visual) and of proximity of the 'other' (e.g. co-present, virtual).

SOCIALITY AND EMPATHY

Sociality implies the capability of one person to feel empathy for another. Empathy is the identification with and understanding of another's situation, feelings, and motives. Parsing this process, two distinct capabilities are required: the ability to perceive the other person's situation and emotions and the ability to experience this perception by sharing the emotion. The first, as discussed before, can involve 'mind reading,' whereas the second is more strictly 'empathic.'[4]

Studies on mental deficits, such as autism and Asperger's syndrome, differentiate clearly parts of the brain that perform these acts. People with autism are fearful to look into another person's eyes, as signaled in hyperactivity of the amygdala. They perceive other people well, but the perception fires the wrong response. They fail to read emotions. Moreover, brain scans show a lack of activity in another part of the brain that signals fascination.[5] The autistic individual is triply in deficit: overly fearful and unable to read emotions and oddly disinterested in the other.

By contrast, an individual who is not autistic is able to read emotions of others and is interested in doing so. But how is this possible? Gallese (2004) proposes a concept of 'embodied simulation' in where there is a range of 'mirror-matching mechanisms' that simulate another person's emotions. He describes experiments in which the same neurons were activated in anaesthetized but awake patients who observed a noxious mechanical simulation applied to their hands *or* to the examiner's fingers. He cites a deficit study of a patient who suffered stroke damage to cortical and subcortical structures. The patient could therefore neither experience nor express disgust and could not represent and detect this emotion in others. This conclusion implies that the pathological case of 'no disgust' implies conversely that the feeling of shared disgust, or empathy, is a taken-for-granted attribute of fundamental sociality.

IDENTITY AND SOCIAL CATEGORIES

An important claim in the theory of the firm as embedding knowledge in social communities is the importance of identity. There is a very large literature on identity in the social psychology and organizational behavior (see, e.g. Ibarra 1999). I will confine my attention to the studies that *imply* a neural basis of identity and categorization. These studies have largely focused on the differences in neural processing in response to racial priming.

The studies are rather simple and yet provocative. In one study, people were tested for racial bias (Richeson et al. 2003). White subjects interacted with white and black partners. Those testing higher for racial bias showed they were more impaired in their executive control when interacting with black counterparts, thus indicating that they exhausted these mental resources momentarily. By implication, interactions with black partners caused those with racist indications to rely less on automatic cognitive processes and more on reflective processes. A subsequent study by Fehr and Fishbacher (2003) used brain scanning to show that indeed the executive control resources were more expended by those testing higher for race. Phelps et al. (2000) found racist attitudes were found to be associated with amygdala and emotional activation.

These studies suggest the following interpretation. Individuals have identities defined in reference to 'others.' These others are classified into groups, such as those like me and those not like me, or those I know and those I don't know. When we encounter a person whom we classify as sharing an identity, our response is automatic. When we do not classify the person as sharing our identity or as unfamiliar, we rely more upon our non-automatic processes.

Studies on race are convenient insofar as race, being primed by visual attributes (e.g. color), provides an obtrusive stimulus to self-and-other categorization. The above studies indicate that people vary in their racial attitudes, and these lead to different cognitive responses. More broadly, the mechanism is stereotype activation, in which we categorize relative to self-identity, thus activating a stereotype.

There are also many studies that indicate 'contagion.' We have all known that laughter, yawning, and tears can be contagious. Interestingly, identities also seem to be oddly influenced, however temporarily, allowing emotions and stereotyping to be jointly triggered indexically. Thus Dijksterhuis (2005) notes that people who are primed by watching soccer (football) hooligans score subsequently worse on mental tests; conversely they do better when primed by videos of professors of whom they hold a stereotype of being smart. Barring students from faculty meetings prior to their exams appears to be the sensible recommendation.

SOCIALITY AND ALTRUISM

Zander and I borrowed an expression from Kant that people are marked by an 'unsocial sociality' (see Chapter 4). In fact, people are not the most sociable of animals; many animals evidence far more preference for sustained group membership than humans. This standpoint of an unsocial sociality has provoked the criticism that it implies a utopian view of human motivation (see Foss, 1996, for example), whereas it is fairly neutral in this regard. In fact, the dark side of identity—as we all painfully know—is that outsiders are often castigated and maligned.

Still, there is evidence that people feel rewarded when doing good and when their good deeds are reciprocated. Fehr et al. (2005) found by neural imaging that people received positive utility from cooperating with people relative to computers. Moreover, Singer et al. (2004) observed that likeability increased for people who were seen as cooperators; people like those who seem to be morally good. In another experiment, Zak et al. (2005) took blood samples from subjects who played a generous/selfish game, and found those dyads in which the exchange was generous had higher levels of ocytoxin—a hormone associated with feelings of happiness.

Clearly, cooperation and emotions are linked by an implied sense of moral judgment. As noted in Chapter 4, experiments among students show a tendency to over-punish defectors; people choose sanction levels in excess of deterrence and at an excessive (economically irrational) cost. Fehr et al. (2005) observe neural activity indicating positive utility in sanctioning defectors. People enjoy sanctioning those who they perceive as acting immorally. In analysis of that sentiment, many a novel has been written.

Micro-Foundations: Division of Labor and Coordination

My intention in reviewing the studies in neuroscience is to establish that sociality is a foundational concept that is linked to such processes as imitation and transfer, categorization, and identity. Having made this argument, I now turn to analyzing the social interactions among people and to what extent such interactions can be said to constitute 'knowledge.' In this regard, I would like to state clearly that I disagree with the claim that knowledge is only an individual level concept. Sometimes, this claim is stated as 'organizations don't think.'

First, I view one valid analysis of knowledge as the fuzzy partitioning of people, objects, and tasks and the categorical relationships among these partitions.[6] In the context of an economy, we call this partition the division of labor; their relations can be expressed as an input–output table. These specializations can be coded as industrial–such as in the industrial nomenclature used by governments, but this nomenclature is misleading. More telling is that as the treelike partitioning of the division of labor proceeds, specializations appear, some unique to the branch, some common across branches. These specializations are occupational (e.g. the accountant, the steelworker) and organizational (e.g. steel firms, divisions within firms). If we choose to, we could also assign work associations (e.g. unions) or professional associations (e.g. chartered accountants) to these industrial trees. It is in fact the crossing of these specializations—their concatenations—that Harrison White (1992) claims creates the spaces of conflict and innovation.

The complexity of these relations is difficult to understand statically and even more difficult to grasp dynamically. The last chapter of this book provides a perspective on how to understand knowledge as evolving from simple rules. Here, I wish to make the observation is that it is farfetched to view diverse individuals as holding shared templates, or engaging in processes of socialization, that lead to a sort of a holographic understanding. A division of labor is also a cognitive division, in which I understand only my local environment and have mastered only a few competences. The advancement of society depends upon the structuring of my interactions with competent others. This structuring depends first upon the partition (categories in the division of labor), second upon our compliance to norms of exchange (institutions), and third to the processes (capabilities) in which we are engaged.

KNOWLEDGE IS ENCODED IN STRUCTURE

Before explaining these ideas, let me use a parable of the brain-chip to explain why knowledge is more than just individuals. Imagine that a technology has been invented that scans our brains and each one of us is individually encapsulated in a 'chip.' These chips are thrown into one large bin. A powerful computer then simulates an economy by assigning randomly each chip to a category (e.g. accounting) and to an organization (e.g. a car company). Even if we could be identified categorically (Paul does finance), or by a partial order (Betty is smarter than Jean Pierre), our joint contributions would not 'add linearly' but interactively. No individual could possibly understand a priori the best outcome, and indeed it would take even our imaginary computer an infinite time to work out the best solution even for a very small population.

Yet, it is this allocation that economies and organizations make. Major innovations, such as partnerships or secondary markets, have nothing to do with the knowledge in the head of particular individuals but simply in establishing new organizational and institutional technologies. In a very elegant set of experiments, Rao and Argote (2005) showed that even for a simple economy, a division of labor resulted in better performance when turnover of people was high. Structure *structures* the routine interaction among people; structure encodes knowledge.

Let's rephrase this debate between knowledge as located only in heads or also in structures by posing a question: do societies and economies think? Yes, they think if it is meant that they are computationally exploring better connections and allocations. We have in fact rather intriguing models by which societies and economies evolve by computing better allocations through local decisions but in the context of particular structures and institutions (see for example Axtell and Epstein 2004). The system dynamics drive the evolutionary process of which individuals (including social scientists) can have only partial knowledge. If we have only partial knowledge, then the residual is the knowledge in the system, or as I explain in the final chapter, of the network. The network, being structure and hence generatively an expression of structuring, is knowledge.

Perhaps what people mean in objecting that only people think is that economies, firms, and organizations are not 'conscious.' It seems correct that consciousness is not a property of social systems. At the same time, consciousness in terms of the 'shared template' or of the contents of the 'socialization' is not an obvious property of individuals and teams either. In other words, consciousness is neither well defined in these studies, nor obviously relevant. At the same time, thinking—if it is meant the process for evolving better solutions—is a property of both individuals and social systems.

SMITH AND BABBAGE ECONOMIES AND THE SELFISH POSTULATE

Let's leave this digression, and turn to the explanation of why sociality, categories, and identities are primary dimensions to understanding social and economic behavior. Given our discussion of a division of labor, one can not choose a more pertinent contextualization than considering Adam Smith's discussion. Smith describes an economy where tasks are specialized. Borrowing from his reading of a French text in the *Encyclopédie*, Smith used the example of the pin factory, in which the drawing of the wire, its cutting, its hammering were done through a process of discrete and sequential steps. It was early recognized that as much as a division of labor implied specialization, it also implied coordination. Specialization and coordination are analytically joined.

In his discussions of the labor problems of the early and mid-1800s, the brilliant engineer called the father of the computer, Charles Babbage, proposed a related concept of a 'division of mental labor.'[7] He borrowed with full recognition a French example, this time of the renowned mathematician de Prony. De Prony was asked by Napoleon to tabulate logarithmic and trigonometric tables to comply with the adoption of the decimal system. By one of the interesting quirks of history, de Prony fell upon Adam Smith's book and the introduction of the division of labor of pins and decided to apply the principle to calculate logarithms. He did so by organizing workers into three groups who performed the calculations of an algorithm. This algorithm entailed taking the second differences of the squares of numbers. The first consisted of a few mathematicians, including de Prony and Legendre, who designed the formulae (or algorithms to be used). The second group, consisting of six to eight people, supplied the numbers to the formulae. The largest group of about 60 people simply took first differences. From this human calculating organization, logarithms were calculated to several decimals.[8] This human organization employed the algorithm that formed the basis for Babbage's mechanical invention, his 'difference engine.'

In this story of de Prony, we have the exemplary illustration of the generation of economically—and socially—valuable knowledge by organizing principles which are only locally understood by individuals who are (partially) ordered categorically and hierarchically: mathematicians, skilled labor, relatively less skilled. The engineer Babbage noted that Smith did not have an economic concept of the division of labor, noting that tasks required different skill levels and it would thus be economical that the more skilled should specialize in the more difficult tasks and be differentially paid for it. Thus, arguing from scarcity in skills and the variation of difficulty in tasks, Babbage arrived at an economic argument for the hierarchical division of physical and mental labor.

Smith and Babbage expressed in their treatises on the division of labor disparaging views of human motivation. I call this the erred postulate of selfishness. Smith's portrayal of the selfishness of human pursuit contradicts his earlier writings and even passages in the *Wealth of Nations*. Rhetorically, the argument is brilliant: let's assume you are right, he said to his critics, that people are bad, and I will show you nevertheless that a liberal market economy will harness individual selfishness to create collective wealth. Babbage, it is required to note, had a far more pessimistic view of workers, believing that machines disciplined their idleness.

Is selfishness important to understanding the working of the Smith and Babbage economies, or simply a rhetorical device for Smith and bad temperament of Babbage? This question brings us to a central claim in many of the papers included in this book, namely that selfishness is not logically necessary for the explanation of firms and organizations. By necessary, we mean the logical statement that when you see an organization, you will *always* find selfishness as the explanation (or part of the explanation) for its existence.

Not necessary does not mean that there are no cases where selfishness leads to organizational solutions. It just means that it is an empirical question when selfishness leads to organizations, and when something else leads to organizations.

CATEGORIES, IDENTITIES, AND COORDINATION

What Udo Zander and I proposed is that an organizational sociology of knowledge provides an alternative explanation that does not rely on the necessity of selfishness as a motivation. This knowledge is held in social communities that attach meaning to categories and to organizational boundaries. Social value and meaning are ascribed to the division of labor in knowledge, such as physics and chemistry, finance and marketing, skilled and unskilled. Attached to these categories are invariably strong values, if not about status, then about what constitutes membership and how members talk, communicate, and coordinate their activities.

Identities are an emotional commitment to a community and its categorization. As an emotional commitment, there are associated pleasures of interacting with other category members and the associated displeasure of witnessing violations of normative expectations. The moral attributions caused by the identification with a firm are critical to understanding why people often volunteer their labor to a firm and often feel betrayed by it. Whereas an economics that focuses only material incentives struggles to convert status rankings into potential monetary rewards captured through future job offers, an organizational sociology has less qualms in observing the dialectic between 'intrinsic' and 'extrinsic' incentives.[9]

A fair objection to this perspective is that some social and economic categories are socially neutral but simply computationally necessary. Our brains use tricks of categorization to save on limited memory. Work in memory affirms that we have limited 'registers' for storing information; a famous doctrine was that the typical person stores only seven digits plus/minus two in short-term memory (Miller 1956) It is easier for us to classify companies as energy generation or services than by smaller and multiple aggregations. Ezra Zuckerman (1999) found evidence that analysts discount conglomerates because of the difficulty of assigning them to a single category; these overworked analysts effectively taxed the valuation of a corporation for having taxed their cognitive capabilities.

Even though there are neurological limitations to memory, categories are not semantically 'pre-existing' (see Lakoff 1987; and Chapter 4, this volume). Our minds may be categorizing instruments, but the categories are learned. Not surprisingly, to those that work in these classifications, being a nuclear engineer means something different than being a mechanical engineer. According to our earlier review of neuroscience studies, it does not surprise me that we find people relying upon automatic neural processing when talking among those of the same category and upon the pre-frontal cortex when encountering the other category.

The claim of the essays in this book is that the coordination problems posed by a division of labor ensue from collective impediments of identities lodged in social categories. To suffer coordination failure, it is not necessary for physicists to be conniving, or chemists possessed by guile. Groups can fail to coordinate because they fundamentally do not understand the corresponding codes and domains of expertise.

Coordination can have a very technical meaning in economics. The classic treatment of the problem is a situation of two parties choosing the right decision when they can neither communicate, nor signal each other. Thomas Schelling won the Nobel Prize for recognizing that these types of problems could only be solved if there was prior knowledge, or what is sometimes called 'common knowledge.' By design, Schelling's analysis removed incentive conflicts and hence selfishness as a motive. Failure occurs simply because people do not share sufficient 'common knowledge' to predict what the other wants or will do. As a result, coordination proceeds by heuristics based on norms, for example when lost, go to the biggest building in town. But since norms are local, this heuristic would fail us in the woods. Thus, Schelling created by implication a very rich insight, namely that institutions are coordinating devices in societies in which knowledge is specialized and local.

Stephen Postrel (2002) provides a simple and insightful model along these lines to show that communication errors can lead to coordination failures independent of incentive conflicts. The model consists of two divisions, production and marketing, who communicate with some error. If the divisions were perfect in their capabilities, they would not need to communicate. However, if they commit errors, an organization needs a transpecialist to translate so that marketing knows when production has erred, and vice versus. In this way, a transpecialist is a valuable substitute in organizations in which individual division capabilities are rather low. This coordinating contribution is valuable without consideration if one division is trying to cheat the other.

Game theory as applied to coordination has usually very restrictive assumptions. We use a broader definition of coordination in these papers, though I find it very useful to keep this stylized treatment of coordination as a baseline. The following essays propose that a firm qua community has the property of enhancing coordination, communication, and learning. In contradistinction to many economic theories that emphasize how firms via incentives solve failures, these essays present a theory of why firms are sometimes more capable than 'markets' (meaning other firms!) in performing their activities. Economic value is derived from the social knowledge held by individuals who are heedful of their membership in a social entity, be it their immediate working group, division, or firm.

Meso-Organizational Behavior: Knowledge in Research and in Practice

The last section addressed the issue of the division of labor and the relation to the learning of social categories through identity. The social learning of categories, and their relations among each other, can be construed as supporting a 'social construction of knowledge.' It is useful to understand my agreement and objections to this approach as a preface to my definitions of organizational knowledge.

A beautiful example of this approach is the essay by Pinch and Bijker on the evolution of design in bicycles (Pinch and Bijker 1984). An amusing part of the history is the many attempts to invent a bicycle that would permit a lady to peddle without having to straddle it. Here we have a clash between the category of behavior appropriate to a lady and the mechanical demands to produce feasible and efficient machines. Eventually, these efforts to maintain social norms were too costly, and more efficient compromises were found.

However, as much as I admire this work for its brilliance in curbing the strong technological determinism that is rooted very deeply in economics, management, and in specialized fields of engineering design, it does not prove the counter position that 'all is socially constructed.' A physical world consists of important constraints on the realization of the human imagination. Gravity and death are two examples.

The distinction between physical facts and social facts is fundamental. John Searle (1995) notes that some facts are physical: the weather is warm today. Other facts are social: this piece of paper money is worth €5.[10] To some, the latter seems to imply that because the world is socially constructed, there is no realism. To the contrary, Searle argues that the common recognition of a social fact is the foundation for realism. Searle notes that 'institutions' are social facts that are real: the Prime Minister is Gordon Brown and the Prime Minister's is the highest political office in the United Kingdom government are physical and social facts, respectively. Institutions are social facts that express legitimated assignation of authority and normative rules. They are not physical facts, but they exist in reference to assigned roles and constitutional rules.

CATEGORIES AS PROTOTYPES

The chapter with John Paul MacDuffie and Charles Ragin in this book represents the most explicit statement of an investigation of truth claims of social categories despite incomplete knowledge. The chapter deals simultaneously with two interests: the categorization by *prototype* and the contingent *truth* claims of social science. This chapter consists of an analysis of whether a prototype category, called the Toyota Production System, is associated with superior performance. The category is socially constructed, as is the performance metric, but we can nevertheless ask if there is a relation between category and metric. I agree with Ragin that knowledge in social sciences is comparative; I am referring here to his two path-breaking books on methodology (1987, 2000). Social science is an iteration between a researcher and a domain of physical and social facts, to which we attach a domain of plausible logical relations. I am content with a notion of 'plausibility' in place of 'causality' in which the inquiry is to establish a set of empirical or logical relations whose truth claims are valid in one or many possible worlds. An ideal goal of an inquiry is to establish a logical relation whose truth claim applies to all worlds. This is unrealistic. In the world of automobile manufacturers who are engaged in constructing more efficiently automobiles, auto plants having a higher category membership in Toyota methods performed comparatively better than those that did not. The result surely is not true of all possible worlds, such as plants existing before or in the future.[11]

The strength of comparative research is to investigate truth claims across possible worlds. Of course, as Galton taught us in the nineteenth century, observed worlds are often contaminated by diffusion. Armed with this proviso, it is useful to ask: do I observe X when I see outcome Y? This question poses whether the requirements to establish necessity are met. Or we can ask, when we see the outcome Y, do we observe also X? Here we are asking if X is sufficient for Y.

These are old concepts in logic, which are bread and butter of mathematical proofs found in formal social science. In many instances, they imply a definition that knowledge is justified belief. The justification is conformity with logic. From an empirical perspective, however, the data given to us for social science research rarely are sufficient to establish this justification. The best we are usually (always?) able to say is that, in the world of experimental design in which we can isolate undergraduate students in a laboratory, we find that

X is necessary for Z with a probability of 0.95 or more. However, this possible world of laboratory experiments may be quite far removed from the world of interest, namely the uncontrolled reality of every day life.

KNOWLEDGE IN PRACTICE

In practice, knowledge is rarely if ever justified by meeting even implicitly the criteria of logic. The epistemological requirements are too strenuous and are also likely to discount a lot of knowledge validation that happens 'on the side'; see, for example, Ziman (1978). In part, this objection is a restatement of the classic debate between Hempel and others, such as Dray, on whether covering laws can be given to unique events. But this is old and familiar ground.

My larger observation is that the world does not really care a lot about epistemology but more about pragmatic knowledge as defined in social communities. Brown and Duguid (1991) have argued this position eloquently. An alternative approach to epistemological considerations, then, is to consider how knowledge is used, validated, and valued in practice. We should not confuse our social science desire to establish justification with the pragmatic task of using knowledge in given contexts. Henry Ford did not know if mass production would work in every possible world, but it surely worked in early century American auto production. Of course, mass production does not work for all worlds. Herein lies the relevance of what is called 'negative transfer' in learning theory: knowledge that works in context A fails when transferred to context B. I propose the definition from this pragmatic view that knowledge is social belief validated contextually (indexically) by shared experience.

For this reason, knowledge as the 'object' of social science inquiry is 'ontological': we want to understand the use of knowledge in reference to defined social contexts and social categories. The initial forays into this research lead Udo Zander and me to try to understand knowledge as used by Swedish companies transferring manufacturing capabilities to foreign locations. Zander in particular did a lot of field research observing, for example, how Atlas Copco's manufacturing know how was altered when transferred to a country that did not have the same geology. Technology transfer is a type of 'fruit fly' setting for knowledge research, for it is feasible to observe how entities—companies and other organizations—package and transfer their knowledge from one setting to another on a fairly frequent basis. This transfer is very often negative, as 'things just don't work there as they work at home.'

One of the observations Udo Zander made was that the experiences of drilling in different countries permitted the gathering of a lot of information, such as the relation of the qualities of the rock and the design of the drill. This information was proprietary. To my knowledge, epistemology does not consider the category of proprietary as relevant, but it is surely an important ontological category in economic affairs. To the practitioner, proprietary information is what came to be known as a 'knowledge asset.' It can be packaged and sold, without either party to the transaction knowing how to use the information. It was based upon these observations that we decided information belonged to the category of economically valued knowledge, no matter its epistemological status.

The other term that arose in studies on technology transfer is 'know-how.' Know-how has a legal status, that is, it has a legal ontological status to which a body of law refers. As a result, it is a term that is found in legal contracts. Even though many languages, such as German and French, distinguish between knowing and knowing-how, it is interesting that 'know-how' is often used without translation in many foreign countries. My informed guess is that in recent history, the US has been the source of considerable know-how transfer and this historical contingency shows up in the importation of the English words. We came to understand that this distinction had been brilliantly discussed by Gilbert Ryle in reference to his notion of a 'category error' indicating the mistaking, in my interpretation, of knowledge as justified from knowledge as validated.

We noted in this first article that this distinction between information and know-how has a parallel in the treatment in computer science of 'declarative' and 'procedural' knowledge. As noted before, these types of knowledge are stored in long-term memory but are located in different parts of the brain; procedural memory is implicit and associated with automatic motor skills. I recall being perplexed in trying to figure out how to handle the problem that the communication and replication of knowledge can be impaired if you don't know the language. It was useful to consider this problem as allied to the portability of software programs from one machine to another.

I confess fully that I did not expect that the 1990s would be marked by an explosion in the development and commercialization of 'knowledge management' as a body of consulting practice and as software business. Amid this explosion came two central learning. The first was that information technologies and computer science were aggressively trying to attack some of the very same problems under such labels as 'universal grammars' and 'semantic ontologies.' The second was that knowledge was generative and thus both technological and social. Some of the most thoughtful practitioner/academic theorists, such as Larry Prusak and Tom Davenport, understood early that knowledge required encrypting in stories and could not be captured fully in information technologies. These two learning represent, then, a continuing debate between humanists and technologists regarding the question if machines can be knowledgeable in the same way humans are. My primary observation from this debate is that it *should* be an eternal debate in order to defend the human domain against the ever-expanding reach of non-human intelligence. Still, the strides being made in computer sciences in understanding domain knowledge, semantics, ontologies, universal grammars, weaved within a growing appreciation of social networks and community, deserve far more attention that what is evident in social science journals.

OPERATIONALIZING KNOWLEDGE BY LEARNING FROM TRANSACTION COST ECONOMICS

At the time we wrote the articles that appear as Chapters 2 and 3, it was not evident that one had a good definition of knowledge that could lead to grounded empirical work. Udo Zander and I had then the goal in this early work to show that knowledge could be operationalized in useful ways. There had been an under-appreciation of the concept of 'tacit knowledge' since Michael Polanyi's introduction of the term, by which he meant to indicate that scientific knowledge could not fully articulate experiential knowledge. This concept was picked up in economics precociously by Friedrich von Hayek and Fritz Machlup—perhaps their Austrian roots and exposure to philosophy in Vienna made them disposed in this direction. However, the concept lay dormant in economics until Richard Nelson and Sid Winter emphasized Polanyi's contribution in their book *An Evolutionary Theory of Economic Change*. They both had the opportunity to think deeply about tacit knowledge while at the Rand Corporation, which documented many case studies of failed transfer of American military technology to allied manufacturing plants.

The concept of tacit knowledge was also largely dormant in other fields, with notable exceptions. One exception is the brilliant essay by Harry Collins (1982) on the transfer of laser technology, an essay that came to our attention only after our work was long published. The other exception was psychology. Tacit knowledge had a very close parallel to the 'implicit learning' developed by Arthur Reber, who made the link explicitly in his 1993 book. In his arguments against formal intelligence testing, Robert Sternberg proposed measures for tacit knowledge at the individual level at about the same time as Udo and I proposed measures at the organizational level.[12]

The sociologist Reinhard Bendix often said in his classes on political sociology which I took as an undergraduate at U.C. Berkeley that to understand a position, it helps to understand what one is arguing against. In particular, we were arguing against the view that an understanding of why firms, and organizations, could only be derived from an assumption that people are selfish and cognition is bounded. This perspective was championed by the economist Oliver Williamson, who courageously sought to broaden his discipline's presumption that people had full knowledge of the choice set, while he sought to retain the deep attachment to individuals as isolated maximizing utility agents. Williamson proposed that selfish behavior lead people to take advantage of each other and that this problem was most pronounced in market as opposed to within-firm transactions.

In his 1981 article, Williamson had transformed this rather general view into clear concepts that permitted empirical testing. It was the testability of his ideas that interested researchers in management departments. A successful research program has to provide 'rails' upon which other trains can ride. By the early 1980s, a number of researchers showed that data could be collected, persuasive statistics could be estimated, and the propositions tested. Within a decade, there had been hundreds of studies that showed transaction costs influence the contracting and boundary decisions of the firm. The journals were filled with transaction cost articles.

Udo Zander and I wanted to replicate this model for the study of knowledge. Despite our admiration for transaction cost economics, we ironically desired to achieve four objectives contrary to this perspective. The first was that we wanted to emphasize 'capabilities,' or what Williamson called 'production costs,' as the determining factor for the boundaries of the firm. If one reread the principal empirical findings for transaction costs, capabilities appear generally as the most important factor. In other words, firms tend to do in-house those activities which they do better.

The second was that we asked, could we construct a theory of a firm that did not rely upon selfishness. We don't doubt that people act selfishly and at times dishonestly. It might be that to understand heaven, one has to understand the underworld as well. Or, can a theory of the firm be constructed without this Manichean duality? We observe in any complex society, such as a university, cases where well-meaning people fail to understand each other, because one is a lawyer and the other is poet, or one is a physicist and the other a geneticist. Coordination failure can rest on the absence of codes.

Third, we wanted to construct measures of tacitness, as I noted above. These measures consisted of 'codifiabilty' or 'teachability,' for which we created items and built scales. Others have used these scales, with similar results (see, for example, Hansen 2002). Of course, others developed other measures, related to allied concepts, such as stickiness. Some of this work had access to data we could not get, namely, both sides of the transfer. However, I felt then, and still do now, there has not been sufficient unity in approaches. The studies in this area are less comparable than the achievement in transaction cost economics that have more—though still heterogeneous!—unity in empirical approaches. Parenthetically, I will add that studies in learning have often proceeded without reference to the work on technology transfer (a well studied and defined domain of intentional learning) and without a theory of knowledge. No wonder then that so much of learning studies are oriented towards social construction accounts in which there are flows but no outcomes (such as fads), for there is a lack of historical appreciation of accumulation of social and economic knowledge.

Last, we sought to shift the focus of research from the transaction to the relationship in order to answer the question of 'what firms do.' Economics often focuses on incentive conflicts in transactions as opposed to analyzing why there is heterogeneity in capabilities. Nelson and Winter (1982) sounded the trumpet to launch this type of investigation. Initially, I thought of this problem in the context of multinational corporations, whereby I re-defined foreign direct investment as the transfer of organizing principles (Kogut 1987). Increasingly, my attention turned to joint ventures (which proved to be more of a growth field than anyone could have guessed) in which I established two results: (1) it was the *relationship*, not the transaction that mattered (Kogut 1989); and (2) firms treated joint ventures as investments in new capabilities and hence joint venture contracts explicitly allocated the control rights to buy out the other partner when these investments were 'in the money' (Kogut 1991; Chapter 6 this volume).

GROWTH OPTIONS AND THE PROBLEM OF SCALING

Through these empirical studies, I began to treat combinative capabilities and knowledge, formally and empirically, as investments that provided organizations with *options* on the future. The chapters in this book on options consequently sought to establish the tacitness and uniqueness of a capability (e.g. routines that enable multinationals to switch production efficiently) in relation to their economic value in addressing future markets (Chapter 7). In an article not included in this volume, Dong-Jae Kim and I (1996) showed that some technological capabilities were 'dead-ends' while others proved to be fecund platforms for expansion. Sea Jin Chang and I (Kogut and Chang 1996) similarly found that multinational corporations developed platforms in countries that provided the hysteretic option to expand or to withdraw. This concept of platforms is the conceptual bridge between capabilities as knowledge and the realization of their uncertain economic value (see Chapter 8).

In the spirit of this introductory chapter, let's focus on the behavioral underpinnings and leave the technical details to the chapters. In the context of organizational sociology and knowledge, dynamics requires that we understand how capabilities *scale*, that is, how they grow and evolve with successful feedback from the market. Roberto Weber (2006) finds for example that students who learn to coordinate in the first set of games are more likely to cooperate in later games when the group size is much bigger.

Experimental studies show that people are far more selfish in large groups. Thus, Weber claims to show that students learn norms in small group settings, their learned norms scale to larger groups.[13] These results are not especially surprising unless you start from the economics perspective that the breakdown in cooperation is the canonical norm. The results are nevertheless interesting to show how cooperation scales with the growth of the firm.

The Weber experiment concerns *transactions* and is an investigation essentially of how participants learn that Pareto-improvements in collective outcomes require tempering the selfish instincts to defect. For studying what organizations do, it is more interesting to study production (or what we call capabilities) than transactions (which are markets). For example, we would like to know if better techniques of production can be discovered and learned. We put aside the economist obsession with whether people are good or bad, altruistic and selfish, and instead we just want to know whether people learn better ways to coordinate (i.e. routines) in memory. Cohen and Bacdayan (1995) offered one of the most insightful investigations of the learning organizational routines based on a very elegant design. A routine is a learned repetition of a menu of interactions among people, for example when I put butter on the bread, you then add jam. The assignment and coordination of these tasks constitute the structuring of interactions. Cohen and Bacdayan asked participants in an experiment to play a very simple card game, in which the amount of their award was indexed by how many hands they completed in a finite period of time. Through repeated play, they showed how routines evolved which were characterized by improvements in reliability and speed. At the same time, the participants made errors when the rules were changed, evidencing 'negative transfer,' that is, mistakes due to using learned routines in inappropriate contexts.

The Weber experiments established scaling by the transfer of norms, in which the focus was trying to understand the transition from selfishness to cooperation. This line of work was influenced by the very thoughtful essay of David Kreps on culture as a type of Schelling focal point that coordinated decisions (Kreps 1990). Yet, Kreps's solution did not rely (in this context) on a presumption that considerations of selfish defection was relevant; he just wanted to know how people knew what decisions to take which could be anticipated by others. The organizationally more relevant work of Cohen and Bacdayan assumed people care about incentives and rewards; after all, the participants earned money. But the incentives were collectively indexed. Their contribution was to show that coordination is learned in procedural memory, and becomes part of the unconscious social knowledge that neuroscience indicates is stored in specific parts of the brain. We have thus the sketch of a powerful psychological foundation to organizational knowledge based upon sociality, procedural memory, and priming.

ORGANIZATIONAL SOCIOLOGY AND NETWORKS

However, in what sense is this organizational sociology? By now, we have hundreds of studies that investigate the problems of transfer, of codifiability, of knowledge inside and between organizations. In all, Zander's and my advocacy to replicate the success of transaction costs in creating a large body of empirical knowledge based upon common measurements has surely been answered. However, since knowledge is insufficiently recognized to be structural, as well as personal, there has not been yet an appealing marriage of knowledge creation and transfer with organizational sociology and its concern with structure, prestige, and authority. Surely, the magisterial study by MacKenzie and Spinardi (1995) of the transfer of nuclear bomb technology—and the precocious analysis of whether Iraq could acquire such technology—indicated explicitly the conceptual importance of tacit knowledge. Such explicit studies are though rare. The many managerial studies of diffusion (e.g. mergers, poison pills, etc.) in social networks should differ among the types of knowledge and how much gets diffused. Generally, they do not.

If we worry less about terminology and consider studies in sociology that are equivalently concerned with knowledge, then there is no shortage. One category of studies focus on the search for knowledge in distributed organizations. The expansive literature on search in the web is a broad example, but we can find a long history of such studies in sociology. This literature includes the studies by Rapoport on 'biased' search, to Granovetter's studies on weak ties, and to more recent work by Watts and Strogatz. An approach that investigated this bias in relation to tacitness is Hansen's (1999, 2002) studies on the search for knowledge in a global multidivisional firm. Hansen found that the transfer of tacit knowledge was facilitated by 'strong ties' among people; he also in his subsequent study analyzed more carefully the relation of tacitness to structure and search. These studies are among the few that showed the quality of the knowledge transferred influenced the type of network channel that was utilized for search.

Another equivalence to knowledge is social capital, which entails a structural component and a relational one. The structural component is contested along the lines of brokerage and closure, by which it is meant whether Bob is the unique bridge for communication with Suzie and Ralph who don't talk with each other (brokerage) or whether they are all connected (closure). Brokerage is associated with Ron Burt; closure with James Coleman (see the discussion in Chapter 13). Gordon Walker, Weijian Shan, and I (Walker et al. 1997) published the first comparison of brokerage and closure in relation to claims about social capital, and it was one of the few studies up to then to look at the over time dynamic processes. We found that certain kinds of networks— in this case, biotechnology—tended towards closure through repeated ties. Again, we find that relationships lead to structures, and structures lead to repeated relationships. It is this structural replication that encodes for enduring coordination among people and organizations.

The above studies are essentially investigations of the relation between topology (e.g. are firms organized by hierarchy or horizontally) and information and its access. As mentioned early, computer and natural sciences made considerable advances in the 1990s in the area of management. It might be useful here to comment briefly on one area of advance in relation to disentangling important concepts in distributed knowledge. From economics, we have already noted the importance of 'common knowledge' in coordination games. The logical complement to common is 'asymmetrical information' in which two players do not share common knowledge: I don't know what you know. The standard economics views asymmetries as 'information relevant' to the decision to cooperate or defect; in my view, asymmetries are also procedural. In other words, whether one person knows how to do what another person does is relevant to the resolution of how to coordinate. The idea of common knowledge and information asymmetries are quite powerful, but often empirically disappointing because they miss key contextual elements: people are located in the same or different divisions, or in the same location or different locations. We may think then of knowledge as distributed in a network, in which people (or agents) share local but not global knowledge. Knowledge is thus 'distributed.' Locally, people in the same division share common knowledge but they do not share knowledge globally.

In other words, the asymmetry in knowledge is given by the topology of the network. We can view local as a 'cluster' in which people who have direct social relations (one step away) share common knowledge. At two steps away, knowledge is more asymmetrical, and at further steps, the degree of common knowledge decays further. These ideas of cluster and steps (or path length) have become an important way to understand how a particular type of topology called 'small worlds' can matter to *information* diffusion (Watts and Strogatz 1998). The interesting dynamics of small worlds is that *procedural* knowledge and social interactions are denser within clusters than between them.

By encoding knowledge in structures, organizations and societies are rendered robust. This robustness is a property of 'small worlds': most URLs are fairly close proximity to each other (i.e. short path length) and links among they are 'clustered.' Knowledge is preserved in structure because structure, being clustered and marked by redundancy, is resilient to perturbations. Thus, where formal hierarchies may be efficient for transmitting information, distributed social networks are good for achieving robustness.

In an article on German corporate ties, Gordon Walker and I (Kogut and Walker 2001) unveiled corporate ownership ties to be a small world; the network of ties among owners had a short average path length (owners were only a few steps away) but these ties also were clustered (owners tended to own many firms together). By a simulation that rewired the network by randomly reassigning ownership ties, we showed that small world properties are surprisingly robust. These results are pertinent to other empirical domains. If knowledge was only in the heads of people, then Indian software companies experiencing 25 percent rates of annual labor turnover would dissolve. Fortunately, organizational structure is robust (Kogut and Walker 2001) and resilient to turnover (Rao and Argote 2005).

In the context of the literature on common knowledge, information presumes a high degree of articulation and consciousness on the part of the 'knower.' It fits well the game theoretical treatment of a coordination problem as a transaction in trying to know if you know what I know. But it does not fit the type of situation when knowledge is tacit and poorly understood, yet coordination is possible through the priming of autonomous responses and the creation of shared identities that are acquired over long histories of interactions. In other words, we want to understand knowledge at two levels: the learned interactions (routines) among people and the structuring of interactions through organizing principles of design—or what we could call the generative rules for producing organizational topologies.

Using this lens, we can see now why the claim that coordination is learned in small groups and can be scaled to the large organization is extreme, unlikely, and unnecessary. In a distributed view of knowledge, local interactions will produce rich and tacit knowledge. This type of knowledge is not 'common' in the sense of economics, but rather is stored in learned repertoires, as the Cohen and Bacdayan experiment indicates. Despite the absence of common knowledge, organizations do scale, because of higher order organizing principles that structure work into local clusters while providing mechanisms of coordination by formal authority and informal social connections.

RESOURCE-BASED VIEW OF STRATEGY

The claim that knowledge is encoded in structure and social networks brings us to the relationship of the organizational sociology of knowledge to the 'resource-based' view of strategy, or RBV. The resource based view is a dominant school of thought in the area of strategy. This approach responded to the framing of strategy formulation as 'industry analysis,' in other words, the determination of the forces that make some industries more profitable than others and what are the appropriate means for a firm to build competitive advantage and to attain sustained profits in a given industry (Porter 1981). The simple observation of RBV is that since firms need to have the resources and capabilities to compete effectively, telling them what makes money in their industry can be like telling a fish to learn how to run.

As it is not my job to give the history of this view, I will restrict my comments to a few papers and then turn to answering the question. It is conventional to cite Edith Penrose's magisterial book *The Growth of the Firm* as the seminal source, with secondary reference to a brilliant article by Steven Lippman and Richard Rumelt. Penrose's book established that firm's growth consist of various components which do not scale proportionally, hence while a firm's marketing resources may be exhausted, it might have unexploited capacity in production. This unbalanced growth promotes diversification to employ the excess capacity. It is hard to render justice to this book, except to remark that it was modern in its use of counterfactual and off-equilibrium reasoning.

The Lippman and Rumelt article presented an original argument, whose core idea was captured by an appealing mathematical model. Assume that firms are given a productivity parameter; this parameter says you need a 100 or 50 workers to produce a car. Some draw high productivity (50 workers), and others low productivity (100 workers). By luck, then, firms are endowed *heterogeneously* with varying productivity. They compare their productivity to the market price and decide whether to enter the market. As more firms enter, the price falls, causing some firms to exit. At equilibrium, price equals the marginal cost of the least productive firm. Marginality of classic microeconomics prevails, but a central result of the standard economics is dismissed: in equilibrium, the surviving firms have positive profits on average.

The title of the paper contains the phrase 'uncertain imitability.' This concept plays the role of explaining why firms cannot simply enter by imitation, but it plays no further role. In a subsequent paper, Rumelt (1984) provided the additional explanation that firms can profit from many potential sources of rents that are protected by 'isolating mechanisms,' one of which is uncertain imitability. Somewhat buried in this chapter is the recognition that this simple model contains a real option in two forms. The first is that the expected value of entry contains an option calculation. Any mean-preserving increase in volatility increases the value of entry since there would be a bigger potential gain and the loss remains the same. The second real option is an 'embedded' growth option. Rumelt notes that if a firm were given a chance to draw again from a bin of productivity parameters, it would want the second bin to be correlated with the first draw. He notes 'new activities should be added until the point where further additions would not add sufficiently large expected profits or profit variance to justify the added sunk capital.' By the phrase 'profit variance,' Rumelt implies the argument that the current capabilities generate options on subsequent markets. Thus, options are at the core of this early investigation into resources.

Not surprisingly then, Lippman and Rumelt did not say that 'the resource view' contradicted industry or market analysis. To the contrary, we see that markets, prices, demand interacted with resources. Neither did the 1986 Jay

Barney article on scarce resources deny markets. To the contrary, Barney elevated the financial market to a level of efficiency that would make financial economists blush. In this achievement, he neglected that heterogeneity among firms would result in variance in the financial valuations of the same resource. To paraphrase Rumelt, because of 'postentry efficiencies,' two firms will have different capabilities and will thus place different valuations on a given resource and its acquisition. In this sense, he missed the Lippman and Rumelt point that once markets and prices are in equilibrium, homogeneous firms cannot profit by buying resources from these markets, but that heterogeneous firms can realize excess profits through the combination of the acquired resource and its current resources.

During this time, as we have seen above, a few seminal publications on knowledge began to appear. The book of Nelson and Winter, appearing in 1982, discussed at length skills and routines and idea of tacit knowledge. In 1987, Winter published his article on knowledge and strategy, where he adopted the scales of Rogers in terms of the diffusion of innovation to understand the dimensions of tacit knowledge. In an article on joint ventures (1988; Chapter 5 this volume), I had offered the framing of alliances by three motivations, the third one being 'organizational learning' which relied upon the transfer of tacit knowledge. Along with Udo Zander's ideas, this insight was developed further in the article on knowledge submitted in 1988 to *Organization Science* (the sixteenth article to be submitted in that journal's history), but it was not published until 1992 (after having been even queued over a year following acceptance). (See Kogut and Zander 1992.) The empirical part was submitted by 1990 and published in *Organization Science* in 1995; a second study was published in the *Journal of International Business Studies* in 1993. Parenthetically, then, RBV did not precede the work on knowledge.

More importantly, there is a substantive difference in theorizing that has had important implications. The work on knowledge did not define 'competitive advantage' but instead asked if the premise that knowledge shared in a social community could compose a theory of the firm. We sought to understand the sociology of why knowledge is embedded in communities and encoded in organizing principles. The causality was that factors X lead to the creation of capabilities Y which enabled firms differentially to compete against each other. Thus, from the start, market demand and competition were integral to an evaluation of the economic value of a capability. We can call this capability a 'competitive advantage,' but it is in turn the expression of the tacit and explicit knowledge resources inside a firm. Through the recombination of these resources—though subject to restraints of identity, a firm posseses the option to evolve new capabilities (see Kogut and Kulatilaka Chapter 8, this volume.)

Arguably, via organizational economics, one could also analyze a set of capabilities as resulting from appropriate design of incentives in relation to the chosen technology. Like the organizational sociology view, the argument is not crude functionalism. There are two levels of analysis, one consisting of an incentive problem, the second consisting of the disposition of a competitive asset to compete in markets. In this sense, organizational economics and organizational sociology provide two distinct, at times complementary theories of resources and competitive advantage. Neither of them denies the importance of demand and competition in the determination of economic value of a capability.

This equality of competitive advantage and resource was the central claim of the most seminal article in the RBV literature, namely, the 1991 article by Jay Barney in the special issue of the *Journal of Management* that he edited. The article posited a simple functionalism in which an asset that is not imitable and is scarce and valuable constitutes a competitive advantage. The central idea of this article is the acronym VRIN, which defined a competitive advantage as valuable and rarity. The sustainability of a competitive advantage is defined by a competitive advantage that is neither imitable, nor substitutable; some also add in non-transferable. The excellent articles by Priem and Butler (2001a, b) argue very effectively that these statements are tautologies, analytically and synthetically. Since value and competitive advantage are definitionally equivalent, the tautology is synthetically trivial. Construct validity is thus vacuous.

Priem and Butler offer the solution of rendering 'value' external to the resource. In other words, they suggest that markets should determine value. This commonsensical perspective states that strategies should be chosen in reference to the value of good and services and to the non-imitable competitive. This commonsense is the same position that is taken in the chapters that follow, especially in the Kogut and Kulatilaka in this volume (Chapter 8). However, this solution does not go far enough.

VRIN after all is a typology, not a theory. It is a view, and in this sense, the resource based view is aptly named. The danger is that a typology leads to a treatment of resources as *lego* pieces (Kogut and Zander 2003). The job of the mythical strategist in RBV is to recognize that the dish needs more carrots, and carrots are purchased and added. Teachers of strategy like this view, because it is engineering; it says you can take a bit of salt and sugar, buy some flour and yeast from the market, and then you get bread.

Unfortunately, human systems do not behave this way. Consider the finding that many, if not most, acquisitions destroy value. The studies of post-acquisition costs recapitulate the learning from those of technology transfer, that is, these costs can be substantial and vary by the codification of knowledge and by organizational conflicts. What are these conflicts? One is that employees of the two firms have had different identities and loyalties. Second, they also have established local understandings of merit and worth. When a retail bank and an investment bank merge, the difference in pay among employees is no longer abstract. It no longer is that investment bankers are paid more, but the person now in my firm is paid a multiple of my salary.

Nickerson and Zenger (2004) view this behavior as envy arising from social comparison. This is a welcomed analysis insofar as limits to a strategy (that is diversification) are motivated by an organizational sociology theory. Indeed, studies on salary and remuneration show that people are largely paid by 'category,' and less so by individual performance. However, their argument misses the significance of the relevance of social proximity: envy is triggered by a social comparison circumscribed by the borders of the firm. As discussed in Chapter 4, one can always compare one self to better paid managers in other firms and industries. So the argument begs why envy is restricted to within-firm comparisons. What makes the comparison to *salient others* in the same category salient is *identity*, for it is by identification that membership to a *normative* community is determined.[14] The community is those members who feel they are socially proximate. Nickerson and Zenger thus have implicitly assumed the borders of a firm to be meaningful for social comparison because of shared membership in a community with normative expectations.

ORGANIZATIONAL ECONOMICS: BABBAGE ECONOMY REVISITED

There are two theoretical ways to break out of this lego impasse, as suggested above: organizational sociology of knowledge and organizational economics. Organizational economics has treated knowledge largely as 'human capital.' This capital might be firm-specific or market-specific, individual-specific or team-specific. No matter the characterization, this specificity implies a governance problem of how to incentivize workers to invest in knowledge given imperfect contracting. The article of Becker and Murphy (1992) is an excellent illustration of this problem for the case of 'weak-link production.' As discussed above in the discussion of Weber's coordination argument, weak-link production problems do not need to assume contracting difficulties in order to motivate coordination failure. Thus, here is an inkling of an intuition that contracting problems may not be necessary to understand the division and hierarchy of knowledge.

The economics of knowledge generally assumes incentive or contracting difficulties. For example, Luis Garicano's work has focused more on the sorting of knowledge by hierarchy. In brief, his work is a formalization of the *Babbage economy*, since he matches essentially the division of mental labor to a hierarchy reflecting gradations in skills. However, incentive conflicts are not always integral to the explanation of knowledge. One of the core ideas in the knowledge literature is that people within a community speak a coded language. The Postrel paper above proposed that transpecialists arise to coordinate knowledge across a division of labor. This transpecialist shows up in the Cremer, Garicano, and Prat (2007) paper as a 'translator.' They show that a common code can provide a cooperative gain to specialists depending upon the richness of the language and the complexity of the environment. Where the environment is specialized—such as two distinct clients, it is best to have two organizations serve each client rather than mix codes. They reach the conclusion that there are declining returns to variety—which is consistent with the informal claims in Kogut and Zander (1996) and Kogut (2000).

These conclusions do not rest on incentive conflicts. Of course, there is a literature that shows incentives and knowledge are complementary; see, for example, Azoulay (2004). The very interesting study of Nicholas Argyres (1999) on the B-2 stealth bomber found that project teams became more efficient by developing a 'technical grammar' for communication, thus reducing the need for hierarchical supervision. He makes the observation this grammar reduces asset-specificity, thereby reducing contractual holdup. This last observation appears as a slight leap of logical faith, for the difference in knowing a language and knowing how to do anything is abundantly clear to anyone who has followed all the steps in a math proof and yet cannot replicate it the day after. Still, the point that an increase in 'common knowledge'— such as knowing the conventions—lowers agency costs is true by most logical constructions. The contention again is whether it is necessary to the analysis of the relation of common language and hierarchy. By the Cremer, Garicano, and Prat paper on language, the answer is no.

MERGING INCENTIVES AND KNOWLEDGE: COGNITIVE TEMPLATES

The debate over the primacy of incentives bears frequently similarities with historical conflicts in which violent conflict leads to territorial separation based on ethnic affiliation. The United Nations approach to knowledge is to consider incentives as motivating selfish agents in conjunction with coordination problems. A useful insight into coordination problems is to start with a simple census that asks if I do A, does this make it more valuable for you to do B, or to do less of B. The first case says A and B are complements; the second, says they are substitutes. This is useful knowledge to have if you wish to design an organization.

The elegant book by John Roberts (2004) is a thoughtful treatment of the interaction of capabilities as design and incentives as motivation. In its comparative static form, the theory of complementarities permits a useful census of the interactions in a firm, namely whether A and B are complements or substitutes or independent. A piece rate incentive is difficult to implement on an assembly line (though it is quite amazing that the historical record shows many firms in many countries surely tried). Thus, an increase in piece rate incentives should encourage a decrement in assembly lines; they are substitutes. In an organization consisting of many potentially interacting parts, these interactions pose a problem that is usually not solvable in finite time. The real-time problem belongs to a fascinating domain of the new science of complexity, because it is impossible (as I noted earlier) to solve this problem realistically in any relevant horizon. Instead, managers rely upon prototypical classifications by which to reduce this complexity to making the best guess based on observable data and existing cases. It is this analysis that the article by MacDuffie, Ragin, and I (Chapter 10) provide, including a methodology by which to determine not only complementarities, but also a method to reduce complexity to smaller dimensionality and to explore new combinations.

The more radical claim is that organizational design evolves along with their product architectures. Giovanni Dosi and I (1992) were the first to propose a co-evolutionary argument of organizing principles and technologies in relation to national trajectories. A co-evolutionary argument is distinct from extreme technological determinism of some theories of organizational design, such as those proposed by Baldwin and Clark (2000) and by Levinthal (1997). The claim that product modularity correlates with organizational structure is appealing in the context of computer companies (but even so, doubtful), yet is surely dubious for multiproduct, multitechnology companies. The more appealing formulation is given by Henderson and Clark (1990) that technologies lead to particular information filters, mental models, and problem-solving strategies. Because those who love technologies are so beguiled by the object of their study, it is useful to remember that the same case could be made for marketing. The match of product module to organizational structure is bound to be more contingent.

In this regard, we should keep in mind the studies on multinational corporations, because they are multiple-product, multiple-technology, and multiple-market companies, thus providing a lovely experimental design. In one of the earliest studies of their strategy and structure, Wells and Stopford (1972) made the simple but fundamental observation that advertising-intensive firms organize by geographies and technology-intensive ones by product. Is it unfair to conclude from this discussion that firms tend to organize around the information they require and the capabilities they need to harness?

This multidimensional variant on the coupling of organizations to technologies and environments makes too much of a claim. The engineering design perspective just doesn't like sociology. After all, the studies by Morten Hansen, discussed earlier, of knowledge flows used a multinational corporation as the field site. His conclusions, backed by extensive data collection, indicated that social networks mattered to knowledge sharing, independent of formal hierarchy. To organizational sociologists—such as Ron Burt or Mark Granovetter—this finding is the justification for their theoretical livelihood.

Social networks and organizational structure offer solutions to theoretical quandaries that beguile otherwise beguiling concepts. An example is the re-introduction of 'cognition' (or 'cognitive maps,' 'cognitive templates,' 'schemata') into the recent discussion of organizations and strategy. These concepts provide an alluring solution to the coordination problem: we know what to do because we all have common knowledge, or we fail to do because we have the wrong common knowledge.

Interests and cognition are the substance of the new sociological institutionalism that dresses Émile Durkheim and his *Elementary Forms of the Religious Life* in new clothing. Durkheim proposed a correspondence between social categories and cognitive categories. Thus, the micro–macro problem that has been the bane of sociology theorizing was resolved by positing there is no problem: the partitions of society are the same as the categorical partitions held by individuals. This resolution by imposition is not appealing. Instead, we would like to know, as explained earlier, the relation of local knowledge and macro structures.

The area of strategy has cyclically been concerned with shared cognitive templates, sometimes located in the heads of top management, sometimes in the organization. In a well-argued and thoughtful article, Sarah Kaplan and Rebecca Henderson (2005: 513) propose that 'that incentives cannot be understood separately from the cognitive frames and interests of both employees and employers in any complex organization.' Change is difficult, because 'managers have developed the kinds of local, focused cognitive frames that are likely to get them promoted, then they may plausibly reject information alerting them to radical shifts in the environment as unimportant.' In this sense, their proposal echoes the behavioral psychology of B.F. Skinner in which people, and mice, are manipulated by incentives. Once trained, behaviors are hard to alter according to this tradition.

There is though also a hidden structural component to it as well, which not surprisingly I view as fundamental to carry their proposal further. Supposedly the careers of managers followed a pattern by which they were hired into a department, made associations, were promoted, etc.; mobility ladders is a staple industry of organizational sociology and especially of that great network theorist Harrison White (1970). Their companies might have employed open space environments, where they worked in cross-functional teams, or transferred to different locations. These personal experiences generated *biographies* across interpersonal networks which reflect a combination of organizational rules (e.g., transfer people, put people into spatial proximity without walls) and idiosyncratic histories that relational knowledge. Across these biographies, people develop identities. When we see once great firms fail, it is very often because managers don't want to give up their definition of social worth rather than their failure to recognize that policy A is now needed to replace policy B. You can tell a sexist that the firm would recruit better talent if they could attract more women, and here is an incentive to hire more women because it is Pareto-optimal. A lot of research says, this is not enough to cure the problem of sexism, or racism, or social ills in general; inequalities are enduring because social categories segregate identities (Tilly 1998; Akerlof and Kranton 2000).

The Henderson and Kaplan argument proposes the weak test that the absence of organizational change is explained by the persistence of mental models. If we were to study how organizations change instead of why do they fail to change, we would need to show that change in mental models occurred and these changes were causal. An evolutionary approach might help. In the process of organizational change, we would probably observe people being fired, hired, or moved about; they might also observe new organizational groupings being tried out. An interesting question is would the firm change if the organizational structures and processes did not change? A reasonable answer is perhaps, but it would be easier if such structures and processes changed too. By now, you know what I am getting at: individual cognitive changes are the secondary effects; the primary effect is changing the structure and local interactions.

Part of what people know is generated by the history of their interactions embedded in local structures, and structures therefore encode cognition for the firm. Since much knowledge is procedural (recall Cohen and Bacdayan), procedures have to be changed. Since structures code for coordination, changing people alone is not sufficient (Rao and Argote). Since much economic value is lodged in social capital, social networks may persist even if formal structures are changed (Hansen). If you want to change mental models, then enlarge social networks, induce new interactions, and alter life experiences. The price though is not minor, as people carry personal attachments and professional identities.

Positing shared templates as blocking change repeats the Durkheim error of wishing the tough theoretical work to go away. The good news is that cognition is part of organizational economics (e.g. what is the common knowledge among actors) and part of organizational sociology (e.g. what are the identities, social networks, and procedural knowledge). We are thus spared trying to answer irritating questions such as does everyone in the organization share the mental model and if not, who shares what templates. It is to be expected that in this complex dynamic, shared mental models are not very shared after all.

Leadership might usefully be treated as creating new mental models, and yet even here, such an argument is liable to be overstated. Robert Burgelman's remarkable paper on the evolution of Intel from memory to processors provides the instructive lesson that no one knew ahead of time a new mental model (Burgelman 1994). Emergence of a new strategy and new capabilities proceeded instead by a rewiring of the social network guided by incentives and a capital allocation process that rewarded experimentation. Incentives mattered as signals as much as for motivation. The organization re-aligned. Ex-post, managers have a mental model of a computer processor firm, but ex-ante is the harder and more important claim to prove. Burgelman's study shows that organizational change can precede the change in mental models.

Macro Behaviors: Norms, Institutions, and Practical Knowledge

To come now to the level of society after having covered the brain, the social individual, and the organization is a daunting task for this introductory postscript. I will utilize, then, a card borrowed from Harrison White (1992) and Andrew Abott (2001) by noting the fractal principle of self-similarity. For much of what is to be said about norms and institutions at the level of society has already been said about individuals and organizations. Since the following articles do not included any studies of industrial economics or inter-organizational networks, I will not extend the earlier discussion on economics and sociology into the macro domain.

Much like our discussion on mental templates, there is the *strong presumption of multi-level isomorphism* in much of the new institutional economics, of all places. The presumption is conditioned on the following logic: Economic growth depends upon the resolution of collective action problems. Adherence to good norms and institutions resolve such problems. Thus, good norms and institutions lead to economic growth. Institutions at the macro level appear isomorphic to norms at the micro level.

By this logic, there has been an interesting and recent growth industry producing articles that show societies that have strong rule of law have better developed financial markets and better developed financial markets lead to higher growth (La Porta et al. 1997; Levine 1997); belief in heaven and/or hell (the latter belief is more effective) leads to higher economic development (Barro and MacCleany 2003); cultural beliefs, including Christianity, leads to better economic growth (Guiso et al. 2006); importation of European institutions into colonies is a good thing for development (Acemoglu et al. 2001). All of these studies are characterized by close attention to instrumental variables and endogeneity issues, and they all show, with some disagreement, that institutions, laws, and norms matter for economic progress.

Again, to be clear, these results pretend to show that *particular* social values and institutions make people more honest and societies richer. This demonstration is not as observationally strong as the earlier studies in economics that we cited, such as the Bowles et al. (2003) study of the ultimatum game played in the field, because our institutional authors don't observe the intermediary variables (e.g. certain values make you more honest). On the other hand, the

Bowles study did not claim to know what values lead to higher economic development; their modesty is to be admired. However, we could imagine experiments designed in different country settings that could lend their results to such extrapolations. Indeed, the study notes that their estimates of altruism have less measurement error than most alternatives and hence could be useful, when enough societies are sampled, in providing a variable of altruism that could be used in cross-country regressions.

DURKHEIM FALLACY RE-EXAMINED

Despite the parallels between thinking about micro experiments and these larger societal studies, there are many differences across these levels of analysis and these differences are exceedingly hard to integrate. The postulate of an identity between social and individual cognitive categories is what we earlier called the Durkheim fallacy. It is a potent observation that much of the source of conflict and change in societies is the disjoint between social institutions and personal values. Social institutions such as the state and its monopoly on violence (to use Weber's phrasing) or the church and its desired monopoly on faith do not always win the compliance from some members of society. Nor do economic standards, such as software operating standards, win always the compliance of competitors and users. The difference of course is that to reject the State's monopoly of violence or the Church's teachings is dramatically different than rejecting an economic standard. Similarly, while people can often—assuming free markets and some degree of choice—opt in or opt out of working for a given corporation, one cannot opt out of a country easily. Violation of its rules (e.g. laws) carries sanctions of a different magnitude than a loss of pay or job.

Societies are internally far more heterogeneous than organizations and they are marked by fairly complicated institutions, constellations of power, and relationships. A lot of the misconception regarding similarities stem from the imprecision of terms institutions, norms, and conventions. Institutions are commonly defined in economics as 'rules of the game' (North 1990). One might think rules are better called conventions, e.g. driving on the left side of the street when in the UK. Institutions might be reserved to refer to abstract Hegelian entities, such as the law, the state, labor, or the religion, with institutional actors being the judicial and enforcement system, the government, the union, and churches. Norms are cultural values and institutionalized beliefs which people non-reflexively hold, such as beliefs in family loyalty, honesty. These are my proposals.

It might seem that the levels of analysis are connected by identities, that is, they are isomorphic. It is a fair abduction from the economic studies on religion and culture cited above that they imply people abide by Catholic or

Muslim beliefs in their daily lives, and that these beliefs are lodged in personal identities. Thus, by this argument, even though Italians show high rates of divorce, of pre-marital and extra-marital sex, and of corruption (by the same indices economists use in their studies), they nevertheless are Catholic in their economic transactions. There might be a way to resolve this tenuous argument along the lines of a path dependence in which Catholic values were necessary for bootstrapping the Italian society into a higher economic equilibrium. Once achieved, such values could be nostalgically recalled during festivals during the year, paraded like saints in the streets, and then returned to the closet in order to permit a return to a secular life. This complicated argument, though, is not the one given in the economic papers cited above. To the contrary, Guideo, Sapienza, and Zingales define culture as consisting only of enduring values; thus this resolution suggesting the inheritance of particular values without all the original beliefs is incompatible with their proposal. My forecast for this literature is that static cross-sectional results are very misleading, and we will need evolution of individual and societal values.

COMPARATIVE SYSTEMS

People are, as we noted at the start, highly capable at navigating across multiple domains of social identity. At times, a particular identity becomes inflamed, as when prejudice against a minority causes a critical threshold to be passed. At other times, institutional actors compete for identities and loyalties, such as the famous socialist debates in late nineteenth century Germany regarding loyalties to the party, to democracy, and to the nation. The competition between state and church in France is a battle across centuries; 'laicisme' is a body of secular values taught at the prestigious state schools of higher education, for which the Jesuits offer some of the best preparatory training.

An interesting body of work ignores the dimension of values and focuses precisely on the cooperation and conflict among institutions. The book by Hall and Soskice (2001) has been especially influential in political science. The starting point for this book is a reiteration of Richard Nelson's (1956) precocious model of development as characterized by a passage from a low equilibrium to a high equilibrium economy. Finegold and Soskice (1988) made a similar observation for even developed countries by arguing the UK was trapped in a low-level training equilibrium. Hall and Soskice aggregated these and other studies to propose that countries consist of several *complementary* institutions. We have already seen this argument earlier in connection with John Robert's book on firms; Roberts, along with Paul Milgrom, is a chief architect of the formal theory of complements. Thus, countries, like firms, change only precariously because each institution functions in relation to other institutions. The final step in this intellectual history is now underway, that is, dropping the empirical claims that one constellation of institutions (e.g. German) is better than another (e.g. Anglo-Saxon). Rather it is sufficient to state the good configurations, which are many, among the very large combinatorial possibilities. After all, if you have six institutions (unions, common law, corporate associations, work councils, stock markets, independent central banks), you have a 2^6 (or 64) combinations. It is an achievement to be able to say here are two or three good systems, and the rest are bad.

This modest yet insightful literature contrasts impressively with the earlier institutional economic studies that tend to rely on what I call in Chapter 9 'silver bullet theories.' They say, if you are religious, you grow; if you have common law, you grow; if you have European institutions, you grow. Hall and Soskice have gradually moved in the course of their journey to a more reasonable proposition: there are more than one and less than many ways in which countries can configure their institutions in order to enjoy economic success.

My starting point in the relation of country, society, and firms differed from the above literatures. I noted early in my career that country economic leadership persisted far longer than the leaderships of firms; since technologies were relatively rapidly copied by other firms even in different countries and organizational capabilities were not, the latter must be the source of the explanation for persisting country leadership; hence a central question must be why do organizational capabilities diffuse slower across the borders of countries than across the borders of firms (Kogut 1987). These thoughts were the substance of the Crawfoord Lecture organized by Lund University which was republished in a revised form in 1991 in the *Strategic Management Journal* (Kogut 1991; 2000).

There is, I hold, a difference in the economic focus on norms supporting cooperation and the organizing principles that are entailed in the design and coordination of work. It is this link of practice and procedural knowledge that is missing in these econometric studies that seek the secrets of growth in variations in altruism and honesty across societies. I am surely inclined to give an explanatory role to honesty, but in watching countries such as China and India grow, I doubt the claim that their growth is explained by a sudden conversion to honesty and transparency. Rather, what you see is that in this age of modern communication and mobility of skilled talent (e.g. engineers, consultants, managers) is a diffusion and arbitrage of practice and knowledge that is considerably faster than what the UK or the US experienced in their histories as industrial giants.

Rather than norms alone, I proposed, as seen in Chapter 9, a schema in which institutions and practices interact as complements but they are loosely coupled. Often, practices are easily diffused, because their knowledge is well codified and because they are 'institutionally neutral.' Sometimes, they are not neutral complements, such as when the importation of Japanese team concepts to Germany conflicted with prevailing powers of work councils.

In addition to institutional neutrality, this chapter notes that the process of diffusion often causes institutions and practices to 'decouple' and 'recouple' (Kogut 1997). A simple way to express these ideas is by a Boolean algebra. It is this conceptualization that is explored, although by fuzzy set inferences, in Chapter 10.

Diffusion implies the possibility of institutional change, and in this regard, conflicts strongly with the implied predictions of the new institutional economics and of Hall and Soskice. The primary difference is that I reject this isomorphism between the societal and micro levels; they are more decoupled than commonly proposed. There is an important policy implication as well, for I am far more skeptical of our ability to change societies by mandating that they adopt particular kinds of institutions, such as common law or free labor markets. Institutional neutrality permits, in a technical and empirical sense, far more avenues of adaptation than these literatures permit.[15]

GENERATING RULES: GROWING SOCIETIES AND NETWORKS

The analytical basis of understanding exactly how such adaptations occur seem to me far from established, perhaps because we have been too busy looking for self-similarities across levels of analysis. Noting the problem of low and high equilibria, Robert Boyer and Andre Orleans (1992) propose an insightful suggestion that transition from low to high could take place by local diffusion processes. Such a process might take the form of diffusion in isolated islands, with eventual diffusion to the rest of the population (see Scott Boorman and Paul Levitt 1980). It is this type of invasion that is suggested by a frequency-dependent process, such as Axelrod's and Hamilton's (1981) analysis of the diffusion of cooperation and defection. The models we discussed earlier, such as Weber's on coordination, are in many ways a discrete-time approximation of these arguments. Coordination begins in small groups (islands) and then scales to larger groups (societies). This frequency-dependent process, so central to Axelrod, Hamilton, Boorman, Levitt and many others in artificial intelligence and computer science communities, is now diffusing into economics, which has re-invented it (Camerer and Fehr 2006).

Diffusion has, however, its limits, because not all institutions and practices are neutral or easy to transport. Paul Almeida and I applied for a National Science Foundation grant to study the relation of the mobility of star innovators to the diffusion of knowledge across firm and geography borders. This question represented an attempt to understand why knowledge appears to be spatially circumscribed. The grant was turned down, with one explanation being that because it focused on one industry (semiconductors), it lacked generalized validity. This objection is interesting, because clearly the NSF understood the experimental design (hold technology constant and vary the region) but did not see the importance of understanding the sources of heterogeneity. This article (Chapter 11) showed that contrary to very innovative prior work by Jaffe et al. (1993), knowledge (as measured by patents) and diffusion (measured by citations) differed by geography. Clearly the Silicon Valley was performing more successfully in building on local knowledge than other regions. We then showed that this region had higher rates of mobility of big innovators, that these innovators went on to do more innovations, and then tended to stay local even when changing jobs. Clearly, local labor markets, and implicitly social networks, differed among regions and hence influenced the diffusion of knowledge. One takes some satisfaction that Thompson and Fox-Kean (2005) published an article showing that the Jaffee et al. results overstate the effects of localization by aggregating across heterogeneous sectors.

On the other hand, new institutional forms are now being created that represent a weakening of spatial constraints on diffusion. The open source software movement is the outcome of a major institutional innovation: the General Public License (GPL). Just like venture capital received its institutional vehicle of diffusion through partnership agreements, open source communities grew only when a complementary institution was innovated. These communities, now much more studied, are not homogeneous; they are not utopian communes; they have formal structures and informal networks that explain the large differences in behaviors and type of innovative outcomes among them.[16] However, because such communities are built partly upon a shared global culture (i.e. hackers), their members are impressively diverse in their geographic origins. They represent the globalization of innovation and the increased possibility for bright minds at the periphery of the dominant economies to make use of their human capital that otherwise would be left dormant. It is more obvious now than a few years ago how much of the expansion of the world economy is based upon the arbitrage of brains, the most wasted world resource.

The past few years have seen exciting new intellectual currents in the social sciences. Because of advances in neurosciences, we see a greater sophistication in psychological foundations relevant to the social sciences. These foundations are too important to be left only to neural scientists and (social) cognitive psychologists. To establish finally a more integrated social science, the opportunity of this technological disruption should be used to create a scientific agreement on the motivations of people, their sociality, their individuality, and the rules by which they engage in the world.

These rules will be hard to determine, but we can start by the easy stuff first. The final chapter of this book proposes a framing that calls for the introduction of dynamic methods into the study of behavior and organizations. In recent years, there has been considerable technical progress in the understanding of micro-rules and emergence. The digitalization of historical, archival, and current data is changing the frontiers of academic research.

Increasingly, we do not have to rely upon suggestive relationships drawing on aggregate data, for example, culture leads to economic growth, that do not match the theoretical arguments of micro beliefs and macro outcomes. By understanding spatial and social localities, we can explore by a process of statistical estimation and simulation how rules of coordination and social processes (e.g. homophily, preferential attachment) generate complex macro outcomes.[17]

These new technological possibilities for research are imposing significant changes on the social sciences. The availability of large datasets makes academic conventions of measuring important findings (e.g. T-statistics, explained variation) senseless. The technical challenges are stimulating and difficult, requiring learning across the sciences. In evaluating careers and promotions, one can envision greater appreciation for the contribution made by an individual to research teams. It is a fitting conclusion to this introductory postscript to note that academic communities can thrive by lowering individual incentives and increasing collective contributions. For if one thing is common across all disciplines, sociality, identity, and the participation in communities are sources of inspiration and sustained creativity.

⬜ ENDNOTES

1. A good review is given in Cohen (2005). A more precise description can be found at http://brainmind.com/BrainOverview.html

2. There are several instruments used in neuroscience studies. Traditionally, studies relied upon cases of accidental damage to the brain, such as those used in the popular book by Oliver Sacks (c.1985).

3. Singer et al. (2004) cite the 'mirror neuron' evidence as supporting a particular theory of mind ('theory theory'), whereas in the same volume, Gallese (2004)—one of the discovers of these neurons—poses two objections: one is that mirror neuron are found in infants who do not have the cognitive development necessary to simulate according to a theory of mind and two is that the imitation is non-reflexive and automatic.

4. Gallese (2004) provides an excellent treatment of the developmental psychology work that supports a view of empathy as based upon mindreading and interpersonal relations.

5. Goleman provides a brief summary (2005: 141–2).

6. For an introduction to common knowledge that accounts for its distributed and implicit qualities, see Fagin et al. (2003). I thank Tim van Zandt for useful conversations on this topic.

7. See Babbage (1835). Nathaniel Rosenberg has a characteristically insightful interpretation of Babbage's ideas on the division of labor; see Rosenberg 1994: 24–46.

8. I recall reading in the American magazine *Life* that the Chinese in the 1960s or 1970s created a computer based on human organization. The accompanying photo showed a large field populated by Chinese in Maoist uniforms organized in a distributed organization and performing rudimentary calculations through the application of an algorithm.

9. For the conventional view, see Lerner and Tirole (2002); for an expansive view of economic motivation, see Osterloh and Frey (2000).

10. In addition to Searle, Hacking (1999) provides a very clear argument for realism.

11. This concept of 'possible worlds' is due to Leibnitz, though the more relevant development is due to Saul Kripke and David Lewis. An accessible and as always intriguing investigation is given in Elster (1978).

12. He offered in fact a guide to managers on this topic as early as 1987 (Wagner and Sternberg 1987).

13. Weber makes various inferences on the 'transfer' of behaviors—oblivious to the studies in the field that have examined transfer at length. See, for example, Zander (1991); Szulanski (1996); and Argote et al. (1990).

14. See the lovely book by Charles Tilly (1998) on inequality and classification.

15. See Amit Jain and Bruce Kogut (2006).

16. See also Gittelman and Kogut (2003) where we show that because industrial scientists live in professional communities, they live by a logic relevant to their community and at conflict with market incentives.

17. This final chapter is the introduction to my current work (e.g. Kogut et al. 2007).

Part I

Knowledge, Coordination, Categories, Identity

2 Knowledge of the Firm, Combinative Capabilities, and the Replication of Technology*

with Udo Zander

A fundamental puzzle, as first stated by Michael Polanyi (1966), is that individuals appear to know more than they can explain. That knowledge can be tacit has broad implications for understanding the difficulty of imitating and diffusing individual skills, a problem lying at the heart of artificial intelligence to the competitive analysis of firms. Though the idea of tacit knowledge has been widely evoked but rarely defined—as if the lack of definition is itself evidence of the concept, it represents a dramatically different vantage point by which to analyze the capabilities and boundaries of firms.

This article seeks to lay out an organizational foundation to a theory of the firm. To rephrase Polanyi's puzzle of tacit knowledge, organizations know more than what their contracts can say. The analysis of what organizations are should be grounded in the understanding of what they know how to do.

It is curious that the considerable attention given to how organizations learn has obscured the implication that organizations 'know' something. In fact, the knowledge of the firm, as opposed to learning, is relatively observable; operating rules, manufacturing technologies, and customer data banks are tangible representations of this knowledge. But the danger of this simple characterization is that everything that describes a firm becomes an aspect of its knowledge. While this is definitionally true, the theoretical challenge is to understand the knowledge base of a firm as leading to a set of capabilities that enhance the chances for growth and survival.

In our view, the central competitive dimension of what firms know how to do is to create and transfer knowledge efficiently within an organizational context. The following article seeks to describe these capabilities by analyzing the contention put forth by Winter (1987) that technology transfer and imitation are blades of the same scissor. The commonality is that technology is often costly to replicate, whether the replication is desired by the firm or occurs by imitation and unwanted diffusion. Though the terminology may differ, the underlying phenomena impacting the costs of technology transfer and imitation share similarities, regardless whether the replication occurs within the firm, by contract, or among competitors.

That similar factors may determine both the costs of imitation and technology transfer presents an interesting dilemma to the firm. In the efforts to speed the replication of current and new knowledge, there arises a fundamental paradox that the codification and simplification of knowledge also induces the likelihood of imitation. Technology transfer is a desired strategy in the replication and growth of the firm (whether in size or profits); imitation is a principal constraint.

Our view differs radically from that of the firm as a bundle of contracts that serves to allocate efficiently property rights. In contrast to the contract approach to understanding organizations, the assumption of the selfish motives of individuals resulting in shirking or dishonesty is not a necessary premise in our argument. Rather, we suggest that organizations are social communities in which individual and social expertise is transformed into economically useful products and services by the application of a set of higher-order organizing principles. Firms exist because they provide a social community of voluntaristic action structured by organizing principles that are not reduceable to individuals.

We categorize organizational knowledge into information and know-how based, a distinction that corresponds closely to that used in artificial intelligence of declarative and procedural knowledge. To move beyond a simple classification, these types of knowledge are argued to carry competitive implications through their facility to be easily replicated within an organization but difficult to imitate by other firms. Following the suggestions of Rogers (1983) and Winter (1987), the characteristics of both types of knowledge are analyzed along the dimensions of codifiability and complexity. By examining first personal expertise and then social knowledge, the capabilities of the firm in general are argued to rest in the organizing principles by which relationships among individuals, within and between groups, and among organizations are structured.

But organizations serve as more than mechanisms by which social knowledge is transferred, but also by which new knowledge, or learning, is created. The theoretical problem is that if the knowledge of the firm is argued to be competitively consequential, learning cannot be characterized as independent of the current capabilities. To explore this dynamic aspect, we introduce the concept of a *combinative capability* to synthesize and apply current and acquired knowledge. This concept is, then, explored in the context of a competitive environment. By this discussion, we ground such concepts as localized

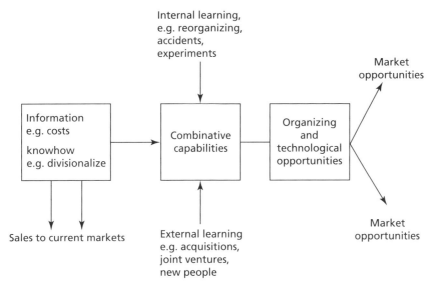

Figure 2.1. Growth of knowledge of the firm

learning to path dependence by developing a micro behavioral foundation of social knowledge, while also stipulating the effects of the degree of environmental selection on the evolution of this knowledge.

To ground the abstraction of the argument in an example, we reexamine the empirical findings on the make–buy decision of firms. The importance of the ability to generate new knowledge suggests a different view on the 'boundaries' of the firm, that is, what a firm makes and what it buys. Firms invest in those assets that correspond to a combination of current capabilities and expectations regarding future opportunities. Or, in other words, the knowledge of a firm can be considered as owning a portfolio of options, or platforms, on future developments.[1]

Figure 2.1 provides a roadmap to our argument. We begin by analyzing the knowledge of the firm by distinguishing between information regarding prices and the know-how, say, to divisionalize. This static portrait is the basis by which we explore how knowledge may be recombined through internal and external learning. An important limitation to the capability of developing new skills is the opportunity (or potential) in the organizing principles and technologies for further exploitation. Eventually, there are decreasing returns to a given technology or method of organizing, and there, consequently, results in an incentive to build new, but related skills. These investments in new ways of doing things, we suggest, serve as platforms on future and uncertain market opportunities.

It is important to underline the presumption that the knowledge of the firm must be understood as socially constructed, or, more simply stated, as resting in the organizing of human resources. The issue of the organizing principles underlying the creation, replication, and imitation of technology opens a window on understanding the capabilities of the firm as a set of 'inert' resources that are difficult to imitate and redeploy.[2] It is the persistence in the organizing of social relationships in which knowledge is embedded that is the focus of inquiry developed in this article.

Information and Know-How

There have been many suggestions as to how the knowledge of the firm might be categorized. Nelson (1982), for example, separates techno from logy, the former belonging to a firm, the latter to the public arena. A more common distinction is between research and development, or that between process and product.

For our purposes, we distinguish between two categories of knowledge as information and know-how.[3] By information, we mean knowledge which can be transmitted without loss of integrity once the syntactical rules required for deciphering it are known. Information includes facts, axiomatic propositions, and symbols. Nelson's idea of logy is, in fact, a recognition that within scientific communities, there exists a social agreement regarding the factual evidence by which to communicate the reliability of scientific findings. Similarly, public firms are required to report data to shareholders in a common format so as to facilitate analysis and appraisal. For the objective of public dissemination, information is standardized and released in order to be understood at minimal cost to those with the requisite training.

Of course, information is often proprietary. Firms maintain, as a rule, two sets of accounting data, one for external use, the other to aid managerial decisions and evaluation. Data can also be of competitive value. An obvious example is the value of information to traders of financial securities, but a more prosaic example is the data acquired by grocery stores on consumer expenditures.

Know-how is a frequently used, but rarely defined term. Von Hippel offers the definition that 'know-how is the accumulated practical skill or expertise that allows one to do something smoothly and efficiently' (von Hippel 1988). The pivotal word in this definition is 'accumulated,' which implies that know-how must be learned and acquired.

Knowledge as information implies knowing *what* something means. Know-how is, as the compound words state, a description of knowing *how* to do something. In economics, this distinction is, implicitly, preserved in the often made distinction between exchange and production economies, where the former consists of only traders responding to prices, and the latter to how inputs are transformed into outputs. To use a current example, the problems of the adoption economy in Eastern Europe consist not only of just finding the right prices, but also learning how to organize a market and a firm efficiently.

Though this distinction between information and know-how appears to be a fundamental element in the analysis of organizational knowledge, most efforts in this direction have tended, following March and Simon (1958) and Cyert and March (1963), to investigate the notion of routines in the context of organizational learning. Yet, this vantage point for the investigation of firm knowledge is ill-chosen. Learning has little significance in the absence of a theory of organizational knowledge.

A routine is in itself an insightful but incomplete characterization of knowledge. Because of the broad coverage of the term routine, an appeal is often made to the analogy of a blueprint, an analogy favored by a number of authors.[4] But a blueprint favors much more a description of information than know-how. Knowing how to do something is much like a recipe; there is no substantive content in any of the steps, except for their capacity to produce a desired end.[5] The information is contained in the original listing of ingredients, but the know-how is only imperfectly represented in the description.

It is revealing that this distinction between information and know-how as blueprints and recipes is similar to that made between declarative and procedural knowledge used in computer science. Declarative knowledge consists of a statement that provides a state description, such as the information that inventory is equal to a 100 books. Procedural knowledge consists of statements that describe a process, such as a method by which inventory is minimized. This distinction is robust to other phenomena than software, even to a furniture set where the inventory of parts is first described and then the recipe of assembly laid out.

Know-how, like procedural knowledge, is a description of what defines current practice inside a firm. These practices may consist of how to organize factories, set transfer prices, or establish divisional and functional lines of authority and accountability. The knowledge displayed in an organizational chart, as in any blueprint, is limited to providing information on personnel and formal authority. The know-how is the understanding of how to organize a firm along these formal (and informal) lines. It is in the regularity of the structuring of work and of the interactions of employees conforming to explicit or implicit recipes that one finds the content of the firm's know-how.

The Inertness of Knowledge

Firms differ in their information and know-how and these differences, when they are economically interesting, have persisting effects on relative performance. Thus, a central characteristic to be explained is the persisting difference in capabilities, that is, the difficulty in their transfer and imitation. The persistence of differentials in firm performance lies in the joint problem of the difficulty of transferring and imitating knowledge.

There is a need, therefore, to go beyond the classification of information and know-how and consider why knowledge is not easily transmitted and replicated. The transferability and imitability of a firm's knowledge, whether it is in the form of information or know-how, are influenced by several characteristics (Kogut and Zander 1990). Rogers (1983) and Winter (1987) have proposed that knowledge can be analyzed along a number of dimensions.

Consider the two dimensions of codifiability and complexity. Codifiability refers to the ability of the firm to structure knowledge into a set of identifiable rules and relationships that can be easily communicated. Coded knowledge is alienable from the individual who wrote the code. Not all kinds of knowledge are amenable to codification. Drafting a recipe for the manufacturing of a musical instrument is unlikely to capture the requisite skills of a craftsperson.

Nor is this limitation only applicable to know-how. It is not always possible to identify the relevant information which operates as the data to an actor or set of actions. There may be no 'theory' (in the sense used above) by which to identify the relevant information, such as drawing the blueprint. This argument bears similarities to the artificial intelligence debate on the obstacles to formalizing noncodified 'background knowledge' to scientific theories (Dreyfus and Dreyfus 1988). Codifiability is a question of the degree that there exists an implied theory by which to identify and symbolically represent knowledge. A theory may be as lacking for information as for know-how.[6]

Though codifiability is a central characteristic, it does not capture other aspects of knowledge. Knowledge can vary in complexity. There are many ways to define complexity. From a computer science perspective, it can be defined as the number of operations (or CPU time) required to solve a task. Indeed, Simon's notion of nearly decomposable systems is closely related. An ordered system reduces the cost and necessity of complex communication patterns. Drawing upon information theory, Pringle (1951) draws the distinction between order and complexity, defining the latter as the number of parameters to define a system. Within any given ordering (or what we call a code), complexity can be accommodated, but at a cost.

These dimensions are not independent. Codifiability and complexity are related, though not identical. To return to Pringle's definition, it is obvious that the number of parameters required to define, say, a production system is dependent upon the choice of mathematical approaches or programming languages. For a particular code, the costs of transferring a technology will vary with its complexity. A change of code changes the degree of complexity.

	Individual	Group	Organization	Network
Information	• facts	• who knows what?	• profits • accounting data • formal & informal structure	• prices • whom to contact • who has what?
Know-how	• skill of how to communicate • problem solving	• recipes of organizing such as Taylorist methods or craft production	• higher-order organizing principles of how to coordinate groups and transfer knowledge	• how to cooperate • how to sell and buy

Figure 2.2. Who has what knowledge?

Transformation of Personal to Social Knowledge

The final element in our characterization of the static properties of organizational knowledge is the distinction between the knowledge of an individual and that of the organization. Any discussion of firm knowledge confronts, ultimately, the problem of unit of analysis. We leave to the side the important task of specifying a more explicit integration of individual and organizational knowledge (such as via a shared culture, mechanisms of socialization, or an assumption of affiliative needs), but turn rather to laying out a description of the problem by distinguishing between personal, group, organizational, and network knowledge. The following discussion is summarized in Figure 2.2.[7]

Nelson and Winter (1982) have provided an important contribution by separating skills from routines. Individuals can be skilled in certain activities, such as driving a car or playing tennis. These skills may indeed be difficult to pass on. Variations in human intelligence alone may render difficult the transfer of technology, especially if intelligence is decomposed into aptitudes for solving differentiated tasks.

It is, in fact, the problem of communicating personal skills that underlies Polanyi's (1966) well-known idea of tacit knowledge, an idea similar to the dimensions of noncodifiable and complex knowledge. As noted earlier, to Polanyi, the central puzzle is the following: why do individuals know more than they can express. An interpretation of his argument is that tacit knowledge consists of search rules, or heuristics, that identify the problem and the elements consisting of the solution (Polanyi 1966: 23–4). The act of solving a problem rests on a sense of how the phenomena function; the formal expression of the solution is unlikely to capture fully this procedural knowledge, or even the data and information (or clues, as Polanyi describes it) leading to the solution. Thus, even in the arena of problem identification and solving, the know-how of heuristic search precedes the formal knowledge of the solution.[8]

The teaching of know-how and information requires frequently interaction within small groups, often through the development of a unique language or code. Part of the knowledge of a group is simply knowing the information who knows what. But it also consists of how activities are to be organized, for example by Taylorist principles.

It is the sharing of a common stock of knowledge, both technical and organizational, that facilitates the transfer of knowledge within groups. This view is widely held across a disparate literature. Arrow (1974) views one of the advantages of the organization as its ability to economize in communication through a common code. Piore (1985: xxv) likens the theory of internal labor markets to a 'conception of production knowledge as being like a language' common to a particular group of workers. By shared coding schemes, personal knowledge can be transmitted effectively within close-knit groups (Katz and Kahn 1966). Personal knowledge can be transmitted because a set of values are learned, permitting a shared language by which to communicate (Berger and Luckmann 1967). It is this language which provides a normative sanction of how activities are to be organized or what information is to be collected and evaluated.

But whereas the accumulation of small group interactions facilitate the creation of shared coding schemes within functions, a fundamental problem arises in the shifting of technologies from research groups to manufacturing and marketing (Dougherty 2007). At this point, the identification with a professional orientation conflicts with the need to integrate within the organization. The problems of different professional languages are attenuated when technology transfer is horizontal, that is, within the same function, as when a second plant identical to the first is built. To facilitate this communication, certain individuals play pivotal roles as boundary spanners, both within the firm as well as between firms (Allen and Cohen 1969; Tushman 1977).

The vertical transfer of technology, as when a product is moved from development to production, poses additional problems insofar as the shared codes of functional groups differ. Leonard-Barton's (1988) finding that technology transfer success is dependent upon the mutual adaptation between the two parties highlights the critical transformation of personal and group knowledge in the process of codification. To facilitate this transfer, a set of higher order organizing principles act as mechanisms by which to codify technologies into a language accessible to a wider circle of individuals. These principles establish how the innovation is transferred to other groups, the responsibility of engineers to respond to complaints, and the allocation of incentives to establish authority over decisions. These organizing principles, which we call higher order as they facilitate the integration of the entire organization, are also supported by data regarding profitability, costs, or task responsibility (as represented in an organizational chart).

In this sense, a firm's functional knowledge is nested within a higher order set of recipes that act as organizing principles. Complex organizations exist as communities within which varieties of functional expertise can be communicated and combined by a common language and organizing principles. To the extent that close integration within a supplier or buyer network is required, long-term relationships embed future transactions within a learned and shared code. In fact, the trading of know-how among firms often requires the establishment of long-term relationships (von Hippel 1988). In this wider perspective, a firm's knowledge consists also of the information of other actors in the network, as well as the procedures by which resources are gained and transactions and cooperation are conducted.

The Paradox of Replication

There is an important implication for the growth of the firm in the transformation of technical knowledge into a code understood by a wide set of users. An individual is a resource severely restrained by physical and mental limitations. Unless able to train large numbers of individuals *or* to transform skills into organizing principles, the craft shop is forever simply a shop. The speed of replication of knowledge determines the rate of growth; control over its diffusion deters competitive erosion of the market position.

For a firm to grow, it must develop organizing principles and a widely held and shared code by which to orchestrate large numbers of people and, potentially, varied functions. Whereas the advantages of reducing the costs of intra- or inter-firm technology transfer encourage codification of knowledge, such codification runs the risk of encouraging imitation. It is in this paradox that the firm faces a fundamental dilemma.

The problems of the growth of the firm are directly related to the issues of technology transfer and imitation. Once organizing principles replace individual skills of the entrepreneur, they serve as organizational instructions for future growth. Technology transfer is, from this perspective, the replication of existing activities. The goal of the firm is to reduce the costs of this transfer while preserving the quality and value of the technology.

Because personal and small group knowledge is expensive to recreate, firms may desire to codify and simplify such knowledge as to be accessible to the wider organization, as well as to external users. It is an interesting point, with far-reaching implications, that such a translation rarely occurs without a transformation in the nature of the knowledge. Computer software packages not only reduce the complexity of the knowledge required to use a computer's hardware; knowing how to use software is, in fact, substantively different from knowing how the computer works.

The reason why software has been successful is that it is codified so as to demand a lower fixed cost on the part of the general user. The user is required to understand the function of the program without knowledge of the substantive technology. (A function is an attribute to the product; substantive technology is the knowledge by which the product is created or produced.) The cost of this transformation is that the user's choices are restricted to the expressed functions. The specificity of a software language cannot expand the capabilities of the hardware; rather, it can only reduce the costs of its accessibility. It is, in fact, the possibility to separate the expertise to generate the technology and the ability to use it that permits the nesting of a firm's knowledge, as described above. But it is also this separation, as discussed below, that facilitates the ease of imitation. Being taught the functional skills of how to do something is different than being taught how to create it. We turn to these static and dynamic considerations below.

Combinative Capabilities

The issue of being able to use and being able to create software reflects a distinction commonly made in the literature on technology transfer regarding know-how and know-why.[9] It is, in fact, this distinction between exploiting and developing capabilities that lies at the foundation of Rosenberg's (1976) observation that 'reliance on borrowed technology (by developing countries) perpetuates a posture of dependency and passivity.' For example, activities involved in a manufacturing production process can be codified and imitated without requiring the knowledge of how the machinery functions. A Japanese factory shop might, conceivably, be organized by rules for inventory management and these rules might be transferred to American operations. Yet, the knowledge that leads to the development of such practices is unlikely to be transferred as easily.

To return to the development of software as a problem in codifying knowledge, Papert (1979: 77) notes the paradox that some languages are simple to learn but become complex in application. He writes:

But what do we mean by 'simpler' and what do we mean by 'learn the language'? Indeed, the [user] ... would learn its vocabulary very quickly, but they would spend the rest of their time struggling with its constraints. They would have to search for devious ways to encode even mildly complex ideas into this small vocabulary. Thus it is well-known that the programming language BASIC ... is quickly learned, but its programs quickly become labyrinths.

Papert's objection raises two important points. Some codes may be qualitatively better than others. They might facilitate certain technologies or practices better; the language of chemical pharmaceuticals may be inadequate for the development and transfer of biotechnologies. Even for the same technology, some firms may have evolved codes that differ in their efficacy.

The observation that some languages are more 'easily learned' suggests, superficially, a contradiction in the argument. Basic is 'simpler' but becomes quickly complex. But in what sense is it simpler other than through its familiarity to what the user already knows and through its design to address specific applications familiar to the user? Then why does it become a 'labyrinth'? The implicit suggestion is that Basic does not provide an efficient capability to address a change in the required application.

Let us migrate the argument from the individual to the organizational level by sorting out the two issues of familiarity to the user and, as discussed later, of the capability to create new applications to address changes in the environment, such as changes in market demand. Creating new knowledge does not occur in abstraction from current abilities. Rather, new learning, such as innovations, are products of a firm's *combinative capabilities* to generate new applications from existing knowledge. By combinative capabilities, we mean the intersection of the capability of the firm to exploit its knowledge and the unexplored potential of the technology, or what Scherer (1965) originally called the degree of 'technological opportunity.'

In the technological literature, the determinants of 'opportunity' are often regarded as physical in character; the speed of electrons is inferior to that of light. But since physical laws are eternally given, the critical question would then seem to be the social laws of their discovery and innovative application. Schumpeter [1911] 1934 argued that, in general, innovations are new combinations of existing knowledge and incremental learning.[10] He writes: 'To produce other things, or the same things by a different method, means to combine these materials and forces differently...Development in our sense is then defined by the carrying out of new combinations' (Schumpeter [1911] 1934: 65–6).

As widely recognized, firms learn in areas closely related to their existing practice. As the firm moves away from its knowledge base, its probability of success converges to that for a start-up operation (as implicit in Lippman and Rumelt 1982). The abstract explanation for this claim is that the growth of knowledge is experiential, that is, it is the product of localized search as guided by a stable set of heuristics, or, in our terminology, know-how and information (Cyert and March 1963; Nelson and Winter 1982). It is this local search that generates a condition commonly called 'path dependence,' that is, the tendency for what a firm is currently doing to persist in the future.

It should be clear that individual limitations in learning new skills are not a sufficient explanation. For even if mature individuals do not re-learn—as psychological evidence suggests, an organization may reconstitute its knowledge by recruiting new workers with the requisite skills. The problem of the 'inertness' of what an organization knows is not reduceable to individuals, except for the degenerate case of restrictions on the recruitment and retirement of human resources.

What makes the innovative search localized is that 'proximate' technologies do not require a change in an organization's recipes of organizing research. If current knowledge is inadequate, it may well be that a firm does not know what changes are required in the existing principles and structure of relationships. Even if identified, they may not be feasible, because the relational structure in the organization would be disturbed. Knowledge advances by recombinations because a firm's capabilities cannot be separated from how it is currently organized.

Selection Environment

Up to now, we have been concerned with explaining the role of organizing principles to facilitate the transfer of technology and ideas within the organization of the firm. The distinction between the ability to produce a product and the capability to generate it is fundamental to broadening our perspective to the competitive conditions of imitation. The ability to build on current technology is instrumental in the deterrence of the imitation of a firm's knowledge by competitors.

Imitation differs from technology transfer in a fundamental sense. Whereas technology transfer is concerned with adapting the technology to the least capable user, the threat of imitation is posed by the most capable competitors. In abstraction from a particular technology, it is, a priori, impossible to state in general what aspects of the transformation of ideas into marketable products will deter imitation. No matter which factor, however, is the most important, imitation is impeded by the possession of at least one bottleneck capability, as long as this capability is rewarded in the market.[11] This bottleneck can possibly arise through the benefits of reputation among consumers, patent protection, or the exercise of monopoly restrictions.

When these entry-deterring benefits are absent, competition switches from traditional elements of market structure to the comparative capabilities of firms to replicate and generate new knowledge. The nature of this competition is frequently characterized as a race between an innovator and the ability of the imitating firm either to reverse engineer and to decode the substantive technology. The growth of the firm is determined by a combination of the speed of technology transfer and of the imitative efforts of rivals.

Reverse engineering is often not a required response by competitors to new innovations. Incumbent competitors may simply respond to new product innovations by relying on other capabilities, such as brand labeling or distribution channels. Of more interest to our concerns, some competitors can imitate the function of the technology without necessitating reverse engineering of the substantive code. (As an example, many distinctive kinds of software can provide a spreadsheet function; the function is imitated, but not the underlying technology.) Many new products are only re-designs (i.e. recombinations) of existing components (Henderson and Clark 1990). In this kind of competition, the need to decipher the elements of the innovator's knowledge that generated the product can be simply bypassed.

In this ongoing competition, there is a short-term consideration, i.e. at what speed and cost can a firm replicate its current technology and imitate others. In innovative industries, competition is frequently a question of the speed and efficiency by which diverse groups within a corporation cooperate, a problem exacerbated when multifunctional coordination is required in order to increase transfer times to the market (Dougherty 1990). Over time and across multiple products, small differences in efficiencies can generate significant variations in profitability and (as well established in evolutionary biology) survival.

Short-term competitive pressures can, however, draw from the investments required to build new capabilities. The direct effect of selection is on the acceptance and rejection of new products, but indirectly it is operating to reward or to penalize the economic merits of the underlying stock of knowledge.[12] Knowledge, no matter how resistant to imitation, is of little value if it results in products that do not correspond competitively to consumers' wants. Selection on product types acts to develop and retard the capabilities of firms.

The ability to indulge in a forward looking development of knowledge is strongly contingent on the selection environment. Long-term survival involves a complex tradeoff between current profitability and investing in future capability. Future capabilities are of little value if the firm does not survive. In this sense, we have returned to Papert's concerns. Basic may be a poor language by which to address new applications or changes in the market. But for the student facing a deadline, programming in Basic may have clear survival value.

An important question, then, is the critical balancing between short-term survival and the long-term development of capabilities. A too strong reliance on current profitability can deflect from the wider development of capabilities (Stiglitz 1987). By their ability to buffer internal ventures from an immediate market test, organizations have the possibility to create new capabilities by a process of trial-and-error learning.

Thus luxury is often too exorbitant for companies or, for that matter, developing countries facing strong survival pressures. Yet, because investments in new ways of doing things are expensive, it is possible for a firm to continue to develop capabilities in ways of doing things which it knows, in the long run, are inferior (Arthur 1989). A too rigid competitive environment, especially in the early years of a firm's development, may impede subsequent performance by retarding a firm's ability to invest in new learning.

The Make Decision and Firm Capabilities

The merits of the above argument can be better evaluated by considering an example. An interesting application is the make–buy question, that is, whether a firm should source a component from the outside or make it internally. The examination of this problem throws into relief how an approach based on the knowledge of the firm differs from a contracting perspective.

It has become standard to argue that markets for the exchange of technology fail because of an appeal to a poker-hand metaphor; once the cards are revealed, imitation rapidly ensues since draws from the deck are costless. Because of the work of Teece (1977), Mansfield et al. (1981), and Levin et al. (1987), it is widely recognized this argument is a shibboleth. Yet, the consequences of this recognition are scarcely to be seen in the literature on technology transfer.

In fact, the costliness of its transfer has often been reconstrued as market failure (Teece 1980). Because a buyer cannot ascertain its value by observation, technology cannot be priced out. Thus, markets fail for the selling of technology since it is costly to transact.

The problem of this market failure argument is not only that markets for technology do exist, but also that it is over-determined. The public good argument turns on the opportunism of the buyer; the costs of transfer do not necessitate a similar behavioral assumption, though one can always throw it in for good measure. Opportunism is not a necessary condition to explain why technology is transferred within a firm instead of the market. Rather, the issue becomes why and when are the costs of transfer of technology lower inside the firm than alternatives in the market, independent of contractual hazards. The relevant market comparison, in this sense, are the efficiencies of other firms.

This issue extends to the more commonly studied case of contractual hazards affecting the make or buy decision, that is, whether to source from outside the firm. In the seminal empirical study of Walker and Weber (1984), evidence was found for the claim that the transaction costs of relying on outside suppliers lead to decisions to source internally. Yet, the most important variable is the indicator of differential firm capabilities, that is, whether the firm or the supplier has the lower production costs. Transaction cost considerations matter but are subsidiary to whether a firm or other suppliers are more efficient in the production of the component.

In the Monteverde and Teece (1982) paper that also supported the transaction cost argument, the most significant variable is the dummy for the firm. In other words, despite controls, the heterogeneous and unobserved firm effects were the dominant influence on the make–buy decision. Yet, both firms faced the same environment and transactional hazards.

While the boundaries of the firm are, unquestionably, influenced by transactional dilemmas, the question of capabilities points the analysis to understanding why organizations differ in their performance. The decision which capabilities to maintain and develop is influenced by the current knowledge of the firm and the expectation of the economic gain from exploring the opportunities in new technologies and organizing principles as platforms into future market developments. (See Figure 2.1.) We propose that firms maintain those capabilities in-house that are expected to lead to recombinations of economic value.

The evaluation of this economic gain rests critically upon a firm's ability to create and transfer technology more quickly than it is imitated in the market. Many investment decisions inside a firm do not include a make–buy calculation, for the presumption is that the new assets are extensions, or combinations, of the existing knowledge base.[13] Nor should it be surprising that there is a sense of ownership over the right to make and control the investment, for the physical assets are embedded within the replication of the existing social relationships and political structure of the firm. Because these relationships exist, an ongoing firm should have a greater capability to expand in current business than new entrants.

Path dependence is a rephrasing of the simple statement that firms persist in making what they have made in the past; for existing firms, knowledge advances on the basis of its current information and ways of doing things. To return to the Monteverde and Teece study, the finding that firms tended to produce internally those parts with high engineering content is a confirmation that auto companies specialize in engineering design and production. They make those parts that reflect their knowledge. (In fact, we should expect that they imitate those technologies which correspond closely to their knowledge.)

There are, of course, investment opportunities which are uncertain in terms of the applicability of a firm's current knowledge. Internal development, and imitation, are deterred because the organizing principles and information cannot be easily identified. Thus, investments in new knowledge often have a characteristic of trial-and-error learning, much like buying options on future opportunities.

Joint ventures requently serve as options on new markets distantly related to current knowledge by providing a vehicle by which firms transfer and combine their organizationally embedded learning. A common purpose of joint ventures is to experiment with new ways by which relationships are structured. That they frequently end by acquisition is a statement of their value as an ongoing entity of enduring social relationships which serve as platforms into new markets (Kogut 1991).

The decision to make or buy is, thus, dependent upon three elements: how good a firm is currently at *doing* something; how good it is at *learning* specific capabilities; and the value of these capabilities as *platforms* into new markets. To formalize the implications of these elements in terms of propositions, we would expect the following to hold:

1. Firms make those components that require a production knowledge similar to their current organizing principles and information.

2. The purchasing of technologies is carried out by the market when suppliers have superior knowledge which is complex and difficult to codify; by licensing when the transferred knowledge is close to current practice.

3. Firms develop internally projects that build related capabilities leading to platforms into new markets or rely on joint ventures (or acquisitions) when the capabilities are distantly related.

4. Immediate survival pressures encourage firms towards a policy of buying.

Similar propositions could be made in reference to other applications, such as acquisitions, the composition of a technology portfolio, and the sequence by which a firm invests in a foreign market.

Conclusions

The study of the knowledge of a firm raises issues, such as relatedness, technical core, or corporate culture, that are familiar to organizational theorists, but that have been hard to pin down. To a large extent, the theory of firm knowledge, as we have sketched it above, neglects the problem of individual motivation by focusing on organizing principles as the primary unit of analysis for understanding the variation in firm performance and growth. Because these principles are expressions of how a firm organizes its activities, they represent the procedures by which social relations are recreated and coordinated in an organizational context.

In contrast to a perspective based on the failure to align incentives in a market as an explanation for the firm, we began with the view that firms are a repository of capabilities, as determined by the social knowledge embedded in enduring individual relationships structured by organizing principles. Switching to new capabilities is difficult, as neither the knowledge embedded in the current relationships and principles is well understood, nor the social fabric required to support the new learning known. It is the stability of these relationships that generates the characteristics of inertia in a firm's capabilities.

Without question, there are issues, such as the creation of compatible incentives to induce behavior from individuals in accordance with the welfare of the organization, that can be fruitfully examined from a contracting perspective. But the transaction as the unit of analysis is an insufficient vehicle by which to examine organizational capabilities, because these capabilities are a composite of individual and social knowledge. After nearly two decades of research in organizational and market failure, it is time to investigate what organizations do.

Acknowledgments

We would like to thank Ned Bowman, Farok Contractor, Deborah Dougherty, Lars Hakanson, Gunnar Hedlund, Arie Lewin, and the anonymous referees for their comments. Partial funding for the research has been provided by AT&T under the auspices of the Reginald H. Jones Center of The Wharton School.

▢ ENDNOTES

* This chapter is a revised version of B. Kogut and U. Zander (1992) 'Knowledge of the Firm, Combinative Capabilities, and the Replication of Technology,' *Organization Science*, 3: 383–97.

1. This notion of a platform is investigated in Kogut (1991) and Kogut and Kim (1991).

2. See Lippman and Rumelt (1982), Rumelt (1984), Wernerfelt (1984), Barney (1986), and Kogut (1987), as well as the publications that appeared while this article was under review by Dierickx and Cool (1989) and Prahalad and Hamel (1990).

3. Steve Kimbrough has pointed out in conversation that the terms are similar to Bertrand Russell's distinction between know-that and know-how.

4. See March and Simon (1958); Hannan and Freeman (1977); Nelson and Winter (1982).

5. In light of the wide appeal genetics has for organizational analogies, it is of interest to refer to Dawkins's (1987) discussion of genes as recipes (and the phenotype as a blueprint). See also Simon ([1962] 1979).

6. Contrary to Dreyfus's and Dreyfus's doubts, the organization behaviorists, Argyris and Schoen (1978: 11), believe it possible to derive the 'theory-in-use' from 'directly observable data of behavior ... to ground ... construction of the models of action theories which guide interpersonal behavior.'

7. As a way of summarizing our argument, this figure was suggested to us by Gunnar Hedlund. See also Hedlund and Nonaka (1991).

8. In the philosophy of the science, this distinction corresponds to the difference between the logic of discovery and the logic of demonstration. See also Dreyfus and Dreyfus (1988) for a discussion in relation to artificial intelligence.

9. In the interest of avoiding a proliferation of terms, we would add the caveat that since formal science is characterized by recipes through which causal relationships are identified, this distinction may be simply a restatement of the question, identified in note 8, whether the methods of scientific discovery can be codified.

10. The view that knowledge can be created only as combinations of what is already known has a long lineage, from Plato's *Meno* to Polanyi's (1966) idea of tacitness.

11. This point is captured in empirical work using the survey results, whereby appropriability is defined as the item that indicates the maximum deterrence to imitation (Levin et al. 1987).

12. This point, of course, lies at the heart of the genes versus phenotype controversy in biology. See, for example, Dawkins (1976).

13. We would like to thank Gordon Walker for emphasizing that many new investment decisions entail only whether to and not to make internally; there is often no external evaluation.

3 Knowledge and the Speed of the Transfer and Imitation of Organizational Capabilities: An Empirical Test*

with Udo Zander

That innovation is the central feature of competition in capitalist economies is a widely held view. It is especially emphasized in the work of Schumpeter (1942) and the evolutionary theory of the firm of Nelson and Winter (1982). Due to the force of competition and changes in consumers' wants, the firm's long-run survival and growth depend on its ability to develop new products and new methods of organization. Yet, what is frequently underemphasized is that the expansion of an innovation rests upon the capacity to replicate the capability of the production and sales of the new service or product. This replication can occur by the voluntary transfer of this capability within the firm or to other firms (e.g. by a license), or by the unwanted imitative efforts of competitors. Transfer and imitation of the organizational capabilities are the twin elements of competition in innovative and growing markets.

In an earlier article, we proposed that the firm should be understood as a repository of social knowledge, where a competitive set of capabilities is replicated over time while subject to imitation. This present article examines a central proposition that the characteristics of social knowledge should influence the time to transfer and the time to imitation of major product and process innovations. In general, the knowledge of the firm can be categorized into 'information' and 'know-how.' It consists of the competence of individuals and of the organizing principles by which relationships among individuals, groups, and members to an industrial network are structured and coordinated. These principles of coordination of individual and functional competence generate the capabilities of a firm.[1]

In the examination below, these capabilities concern the ability to man-ufacture major industrial innovations. The issues we explore lie at the core of an evolutionary theory of the firm. In such a theory, the competitive dynamics of an industry are driven by the rates of the transfer and imitation of new products and organizational capabilities.[2] In this dynamic perspective, internal transfer and imitation of an organizational capability are alternative mechanisms of serving a market. They, in this regard, represent joint processes of diffusion whose paths are partly determined by the ease of the replication of underlying knowledge. Other factors obviously influence the rates of transfer and imitation. Particularly important, as discussed below, is the degree to which firms share common manufacturing capabilities, on the one hand, and the degree to which they differ in their distinctive abilities to *recombine* their knowledge to improve the innovation, on the other.

In the first part of the paper, the perspective that capabilities of the firm consist of the cumulative experience in understanding a class of knowledge and activities is developed. Subsequently, drawing on the work of Rogers (1980) and Winter (1987), a set of dimensions by which to characterize a firm's capabilities (e.g. codifiability and teachability) is developed. Through questionnaires, data on the transfer and imitation times of 35 major Swedish innovations were collected. The questionnaire responses were then used to construct scales describing the *manufacturing capability* used for the production of these innovations. The time to transfer of manufacturing capabilities to new sites and the time to imitation by competitors were then regressed on these scales.

Strong support is found for the effects of different characteristics of capa-bilities on the time to transfer, while results for imitation are mixed. The empirical tests confirm that the degree to which capabilities are codifiable and teachable influences the speed of their transfer. These factors are not important for determining the rate of imitation. Imitation rates are influenced by the extent to which important aspects of the capabilities are possessed by many firms and by the ability of the innovator to improve the product. These results support the broader argument that firms exist and compete on the basis of their abilities to create, further develop, and transfer capabilities.

Knowledge of the Firm and the Dissemination of Capabilities

The transfer of technology is a topic that has received considerable attention. The term is often misleading, because technology is frequently associated with the application of scientific knowledge. Yet, these applications represent a special case of a wider phenomenon. Technology, as the many case studies on transfer of manufacturing know-how to other countries show, consists of the principles by which individual skill and competence are gained and used, and by which work among people is organized and coordinated.[3] The successful transfer of technology results in the receiving unit implementing *new techniques of production*. These capabilities can be used and economically exploited in the marketplace. Transferred knowledge can reside in design, production, installation, sales and distribution, operation and maintenance, or management.

Much as skills define the competence of individuals, organizing principles underlie the capabilities of a firm. The relationship between principles of organization and capabilities can be seen in revolutionary innovations of this century in the area of work organization. As Chandler (1977) has documented, the Taylorist principles of incentives and staff organization supported the capability to accomplish standardized production at lower costs. The Toyotist principles of decentralized authority and lateral communication across functions, buyers and suppliers generate the capability of speed and flexibility.

Organizing principles underlay what firms can do. To be flexible requires rules by which work is coordinated and by which information on the market is gathered and communicated. Just-in-time manufacturing, designing for manufacturability, or decreasing time to the market are capabilities which presuppose a certain social knowledge regarding who is competent, how work is coordinated, and what information is shared.

The endeavors of firms to create, apply, and replicate this social knowledge do not proceed with the purpose of rapid public dissemination. Largely, the construction of knowledge in a firm should be more idiosyncratic, reflecting the firm's particular history and experience. Technology is indeed often firm-specific, differentiated knowledge about specific applications, which is largely cumulative within firms.[4] Moreover, through experience, a multiunit firm develops a set of rules or higher ordered organizing principles by which new capabilities are created, improved, and transferred in the organization.

There are also other important aspects of developing capabilities which are idiosyncratic to individuals and to small groups.[5] Competitive pressures create a value in developing a capacity of replicating knowledge within the firm faster than the similar efforts of competitors. When a new market is created through an innovation, a central limiting force on the growth of the innovating firm is the speed by which competitors imitate the new products.[6] In the simplest evolutionary models, profit-seeking firms imitate in response to the prevailing market signals that it is profitable to do so. As a form of public information, market signals are not always sufficient to engender imitation. In many cases, imitation requires the acquisition of new know-how, that is, of new ways of doing things.

It makes sense that the competitive pressures of imitators create an incentive for the innovator to expand rapidly by speeding the voluntary transfer of what is commonly called technology. Here lies the interesting dilemma that a technology that is easily transferred and replicated may also be easily imitated. Since the transfer and imitation are alternative and exhaustive mechanisms by which capabilities are disseminated, they should, as Winter (1987) has argued, be linked in their ease through which the relevant knowledge can be identified and communicated.

The ability to transform tacit capabilities into a comprehensible code, understood by large numbers of people, is derived from the collective experiences of members to a firm organized by persisting rules of coordination and cooperation.[7] The relationship of accumulated experience in facilitating the communication and understanding of a new technology is a consistent finding in studies on the transfer of technology. Teece (1977) found that the costs of technology transfer were determined by the age of the technology, the recipients' previous experience with transferring the technology, and the number of firms using similar technologies. All three variables point to a latent factor involving the codification of knowledge (Teece 1981). Since older technologies are better codified, they are less costly to transfer. Experience with transferring the technology points to the importance of learning how to codify the technology effectively for subsequent transfers.[8]

An interesting and overlooked factor is suggested by Teece's (1977) finding on the negative association between the number of other firms using the technology and the costs of transfer. In effect, technologies which are widely diffused are less costly to transfer, because, one can speculate, the knowledge of their properties is well understood and codified. This finding has come out in other studies as well. For example, Contractor (1981) found that technology transfer (via licensing) to a country increases with the sophistication of its manufacturing and engineering base.[9] The relationship between past use and ease of the transfer underscores the explanation advanced by Hall and Johnson (1970), Westphal et al. (1985), and Pavitt (1985), that the cumulative experience with a technology is a critical factor determining the learning capability of the recipient to understand new technologies.[10] An issue related to imitation is that because firms differ in their history of experience with different technologies, they will vary in the costs for understanding and assimilating new technologies.

Experience is important both at the individual and organizational level. From studies on individual learning, we know that new skills are more quickly learned the more they share elements with already acquired knowledge. In their study of the acquisition of computer programming and calculus skills, Singley and Anderson (1989) concluded that procedural knowledge (e.g. riding a bike) is more slowly forgotten than declarative knowledge (e.g. facts or propositions). The trade-off is that procedural knowledge is useful to a more limited number of activities. For learning radically new applications, declarative knowledge of a theoretical nature proved more robust.

The reason procedural knowledge is easily remembered and yet useful is probably due to the facility by which it can be stored in chunks. It is easier to remember modules than to figure out new ways to recombine many propositions. In an intriguing experiment, Cohen and Bacdayan (1995) found that their subjects tended to repeat similar sequences of actions; procedures often consisted of a learned repertoire of associated behaviors. Importantly, due to the experimental condition of penalizing slower decisions, these learned sequences were used when more optimal, even when obvious alternatives were available.

The pressure of competition is the pressure of limited time to decide. Firms rely upon routinized behaviors because they are efficient ways of doing things given what they already know how to do. The classic study of Bavelas (1950) reported that different structures of communication among subjects to an experiment influenced the number of errors (performance) and morale. Moreover, the initial distribution of resources and communication structures greatly affected the ability to arrive at an optimal solution.

It is not surprising that given the difficulty of arriving at optimal solutions for relatively simple tasks in small groups, the pressure of competition forces behavior toward the reiteration of learned behaviors that have been successful in the past and that speed the coordination among individuals. Technology transfer from developed to developing countries has often been found inappropriate to the receiving country (Davies 1977). It follows from our reasoning that they are inappropriate because firms transfer the procedures they already know how to do.

The Dimensions of Knowledge

We have developed the argument that the accumulation of experience in an activity leads to the facility to communicate and understand the relevant knowledge. This facility, in turn, should reduce the cost of acquiring new related capabilities and speed the time to transfer and imitation. Usually, the effect of experience has been framed in terms of its relationship to the costs of transfer and imitation or, more commonly, on the frequency of transfer. We propose, instead, to analyze directly the effects of the extent to which capabilities can be communicated and understood on the time to their transfer and imitation.

Technologies and innovations have, of course, been described and measured according to several dimensions in previous studies. There have been, however, few investigations of the effects of these characteristics on the rate of dissemination, whether by voluntary transfer or imitation. Rogers (1980) and, more recently, Winter (1987) have proposed similar ways by which to link the attributes of an innovation to the rate of dissemination. While these approaches have not been tested on the rate of dissemination, they offer consistent advice on the properties of a technology that should influence the degree to which an innovation can be communicated and understood.

In his major work on the diffusion of innovations, Rogers (1980) proposed five dimensions by which innovations can be described: 'relative advantage' (or 'profitability'), 'communicability,' 'observability,' 'complexity,' and 'compatibility.' The latter indicates the similarity of the innovation to current experience, knowledge, and values. More recently, Winter (1987) suggested a similar taxonomy, which identified four dimensions of a firm's knowledge: 'tacit/articulable,' 'observable/not observable in use,' 'complex/ simple,' and 'dependent/independent of a system.' The first dimension is further broken down into whether the knowledge is articulated (e.g. whether records are kept), and whether it can be taught. It is suggested that even if knowledge is tacit, it may be taught by apprenticeship.

We follow the Rogers and Winter taxonomies by developing five central constructs by which to characterize a firm's knowledge at the levels of individual competence and group and organizational capability. These constructs are 'codifiability,' 'teachability,' 'complexity,' 'system dependence,' and 'product observability.' The fifth construct, 'product observability,' developed in reference to imitability, captures the degree to which the technology is common to a network of industrial competitors; observability of the technology is important for the imitation by reverse engineering (i.e. copying the components by inspection), but should not be important for voluntary capability transfer.

The five constructs are ways to measure the degree to which a capability can be easily communicated and understood. These constructs measure different qualities of the knowledge of the firm. It would be nonsensical to believe that there is a single dimension called tacitness. Neither is there a reason to believe that there is a body of knowledge that is univariate across levels of analysis of the individual, the organization, and the network.

'Codifiability' captures the degree to which knowledge can be encoded, even if the individual operator does not have the facility to understand it; software controlling machinery is a good example. 'Teachability,' to the contrary, captures the extent to which workers can be trained in schools or on the job; it reflects the training of individual skills. 'Complexity' picks up the inherent variations in combining different kinds of competencies; knowledge, no matter the education of the worker, is simply more complex when it draws upon distinct and multiple kinds of competencies. 'System dependence' captures the degree to which a capability is dependent on many different (groups of) experienced people for its production. 'Product observability,' finally, captures the degree to which capable competitors can copy the manufacturing capability, because they are able to manufacture the innovation once they have understood the functions of the product.

These characteristics of knowledge measure different aspects that underlie the facility by which manufacturing capabilities are transferred and imitated. To test for the effect of these characteristics on the rate by which a capability is transferred or imitated, we created a design, described below, that employs the time to transfer and the time to imitation (or, more precisely, their hazard rates) as the dependent variables. These measures differ from Teece's calculations of transfer costs (Teece 1977), as well as from the more common measures of counting the number of transfers adopted by countries (Contractor 1981), or the age of the technology at the time of imitation (Mansfield 1985). Our method has the advantage of avoiding the problems of estimating transfer costs, as well as of incorporating censored observations, i.e. those capabilities that were not transferred or imitated.

To summarize, our design is to analyze the following central proposition:

P1. The more easily a capability can be communicated and understood, the shorter the times to transfer or imitation.

The dimensions used to measure the ease of communication and understanding are 'codifiability,' 'teachability,' 'complexity,' and 'system dependence.'

There are, of course, other factors than the ones just mentioned which influence the time to transfer and imitation. As reported above, previous studies on the transfer of technology have argued that a large number of firms using a similar technology suggests that the capability to receive and assimilate the technology is widely spread. Another possibility, suggested by our argument, is that competition should encourage rapid expansion by capability transfer, as well as imitation, due to the threat of competitive preemption in the market. This leads to our second proposition:

P2. The more there are competitors engaged in developing similar products, the shorter the times to transfer and imitation of the capability.

It is important to note that the comparison between the transfer of manufacturing capability and imitation is inexact, for imitation may be possible even if the innovator's manufacturing knowledge remains proprietary. The importance of manufacturing varies by innovations. In some industries, the key capability is knowledge of the customers' needs; knowledge of how to manufacture may be 'common' among competitors.[11] One way to address this aspect of the determinants on imitation is to assess directly the degree to which principal aspects of a manufacturing capability are well dispersed among a group of competitors. The extent to which imitators can pull from a general pool of knowledge regarding how to manufacture this product should influence imitation.

P3. The more the principal aspects of the manufacturing capability have spilled over the boundaries of the firm, the shorter the time to imitation.

Finally, we also look at the effect of continuous improvement in innovations as a way to deter imitation. As argued by Gilfillan (1935), Usher (1971) and Abernathy and Utterback (1975), innovations at the time of introduction undergo a period of incremental improvement. Whether it pays to invest in appropriating a technology is also a question of how rapidly it becomes obsolete. Imitation is often deterred based upon the *combinative capabilities* of a firm to innovate incrementally on its innovations (Kogut and Zander 1992). The ability of the innovating firm to improve the product should deter imitation, even if important aspects of the manufacturing capability are widely diffused.

P4. The more the innovating firm has subsequently improved the product or the production process, the longer the time to imitation.

Empirical Design

THE SAMPLE

To test the thesis that the transfer and imitation of capabilities are related to the dimensions of the underlying knowledge, we developed a questionnaire instrument to distribute to project engineers knowledgeable of the history of a major innovation. The innovations were identified from a study by Wallmark and McQueen (1986) on 100 major Swedish innovations which achieved a major share of world markets.[12] To satisfy the need to observe the history of the innovation over a long period of time and to question engineers familiar with this history, the target sample was narrowed to innovations occurring after 1960; this process identified 44 innovations for which, due to multiple innovations, 20 firms were responsible. For each 44 identified innovations we sent out a questionnaire.

The respondents were selected by asking the technical director at the group level to identify key respondents.[13] The technical directors recommended individuals who were contacted by phone to verify their knowledge of the innovation and prepare them for the questionnaire. Multiple respondents for an innovation were not used, though, for some questionnaires, one individual scored the basic information and another answered the section dealing with the manufacturing process. (As the questions did not reflect on the performance of the respondents, the risk of misattribution is low.)[14] In nine cases, the respondents were the primary innovators. When an original innovator did not exist or was no longer accessible, individuals were contacted who had been directly responsible for manufacturing and product management internationally since the introduction of the innovation.[15] Of the 44 questionnaires sent out, a response rate of 80 percent was attained; the remaining 20 percent were similar in size and industry affiliation to the responding organizations. (For a list of the 35 innovations for which completed questionnaires were received, see Appendix 3.2.)

Besides being a novel sample, the data on Swedish innovations had clear advantages. All of the companies are Swedish-based, competing in industrial markets. Because Sweden is a small country, these companies were forced to expand in international markets. Transport and communication costs generally encourage the transfer of technology, and the enforceability of patents is less binding in world markets. These conditions increased the attractiveness of technology transfer and the possibility of imitation.

The focus on major innovations made it more likely to gather accurate information on the year of the first product delivery and the subsequent incidents of transfer and imitation. These data would not be as easy to reconstruct for less important or successful innovations. Since all of the innovations were chosen on the basis of their success, there is likely to be little variance in what Rogers called 'relative advantage.' This selection criterion, in one sense, imposes an implicit control for variations in demand and profitability. While restricting attention to very successful innovations, the sample may overstate the speed to transfer (successful innovations require more manufacturing capacity) and also affect the speed to imitation. As we are, however, not estimating the regressions on time to transfer and time to imitation simultaneously, this effect (which is common across the whole sample) should not bias the estimates.

Some factors which would have been of interest could not be easily investigated. In particular, we did not measure how widely spread the relevant technological capabilities of imitators and recipients of technology were or whether they understood the same codes; what is codified for one firm may thus be incomprehensible to the next. At present, we are not able to control directly for this possibility, but the problem may not be too severe. Since the firms were expanding first in developed markets, recipients and imitators originate in countries with comparable levels of technological capability. We assume, in the terminology of Hall and Johnson (1970), that general capabilities are present in developed countries to allow the assimilation of the technology and to pose the threat of imitation. Moreover, we introduce in subsequent regressions variables which indicate the degree of spillover of important aspects of the manufacturing capability.

THE QUESTIONNAIRE

The questionnaire was developed, first, through field research, which resulted in eight case studies of innovations developed in three firms.[16] Following these case studies, an initial instrument was drawn up and pretested on respondents from five of the case studies, as well as on academic colleagues from Swedish technical universities. (The instrument was written in Swedish, with all respondents being fluent in this language.) This process generated a two-part test instrument.

The first part of the questionnaire simply asked for factual data, e.g., the date at which the innovation was first introduced into the market, the number and timing of transfers, the occurrence of the first imitation, etc. These data provided the information required constructing the hazard rate specification for estimating the effects of the covariations on the time to transfer, as well as on the time to imitation.

The second part of the questionnaire drew upon a design common in psychometric studies. A list of questions was developed, and characteristics of manufacturing capabilities were measured by 43 questions regarding the nature of the firm's *manufacturing* of the innovation. Respondents marked on a seven-item scale, as recommended by Cox (1980). The decision to concentrate on manufacturing was motivated by the impracticality of seeking internal experts on all the relevant functions affecting the commercialization of an innovation. This decision poses no difficulty for the analysis of the transfer of manufacturing capabilities. It, however, turned out to be insufficient, as the latter results show, for the study of imitation.

OPERATIONALIZING THE CHARACTERISTICS OF KNOWLEDGE

The items forming the construct measuring characteristics of manufacturing capabilities, technological competition, and the degree of knowledge diffusion among competitors are described in Appendix 3.1. For *codifiability*, the items were designed to capture the extent to which the knowledge could be articulated in documents and software. This knowledge may be substantive, e.g. in blueprints, or it may be procedural, e.g. in a recipe for carrying out a task (Simon [1962] 1979; Kogut and Zander 1992).

Teachability was designed to capture the ease at the individual level by which knowledge, even when it cannot be formally articulated, can be taught to new workers. Capability transfer often requires the sending of engineers and workers from the originating plant to help in the building up of know-how in the sister plant.[17] To the extent that this know-how is easily taught, the transfer is more feasible and can be made faster.

Complexity proved to be one of the more difficult dimensions to opera-tionalize. Simon ([1962] 1979) avoided explicitly to give a definition, though his examples suggest the number of decomposed cells in a system as a mea-sure of complexity. A complementary definition is the number of parame-ters required to describe the function of the technology. Tyre (1991) mea-sures 'technical complexity' as the number, novelty, and technological sophis-tication of new features and concepts in a technology. Along these lines, we defined complexity as the number of distinctive skills, or competencies, embraced by an entity or activity. As the knowledge being dimensionalized concerns manufacturing, we developed a variable by adding the scores on four items indicating the importance of four types of processes, as identi-fied by Hayes and Wheelwright (1984). Thus, we decided upon an objec-tive set of items which indicate the importance of different manufacturing methods. Our approach thus tries to measure complexity as the degree of multiple competencies used to manufacture a product.[18] The more complex a manufacturing capability, the more difficult it should be to transfer or to imitate.

With the dimension *system dependence*, we tried to capture at the organiza-tional level the extent to which transfer or imitation of a capability is impaired due to dependence on many different (groups of) experienced people for its production. Winter's (1987) idea of 'dependence of a system' refers to the possibility for a technology to 'stand alone.' We developed this scale using items on the degree of dependence of manufacturing with other functions. Our measure is related to Tyre's (1991) measure of 'functional overlap' which describes the number of lateral linkages between plant engineering and pro-duction personnel.

Product observability was constructed from items concerning whether the manufacturing capability can be acquired by reversed engineering or from published reports. This construct is used only in the estimates for imitation, since a firm that voluntarily transfers its manufacturing does not need to resort to reverse engineering or generally available documents.

To control for the effect of competition on speeding the time to transfer and imitation, the variable *parallel development* was used. It is measured by the count of competitors perceived as engaged in parallel efforts aimed at devel-oping a similar product at the time of the innovations' release. (A summary of the described variables and the predicted relationships with the times to transfer and to imitation is given in Table 3.1.)

A central issue for imitation, as discussed above, is the extent to which there is already a common manufacturing capability among competitors. To test for these effects, we constructed three measures to capture the extent to which aspects of manufacturing capability spills over quickly and easily among firms. *Proprietary equipment* is constructed from items indicating

Table 3.1. Predicted Signs of Independent Variables

Variable	Probability transfer	Predicted sign of early risk of early imitation
CODIFIABILITY	+	+
COMPLEXITY	−	−
TEACHABILITY	+	+
SYSTEM DEPENDENCE	−	−
PARALLEL DEVELOPMENT	+	+
PRODUCT OBSERVABILITY		+

the extent to which machinery and software developed and kept within the company embody principal manufacturing capabilities. *Outsourced equipment* indicates the extent to which machinery or software purchased from external vendors embody principal manufacturing capabilities. The third measure, *key employee turnover*, is derived from the question whether any of the firm's knowledgeable manufacturing employees had left the firm (coded as one or zero).

An important finding in the literature has been that one of the most significant deterrents to imitation is the capacity of the innovating firm to improve consistently on its original design (Levin et al. 1987). The measure *continuous development* is constructed to capture the importance of subsequent improvements of the innovation through recombining current knowledge. It is created by taking the maximum standardized value of how important subsequent modifications are perceived to be for preventing imitation.[19]

CONSTRUCTION OF THE MEASURES

The constructs derived from the questionnaire items were measured by forming scales derived from questions that were chosen a priori to contribute to the same construct. The scales were constructed by transforming the responses into a standard normal deviate, with zero mean and variance of one. Then, the standard scores were summed to form a scale score. By standardizing the scales and locating the mean at zero, it is easier to interpret the results as the effect on the time to imitation or transfer from a departure from the mean. In Table 3.2, the descriptive statistics for the variables are reported.

To test for reliability, Cronbach alphas were calculated for each scale, with the recommended 0.7 used roughly as a cutoff (Nunnally 1978). Cronbach alphas are derived by averaging the inter-item correlations of the off-diagonal entries of the correlation matrix and adjusting these correlations for the number of total items. An increase in either the average correlation or the

Table 3.2. Descriptive Statistics

Variable name	Mean	Standard deviation	Lowest	Highest
1. CODIFIABILITY	0	291	−654	375
2. COMPLEXITY	0	242	−466	381
3. TEACHABILITY	0	370	−713	720
4. SYSTEM DEPENDENCE	0	279	−834	501
5. PARALLEL DEVELOPMENT	0	1	−084	400
6. PRODUCT OBSERVABILITY	0	243	−357	557

Correlation matrix

	1	2	3	4	5	6
1	—					
2	−016	—				
3	002	023	—			
4	003	028	−018	—		
5	008	025	001	006	—	
6	−021	028	047	−001	−001	

number of items improves the alpha score. This test has been shown to set the lower bound to the reliability of an unweighted scale and, consequently, provides a conservative estimate (Novick and Lewis 1967). Questions with low item-to-total correlation were deleted; reliabilities for the final constructs ranged from 0.61 to 0.785.

Because of the high number of items to sample size, discriminant validity could not be estimated by confirmatory factor methods. It is important to verify that the constructs related to the ability to communicate and understand a capability consist of items which are distinctive. We estimated, therefore, the average correlation of intraconstruct items as a 'within measure' and the average correlation of each construct's items with each other construct's items as a 'between measure.' (See Table 3.3.) The 'within' average correlation is higher than the 'between' average correlations, providing a reasonable indication of the discriminant validity of these constructs.[20]

Table 3.3. Average Within/Between Correlations

	COD	TEA	SYS	OBS
COD	0373	—	—	—
TEA	0108	0434	—	—
SYS	0132	0178	0316	—
OBS	0145	0282	0079	0484

Notes: COD = codifiability; TEA = teachability; SYS = system dependence; OBS = product observability.

Table 3.4. Hazard Rates of Major Swedish Innovations

Year	1	2	3	4	5	6	7	8	9	10	11	12	13	14	15	16	17	18	19	20
Int Transfers	017	07	011	0	004	009	005	005	0	0	005	006	006	007	0	008	010	0	029	020
# at Risk	35	29	27	24	24	23	21	20	19	19	19	18	16	14	13	12	10	9	7	5
Imitation	0	003	0	006	013	011	004	005	0	014	0	0	0	0	007	0	027	013	014	033
# at Risk	35	35	33	33	31	27	23	22	21	21	18	17	16	16	15	11	11	8	7	3

SPECIFICATION OF THE STATISTICAL MODEL

As stated earlier, we understand capability transfer and imitation as diffusion processes determined by a common, though not exclusive, set of factors. We estimated the effects of the co-variates on the rates by which manufacturing capabilities were transferred to new sites and by which innovations were imitated. These rates, when expressed as the probability of transfer or imitation *conditional* on no previous event, are called hazard rates. In Table 3.4, we show these rates for the years following introduction of the innovation in the market.

A natural test would be to correlate the hazard rates for imitation and transfer. This problem is statistically very complicated, as the data are censored, i.e. some innovations were not imitated or transferred by 1988 when the period of observation ended. For our purposes, we rely upon a regression format to test whether the co-variates act similarly upon the hazard rates for transfer and for imitation.

To do this, we rely on techniques of likelihood estimation, under which the data are used to generate estimates of the coefficients which maximize the likelihood of the functional specification. Since we are not interested in the exact timing of the event, we specify the hazard model as a partial likelihood. (To specify a parametric function would raise unnecessary questions of the theoretical basis for the specification.) The procedure relies on the partition of the likelihood for events into a baseline hazard rate and an exponential term incorporating the co-variates. Partial likelihood simply discards the baseline hazard rate and treats the coefficient term as depending only on the order in which the events occur. In our case, the method rank orders technologies in terms of the sequence of transfer or imitation times, as measured from when manufacturing first started. This specification is semi-parametric, for the baseline hazard is entirely general, but the co-variates are specified as raised to an exponential and act multiplicatively on the baseline hazard.

The log likelihood function is constructed as the sum of the likelihoods that a capability will be transferred or imitated given that *j* technologies are at risk:

$$L = \sum_t \left[B'X_t - \sum_{j \in Rt} B'XJ \right] \quad (1)$$

where L is the log likelihood and $\Sigma_j \in_{Rl}$ is the sum over all j technologies at risk at time i, X is the covariate vector, and B is a vector of coefficients. (As the baseline hazard is the same for all technologies at risk, it has canceled out from the expression.) The estimates have been shown to be asymptotically consistent (Efron 1977). As long as censored observations are large, ties do not pose any estimation problems (Allison 1984; Cox and Oakes 1984). Our data satisfy this criterion. A positive sign to an estimated coefficient (B) represents that an increase in the variable increases the hazard of transfer or to imitation; a negative sign indicates the converse.

Empirical Results

DESCRIPTION OF THE DATA

The innovations in our sample have generally been exploited rapidly in international markets. On average, around 50 percent of production has been sold overseas within one year after the introduction of the new product. At the time of measurement in 1989, over 70 percent of the new products were manufactured in at least one plant outside Sweden. In total, 85 transfers had been made, with the average number of transfers per innovation being three.

The median time to transfer was five years; without correcting for censored observations, the average was eight years. Reflecting the trade and investment patterns of Swedish firms, the most important recipient countries were the US (nine transfers), Canada (seven), France (seven), Australia (seven), Japan (six), England (four), and Norway (four).

Imitations showed a time profile similar to that of transfers. Despite that all the innovations in the study were protected by patents, approximately two-thirds of the products have been imitated by competing firms. In a vast majority of these cases, the imitating firms had been important international competitors with a long experience in the industry.[21] Rarely, local competitors had copied the new product, while newly established firms, licensees, joint venture partners, subcontractors, or customers had almost never introduced a product based on the same technology.

For the innovations that had actually been imitated, the median time to imitation was five years, with the average being eight years. These medians are larger than those reported by Levin et al. (1987) and Mansfield (1985).[22] A

Table 3.5. Partial Likelihood Estimates of Covariates to Log Hazard of Transfer

Variable name	Probability of early transfer
CODIFIABILITY	019 (215)**
COMPLEXITY	003 (027)
TEACHABILITY	019 (268)***
SYSTEM DEPENDENCE	008 (076)
PARALLEL DEVELOPMENT	081 (336)***

Notes: *** $P < 001$ (t statistics in parentheses, two-tailed tests); ** $P < 005$; * $P < 010$.

possible explanation is that our sample is drawn from a listing of successful and significant innovations. The nationalities of the imitating firms were diverse, roughly similar to the countries of the first transfers.

TRANSFER OF MANUFACTURING CAPABILITIES

The results regarding the determinants of the time to transfer are interesting in that they show that certain characteristics of manufacturing capabilities can be used to explain variations in transfer patterns. Estimates for transferability are given in Table 3.5. The strong results for *codifiability* and *teachability* act as a bellwether. These two constructs provide the most direct insight to the degree to which capabilities are tacit and difficult to communicate, and have significant effects on the hazard of transfer; the more codifiable and teachable a capability is, the higher the 'risk' of rapid transfer.

Parallel development has a highly significant effect (as measured by the coefficient and T-statistic) on the hazard of transfer. This result underscores clearly that a high level of 'technological competition' and the fear of losing the technological edge to competitors speeds the transfer of capabilities. The strong result regarding parallel development is especially interesting given the relative neglect of this type of variable in earlier studies of technology transfer.[23]

The coefficient estimates to *system dependence* and *complexity* are insignificant.

IMITATION AND GENERALIZED KNOWLEDGE

Results for imitation, given in Table 3.6, show that the characteristics of the manufacturing capability *do not* affect the hazard rate. This result suggests that the view of capability transfer and imitation as mirror phenomena needs to be refined. It is easy to see by our earlier discussion why this is the case,

Table 3.6. Partial Likelihood Estimates of Covariates to Log Hazard of Imitation (A)

Variable name	Risk of early imitation
CODIFIABILITY	−011 (−137)
COMPLEXITY	018 (143)
TEACHABILITY	−010 (−146)
SYSTEM DEPENDENCE	010 (120)
PARALLEL DEVELOPMENT	−008 (−030)
PRODUCT OBSERVABILITY	009 (075)

Notes: *** $P < 001$ (t statistics in parentheses, two-tailed tests); ** $P < 005$; * $P < 010$.

though the implications are not, as discussed below, fully reflected in the wider literature.

The imitation of innovations does not necessarily involve the imitation of capabilities, while transfer, by our definition, is the replication of manufacturing capabilities. For this reason alone, imitation and transfer are not identical phenomena.

In many industries, manufacturing capabilities may be widely diffused among the principal competitors. Successful imitation is often determined more by the access to a broad range of capabilities (e.g. how to design, test, modify, manufacture, market, and service the product). Moreover, industry conditions, such as reputation, government policy, and retaliation, will also influence imitative activities.

The omission of the effect of competitors' capabilities on imitation can be partly addressed by capturing the extent to which manufacturing knowledge is common to a group of competitors. Imitation should be quicker in industries where important capabilities, whether embodied in individuals or in machines, are more accessible. Possessing knowledge of manufacturing has little importance if this knowledge is widely dispersed.

We capture the extent to which certain aspects of the manufacturing capabilities are common knowledge by regressing the hazard of imitation on measures of labor turnover, inside sourcing of equipment and software, and external sourcing of specialized machinery and software. Simultaneously, we include a measure of the degree to which the innovator improves the product or the production process in response to imitative threats.

The results, presented in Table 3.7, indicate that the degree to which important aspects of manufacturing capabilities spill over among firms has a significant effect on the speed by which innovations are imitated. As in Tables 3.5 and 3.6, we use a conservative two-tailed test although our hypotheses are directional. *Key employee turnover* is significantly associated with faster imitation times. The coefficient to *continuous development* is just shy of significance at the 0.05 level. The result suggests that building on current capabilities creates

Table 3.7. Partial Likelihood Estimates of Covariates to Log Hazard of Imitation (B)

Variable name	Risk of early imitation
PROPRIETARY EQUIPMENT	−019 (−128)
OUTSOURCED EQUIPMENT	011 (071)
CONTINUOUS DEVELOPMENT	−031 (071) (−194)*
KEY EMPLOYEE TURNOVER	108 (199)**

Notes: *** $P < 001$ (t statistics in parentheses, two-tailed tests); ** $P < 005$; * $P < 010$.

an effective deterrent to imitative efforts. The use of *proprietary equipment*, i.e. machinery and software developed and kept within the company lowers the risk of early imitation, but the result is weak. The sign to the coefficient of the variable *outsourced equipment* is as expected, but the result is not significant.

Insights from the Field

The case of imitation can be further understood by turning to the field research that preceded the study. Consider the following examples derived from an indepth study of three innovations in rock drilling and pulp and paper drying (innovations 13, 22, and 32 in Appendix 3.2.) The three innovations, the compact pulp dryer, the flash dryer, and the hydraulic rock drills, display quite different characteristics of manufacturing technology, although they were developed in similar firm environments.

Fläkt's[24] compact pulp dryer (the FC dryer) and Atlas Copco's[25] hydraulic rock drill have not been transferred outside Sweden. Manufacturing has been centralized in Sweden, with some sales and after-sales service assigned to the foreign subsidiaries.

As to the FC dryer, the decision to centralize manufacturing was driven by the difficulty to codify the information by blueprints and by the difficulty to teach manufacturing employees.[26] Production has depended upon well-trained, experienced manufacturing teams which worked for long periods of time together.

In the case of hydraulic rock drills used for the piercing of hard rock in mining, the competence to design, manufacturing and improve the metallurgical qualities of the parts was heavily dependent on a few key employees.[27] For example, it was not uncommon that design engineers brought blueprints down to the shop floor for revision by key employees, who applied their hands-on experience to correct flaws in the proposed design.

To manufacture Fläkt's flash dryer[28] used to sort and fluff pulp for paper production, it was possible to write comprehensive manuals describing the manufacturing technology and the relatively uncomplicated nature of man-ufacturing. The accumulated knowledge about designing the dimensions, which is the more problematic part of building the flash dryer, was codified and stored in a computer program. The data and software, drawn from the cumulative experience from worldwide installations, have never been trans-ferred to foreign units but are kept at central level in Sweden. Easily imitated, access to the computer-driven system is highly restricted.

Examining information from the three innovations, there is no clear rela-tionship between the characteristics of manufacturing technology and imita-tion by competitors. The examples consist of two innovations where manufac-turing was complex and based on the competence of manufacturing personnel (the FC dryer and the hydraulic rock drill). In the third innovation (the flash dryer), manufacturing was uncomplicated and easy to understand and communicate.

However, complexity and the requirement of personal skills in manufac-turing did not prevent imitation of the hydraulic rock drill. In spite of the uncomplicated and easily understandable manufacturing technology, the flash dryer was not imitated. The case of the flash dryer illustrates how the codifi-cation of critical knowledge does not necessarily increase the risk of imitation. The software and database, containing critical information about different installations and how they work, are tightly held secrets based on cumulative learning; Fläkt has been aggressive in driving competitors out of business.

Other variables related to actions taken by the firms to protect the technol-ogy affect imitation patterns. As the flash dryer case shows, secrecy sometimes relates to codified knowledge, but it might also relate to the retention of key employees. There are indications in the hydraulic rock drill case, and also in Fläkt's earlier generations of dryers, that the losses of key employees were detrimental to keeping the technology from the hands of competitors. The loss of skilled engineers also negatively affected the ability to refine the product or the manufacturing process.[29]

In all three examples, continuous improvements of products and manufac-turing processes were cited as discouraging would-be imitators. As illustrated by Fläkt in the flash and FC dryer case, the product was continuously devel-oped after the introduction of the innovation. The perception was that com-petitors might have the capacity to imitate individual generations of the prod-uct, but that they could not keep up with a high pace of product development.

Conclusions

The empirical analysis points to both simple and more complex conclusions. The transfer of manufacturing capabilities is influenced by the degree to which they may be codified and taught, and the threat of market preemption. Both the nature of the capabilities and the nature of industry competition matter.

The principal difficulty in the argument which we have advanced regarding imitation is not the logic, but the empirical complexity. Imitation encompasses a complex comparison between the full array of the capabilities of the innovator and competitors. The requisite aspects of manufacturing capabilities may be widely spread among competitors, each of which may be competing upon differentiated and cumulative experience.

There is an insightful lesson in these simple conclusions from a complex matter. The capability to produce a product is obviously different from the nature of the product itself. There is no reason to believe that a given product quality, or attribute, must map uniquely onto a set of capabilities. For example, cars are manufactured by many different production methods. Of course, the mapping of product qualities onto capabilities is not unbounded; we do not expect craft production methods of 1890 to produce high volumes of low-cost cars. But the variations in wage and capital costs, and in the accumulation of firm-specific experiences, can generate a substantial heterogeneity in the organizing principles and capabilities in a market.

In this study, we have been able only circumspectly to examine the dynamics by which knowledge evolves over time. The ability to improve a product, we know from the field research, rests on the recombination of already learned skills. In fact, the evidence suggests that a set of capabilities serves as a platform into other markets and related product areas.

This study has concentrated largely on the horizontal transfer of knowledge from one manufacturing site to another. The analysis of the transfer of manufacturing capability, and the relationship of this capability to imitation, is limited only to a single function. We have omitted considerations of the structuring of roles and the attribution of power in an organization. If we are to understand why capabilities are 'inert,' such as happens in adopting radically new ways of doing things, we need have a better understanding of problems of collective choice and coordination. However, understanding the resistance to change only as a problem of stalemate among different groups inside a firm provides limited, albeit important, insight into inertia.

An organization is, obviously, more than a collection of disjointed manufacturing sites and functional groups. There is, in this larger sense, an organizing knowledge that provides a unity to the firm. At this point, we offer only the guess that the partition of firm knowledge into modular 'chunks' of expertise is valuable for speeding the coordination and codification of diverse capabilities. Modular components of the firm can be seen as an efficient decomposition of knowledge into learned sequences (or chunks) of behavior that serve to speed coordination and communication among groups. Understanding how modular capabilities can be recombined may well lead to a better theory linking incremental innovation to the design of organizational knowledge.

The assembly of diverse functions within a single firm raises the question of why coordination and communication between functional groups are better handled within a firm than between specialized firms. We have proposed that the appropriate vantage point by which to analyze this question is to understand the firm as competing on the speed by which knowledge is created and communicated. Why this replication is qualitatively altered at the boundaries of a firm is a central issue in understanding long-term differences in the growth among firms.

The claim that firms act as social communities for the creation and communication of knowledge requires a more explicit description of the motivation and cooperative choices of the individual members. It also requires an understanding of the basis of social knowledge and shared language.[30] It may be that an appeal to the idea of an individual as a reed but a thinking one, is a necessary precondition to developing a pragmatic notion of social knowledge and its accumulation. But sufficiency will certainly require also the development of a notion of the inherent sociality of sometimes selfish individuals. As far removed as it may seem from the concerns of knowledge and organizational capability, the presumptions of people as selfish and sociable, as myopic and pragmatic, form the logical foundations of the views of firms as social communities.

Acknowledgments

The authors would like to acknowledge the support of IMIT and the Reginald H. Jones Center of the Wharton School and the advice and comments of Howard Aldrich, Erin Anderson, Ned Bowman, Bob House, Mitch Koza, Arie Lewin, Dennis Mueller, and Gordon Walker, and the anonymous referees, and comments of participants in seminars at Max Planck Institut fuer Sozialforschung in Cologne, Wissenschaftszentrum in Berlin, New York University. Georgetown University, and INSEAD. Bruce Kogut, who spent a sabbatical year at the Centre de Recherche en Gestion of the Ecole Polytechnique during the process of revising this paper, would like to thank his colleagues, especially Herve Dumez and Jacques Girin, for many helpful discussions.

⬜ APPENDIX 3.1: THE CONSTRUCTS AND VARIABLES

Codifiability

PERCEIVED CODIFIABILITY

1. A useful manual describing our manufacturing process can be written.
2. Large parts of our manufacturing control are embodied in standard type software that we modified for our needs.

3. Large parts of our manufacturing control are embodied in software developed within our company exclusively for our use.
4. Extensive documentation describing critical parts of the manufacturing process exist in our company.

Coefficient alpha: 0.678

Teachability

PERCEIVED TEACHABILITY

1. New manufacturing personnel can easily learn how to manufacture the product by talking to skilled manufacturing employees.
2. New manufacturing personnel can easily learn how to manufacture our product by studying a complete set of blueprints
3. Educating and training new manufacturing personnel is a quick, easy job.
4. New manufacturing personnel know enough after a normal high school education to manufacturing our product.
5. New manufacturing personnel know enough after vocation training to manufacture our product.

Coefficient alpha: 0.785

COMPLEXITY

DIFFERENT TYPES OF MANUFACTURING PROCESSES

How important are the following to manufacturing:

1. Processes for changing physical characteristics of a material (e.g. chemical reactions, refinement, heat treatment).
2. Processes for changing the shape of material (e.g. casting, pressing, rolling, bending).
3. Processes for giving materials certain dimensions (e.g. turning, milling, drilling, sawing).
4. Processes for assembling different parts to a whole (e.g. welding, soldering, gluing, screwing).

System Dependence

PERCEIVED IMPORTANCE OF SYSTEM DEPENDENCE

1. It is impossible for anyone in our firm to know everything about the entire manufacturing process
2. To get high product quality it is very important that our manufacturing personnel has long experience from the specific plant where they are working.
3. Workers in important parts of the manufacturing process have to be in constant contact with engineers or product quality will go down.

Reversed:

4. Our product can be manufactured in a unit isolated from all other production without quality being influenced at all.

Coefficient alpha: 0.637

Product Observability

PERCEIVED PRODUCT OBSERVABILITY

1. A competitor can easily learn how we manufacture our product by analyzing descriptions of our product in product catalogues, etc.
2. A competitor can easily learn how we manufacture our product by taking it apart and examining it carefully.
3. A competitor can easily learn how we manufacture our product by testing in use.

Coefficient alpha: 0.772

Parallel Development

EXTENT OF PARALLEL DEVELOPMENT

1. Were any of your competitors engaged in developing products similar to yours at the time of your innovation?

   - No.
   - Yes. # of competitors: ___

Proprietary Equipment

PERCEIVED USE OF PROPRIETARY EQUIPMENT

1. Large parts of our manufacturing technology are embodied in machines built within our company exclusively for our use.
2. Large parts of our manufacturing control are embodied in software developed within our company exclusively for our use.

Coefficient alpha: 0.61

Outsourced Equipment

PERCEIVED USE OF OUTSOURCED EQUIPMENT

1. Large parts of our manufacturing technology are embodied in machines that are tailor-made by other firms for our purposes.
2. Large parts of our manufacturing control are embodied in software tailor-made by other firms for our purposes.

Coefficient alpha: 0.97

Continuous Development

PERCEIVED EFFECTS OF CONTINUOUS DEVELOPMENT

1. Continuous modification has been very important in preventing imitation of our product.
2. Continuous development of the manufacturing process has been very important in preventing imitation of our product.

Loss of Key Employees

EXTENT OF LOSS OF KEY EMPLOYEES

1. Have any of your skilled manufacturing people left your company to the benefit of competitors after the introduction of the product?
   - No
   - Yes, in the year(s): ___

⬜ APPENDIX 3.2. LIST OF INNOVATIONS

1. Exchangeable Inductor for Steel Melting 1960 (Asea)
2. Pressductor 1960 (Asea)
3. Emulsified Fats for Intravenous Injection Intralipid 1960 (Kabi Vitrum)
4. Rail-Bound Hauling Car for Mines 1961 (Hägglund & Söner)
5. Rubber Details for Rotating Drums 1961 (SKEGA)
6. Milk Sterilizer 1961 (ALFA-LAVAL)
7. Machine for Fluidized Freezing of Foodstuffs: Flofreeze 1961 (Frigoscandia Contracting)
8. Quintus Type Steel Press for Use in the Asea-Stora Process 1962 (Asea)
9. Air Cushioned Lawn Mower 1963 (Electrolux)
10. Cross Cable 1963 (Ericsson)
11. Matrix Printer 1964 (Facit)
12. Beta-Blocker: Aptin 1965 (Hässle)
13. Pulp Dryer with Airborne Pulp Web: Type FC 1966 (Fläkt)
14. Drug for Expansion of Bronchi: Bricanyl 1966 (Draco)
15. Thyristor-Controlled Spin Control System for Locomotives 1967 (Asea)
16. Isostatic Press for Steel Processing 1967 (Asea)
17. Explosive: Dynamex 1967 (Nitro Nobel)
18. Gel for Filtering: CNBr-Method 1967 (Pharmacia)
19. High Resolution Copying Machine Multinex 1968 (Misomex)
20. Ball Bearing: HUB 3 1969 (SKF)
21. Ore Transporter: Häggloader 1969 (Hägglund & Söner)
22. Flash Dryer for Pulp 1969 (Fläkt)
23. Semi-Synthetic Penicillin: Penglobe 1970 (Astra)
24. Selective Beta-Blocker Seloken 1970 (Hässle)
25. Roller Bearing: CC 1972 (SKF)

26. Ventilation System: Optivent 1972 (Fläkt)
27. Ignition Mechanism for Explosives: Nonel 1972 (Nobel)
28. Machine for Feeding Metal Sheets: Doppin-Feeder 1972 (Volvo)
29. Ventilation System: Dirivent 1974 (Fläkt)
30. High Temperature Steel 153 MA & 253 MA 1974 (Avesta Jernverk)
31. Chemical for Wound Treatment: Debrisan 1975 (Pharmacia)
32. Hydraulic Rock Drill 1975 (Atlas Copco)
33. Telephone Switching System: AXE 1976 (Ellemtel)
34. Stainless Steel: 245 SMO 1976 (Avesta)
35. Self-Emptying Railway Car for Ore 1978 (Lkab)

ENDNOTES

* This chapter is a revised version of U. Zander and B. Kogut (1995) 'Knowledge and the Speed of the Transfer and Limitation of Organizational Capabilities: An Empirical Test,' *Organization Science*, 6: 76–92.

1. See Kogut and Zander (1992). We have been struck by the similarities of this argument to the discussion of expert systems by Hatchuel and Weil (1992) of 'savoir-faire,' 'savoir-comprendre,' and 'savoir-combiner.' See also Starbuck (1992).

2. This perspective shares obvious similarities with the resource school of thought, especially Barney (1986), Reed and DeFillippi (1990), and Dierickx and Cool (1989). We tend to agree with Foss (1992) that this perspective is nested within a broader evolutionary approach. Indeed, Nelson and Winter (1982) lay out a broad schema for looking at competitive dynamics with imitation.

3. The classic study in this vein is Hall and Johnson (1970).

4. Pavitt (1985) and Kogut and Zander (1992).

5. Drawbacks to developing capabilities idiosyncratic to individuals and small groups are clearly transparent in studies of R&D cultures, where moving technology from the laboratory to operations is often impaired by differences in the values and work habits of researchers and others in the corporation. See Allen (1970); Tushman (1977); and Dougherty (1990).

6. See Anderson and Tushman (1990); Mitchell (1989); and Lieberman (1989).

7. Of course, some codes extend beyond the boundaries of the firm, as exemplified in the rules designed to diffuse knowledge within a scientific community. The understanding and acceptance of scientific facts, as Kuhn (1962) and his antecedent Fleck ([1935] 1979) point out, are socially determined through the construction of a set of values widely held among an international scientific community. It is a subtle point, and one we cannot pursue here, that the efficiency of these rules for communication may well be responsible for the tendency to fail to understand other interpretations.

8. Davidson and McFetridge (1984) also find this effect, as well as that experience in internal transfers encourages more internal transfers in the future. This suggests that only once a firm has invested in codifying knowledge for the purpose of licensing are external transfers subsequently promoted.

9. There have been, of course, many qualitative and historical studies which demonstrate this relationship; almost any study on why technology is imitated by some countries and

not others has noted the importance of indigenous experience and capabilities See, for example, Westney (1987).

10. The above studies focused on the horizontal transfer of technology from one plant to another. Importance of communication and codification is apparent also in studies on the costs and time of the vertical transfer of knowledge within organizations. In her study of the transfer of new technologies within a corporation, Leonard-Barton (1988) concluded that adoption was accompanied by an intense interaction between the user and the research and development (R&D) project team.

11. 'Common knowledge' is usually meant to refer to symmetries in information among players to a game. In our case, we extend it to symmetries in capabilities. We thank Jacques Girin for stressing this point.

12. As a criterion for inclusion of an innovation, Wallmark and McQueen used the annual turnover generated by the innovation. To be classified as a major innovation, the annual revenues had to be at least 20 million Swedish Crowns (roughly USD 3.5 million) in real terms. Growth rates of revenues also had to be significant. In addition, the innovation had to be patentable in accordance with Swedish Patenting Law, and at least one significant patent had to exist.

13. Given the large size of the firms where innovations in the sample originated, several technical directors were contacted by phone in each case. The invariable consensus on part of the contacted directors as to the right person to send the questionnaire to supports our confidence in the indepth knowledge and the accuracy of the respondents.

14. It was, obviously, impossible to collect time-varying observations on the technology over time. A potential source of noise, then, is that the manufacturing technology is not stationary. This problem, which should only worsen our results, may not be too severe if the rates of technological change are roughly similar.

15. In a large majority of these cases, the same person had been responsible for the product since it had been introduced. In the cases where management had changed, the person having spent the longest time as manufacturing/product manager was selected as a respondent. In all cases, the respondents had detailed knowledge of the historical development related to the innovation, since the introduction and exploitation of the innovation had been the dominating and most exciting part of their career.

16. See Zander (1991). We would like to thank Erin Anderson and Gordon Walker for their assistance in the questionnaire design, and Robert House for his comments on the reliability and validity tests.

17. See Hall and Johnson (1970).

18. For an interesting and somewhat related measure, see Granstrand and Sjölander's (1990) measure of the width of the technology-base of a firm: the sample average of the number of engineering categories represented in a firm.

19. By taking the maximum, this measure replicates the scale in Levin et al. (1987).

20. Only the correlation between proprietary equipment and codifiability violated this rule, but the two constructs were not entered simultaneously into the same regression. It is, by the way, not unexpected that they should be correlated.

21. In no case did the same competitor imitate several of the innovations in the sample.

22. In these studies, imitation has been found to be surprisingly rapid. The median time to imitation varies across studies between roughly one to three years, though with

considerable industry variation. These rates have been shown to be slightly slower for processes, as implied by the findings on R&D and productivity.

23. For an exception, see Stobaugh (1988).

24. Fläkt is a leading producer of drying systems, heat recovery systems, ventilation controls, air pollution equipment and vacuum cleaning systems. In 1987, total group sales amounted to USD 2 billion, of which approximately 80% were generated outside Sweden. Today, more than two-thirds of the world's marketed pulp is dried using Fläkt equipment.

25. Atlas Copco's traditional businesses are compressors, mining and construction equipment, industrial automation and production equipment. In 1987, 91% of group sales were generated outside Sweden, and almost 80% of the 19,000 employees worked outside Sweden. It has been estimated that the company earned some USD 250 million selling hydraulic rock drilling equipment only between 1973 and 1983.

26. The FC dryer efficiently dries a continuously moving airborne pulp web through impinging hot air through 'eye-lid openings' parallel with the web. The tensionless transporting of pulp on a weak air stream makes it possible to handle pulp webs with very low tensile strength.

27. Hydraulic rock drilling technology has doubled drilling speed, reduced energy consumption by one-third, as compared to pneumatic rock drilling. The use of hydraulics has also reduced noise levels and environmental damage. In addition, it is estimated that the hydraulic technique reduces drill steel consumption by 50%.

28. Flash dryers have gained an increasing share of the pulp drying market because of low investment costs and facilitated operations. In a flash drying system, pulp is de-watered, fluffed, and dried in gases with much higher temperatures than normally used in a conventional web-type dryer.

29. In some of the cases, key employees have been lost because of rather petty reasons, e.g. by moving production facilities to a new location.

30. See Kogut and Zander (1992) and Girin (1990) for a discussion along the lines of viewing the firm as an 'epistemic community' sharing a language and, hence, cognitive rules.

4 What Firms Do: Coordination, Identity, and Learning*

with Udo Zander

At the turn of the last century, the French economist Léon Walras stylized a competitive economy by a system of equations that relied upon the notion of a tatonnement, or of iterative bidding, by which quantities are cleared. This notion of an exchange economy is fundamental, not only in identifying the meaning of equilibrium, but also in suggesting that economic agents learn collectively the correct prices through a pursuit of self-interested bidding. In a more modern time in which computers trade automatically, Walras's vision of a tatonnement has been realized in the electronic markets of nonhuman actors. If ever there was a vision of a brain in a vat, it is the evolution of electronic trading in financial markets.

It is amusing, and yet insightful, to note that the modern firm seems bizarrely resistant to these advances. No where is this resistance so obvious than in Mintzberg's (1973) observation on how much talking managers do. Organizations have a process of tatonnement, but the tatonnement is not that of market clearing, but of procedural coordination and learning. These issues were not neglected by Frederich Hayek, although his 1945 essay on the role of prices as information is considered as one of the most eloquent statements on the superiority of the market to planning. In a lesser known article on tacit knowledge, Hayek noted that '... even decisions which have been carefully considered will in part be determined by rules of which the acting person is not aware' (Hayek 1962: 335).

To investigate these issues, we proposed that a firm be understood as a social community specializing in the speed and efficiency in the creation and transfer of knowledge.[1] This knowledge could be understood as consisting of know-how and information, concepts that correspond to the procedural and declarative distinction made in cognitive sciences. Through the recombination of this knowledge, firms evolve, partly by the generative logic of their capabilities but also by the opportunities and influences of the external environment. In our empirical work, we tested a pair of central hypotheses that, if disconfirmed, would provide strong falsification of these ideas. The results indicated reasonable support for the proposition that more tacit knowledge is slower to be transferred and that firms tend to transfer tacit knowledge within the firm instead of through the market. To summarize these findings, we stress the costs of communication, coordination, and new combinations, not those of transactions, as the primary metric that influences the boundary decisions of firms.

The price of a good or service quoted in a market is related, in some way, to the costs of its provision. By implication, firms face different opportunities in the market and address these opportunities with varying costs (and speed) of transformation. It is not transaction costs, but the social knowledge embedded in the competence of individuals and the organizing principles of work that explains what firms are on the basis of what they know how to do.

The comment by Nicolai Foss on our argument poses an important question. Why is there more knowledge, he asks, inside the firm than outside? He argues that the answer to this question requires coupling knowledge of the firm to the capabilities of hierarchy to resolve agency and transaction cost dilemmas. He allows for differences in communication costs to determine firm boundaries, but then notes that communication cost differences beg the larger question, why they should be lower. His causal reasoning runs from hierarchy to the control of opportunism, allowing for the emergence of trust and, consequently, superior performance. This perspective is conventional and echoes Williamson's (1975) notion of a quasi-morality and the reduction in transactions costs for trade inside the firm. Because the gains do not flow to the employees, there is less incentive to behave opportunistically.

The question why there is 'more of it' inside the firm points to an omission in our paper. Our implicit causal reasoning runs from identity of the individual with a group to the dynamics by which coordination and learning are facilitated and, consequently, to the superior performance of firms. Higher-order principles are the organizing knowledge that establishes the context of discourse and coordination among individuals with disparate expertise and that replicates the organization over time in correspondence to the changing expectations and identity of its members. We propose that the boundaries of firms demarcate qualitative changes in the reservoir of social knowledge available to economic agents (i.e. people) because coordination and learning are developed within the organizational context of shared identities. This shared identity does not only lower the costs of communication, but establishes explicit and tacit rules of coordination and influences the direction of search and learning.

Our efforts to make explicit a theory of the firm based on a wider notion of human motivation is not alien to the spirit of Coase's seminal contribution. As Coase (1991) himself acknowledged, market failure due to self-interest is not necessary to an argument that a firm organizes those activities in which it is economically favored relative to a market. This insight of Coase is open to interpretation, because the mechanism by which a firm is better at doing certain activities is not addressed. We wish to preserve the spirit of Coase's inquiry by isolating factors that lead a firm to be advantaged, as well as those factors that limit its growth and diversity.

Firms provide a sense of community by which discourse, coordination, and learning are structured by identity. However, identity also generates a cost on limiting the search for new avenues of exploration and on imposing existing procedural rules suboptimally on new activities. People hold multiple identities, and hence discourse and learning occurs in many settings, including market exchange. We start, therefore, with a sociological and historical presumption, that one of the most important identities in modern society is bound with the employment relationship and its location. Indeed, as Bendix (1956) described, the genesis of the modern firm is intrinsically tied to the historical competition over the loyalty of workers and employees between the enterprise and class. Through membership in a social community called the firm, identity is developed that changes the character and quality of human discourse and behavior. From this, the rest of the argument follows.

Identity and the Division of Labor[2]

To avoid false debates, let us be clear that we acknowledge that incentive problems exist and that these problems are sensitive to the appropriate design of governance mechanisms. Firms, because they are also economic entities, necessarily entail a legal definition by which to sort out claims to cash flows. Some governance mechanisms are less efficient because the resolution to achieving compatible incentives may conflict with the optimal design of ownership claims. The classic case is the conflict between the economic advantages of dispersing ownership in order to allow individuals to diversify and the moral hazard of allocating authority to managers who are not owners.

That people respond to incentives is so patently obvious, by virtue of observation or of introspection, that it hardly can be a point of contention. It is not a telling counterfactual to the argument we propose. Any extant treatment of behavior within and among organizations has to address implications of self-interested behavior, and the resolution of resulting conflicts through ownership.

But self-interested behavior is only one aspect of human motivation. There are emotions, such as those associated with friendship, empathy, and loyalty, and abstract values such as notions of good, beauty, and truth. It is odd that Adam Smith's rhetorical device of accepting the charge of conservative opponents to liberal change by arguing for the virtue of capitalism on the basis of self-interest should be taken not as the limiting but the modal case of human motivation. Smith employed other presumptive reasoning in his other writings, particularly in his analysis of sympathy in his work on moral sentiments. This conflicting view of human motivation was crystallized in the debate in Germany on what was called 'das Adam Smith Problem.' His near contemporary Immanuel Kant noted in his essay 'Idea for a Universal History' that:

The means by which nature employs to bring about the development of innate capacities is that of antagonism within society, in so far as this antagonism becomes in the long run the cause of a law-governed social order. By antagonism, I mean in this context the *unsocial sociability* of men, that is, their tendency to come together in society, coupled, however with a continual resistance which constantly threatens to break this society up. This propensity is obviously rooted in human nature. Man has an inclination to live in society, since he feels in this state more like a man, that is, he feels able to develop his natural capacities. But he also has a great tendency to live as an individual, to isolate himself, since he also encounters in himself the unsocial characteristic of wanting to direct everything in accordance with his own ideas.

The distinction that Kant drew has important implications for understanding the division of labor and the firm. The primary dilemma facing the economic treatment of the division of labor is to account for the transition from the pursuit of self-interest at the individual level to cooperation within the firm. For as Adam Smith noted, the gains to specialization is what generates the foundations of capitalism, namely, comparative advantage that leads to mutual benefit in trade.

More than a half-century later, Charles Babbage extended Smith's observations in important directions (1835). He understood the critical role in matching task to ability. It would be inefficient, he notes, to pay high wages to a skilled worker for doing an unskilled task. The division of labor requires a link between skill and pay gradation. By arguing that the implied hierarchy in physical labor can also be applied to mental labor, Babbage motivated an explanation for why there should be a vertical hierarchy and managers in the firm.

Between Smith and Babbage, a theory for the vertical and horizontal division of labor was developed. This theory accounted for the horizontal division of labor by noting that such a division gives rise to increasing returns to specialization. The vertical division economizes on scarcity wages paid to skilled workers by matching task to skill and allowing for wage gradations.

Babbage also suggested that supervision of less skilled task would be assigned to the scarcer skilled labor. Unlike Smith, Babbage implies that variations in the endowments of individuals leads to a hierarchical structuring of authority.

It was Durkheim who recognized the transformation in identity as a consequence of the industrial revolution and, more perceptibly, of the division of labor. Durkheim argued that the traditional societies were held together by a mechanistic solidarity. The division of labor required a different kind of moral order, one based on an organic solidarity in which the individual identifies with society. He saw the division of labor as evolving out of the interplay of the rule towards specialization and that towards the emulation of the collective type. A contribution of Durkheim was to link this evolutionary view of the division of labor as arising out of competition to the establishment of a new moral order consistent with individual choice. In societies sufficiently populated, competition leads to specialization, which in turn engenders a sense of cooperation independent of notions of family, race, or country:

As we advance in the evolutionary scale, the ties which bind the individual to his family, to his native soil, to traditions which the past has given to him, to collective group usages, become loose . . . as intelligence becomes richer, activity more varied, in order for morality to remain constant, that is to say, in order for the individual to remain attached to the group with a force equal to that of yesterday, the ties which bind him to it must become stronger and more numerous. Through it, the individual becomes cognizant of his dependence upon society; from it comes the forces which keep him in check and restrain him. In short, since the division of labor becomes the chief source of social solidarity, it becomes, at the same time, the foundation of the moral order. (Durkheim [1893] 1933: 259)

The sociological tradition established by Durkheim is based on the observation of both sides of Kant's idea of the unsocial sociability of the individual. Durkheim's brilliance was to see that the division of labor increased the individual's longing to belong to a moral order, whose character is neither good nor bad in an abstract sense but represents the perception of justice and identity in an historical context. Yet, because moral order is contextually understood, Durkheim and Marx could agree on this point, while preserving radically different views on whether this identification is to class or to society.

Or could it be to the enterprise? It was Weber, living in a more regulated Germany and during a time of growing dominance of many of the largest German firms, who most clearly recognized that the modern organization could replace the loyalty to the leader by the routinization of rationality.[3] The division of labor creates a classification of status and occupation that competes with the solidarity to class.

If in the first century of industrial capitalism, the ideologies of authority wavered between the view of the firm as the family with a paternal owner and that of the firm as a disciplinary agent, the current century introduced the notion of the firm as a place of career (Bendix 1956). To Weber, the division of labor leads to an increasing differentiation of bureaucratic work within large enterprises. In fact, his treatment of the division of labor consists largely of the enumeration of the various kinds of job classifications in modern society (Weber [1922]1968: 114ff.) It is this Weberian picture of the loyal bureaucrat who conforms to routinized instructions that is the target of later critics as W. Whyte (1956). It is also a statement of the transformation of identities from family, region, and craft to membership in an industrial organization.

Identity: Behavioral Foundations

The division of labor varies widely over time and space. A system that organizes work into serial standardized tasks is the foundation of mass production. Alternatively, work can be organized into cells involving the use of skilled labor in interdependent and discretionary tasks, e.g. in Volvo's experimental Uddevala plant. Division of labor implies organizing principles that structure work and define the task specialization of individuals. More abstractly, the division of labor is the encoding of social knowledge into a structure that defines and coordinates individual behavior.

In this differentiation lies the roots of economic progress: we are all endowed with increasing organizational capital, much like we are endowed with more technology and more physical capital. Yet, the evolving complexity in the division of labor is a reduction in the proportion of social knowledge controlled by an individual, because it transforms a more elemental social structure into one which is differentiated and loosely coupled. In his essay on cognition in organizations, Jacques Girin (1995) notes:

No matter what kind of interviews (are made) in a large organization and even often in a small one, one is struck by the degree to which each person ignores what the others do. It is not rare to note that the superior does not know much what the subordinate really does, and reciprocally. When one asks persons of one service what the others do in a nearby service, the situation is even more dramatic. And when one moves on from these immediate relationships to move on to questions such as 'What do you know of the people of level N of what the people of $N + 2$ do', one knows practically nothing.

If individuals are less informed, then how is the system more intelligent? Part of the answer is traditional, that a division of labor results in gains to specialization, and specialization implies a division of labor based on competence. More importantly, as Smith noted, specialization creates competence as individuals explore locally around their assigned tasks. Since Smith, this tendency has become formalized through the divisionalization of education along skill and professional lines. Consequently, the division of labor generates a learning dynamic in which people increasingly become more competent in their specialization. The expansion of lower order knowledge held by individuals is driven by adaptive behavior organized by a division of labor.

The process by which specialization drives competence implies, though, the problem of coordination. The common practice of two career ladders for managers and scientists points to the difficulty of comparing apples and oranges inside the same firm, and the problems of communication across competences. One does not need to add incentive problems, which surely exist, to identify the costs of coordination.

How then are we to understand the comparative merits of firms? Knowledge, as we have emphasized, is surprisingly tangible, whether it be observed in accounting rules or in nonformalized relational patterns. The concepts of routines, procedures, recipes, and conventions point to feasible empirical inquiry by which to understand coordination. Because we are talking about economic institutions, it is attractive to create a metric by which to evaluate the costs of communication, coordination, and learning. In this sense, the notion of knowledge lends itself to comparable measurement suggested by Coase, Arrow, or Hurwicz on communication.

However, these similarities in metrics hide profound differences in understanding firms as social communities as opposed to efficient communication nets. For, to return to Foss's question, a communication net is qualitatively unaffected by boundaries. A network of firms, wired electronically, is technologically equivalent to the communication capability within a firm. The authority relationship written into a contract can be similarly replicated among independent agents. So what else do firms provide, other than legal mechanisms by which to account for the ownership rights to economic gains or as solutions to incentive problems?

IDENTITY AND ATTRIBUTION

Firms provide the normative territory to which members identify. This identification has two implications. First, it defines the conventions and rules by which individuals coordinate their behavior and decision making. Much like the boys in Piaget's town of Neuchatel who knew they had to change the rules of their game from one neighborhood to the next, people are skilled in shifting their routine behavior from their recognition of the social context (see Piore 1995: 107–8). Second, identification sets out the process by which learning is developed socially through the formation of values and convergent expectations.

It is the inherent dilemma in achieving communication and coordination among individuals with diverse competencies that puts into relief the role of identity in supporting higher organizing principles of a firm. Introspection and observation on world events tell us that identity with a group is associated with a normative implication. Ethnic conflict is often expressed through statements of good and evil. Members are faced with the cognitive dissonance between their normative attachment to an identity and evidence that the group, or other members, have not behaved appropriately. The tendency to rationalize behavior by members to conform to a notion of good is an important mechanism by which a positive identity is maintained.

The act of identifying has important implications for the shared cognitive schemas and moral values that people apply to how others are categorized.[4] Albert and Whetten (1985) have noted that organizational identity provides a sense of a shared central character and also of distinctiveness. Identity does more than provide a definition of membership; it also influences the attribution of self-interested behavior.

Tajfel et al. (1971) tested whether the simple fact of belonging to a group was enough to affect one's judgment. They assigned English schoolboys randomly to two groups on the basis of a test that supposedly measured artistic preferences. No boy knew which others had been assigned to the same group as himself. They were asked to allot rewards to one member of their own group and one member of the other group, choosing pairs of rewards. The average allocations indicated that the subjects were trying to maximize the difference between their group's rewards and the other group's rewards. Simply being told that one belongs to a particular category causes one to discriminate in favor of that category. In this context, it could be posited that behavior that is commonly interpreted as opportunistic also could be seen as loyalty to the group to which an individual belongs.

Studies of behavior of 'insiders' and 'outsiders' to organizations suggest that potential cognitive dissonance between loyalty and opportunism can be resolved through attribution. Interestingly, some studies show that the mere fact of group membership can completely reverse the patterns of attributions made to an individual's behavior. Taylor and Jaggi (1974) asked 30 Hindu clerks in India to evaluate a series of desirable and undesirable events: for example, a shopkeeper who either cheated customers or was generous. The actions presented to subjects were said to have been performed either by a fellow Hindu or by an out-group Muslim. It was found that the positive behaviors performed by members of one's own group were believed to arise from internal dispositions, while the negative behaviors were seen as the result of external forces.[5]

The attribution that people belonging to the same group are less self-interested has reinforcing consequences. Expected cooperation induces cooperative behavior. To a non-trivial extent, this dynamic is driven by the confidence held in the common knowledge that both parties to an exchange have the intention to cooperate. The recursive calculation 'that I know that you know that I know' is resolved through signaling this intent. It is logical to move from this recognition to an argument that members to a club desire to cooperate as long as detection leads to penalties in excess of rewards. If this is the argument, then we have returned to a breakdown in collective action due to unenlightened self-interest.

But we wish to pose a more radical argument, namely, that identity improves coordination, communication, and learning. Let's turn to each serially.

COORDINATION

Of the many implications of identity, the role played by procedures in resolving coordination problems is the most tangible. It is telling that in the market approach to transactions, the canonical model is the prisoner's dilemma. In attempts to understand coordination, the principal analytical engine are focal rules, a concept introduced by Schelling (1960). By eliminating incentive effects through an analysis of 'pure coordination games,' Schelling shows that coordination is nevertheless difficult in the absence of rules. Incentive problems are replaced by a comparison of risk if coordination is not achieved. Consider the difficulties of driving once people having abandoned conventions that dictate cars should drive on the left or right.

A focal rule is an outcome of 'convergent expectations' that solves for the problem of coordinating (see Knez and Camerer 1994). The critical quality of a focal rule is the recognition of its arbitrariness. Schelling writes:

A focal point for agreement often owes its focal character to the fact that small concessions would be impossible, that small encroachments would lead to more and larger ones. One draws a line at some conspicuous boundary or rests his case on some conspicuous principle that is supported mainly by the rhetorical question, 'If not here, where?' ... We are dealing here with the players' shared appreciations, preoccupations, obsessions, and sensitivities to suggestion, not with the resources that they can draw on when necessary. (Schelling 1960: 111–14)

What Schelling is referring to is the notion of a category error in failing to distinguish between 'knowing that' and 'knowing how.' The intellectual heritage of this distinction is long, but is clearly stated, as Foss notes, by Gilbert Ryle in his classic, *The Concept of Mind*. Ryle ridiculed the belief, or what he called the 'intellectualist legend,' that a theory of decision is consciously known to actors prior to action. He notes:

Champions of this legend are apt to try to reassimilate knowing *how* to knowing *that* by arguing that intelligent performance involves the observance of rules, or the application of criteria. It follows that the operation which is characterized as intelligent must be preceded by an intellectual acknowledgment of these rules or criteria; that is, the agent must first go through the internal process of avowing to himself certain propositions about what is to be done ('maxims', 'imperatives' or 'regulative propositions' as they are sometimes called) only then can he execute his performance in accordance with those dictates. He must preach to himself before he can practice. The chief must recite his recipes to himself before he can cook according to them, the hero must lend his inner ear to some appropriate moral imperative before swimming out to save the drowning man, the chessplayer must run over in his head all the relevant rules and tactical maxims of the game before he can make correct and skillful moves ... (Ryle 1949: 29)

In this philosophical protest lies a startling different implication for understanding firms and their growth. Simon ([1962] 1979) has made an important contribution in his contrast of economic logic based on 'substantive' reasoning as opposed to a decision logic that is essentially 'procedural.' This distinction between the substantive and procedural, or the declarative and procedural, lies at the foundation of the distinction we drew between know-how and know-what. As Nelson and Winter (1982) have argued in their seminal work, procedural knowledge represents a dividing line between rational choice theory and behavioral approaches. Firm behavior reflects the enactment of learned skills and routines grounded in the acquisition of procedural knowledge.

Part of the appeal of understanding focal rules as based on learned behaviors is the complementary evidence concerning the physiology of perception, categorization, and knowledge (see the extended discussion in Lakoff 1987: 24ff.) There is substantial evidence that much learning and skill are based on procedural knowledge, with associated neural physical processes. One definition of declarative knowledge is memory that is accessible to conscious recollection (Squire 1987). Procedural memory is contained within learned skills or nondivisible cognitive operations. That procedural and declarative memory is stored in different areas of the brain is revealed by studies on amnesia patients. Amnesia tends to eradicate declarative, not procedural knowledge. Amnesic patients show intact learning and retention of a variety of motor, perceptual, and cognitive skills, despite poor memory for the actual learning experiences. Such patients also respond to priming effects, even when the stimulus is forgotten. For example, brain-damaged people often have trouble recalling recent events. Yet, they respond to priming effects. That is, if they are exposed to gray, they are likely to detect gray subsequently, even though they forgot the original exposure event (i.e. their exposure to gray).

Several studies have shown that priming stimuli are able to evoke the latter recall of procedural memory better than declarative. Reber (1993) has taken to heart that much that is known is implicit knowledge and only tacitly known. Implicit knowledge tends to be veridical but partial isomorphisms of the environment. Reber reports that experiments on transferability across modalities (e.g. audible, visual), show that unconscious knowledge is retrievable but is surprisingly insensitive to stimuli different than the original priming. For conscious knowledge, activation can occur by modality (e.g. speech) other than how it was first stored (e.g. vision), while when the knowledge is implicit, the same mode of initial priming seems required. These results have important implications for understanding not only the transfer of knowledge, but also why geographic proximity, such as a Silicon Valley, appears to be associated with rich contextual environments for the spawning of new innovations.

Procedural knowledge provides the conceptual underpinning to understanding the generation of routines as arising out of sustained interactions. In this regard, Cohen and Bacdayan (1995) carried out an interesting experiment. They designed a very simple card game, or what we can call a coordination game, between two players. The goal was to have two cards of a particular nature match, and the number of cards was quite small, in the order of six. Players derived particular heuristics, or procedures, that were run off like 'chunks' used in the studies on representation and production systems. They found that procedural rules were remembered better than declarative knowledge, speeded cooperation, but were subject to suboptimality and negative transfer. Cohen and Bacdayan posit that dual priming is the basis for procedural action, with individuals triggering coordinated action by their interactions. When the game changed, these same rules were used. In other words, the players established a set of procedures that were transported to new settings. Cohen and Bacdayan found that players also exhibited 'negative learning'; they transported learned procedures to wrong situations.

Similar results on the dominance of procedural rules over declarative knowledge when optimal decisions are not known have been found in other studies. In a setting far from the laboratory, Bowman (1963) found that managers' decisions were better on average when using regression coefficients derived from data on their previous decisions than their actual decisions. Consistent behavior performed better than the search for optimal decisions. Trying to respond to environmental cues, concludes Bowman, explains why managers deviate from consistent behavior. Lewis and Anderson found that non-optimal behavior persisted unless past a certain threshold; in these cases, negative transfer persists, otherwise replaced or weeded out (see the discussion in Singley and Anderson 1989). Because procedural rules are more likely to be suboptimal than incorrect in some formal sense, they are plausibly more prone to persistent use unless discovered. Reber (1993) reported similar findings on the use of suboptimal rules.

The problem of coordination at the individual level also exists at the organizational. While there is a large body of work on procedural learning and transfer at the individual level, there is little systematic evidence on the use of higher order principles, such as the divisionalization of work. If we think of the division of labor as the coding of how work among groups should be organized, then observations on the inert character of structural change (such as the slow diffusion of the divisional structure) suggests that the extension of organizing principles is most likely to be characterized by suboptimal transfer. It is easier to replicate existing routines than to design optimally. Routines enacted at the organizational level may be even more prone to such error, because the manipulation of such routines is rarely open to individual discretion.

Yet, while the transfer of organizational structure is also a source of error, structure itself provides the important property of robustness. The experiment by Rao and Argote (1995) is particularly interesting, for the design highlighted the roles of specialization and coordination in the division of labor. They experimented with the effects of turnover and structure, and found that turnover was more damaging in cases in which work was not well structured. For the particular production system used in the experiment, the knowledge encoded in the structuring of the work made the overall system robust against turnover. It is the inert quality of the coding of knowledge in structure that provides the robustness against the loss of individuals. It is also the source of error.

DISCOURSE

The difficulty in the transmission of social knowledge is how to communicate from highly specialized bases of expertise to provide instructions and tools that are employable by large numbers of people. In our earlier article (Kogut and Zander 1992), we relied upon the metaphor of the shells of software (e.g. machine language, compiler, operating system) that are employed to allow many users to access some of the functions of a computer. We neglected the critical role played by language and discourse, symbol and interpretation in the operation of higher organizing principles that bind the organization. Identity is not only critical for supporting coordination, but also in creating a dialogue by which information and solutions are discovered.

The superiority of coding and decoding within the firm has been claimed periodically, but rarely explained. Frequently, the work of Shannon and Weaver (1949) is cited as a basis for a theory of communication as reliability of encoding information. In his essay introducing a popularized version by Shannon of his theory of communication, Weaver suggests that

the concept of information...leads directly to a study of the statistical structure of language...The idea of utilizing the powerful body of theory concerning Markoff processes seems particularly promising for semantic studies, since this theory is specifically adapted to handle one of the most significant but difficult aspects of meaning, namely the influence of context (Shannon and Weaver 1949).

Although this approach has not been frequently used in organizational studies, it has been important in cognitive sciences. It is not hard to see its applicability to understanding communication as the problem of people knowing the commands and sharing common notions of coding, of the costs and reliability of various channels, and of the actual information content (i.e. the entropic measure of the percentage of words that reflect discretionary choice—letterheads do not count). The view of communication as the transmission of symbolically encoded meanings is especially appealing in an age in which machine manipulation of symbols has proven to be such a powerful aid to human intelligence. The salience of this metaphor is revealed in the application of cybernetic thinking—memory, retrieval, action, feedback—to organizations and institutions. In fact, the algorithmic nature of procedural learning leads easily to computational simulation by symbolic manipulation.[6]

This line of inquiry is useful, but it can also be misleading. Take, for example, the role played by categories in the symbolic representation of knowledge. In a stunning analysis, Lakoff (1987) notes that people hold ideal cognitive models that inform their understanding of their world. The foundation to these models is the classifications imposed on the perception of reality. Whereas logic may apply to the manipulation of symbols within a schema, the reference of these symbols to an external reality is influenced by bodily properties (e.g. color perception) and imaginative processes (e.g. metaphor and metonymy). Borrowing Eleanor Rosch's theory of classification, Lakoff notes that primitives tend to be classified by prototypic effects, i.e. best examples. One of Lakoff's examples is that an 'unmarried man' is a possible prototype for bachelor; priests and men with three wives when four are allowed would be poor best examples.

To adumbrate the implications of this thinking, consider the notion of 'best practices.' Many firms may claim to have installed Japanese production methods; the Toyota system is, however, a best example. Other systems belong to this category, but the prototype is Toyota. The transfer of this system across firms and countries is difficult for many reasons, but a principle reason is that a prototype is not a fixed template. The transfer of JIT systems, by argument of metonymy—a part representing a whole—might lead to the classification of adopters as implementing Japanese systems. Moreover, understanding Toyotism or Taylorism as a philosophy leads to the implementation of the spirit of the system, metaphorically. It is not surprising that transfer usually entails innovation, and disagreement whether it occurred. But because categorization is imprecise, the reliance on imperfect rules entails error and costs.

Organizational identification is frequently described as a process of self-categorization characterized by distinctive, central, and enduring attributes (Dutton et al. 1994). Individuals, of course, may deviate from such behavior, but certain individuals are often cited as best examples of what it means to be a member. Social stereotyping and membership are intrinsically related, even though few individuals may qualify as prototypic 'bachelors.'

Communication is, in its contextual interpretation, better understood as discourse. Through identities, individuals share ideal cognitive models of the world, based upon similar categories. But interpretation of the world is influenced by discourse. Rarely do we see people capable of changing radically their fundamental beliefs, but they do change their interpretations. Discourse, by creating metaphoric extensions based on prior experience, allows the typing of objects and people to be altered.

We can go further than this. Leadership is the act of persuasion, or what Lakoff would call motivation. It is easier to learn new lessons that are motivated by current understanding than by something that appears as arbitrary (Lakoff 1987: 346). Discourse among people who share cognitive models is fruitful because new learning is motivated by existing categories.

To clarify the implications of this perspective for an understanding of what firms do, consider examples of leadership and incentives. In his book on cognition in economic behavior, Piore (1995) observes that the relational interdependency of agent and activity in communities is the basis for meaning and knowing. Unlike the view of a leader by rational choice theory who resolves conflicts through optimal choices, Piore (1995: 134) proposes that 'in a hermeneutic process, the leader is orchestrating a series of conversations.' He notes that in a time in which bridging across different groups is important, a leader becomes a mediator by which new categories are developed and to help in the translation and interpretation between languages.

This perspective on discourse and motivation places a radically different interpretation of incentives that are found in the principal–agent literature. Sabel (1996) makes an intriguing observation that inverts the usual thinking about monitoring. To Sabel, monitoring is more than the way a principal evaluates an agent. It also establishes, much like Piore's emphasis on hermeneutics, a context for discovery and discussion. Monitoring becomes an occasion for learning. Incentives in a firm are not only a way to motivate work and effort; incentives are also symbolic statements that provide the occasion to guide action and to share learning and experience.

LEARNING

Social interaction in groups facilitates not only communication and coordination, but also learning. It is through learning that coordination and communication are facilitated through identity. Both convergent expectations around procedural behavior and discourse based on share categorization are acquired through social learning. Identity is critical to this process.

An important finding in experimental psychology is that learning through identifying is more powerful than attempts to 'teach' individuals via incentives and propaganda. Bandura and Walters (1963) argue that very little social behavior would ever be learned if we had to depend on someone going through a detailed, demanding, and tedious process of conditioning successive approximations to the desired behavior. In an experiment, Bandura and McDonald (1963) showed that the behavior of a role model was a more powerful influence in the behavior of children than was reinforcement of certain behavior, which proved to be a negligible factor. The results showed that the behavior of the model influenced social learning in children more than reinforcement. Reinforcement proved to be a negligible factor. There was no significant difference in the performance of the children in the model-present condition who were reinforced and those who were not.

These studies point to the importance of how things and people are categorized and learned through identifying and behaving in the context of group membership. Recent studies have made these type of observations the foundation to new theories of learning and thinking. Learning is enhanced in firms through what Lave and Wenger (1991) call 'situated learning' that relies upon 'legitimate peripheral participation in communities of practice.'

Learning thus implies becoming a different person with respect to the possibilities enabled by these systems of relations. To ignore this aspect of learning is to overlook the fact that learning involves the construction of identities. Viewing learning as legitimate peripheral participation means that learning is not merely a condition for membership, is itself an evolving form of membership. We conceive of identities as long-term, living relations between persons and their place and participation in communities of practice. *Thus identity, knowing, and social membership entail one another.* (Lave and Wenger 1991: 53, our italics)

Lave and Wenger place considerable emphasis upon interpretation, or hermeneutics, linked to participation in groups. Meaning is the product of speaker's interpretative activities, and not merely as the 'content' of linguistic forms. Meaning, understanding, and learning are all defined relative to action contexts, not to self-contained and abstract structures. But it is because learning is situated in an identity that it is also difficult to unlearn. Here we see again the flip side to the benefits of a firm, namely the inflexibility in changing acquired learning.

OVERVIEW

A simple proposition is that firms lower the costs of communication and coordination, and it is by this metric that the capabilities of firms can be

	Social knowledge	Market
Coordination	Convergent expectations	Transactional
Communication	Discursive	Information
Learning	Situated	Reputational

Figure 4.1. Comparison of knowledge and transactional approaches

evaluated relative to a fictional market. However, the advantage of a firm is more than just economizing on costs, but is also the creation of a context of discourse and learning that promotes innovation and motivated behavior. Figure 4.1 summarizes the differences in what we could call the 'conceptual models' of capabilities versus transactional approaches. In the market model, communication consists of the coding and decoding of information, coordination proceeds through transactions governed by prices, and learning is the revelation of cooperative or dishonest reputations. In the view of a firm as embodying social knowledge, coordination is achieved through convergent expectations, communication is characterized by discourse based on rich codes and classifications, and learning is situated.

Boundaries as Normative Markers

What are the limits on procedural rules or metaphors by which to structure coordination? Consider the following rule. If a worker should be seen as shirking, punish him or her to the point that the increase in labor output is equal to the marginal cost of allocating time to whipping and of the present value of the loss in permanently damaging the capital. No doubt, there is unamity in condemning such a rule, and yet slavery was a socially practiced regime throughout history and many cultures.

In early periods of industrialization, pay and employment were specifically influenced by norms of justice. In France through the first half of this century, men were the last fired, and men's pay were the last to be cut, especially if they had a family (Moutet 1992). In Japan, the flexibility to respond to macroeconomic shocks is built on the marginality of the female and older work force, which are hired and fired in preference to the primarily male and younger workers (Dore 1986).

In contemporary and industrialized settings, norms of equity tend to prevail. These norms influence the acceptance and usage of a rule. Studies on pay and wage dispersion have been especially explicit in documenting the relationship between norms of justice and perceived inequality. Pfeffer and Langton (1993) found, for example, that job satisfaction and research productivity fell in contexts of perceived high dispersion of wages in academic settings.

Invidious social comparisons have been especially linked to deleterious effects of wage dispersion within the same firm. Some of these effects appear to be culturally specific, as in Levine's (1993) findings that Japanese workers are likely to express dissatisfaction if they are overpaid relative to their reference group.

A useful way to distinguish between notions of equity is through the distinction of procedural and distributive justice. Procedural refers in this case to equity in process; distributive, to equity in outcome. Societies differ, obviously, in their preference for these rules. The kind of implicit social contracts to which members of a firm believe are in force tends to be sensitive to context, time, and place (Rousseau and Robinson 1994).

The importance of fairness as a consideration has persistently surprised game theoretic predictions. Studies on ultimatum bargaining (i.e., one-shot offers to take it or leave it) show that individuals are highly sensitive to fairness (see the insightful review by Guth 1995). In a study conducted in the United States, Kahneman and his colleagues (1986) find that people object to use of the market, that is to prices, as a way to ration goods during a crisis. Bies et al. (1993) replicated this study, but include the experimental condition that people were informed why reliance on prices were procedurally correct. Objections to the market as a way to ration fell significantly. The counter-intuitive results of Cappelli and Sherer (1990) on the satisfaction of newly-hired workers who are placed in a lower paid tier than encumbent workers also point to the role played by procedural explanations and by developing different reference groups for social comparison.

There is, of course, an alternative approach to understanding the modern organization as a resolution of agency problems through such devices as rank tournament for pay or reputations.[7] One is particularly struck by the possibility that the liberal heritage of political economy is challenged in trying to understand non-Western firms. Aoki (1990) poses the important question: why can Japanese workers not own the firm and capture the return to their social network? According to his analysis,

the performance of employees of the Japanese firm are evaluated and rewarded in the long run by the elaborate personnel administration system crystallized in the hierarchy of ranks, and this [*implicit long-term contract*] provides to workers the long-run security and the sense of fair treatment they desire. It does not seem obvious, however, how the egalitarian idea of the employee-controlled firm and the centralized management of hierarchy of ranks can be made mutually compatible (Aoki 1990: 19).

Later, in trying to understand why top management does not abuse these contracts, he notes 'their motives may well remain mixed and contain a carry-over from their longer careers as employees in the lower ranks.' In other words, normative values are internalized.

Complementarities, Coherence, and Notional Consistency

Let's consider how the concepts of knowledge, identity, and categorization can shed light on a problem of what limits the diversity of a firm's activities. As noted by Teece et al. (1994), the diversification of firms tends to cluster in particular industry constellations. Abstractly, this clustering suggests that firms with common industry experiences tend to face similar opportunities and constraints; or, to use a popular observation, the evolution of firms reveals evidence of path dependence.

The analysis of the basis of this path dependence faces quickly a number of important stumbling blocks. If coherence is due to limitations in extending, say, steel technology to semiconductors, then the creation of two divisions appears to be a sensible solution. If the firm were simply a device by which to resolve agency problems and create islands of trust in which communication could prosper, then a conglomerate form would, at first blush, appear as efficient as a related but diversified company. But evidence shows that, in the United States, undiversified firms are less efficient, and that diversification tends to follow consistent patterns. What are the limits to coherence when a firm has the ability to decompose itself into multiple divisions?

A plausible answer is that independence of each division is in conflict with the process of identification, social comparison, and consistency in rules that characterize organizations and firms. The well studied phenomenon of post-acquisition integration points to the grave problems posed by trying to merge two firms with different identities and social comparisons. Similarly, organizations that try radically to revamp their pay systems run into severe problems if top managers have the option to enter an efficient labor market.

These problems, as witnessed in the well-publicized case of Salomon Brothers, emerge often in investment banking firms, where the conflict between an external market for talent and the corporate attempt to preserve shareholder value is especially marked. Conflicts have also been observed following the acquisition of investment banks by commercial banks (e.g. Mellon Bank's take over of a Boston investment bank) or the extension across borders from one kind of pay environment to another (e.g. Japanese investment bank operations in New York and London). The conflict occurs because people make pay comparisons in reference to others who are working at the same firm, and less often to others working elsewhere (i.e. 'the market wage'). When a commercial bank acquires an investment bank, suddenly two employees of the same firm earn vastly different wages (often due to the allocation of extensive bonus pay to the investment bank division employees). Thus, equity comparisons arise post merger when in fact nothing else changed from before. The category 'working for the same firm' carries with it a strong demand for equity. No wonder post-merger integration is not simply a 're-engineering' problem.

The merger thus raises a cognitive dissonance: how do we reconcile the conflict between equity and post-merger introduction of large variance in pay among divisions? The concept of cognitive dissonance suggests that the mind requires consistency when conscious of conflictual results, and yet is a resourceful and flexible instrument in resolving conflict. Identity implies similarly that social entities to which members hold their loyalty provide a logic of reliability and consistency in rules and symbolic categorization per our discussion of Lakoff. To a certain extent, technologies drive the coherence of firms, insofar as members value their membership in a *chemical firm* or in a *steel firm*. These identities may be the borders for firms, and individuals also feel a sense of belonging to a steel industry.[8] Identities, as noted earlier, are rarely singular, with identity to a firm being only one. Individuals can also be members to communities of practice (Brown and Duguid 1991), occupational communities (van Maanen and Barley 1984), and guilds (Kieser 1989). With each of these communities, there is an associated view of what is knowledge; hence, the phrase of Holzner and Marx (1985) of 'epistemic communities' is particularly apt. It is possible that a resolution of the cognitive dissonance is salvaged in the identity to different occupational communities that allow the firm to differentiate pay internally by job cagegory. But this passage from identity with the firm to identity with an occupation poses the problem of coordination that we discussed before. There are always fundamental tradeoffs.

That identity is often technological (that is, occupational) does not mean that technologies determine organizing principles, borders, or what firms do (see the comments of Foss (1996) on this issue). However, to the extent that members of a firm identify with these technologies, they influence the notion of complementarities that top managers consider within the set of alternatives, and employees understand in the context of their expectations. Indeed, it is not surprising that corporate change often occurs in conjunction with a change in name, or a change in the definition of the business. Thus, a tobacco company may say that it is no longer in tobacco, but in packaging and promotion. Or a steel company may transform its name from, say, US Steel to USX, with the last letter indicating a variable definition of its identity.

These issues suggest that complementarities and the coherence of the firm are not simply technologically determined. Certainly, chemicals and auto-making are different technologies, involving different competences. Yet, to return to an earlier point, a firm could potentially place each operation in separate businesses. What determines, in part, the coherence of the firm is the notional consistency of its businesses as understood by its members and, for that matter, outside investors and consumers. Here we see the importance of discourse (and leadership): a firm is characterized by the sharing among its members of *their understanding* of what are the categories of work, their identities, and the logics by which they interact (i.e. their complementarities). We reject the strong statement that complements are given and that firms as unitary actors search experimentally or by imitation to find the ones that best match each other.

However, it is also too simple to claim that the logic of coherence is notional. Here is where we disagree with the extreme stance that all is 'socially constructed.' To produce a car requires a different set of organizing principles than to produce chemicals; selling insurance is different than making hamburgers. They might share commonalities, but they will also differ in terms of whether they can use batch or continuous production, incentive or salary pay. The directionality is not technology to organization, or incentives to technology. Nor is the problem simply finding a match between a single element of technology and another of organization. To the contrary, the problem is finding the composed set of many potential elements, or complements.[9]

The operating logic of what goes with what is complicated, because complementarities pose complex interrelationships and, more importantly, consist of more than technologies. Because pay systems focus attention symbolically on different objects, they engender different avenues of exploration and establish different contexts for discourse. In a Japanese production environment, the system pushes inventories to low levels and forces workers to discover quality defects; pay is more group oriented than elsewhere.

Let's illustrate this point by looking at the data developed by Applebaum and Batt (1994). They coded data in binary form from 184 establishments according to their performance, technology, work system, pay, and incentives. Binary data are appropriate for analysis using Boolean comparative analysis, in which logical sets of factors are found (Ragin 1987). In this analysis, both positive and negative complements are found, that is, the output consists of groupings of complements that must be together or absent.

In Figure 4.2, we show the results from applying this technique to pay, work organization, technology, and union variables. The criterion variable is profit. Bold means the 'presence of' this factor; lower case, the 'absence of' this factor. (The acronyms should be obvious, except for sts—socio-technical systems, and bonus/ps—individual bonuses.) New technology shows up in all groups, except one. The results show a few interesting patterns. In the second line, unions, group pay, and new technology are positive complements; teams, among other factors, is a negative complement. In the third line, unions is now a negative complement and teams is a positive complement. In the fourth line, both unions and teams are positive complements, but new technology and group pay systems are negative complements. These are complex results, but they suggest that, for high profits, unions do not do well in conjunction with changes in both technology and pay systems. For firms that are in industries or countries in which union representation is mandated, high performance

---

Effects on profits

---

union grouppay BONUS / PS NEWTECH broadjob rotation teams sts jit +
UNION GROUPPAY bonus / ps NEWTECH broadjob rotation teams sts jit +
union GROUPPAY BONUS / PS NEWTECH broadjob rotation TEAMS sts jit +
UNION grouppay bonus / ps newtech broadjob ROTATION TEAMS STS JIT +
union GROUPPAY BONUS / PS NEWTECH BROADJOB ROTATION TEAMS sts jit

---

Figure 4.2. Technological and organizational complementarities

systems are still possible, but certain profitable combinations are ruled out. Thus, the distribution of power, as well as cognition, influences the determination of the chosen set of practices.

Of course, these results are based on a limited number of variables. (The data set, in fact, includes 49 variables.) Consider that the combinatorial possibilities are given by 2^{N-1}, where N varies by k number of elements. The combination of binary variables generate large numbers. What would happen if we allowed for a quantitative measure as well, along the lines of a bit more team work and bit less group pay? Or, since knowledge is embedded in social relationships, what would happen if downsizing led to the eliminations of particular individuals, or if quality circles consisted of one more or less individuals? These calculations are simply outside computational limits. The feasible set, technically, should be quite large. As a consequence, the realized set will be an outcome of identity, of inherited practice, and of the constellation of power and interest inside and outside the firm. The determination of what constitutes a firm can hardly be unique, or epiphenomenal.

If the lens is shifted from *what is a firm* to *what do firms do*, then there is a line of inquiry to discover what goes with what for specific capabilities. Consider the case where batch production and individual bonuses are coherent complements, but assembly line production with fixed remuneration. A firm that consists of both batch and assembly processes faces a dilemma. To impose different systems of payment leads to potentially invidious social comparison. To impose the same form of payment is to suffer an efficiency loss in matching false complements. The determination of coherence and of what activities a firm carries out is neither technological nor social: it is both.

The above results point to an important issue, namely, that there is a distinction, as Chomsky (1980) noted for grammar, between competence and performance. Firms may be capable in a set of skills, consistent and coherent, and yet unprofitable. A Boolean analysis of what complements are associated with the truth condition of quality (high equal to 1: low to 0) generates a much larger list of groupings than those that are associated with profits. So there are many more combinations that lead to high quality than to high profits. Feasible high quality complementarities are not necessarily those that correspond to the selection environment.

To return to the discussion in the previous section, nonoptimal routines are likely to persist due to the infeasibility of arriving at optimal solutions in real time. But this assessment is even then too optimistic, for the combinatorial difficulty of calculating the profit implications of n elements, when n is large, implies that non-optimal procedures can persist with no obvious feedback that signals how to improve practice. What firms do tends to persist because knowledge is embedded in social relationships, and because the directionality of change in these relationships is usually unknown. To the cognitive limits of working out better combinations, there is the problem of evolving new rules and procedures of coordination in a context that must comply both with norms of justice and with a feasible redistribution of power and authority. Identity creates more than just powerful motivations for cooperation; it also imposes the weighty costs of ruling out alternative ways to organize and to exploit new avenues of development.

It in this way that we provide a similar result to those of organizational economics but by a different mechanism. Organizational economics show that in some cases firms don't make the 'optimal' investment due to agency or contracting costs. In the contracting literataure, managers are constrained by uncertainty over the future and the difficulty of writing contracts. In our conception, managers don't even know what is best now, no less than the future. Identities provide rules for firms to organize around shared beliefs of what works. Yet, there is a cost to identities, for better ways of doing things are not considered. Thus, we also admit a trade-off between the benefits of identity and the costs imposed by ignoring those paths inconsistent with this identity. In our world, managers routinely ignore better combinations, not because of contracting or agency, but because these combinations conflict with identities and with the shared notions of categories and affiliated notions of equity and fairness.

Conclusions: The Constraints of Vision

Firms differ in what they can do. Some produce cars by highly flexible production lines; others mass produce. The capabilities to do one or the other is not the choice variable of classic decision theory. The limitations are not simply that incentives are too weak, or that people too selfish, to motivate changing capabilities. The roots of this inertia lie in the wiring of human cognition to acquire tacit procedural knowledge as the basis of interaction with other individuals.

We have addressed the question why this procedural knowledge should be 'more' within the firm than among firms. What makes a firm's boundaries distinctive is that the rules of coordination and the process of learning are situated not only physically in locality, but also mentally in an identity. Because identity implies an adherence to a symbolic coding of values and rules, the costs and substance of discourse, coordination, and learning are influenced by normative boundaries of firms. Because identity implies a moral order as well as rules of exclusion, the assemblage of elements that compose an organization are subject to requirements of consistency; not all technically feasible complements are permissible within the logic of a shared identity.

People are bounded by what they know and by what they value, and they are sensitive to norms of what is appropriate behavior. Incentives are important symbols influencing organizational and economic behavior. Their salience and design are linked to prevailing property rights and ownership contracts. Because people are influenced by self-interest, incentives are especially powerful symbols in economic life. But they are also, in a semiotic sense, part of the litter of sign and meaning that populate the working life of individuals. As such, they are guides to determining people's (unconscious or conscious) actions.

In his seminal article, Coase ([1937] 1995) noted that the advantage of firm organization is eventually offset by the cost of relying on hierarchic exchange. We have suggested an additional cost, namely, the paradox that creativity works by rules of exclusion. A conceptual model of classification and thought rules out possible combinations and delimits the realm of exploration to what may be more promising avenues of discovery. But such models err in their signposts, and they lead to the suboptimal transfer of practices from one setting to another. Connectivity, as Weick and Roberts (1993) have argued, may be a proper description of how new structures are formed, but this connectivity is almost certain to be subject to a normative vision that constrains the possible to the envisioned.

These comments, already broad, have omitted important literatures. To move from these micro foundations to an understanding of firms in context of particular societies and competitive contexts requires a further consideration of the field of analysis and of society. The sociologies of Bourdieu, Giddens, or Habermas are more attentive to power, action, and language than what we have suggested above. But the roots are the same, a delineation of what social behavior is in terms of discourse, identity, and structure. It is in the notions of identity and the learning of procedural rules and normative boundaries that the foundations to a theory of what firms are in terms of what they do explains why there is 'more of it' inside than outside.

Acknowledgments

The authors would like to thank Manisha Kulkarni for research assistance, Ned Bowman and Sid Winter for the many conversations, and Benjamin Coriat, Giovanni Gavetti, and Andy Spicer for comments on an earlier draft.

☐ ENDNOTES

* This chapter is a revised version of B. Kogut and U. Zander (1996) 'What Firms Do: Coordination, Identity, and Learning,' *Organization science*, 7: 502–18.

1. See Kogut and Zander (1992). Subsequently, empirical support has been published in Kogut and Zander (2003) and Zander and Kogut (1995) See also our reply to criticism in Kogut and Zander (1995) Winter (1987) was the stimulation for these papers; see Szulanski (1995b) for further validation of the ideas.

2. This section draws on Kogut (1995) and has benefitted from comments by Annie Borzeix, Jacques Girm, and Michael Useem.

3. See Chandler (1990) who notes that German corporations were frequently larger than their American counterparts, and Kocka (1981) on employees and managers in comparative perspective.

4. For a discussion of shared schemas, see Weick and Roberts (1993). It is an important issue whether their approach of schemas is reconciliable with the hermeneutics espoused by Piore (1995) and Girm (forthcoming). See footnote 6 for a related discussion.

5. Considerable studies point to the importance of group identity as the basis of sustained motivation. The classic study by Janowitz and Shils on the disintegration of the Wehrmacht showed the durability of small groups of German soldiers in withdrawing from the Russian front to German-occupied territory (Janowitz and Shils 1948). Schein (1956) analyzed the motives of certain American soldiers who cooperated with their Chinese captors; a key turning point in the efforts to indoctrinate a soldier was to break the identity of the soldier with his comrades.

6. There is an apparent debate in cognitive sciences regarding whether situated learning implies that knowledge cannot be symbolically represented in a production schema, such as Simon advocates. The debate has relevance to organization science in elucidating potential inconsistencies between those that hold a view of the organization as mind with stable schema and those favoring organization in the generative of organizing knowledge through discourse and evolving schemata. See Simon and Vera, Clancey, Suchman and others in *Cognitive Science* in 1993.

7. This view certainly captures a portion of the evolution in vertical authority systems. A P. Sloan, chairman of General Motors, could write that the 'corporation [is] a pyramid of opportunities from the bottom toward the top with thousands of chances for advancement' (cited in Bendix 1956: 307).

8. See, for example, the study by Padioleau (1981) on the French steel industry, Spender (1989) on industry recipes, and Dumez and Jeunemaitre (1994) on the sense of industry borders in cement.

9. See Milgrom and Roberts (1990), Dosi and Kogut (1993), and MacDuffie (1995).

Part II

Ventures, Value, and Options

5 Joint Ventures: Theoretical and Empirical Perspectives*

The study of joint ventures has attracted increasing interest in the popular press and academic literature. Though joint ventures are an important alternative to acquisitions, contracting, and internal development, the literature has not been consolidated and analyzed. This article provides a critical review of existing studies and new data in order to establish current theoretical and empirical directions. In particular, a theory of joint ventures as an instrument of organizational learning is proposed. In this view a joint venture is used for the transfer of organizationally embedded knowledge which cannot be easily blueprinted or packaged through licensing or market transactions.

The chapter is divided into four sections. The first section develops three theories on joint ventures from the perspectives of transaction costs, strategic behavior, and organizational theory. The subsequent section reviews the literature on the motivations for joint ventures and empirical trends in their occurrence. Where possible, the findings are related to the three theoretical perspectives. Because there has been such considerable work in the area of international joint ventures, the third section summarizes some of the major findings regarding foreign entry and stability. The final section suggests some avenues for future research.

The theses of this chapter are essentially two. First, it will be argued that most statements on the motivations for joint ventures are reducible to three factors: evasion of small number bargaining, enhancement of competitive positioning (or market power), and mechanisms to transfer organizational knowledge. Second, it will be proposed that the cooperative aspects of joint ventures must be evaluated in the context of the competitive incentives among the partners and the competitive rivalry within the industry.

Theorical Explanations

Narrowly defined, a joint venture occurs when two or more firms pool a portion of their resources within a common legal organization. Conceptually, a joint venture is a selection among alternative modes by which two or more firms can transact. Thus, a theory of joint ventures must explain why this particular mode of transacting is chosen over such alternatives as acquisition, supply contract, licensing, or spot market purchases.

Three theoretical approaches are especially relevant in explaining the motivations and choice of joint ventures. One approach is derived from the theory of transaction costs as developed by Williamson (1975, 1985). The second approach focuses on strategic motivations and consists of a catalogue of formal and qualitative models describing competitive behavior. Though frequently these approaches are not carefully distinguished from one another, they differ principally, as discussed later, insofar as transaction cost arguments are driven by cost minimization considerations, whereas strategic motivations are driven by competitive positioning and the impact of such positioning on profitability. A third approach is derived from organizational theories, which have not been fully developed in terms of explaining the choice to joint venture relative to other modes of cooperation.

Transaction Costs

A transaction cost explanation for joint ventures involves the question of how a firm should organize its boundary activities with other firms. Simply stated, Williamson proposes that firms choose how to transact according to the criterion of minimizing the sum of production and transaction costs. Production costs may differ between firms due to the scale of operations, to learning, or to proprietary knowledge. Transaction costs refer to the expenses incurred for writing and enforcing contracts, for haggling over terms and contingent claims, for deviating from optimal kinds of investments in order to increase dependence on a party or to stabilize a relationship, and for administering a transaction.

Williamson posits that the principal feature of high transaction costs between arms-length parties is small numbers bargaining in a situation of bilateral governance. Small number bargaining results when switching costs are high due to asset specificity; namely, the degree to which assets are specialized to support trade between only a few parties.[1] The upshot of this analysis is that a firm may choose, say, to produce a component even though its production costs are higher than what outside suppliers incur. Such a decision may, however, be optimal if the expected transaction costs of relying on an outside supplier outweigh the production saving.[2]

Because a joint venture straddles the border of two firms, it differs from a contract insofar as cooperation is administered within an organizational hierarchy.[3] It differs from a vertically integrated activity in so far as two firms claim ownership to the residual value and control rights over the use of the assets. An obvious question is why should either firm choose to share ownership? Clearly, the answer lies in the diseconomies of acquisition due to the costs of divesting or managing unrelated activities or the higher costs of internal development. Thus, a necessary condition is that the production cost achieved through internal development or acquisition is significantly higher than external sourcing for at least one of the partners.

If vertical (or horizontal) integration is not efficient, then an alternative is the market or contract. As described earlier, a transaction cost explanation for why market transactions are not chosen rests on potential exploitation of one party when assets are dedicated to the relationship and there is uncertainty over redress. Leaving aside integration as economically infeasible and market transactions as too fraught with opportunistic risk, the final comparison is between a joint venture and a long-term contract.

A transaction cost theory must explain what discriminates a joint venture from a contract, and in what transactional situations a joint venture is best suited. Two properties are particularly distinctive: joint ownership (and control) rights and the mutual commitment of resources. The situational characteristics best suited for a joint venture are high uncertainty over specifying and monitoring performance, in addition to a high degree of asset specificity.[4] It is uncertainty over performance which plays a fundamental role in encouraging a joint venture over a contract.

To clarify why uncertainty over peformance makes the properties of joint ownership and mutual contribution particularly valuable, consider first a joint venture designed to supply one of the parties, and second a joint venture serving as a horizontal extension of one or more links of each parent's value-added chain. In the case where the joint venture represents a vertical investment for one party and a horizontal for the other, the venture replaces a supply agreement. In this case the venture is the outcome of the production advantage of the supplier coupled with the transaction cost hazards facing one or both of the parties.

These hazards pose the problem of how an agreement to divide excess profits (sometimes called the problem of 'appropriability') can be stabilized over time. Transaction cost hazards can face either the supplier or the buyer. Such hazards are likely to stem from the uncertainty in a supply contract over whether the downstream party is providing information on market conditions, over whether both parties are sharing new technologies, or over whether the supplier is performing efficiently or with the requisite quality production. Each of these cases poses the issue of whether, in the absence of the capability to specify and monitor performance, a governance mechanism can be designed to provide the incentives to perform.

A joint venture addresses this issue by creating a superior monitoring mechanism and alignment of incentives to reveal information, share technologies, and guarantee peformance. Instrumental in achieving this alignment are the rules of sharing costs and/or profits and the mutual investment in dedicated assets, in other words assets which are specialized to purchases or sales from a specific firm. Thus, both parties gain or lose by the performance of the venture.

It is by mutual hostage positions through joint commitment of financial or real assets that superior alignment of incentives is achieved, and the agreement on the division of profits or costs is stabilized. Non-equity contracts can also be written to provide similar incentives by stipulating complex contingencies and bonding. A joint venture differs by having both parties share in the residual value of the venture without specifying ex-ante the performance requirements or behavior of each party. Instead, the initial commitments and rules of profit sharing are specified, along with administration procedures for control and evaluation.

A more complex case is whether the joint venture represents a horizontal investment in order to supply both parties or sell in an outside market. The discriminating quality of a mutually horizontal joint venture is that the venture employs assets, such as one party's brand label reputation, which are vulnerable to erosion in their values. This latter aspect is particularly important if the joint venture has potential externalities which influence the value of the strategic assets of the parties, such as through a diffusion of technology, the erosion of reputation and brand labels, or the competitive effects on other common lines of business. It is, ironically, the initial complementarity between the parents' assets which both motivates joint cooperation and poses the transactional hazard of negative externalities, either through erosion or imitation of such assets as technology or reputation.

If two parties seek to resolve this dilemma by contracting to a third party, or to each other, the danger is that the agent will underinvest in complementary assets and free-ride the brand label or technological advantage. As a result the contracting party will undersupply, or mark up its price of, the inputs it contributes. A joint venture addresses these issues again by providing a superior alignment of incentives through a mutual dedication of resources along with better monitoring capabilities through ownership control rights. In summary, the critical dimension of a joint venture is its resolution of high levels of uncertainty over the behavior of the contracting parties when the assets of one or both parties are specialized to the transaction and the hazards of joint cooperation are outweighed by the higher production or acquisition costs of 100 percent ownership.

Strategic Behavior

An alternative explanation for the use of joint ventures stems from theories on how strategic behavior influences the competitive positioning of the firm. The motivations to joint venture for strategic reasons are numerous. Though transaction cost and strategic behavior theories share several commonalities, they differ fundamentally in the objectives attributed to firms. Transaction cost theory posits that firms transact by the mode which minimizes the sum of production and transaction costs. Strategic behavior posits that firms transact by the mode which maximizes profits through improving a firm's competitive position vis-à-vis rivals. A common confusion is treating the two theories as substitutes rather than as complementary.

Indeed, given a strategy to joint venture, for example, transaction cost theory is useful in analyzing problems in bilateral bargaining. But the decision itself to joint venture may stem from profit motivations and, in fact, may represent a more costly, though more profitable, alternative to other choices. The primary difference is that transaction costs address the costs specific to a particular economic exchange, independent of the product market strategy. Strategic behavior addresses how competitive positioning influences the asset value of the firm.

Potentially, every model of imperfect competition which explains vertical integration is applicable to joint ventures, from tying downstream distributors to depriving competitors of raw materials and to stabilizing oligopolistic competition. Of course, not every motive for collusive behavior is contrary to public welfare. Where there are strong network externalities, such as in technological compatibility of communication services, joint research and development of standards can result in lower prices and improved quality in the final market.[5] Research joint ventures which avoid costly duplication among firms but still preserve downstream competition can similarly be shown to be welfare improving.[6]

Many joint ventures are, on the other hand, motivated by strategic behavior to deter entry or erode competitors' positions. Vickers (1985) analyzes joint ventures in research as a way to deter entry through pre-emptive patenting. In oligopolistic industries it might be optimal for the industry if one of the firms invested in patentable research in order to forestall entry. But given free-rider problems, encumbents would tend to under-invest collectively in the absence of collusion. Vickers shows that, for small innovations, a joint venture is an effective mechanism to guarantee the entry deterring investment. For large innovations it is in the interest of each firm to pursue its own research, for the expected pay-off justifies the costs. More generally, Vernon (1983) sees joint ventures as a form of defensive investment by which firms hedge against strategic uncertainty, especially in industries of moderate concentration where collusion is difficult to achieve despite the benefits of coordinating the inter-dependence among firms.

A strategic behavior perspective of joint venture choice implies that the selection of partners is made in the context of competitive positioning vis-à-vis other rivals or consumers. Though this area has not been investigated, the prediction of which firms will joint venture is unlikely to be the same for both transaction cost and strategic behavior perspectives. Whereas the former predicts that the matching should reflect minimizing costs, the latter predicts that joint venture partners will be chosen to improve the competitive positioning of the parties, whether through collusion or through depriving competitors of potentially valuable allies. Thus, two important differences in the implications of a transaction cost and strategic behavior analysis are the identification of the motives to cooperate and the selection of partners.

Organizational Knowledge and Learning

Transaction cost and strategic motivation explanations provide compelling economic reasons for joint ventures. There are, of course, other explanations outside of economic rationality. Dimaggio and Powell's depicture of mimetic processes of firms offers an interesting alternative point of view, for it is premature to rule out joint venture activity as a form of band-wagon behavior (Dimaggio and Powell 1983). In other words, joint venture activity can be analogous to fashion trend setting.[7]

There is, however, a third rational explanation for joint ventures which does not rest on either transaction cost or strategic behavior motivations. This explanation views joint ventures as a means by which firms learn or seek to retain their capabilities. In this view, firms consist of a knowledge base, or what McKelvey (1983) calls 'comps,' which are not easily diffused across the boundaries of the firm.[8] Joint ventures are, then, a vehicle by which, to use the often-quoted expression of Polanyi (1966), 'tacit knowledge' is transferred. Other forms of transfer, such as through licensing, are ruled out—not because of market failure or high transaction costs as defined by Williamson and others, but rather because the very knowledge being transferred is organizationally embedded.

This perspective is frequently identified with a transaction cost argument, even though the explanatory factors are organizational and cognitive rather than derivatives of opportunism under uncertainty and asset specificity. An example of this confusion is the explanation for joint ventures, commonly embraced as a form of transaction cost theory, that the transfer of know-how in the market place is severely encumbered by the hazards which attend the pricing of information without revealing its contents. Because knowledge can be transferred at—so it is claimed—zero marginal cost, the market fails, as sellers are unwilling to reveal their technology and buyers are unwilling to purchase in the absence of inspection.

Yet, as Teece (1977) demonstrated, the transfer of technology entails non-trivial costs, partly because of the difficulty of communicating tacit knowledge. If knowledge is tacit, then it is not clear why markets should fail due to opportunistic behavior. It would seem, in fact, that knowledge could be described to a purchaser without effecting a transfer, specified in a contract, and sold with the possibility of legal redress. In this sense tacitness tends to preserve the market.

Rather, the market is replaced by a joint venture not because tacitness is a cost stemming from opportunism, but rather from the necessity of replicating experiential knowledge which is not well understood. More generally, tacitness is an aspect of the capital stock of knowledge within a firm. In this regard there is an important distinction between capital specific to individuals, and for which there may be an external labor market, and capital specific to organizations, or what Nelson and Winter (1982) call skills and routines, respectively. For transactions which are the product of complex organizational routines, the transfer of know-how can be severely impaired unless the organization is itself replicated.[9]

In this perspective a joint venture is encouraged if neither party owns each other's technology or underlying 'comps', nor understands each other's routines.[10] Or conversely, following Nelson and Winter (1982), a firm may decide to joint venture in order to retain the capability (or what they call 'remember-by-doing') of organizing a particular activity while benefitting from the superior production techniques of a partner. Even if a supply agreement were to operate at lower production and transaction costs a firm may choose a more costly joint venture in order to maintain the option, albeit at a cost, to exploit the capability in the future. What drives the choice of joint ventures in this situation is the difference in the value of options to exploit future opportunities across market, contractual, and organizational modes of transacting. Thus, a joint venture is encouraged under two conditions: one or both firms desire to acquire the other's organizational knowhow; or one firm wishes to maintain an organizational capability while benefitting from another firm's current knowledge or cost advantage.

The three perspectives of transaction cost, strategic behavior, and organizational learning provide distinct, though at times overlapping, explanations for joint venture behavior. Transaction cost analyzes joint ventures as an efficient solution to the hazards of economic transactions. Strategic behavior places joint ventures in the context of competitive rivalry and collusive agreements to enhance market power. Finally, transfer or organizational skills views joint ventures as a vehicle by which organizational knowledge is exchanged and imitated—though controlling and delimiting the process can be itself a cause of instability.

Acknowledgments

I would like to acknowledge the helpful criticism of Erin Anderson, Dan Schendel, and the anonymous referees, as well as the research assistance of Bernadette Fox. The research for this paper has been funded under the auspices of the Reginald H. Jones Center of the Wharton School through a grant from AT&T.

☐ ENDNOTES

* This chapter is a revised version of B. Kogut (1998) 'Joint Ventures: Theoretical and Empirical Perspectives,' *Strategic Management Journal*, 9: 319–32.

1. Asset specificity is not a sufficient condition, uncertainty and frequency of the transactions are also necessary.

2. For a careful analysis of this problem, see Walker and Weber (1984); for an analysis of the downstream choice of using a direct sales agent (employee) or representative, see Anderson and Schmittlein (1984).

3. Subsequent to writing the earlier drafts of the paper this chapter is drawn from, working papers by Hennart (2006), and by Buckley and Casson (2007) came to my attention. The subsequent revisions have benefited from their work, though the substance of the argument has not changed.

4. It is frequently suggested that institutional choices can be linearly ordered from market to firm. Not only is this conceptually unfounded, but the interaction of asset specificity, uncertainty, and frequency is unlikely, to say the least, to result in a linear effect.

5. For an analysis of network externality, see Katz and Shapiro (1985).

6. See Ordover and Willig (1985). Friedman et al. (1979) found, in fact, that firms which joint venture tend to lower R&D expenditures. Their findings, therefore, support the argument that research ventures substitute for internal development and are motivated by efficiency considerations.

7. Indeed, Gomes-Casseres (1988) has found that joint venture waves exist and are difficult to predict by reasonable economic causes.

8. It could be argued that there is no more sustainable asset over which there is, to paraphrase Rumelt (1984), an uncertainty of imitation, than an organizationally embedded source of competitive advantage.

9. Teece (1982) makes a similar point in explaining the multiproduct firm.

10. Harrigan (1985) provides an excellent description by which firms seek to benefit from technological 'bleedthrough.' For example, internal R&D facilities are sometimes created which parallel the joint venture and staff is then rotated back and forth from the parent and joint venture organizations.

6 Joint Ventures and the Option to Expand and Acquire*

A fundamental problem facing the firm is the decision to invest and expand into new product markets characterized by uncertain demand. The problem is exacerbated when the new business is not related to current activities. In this sense, a firm's initial investments in new markets can be considered as buying the right to expand in the future.

In current parlance, the right to expand is an example of a 'real option,' real because it is an investment in operating as opposed to financial capital, and an option because it need never be exercised.[1] For many investments, such as the purchase of new capital equipment to reduce costs in aging plants, the option value is insignificant. In industries where the current investment provides a window on future opportunities, the option to expand can represent a substantial proportion of the value of a project, if not of the firm.[2]

An analysis of joint ventures provides an interesting insight into investment decisions as real options. The task of building a market position and competitive capabilities requires lumpy and non-trivial investments. As a result, it is often beyond the resources of a single firm to buy the right to expand in all potential market opportunities. A partner, especially one which brings the requisite skills, may be sought to share the costs of placing the bet that the opportunity will be realized.

This perspective is related to the use of joint ventures to share risk. Pure risk-sharing arises in cases, such as bidding on oil lots, where firms have committed capital downstream (such as in refineries) but are dependent upon availability supplies of a finite resource. Multiple joint ventures among firms in the oil industry are analogous to collective insurance.[3]

In many industries, however, joint ventures not only share risks, but also decrease the total investment. Because the parties bring different capabilities, the venture no longer requires the full development costs. Due to its benefits of sharing risk and of reducing overall investment costs, joint ventures serve as an attractive mechanism to invest in an option to expand in risky markets.

However, in the event the investment is judged to be favorable, the parties to the joint venture face a difficult decision. To exercise the option to expand requires further commitment of capital, thus requiring renegotiation among the partners. One possible outcome is that the party placing a higher value on this new capital commitment buys out the other. Thus, the timing when it is desirable to exercise the option to expand is likely to be linked to the time when the venture will be acquired.

The exploration of the link in the timing of the acquisition of joint ventures and of the exercise of the option to expand is the focus of the following empirical investigation. The first two sections apply an option perspective to joint ventures. A distinction is made between acquisitions motivated by industry conditions and those stemming from the desire to expand in response to favorable growth opportunities. The third section develops the central hypothesis that the timing of the acquisition is related to a signal that the valuation of the venture has increased. This signal is proxied by two measures derived from the growth of shipments in the venture's industry. The effects of these industry signals on the likelihood of a venture terminating by an acquisition are tested by specifying and estimating a hazard model, while controlling for industry and other effects.

The same model is then tested on the likelihood of dissolution. If the option interpretation is correct, a signal that the venture's value has increased should lead to an acquisition; a signal that it has decreased, however, should not lead to dissolution, as long as further investment is not required and operating costs are modest. Strong support is found for the option argument.

These results run counter to prevailing presumptions in organizational theories that firms engage in cooperative ventures as buffers against uncertainty and that managerial discretion is severely limited by environmental volatility. In the view of Pfeffer and Nowak (1976), joint ventures are instruments to manage the dependency of the partner firms on the uncertainty of resources. Recent work in organizational mortality, as influenced by the seminal articles by Hannan and Freeman (1977) and McKelvey and Aldrich (1983), has advanced the proposition that managers are severely curtailed in their abilities to affect the prospects of survival of their firms.

To the contrary, an option perspective posits that joint ventures are designed as mechanisms to exploit, as well as buffer, uncertainty. Because firms have limited influence over the sources of uncertainty in the environment, it pays to invest in the option to respond to uncertain events. Joint ventures are investments providing firms with the discretion to expand in favorable environments, but avoid some of the losses from downside risk. In this regard, real option theory provides a way to ground the trial and learning aspect to joint ventures.

Real Options

The assignment of the right to buy and sell equity in the joint venture is a common feature of many agreements. For example, in a recent announcement of a joint venture in the area of power generation equipment, Asea Brown Boverie received the option to buy the venture at some time in the future. Westinghouse, as the partner, has the right to sell its ownership interest. In the vernacular of financial markets, the terms of the venture provides a call option to Asea Brown Boverie and a put option to Westinghouse.

In drawing up a joint venture agreement, it is common practice to give first rights of refusal to the contracting parties to buy the equity of the partner who decides to withdraw. Sometimes, one party is given the priority to acquire in the case of termination. The legal clause serves to regulate the assignation of the rights to the underlying option. Such a clause may establish not only who has the first right to acquire, but also may set pricing rules.

The legal clause outlining acquisition rights should not be confused with the real option itself. Legal clauses serve simply as a way proactively to outline ownership rights in response to unspecified contingencies involving the failure of the cooperation. The termination of the venture by acquisition is not, therefore, necessarily equivalent to the creation and exercise of an option similar to those found in financial markets.

However, an economic option is often inherent in the decision to joint venture and the decision to exercise this option, as explained below, is likely to promote the divestment of the venture by one of the parties. Joint ventures are real options, not in terms of the legal assignation of contingent rights, but, like many investments, in terms of the economic opportunities to expand and grow in the future. The value of any investment can be broken into the cash flows stemming from assets as currently in place and those stemming from their redeployment or future expansion (Myers 1977). Because these latter cash flows are only realized if the business is expanded, they represent, as Myers first recognized, the value of growth opportunities.

The intuition behind this argument can be explained by following the notation of Pindyck (1988). Given an investment of K, the value of the venture can be decomposed in terms of both assets in place and the embedded options:

$$V_J = F_J(K, \pi) + O_J(K, \pi), \tag{1}$$

where V is the value of the venture as estimated by the jth firm, $F_J(K, \pi)$ is the value of the assets in their current use, $O_J(K, \pi)$ is the valuation of the future growth opportunities, and π is the current value of an uncertain state variable. The difference between $F_J(K, \pi)$ and $O_J(K, \pi)$ is that the latter is not equivalent to the discounted cash flows of expected earnings, because

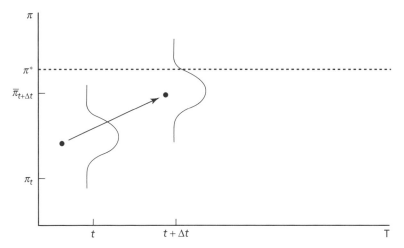

Figure 6.1. Expected change in π_t.

the firm maintains the flexibility to choose among investment alternatives—including not to invest—in the future.

As both the value of the assets in place and the option can be potentially affected by current assets and opportunities of the partner firms, the valuations of the venture will differ among the parties. For example, the venture might source components from one partner and not the other, hence affecting the valuation of assets in place.[4] Differences in option valuation can arise if the potential spill-over effects of the venture's technology complement the product portfolio of one partner more than the other.

Changes in the value of these assets depend on the stochastic process determining the current value of the embedded option, where the state variables are prices, either of production or the inputs. In Figure 6.1, we illustrate the implications of this process by assuming that changes in a state variable (indicated as π) are normally distributed over time and depict a cross-section of the path. The expected value ($\bar{\pi}_{t+\Delta t}$) is the current value plus the expected increase; the variance is σ^2. If realization of $\pi_{t+\Delta t}$ is greater than some critical value π^*, the derived value of the venture is greater than its acquisition price and the option to acquire is exercised. If $\pi_{t+\Delta t}$ is less than π^*, no further investment is made. Nor is it necessary to divest the assets (if operating costs are low), for there is the possibility that future changes will be more favorable. It is for this reason that the downside risk is not consequential.

Below, we consider the conditions which generate the option value, as well as examine motives for acquisitions which are not driven by the underlying option value. We link the value of the option, and, thereby, the venture, to the market demand for new products and technologies. Then, the central issue of the timing of exercise is addressed.

Joint Ventures as Real Options

In the following, we consider two options and examine qualitatively why joint ventures can be viewed as analogues. The first option is waiting to invest, whereby it pays to wait before committing resources. In the second option of expanding production, investment commitment is necessary in order to have the right to expand in the future. These two options, therefore, exemplify two polar types of real option strategies.[5]

It is often the case that an investment decision involves a comparison of both options. Committing engineers or product planners to a risky project incurs the possibility that the market does not develop; it also draws resources from other projects. Clearly, there is a value in waiting before the technology or market is proven. But if there is a benefit in investing today in order to gain experience with the technology or to establish a brand image with customers, then investing generates the valuable option to expand in the future.

A joint venture serves as a way to bridge these options through pooling resources of two or more firms. Because the value of the option to expand is greatest in new markets and technologies, any given firm is unlikely to possess the full repertoire of skills. A joint venture not only shares the investment burden, but sometimes reduces it, as the parties may bring different skills, thereby lowering the total investment cost. In this sense, a joint venture resolves partly the tradeoff between buying flexibility now and waiting to invest and focus later (Wernerfelt and Karnani 1987).[6]

When the market for the technology or new product is proven, the option to acquire, as discussed later, is likely to be exercised. Through the joint venture, the buying party has acquired the skills of the partner firm and no longer needs to invest in the development of the requisite capability to expand into the targeted market. The divesting firm is willing to sell because, one, it realizes capital gains, and two, it may also not have the downstream assets to bring the technology to market (Teece 1987; Shan 1988). In this sense, the divestiture of joint ventures are the buyers' side to the argument and findings of Christensen and Montgomery (1981) that acquisitions are a way to buy into attractive industries.

For one of the partners to make the acquisition, the net value of purchasing the joint venture must be at least equal to the value of purchasing comparable assets on the market. This condition is likely to be satisfied due to the gain in experience in running the venture. If it does not hold, there was no advantage and, hence, no value to the option by investing early. But even if this condition does not hold ex post, a joint venture, as Balakrishnan and Koza (1988) point out, affords the possibility to learn the true value of the assets. As information is revealed, the acquisition is completed or withdrawn. From this perspective, regardless of other motives such as managerial experience, there is a bias to buy out the venture relative to other acquisition prospects simply due to better valuation information.

Timing of Exercise

As apparent from the above analysis, an acquisition or divestment is often a foreseen conclusion to the venture. The investing firms may be indifferent to whether a partner or a third firm purchases the venture. The reward is the capital gains return on the development efforts.

From this perspective, the timing of the acquisition is of critical significance. Simply stated, the acquisition is justified only when the perceived value to the buyer is greater than the exercise price. For a financial option, the terminal value is given by the stock price and the exercise price as set by the initial contract:

$$W = \max(S_t - E, 0]$$ (2)

where W is the value of the option, S is the price of the stock at time t, and E is the exercise price. (In this case, S_t is the state variable which we denoted earlier as π.) As the cost of purchasing the option is sunk, these two parameters determine, ex post, the value of the option when exercised.[7]

The joint venture analogue to equation (2) is:

$$W_J = \text{Max}\left((1 - a)V_J - P, 0\right).$$ (3)

That is, the value of the option to acquire (W) is equal to the value to the jth firm of purchasing the remaining shares in the venture minus P, where $a > 0$ and <1 and is the current share owned by firm j and P is the price of purchasing the remaining shares. (P is either negotiated between the parties or set according to a contractual clause.)[8]

For financial options, it is well established that an option should be usually held to full maturity (Hull 1989: 105–29). Exceptions to this rule depend upon dividend policy on the underlying stock, where it may pay to exercise the option before payment to shareholders. Obviously, in the case of joint ventures, the acquisition is only carried out if $(1-a) V_j > P$.

But the exercise of the option to acquire the joint venture is likely to be immediate for two reasons. First, the value of the real option is *only* recognized by making the investment and realizing the incremental cash flows. If the investment in new capacity is not made in a period, the cash flows are lost. Second, the necessity to increase the capitalization of the venture invariably requires a renegotiation of the agreement, often leading to its termination.[9] The option to expand the investment is likely to coincide with exercising the option to acquire the joint venture.

Consider a pure research venture between two parties. Both parties provide initial funding and a pre-established contribution to costs. As long as the initial investment is sunk and additional capital commitments are not required, increased variance in the value of the technology raises the upside gain. (Of course, variable costs must be paid, but these 'carrying' costs apply as well to some kinds of financial options.) Since the option need not be exercised, the downside is inconsequential. At any given time, whether it pays for one party to buy the venture is dependent upon the buy-out price and the valuation of the business as a wholly owned operation.

But once it is profitable to exercise the option, there are sound reasons not to wait. The option value of the venture is realized by investing in expansion. The requirement to contribute further capital leads to a difficult renegotiation. By now, the partners have information to know that the original equity share may not reflect the division of benefits. This deviation can be expected to be compounded when the option to expand becomes economically viable, as the partners are likely to differ in their appraisal of these opportunities. Thus, the allocation of new capital burdens often forces a revaluation of the distribution of benefits. Buying out the partner is a common outcome.

The timing of the exercise of the option to terminate the venture by acquisition is, thus, influenced by two considerations: the initial base rate forecast underlying the valuation of the business and the value of the venture to each party (or third parties) as realized over time. For the acquisition to take place, the acquisition price P must be greater than the valuation placed on the assets by one of the partners. These considerations lead to the following hypothesis: *The venture will be acquired when its valuation exceeds the base rate forecast.*

Selective Cues and Market Valuation

Unlike the case for a contingent security, there are no written contracts and financial markets that indicate changes in the value of a real option. Testing this hypothesis is, clearly, difficult given the impossibility to collect data on changes over time of both partners' evaluations of the option to expand. Nor is it likely that managers possess clear base-rates and valuation signals by which to guide a decision to exercise the option to expand. Consequently, the specification of the above hypothesis raises important questions about what information and environment cues managers use to time the exercise of the option.

Despite theoretical interest and laboratory experiments, most of the research on environmental cues informing managerial decisions has been oriented to identifying biases in the interpretation of information rather than in the selection of the information itself. Of some guidance is the finding of Bowman (1963) that adherence to a consistent rule derived from previous decisions performs better than the decisions actually made, suggesting that the efficiency of decision-making is impaired due to biases in the selection cues.[10] More recent research has especially pointed to biases derived from base-rate errors and the salience, or availability, of information. Several studies have shown that individuals wrongly calculate probabilities by weighting recent information too heavily or failing to incorporate information on the marginal probabilities.[11] Base-rates are, thus, frequently ignored, especially when the causal relationships are not explicit.

Whereas experimental research has validated a number of heuristics used in selecting information, there is little guidance for establishing the base rates that might be used for irregular decisions, such as the acquisition of a joint venture. We would expect, as Camerer (1981) notes, that individuals rely upon only a few cues of those available. We experiment with two time-varying specifications of the market cues relevant to the acquisition decision: a short-term annual growth rate and an annual residual error from a long-term trend in shipments.

The short-term annual growth rate is calculated as:

$$G_{t,J} = [PS_{t,J} - PS_{t-1,J} / PS_{t-1,J}], \qquad (4)$$

where the growth rate is set equal to changes in the value of product shipments (*PS*) for the jth industry over an annual interval $[t - 1, t]$. The residual error is derived from the error from an estimated regression of the time trend in shipment growth:

$$R_{t,J} = PS_{t,J} - [a_J + b_J t], \qquad (5)$$

where the residual error is the forecasting error from a linear time trend for the jth industry with intercept a and slope coefficient b. (The appropriateness of the linear specification is discussed below.)

It is essential to recognize that the above variables vary with time. Both specifications are derived from a constant dollar series of industry product shipments. The annual growth measure looks at year to year changes, always using the previous year as a benchmark. The residual error indicates that decision-makers establish a long-term base rate for each industry's historical growth and look at year to year departures from this trend. Unlike the growth measure, it assumes that managers act to acquire or divest when a market cue signals a rise in valuation relative to a long-term trend.

These two variables are, by our argument, proxies for changes in the unobserved state variable (given as π earlier) that determines the value of the joint venture. As our interest does not lie, however, in the pricing of the option but in the likelihood (or hazard) of acquisition, differences in the scales of the proxies are unimportant to the estimations, as described below. Positive movements in the value of industry shipments signal improved investment opportunities and an increase in the value of the real option embedded in the venture. Because the exercise of the option requires a decision to expand the investment and, hence, a renegotiation of the capital commitment of the parties to the venture, the likelihood of an acquisition should increase with positive movements of the proxy variables.

Acquisition and Value of Assets in Place

Joint ventures can, of course, be acquired for reasons other than as the outcome to negotiations stemming from exercising the option to expand. In large part, the differences in the reasons to acquire are derived from differences in the original motivations to joint venture in the first place. The motivations to joint venture may sometimes have less to do with building an option to expand into new markets than with the benefits of sharing ownership of assets in their current use. Some ventures provide a mechanism to share scale economies and to coordinate the management of potentially excess capacity in mature and concentrated industries (Harrigan 1986). The option proportion of the total value of these kinds of ventures is likely to be low, that is, the present value of the assets in their current use dominates the option to expand or re-deploy.

There is, though, an interesting aspect to some ventures in concentrated industries which the terminology of the option literature illuminates, for many of these ventures are also partial divestments. A number of recent joint ventures fall in this category: Firestone's sale of 50 percent of the equity of its tire business to Bridgestone, Honeywell's partnership with NEC and Bull in computers, and the above cited Asea Brown Boverie and Westinghouse agreement. In all of these ventures, the call option was given to the non-American firm.

The question of why do the parties not agree to an immediate acquisition underscores the critical roles of learning and pre-emption. Through the joint venture, the divesting party is contracted to pass on complex know-how on the running of the business, as well as to slow an erosion in customer confidence. Since this know-how may be essentially organizational—such as, the procedures by which an American firm are effectively managed, a joint venture serves as a vehicle of managerial and technological learning (Kogut 1988; Lyles 1988). In this case, a joint venture is a phased divestiture with a future exercise date.

The importance of this motivation is especially important in industries where there are few competitors. Tying up a potential acquisition target prevents other parties from making the acquisition, a threat which is particularly troubling in concentrated industries where there are few acquisition targets.

Through the acquisition, full ownership is attained without adding further capacity to the industry by entering with a new plant.

Data Collection

In the above analysis, we related the likelihood of termination of a joint venture by acquisition to increases in the valuation of the embedded option and to industry conditions leading to divestment of existing assets. To test the effect of these two factors on the likelihood of acquisition, data were collected from both questionnaire and archival sources. Information on joint ventures was first acquired from the publication *Mergers and Acquisitions* for the years 1975 and 1983.[12] The sample included only ventures located in the United States in order to eliminate variance in political environments across countries. Moreover, all ventures had at least one American partner given the difficulty of gathering information on non-American firms. Of the 475 firms contacted in two mailings, 55.5 percent responded. However, due to a number of factors, such as misclassifying a contract as a joint venture or announcing a venture which never occurred, only 140 responses were useable. Of these, 92 are in manufacturing; it is this subsample which is used in this paper. Sources for the industry data are given below.

The questionnaire was designed to elicit factual information regarding the starting and, in the case of termination, ending dates for the venture, as well as its primary purpose. On the basis of this information, the percentage of ventures dissolved or acquired by one of the partners or a third party is 43 percent. A follow-up questionnaire was sent one-year later to those ventures reported still alive, which resulted in raising this percentage to 55 percent. A second follow-up was made the following year, with the percentage of terminations rising to 70 percent.

The questionnaire data makes it possible to construct life histories for the 92 manufacturing ventures. Of these 92 ventures, 27 terminated by dissolution, 37 by acquisition, and 28 are censored, that is, they are still in effect. In this study, we treat the ventures that terminated by dissolution as also censored. Such a treatment is reasonable as long as the individual hazards are independent. Given the low density of ventures in a particular industry, the assumption of independence is justified.

From the questionnaire data, we create three dummy variables (*R&D, production and marketing*) indicating whether the venture included any of these activities. These variables are used to control for differences in the contractual terms of the sampled joint ventures due to variations in their functional activities. Clearly, the expectations regarding the duration of the ventures may differ depending on whether they involve investments in production and capital equipment or in joint marketing or product development.

The other data are taken from secondary sources. Drawing on Bureau of Census data, we use the four-firm concentration ratio at the four-digit SIC level (*concentration*) as a proxy for industry maturity that promotes the use of joint ventures as vehicles of planned divestment. Since concentration ratios are published for every fifth year, we employ the ratio nearest the midpoint of the venture's life. (As the ratios are highly correlated across years, there is little difference in results using this procedure or other alternatives.)

As discussed earlier, two different proxies are specified for the central hypothesis that the likelihood of an acquisition is related to the occurrence of a signal of an increase in the value of the venture. The two measures discussed earlier (*annual growth* and *annual residual error*) are estimated from unpublished Department of Commerce data on annual shipments (i.e. goods sold) at the four-digit level in constant 1982 dollars for the years 1965 to 1986. Both of these variables are drawn from industry data.

The annual growth data is derived directly from the shipment series. To normalize the data, each industry time series was divided by the first year of the series; thus each series begins with 1965 set to 100. By first differencing the normalized series and dividing by the lagged year, growth in shipments were calculated for each year. This measure was then entered into the analysis as a time-varying covariate with a one-year lag.[13] The time-varying specification means that for a venture alive in 1978, the value of the growth variable is set equal to the annual growth of the venture's industry for 1977. If the venture survives to the next year, the growth covariate is updated to the realized growth rate in 1978.

The residual error is calculated in several steps. First, we again used the normalized series of shipments for each four-digit SIC industry. Second, a time trend was derived by a linear regression. The residual is calculated as the forecasting error for each year, using the estimated linear time trend as the base-rate predictor and the actual normalized shipment as the realized value. The residual error was also entered into the analysis as a time-varying covariate with a one-year lag.

The use of a linear fit for estimating the time trend is justified on a few grounds. With the exception of a few industries, the F-test indicated that the linear specification resulted in rather good fits. Thus, the simple linear model provides a good estimate of the long-term trend. Moreover, several studies have found that linear rules are commonly adopted by individuals to establish expectations (Hogarth 1982). In some industries, a linear estimate is a poor one and unlikely to be widely maintained. Indeed, as we find below, the exclusion of outliers on the residual measure leads to much better results.

Descriptive statistics are provided for the variables in Table 6.1. The correlation of the variable *acquisition* with the co-variates is misleading, for the later

Table 6.1. Descriptive Statistics and Correlation Matrix

	Mean	Standard deviation	Lowest	Highest
A = Acquisition	0.4	0.49	0.0	1.0
B = Concentration	40.11	20.76	8.0	96.0
C = R&D	0.51	0.50	0.0	1.0
D = Production	0.57	0.50	0.0	1.0
E = Marketing/distribution	0.53	0.50	0.0	1.0

Spearman Correlation Matrix

	A	B	C	D	E
A	—	—	—	—	—
B	0.19	—	—	—	—
C	0.05	−0.08	—	—	—
D	0.05	−0.04	−0.07	—	—
E	0.10	−0.08	−0.05	−0.07	—

regressions use time to acquisition as the basis of ordering the likelihoods. It, nevertheless, provides some insight into the underlying relationships. Evident from the table is the low degree of collinearity among these variables. We do not report the time-varying variables, since it would require reporting a covariate for each year of the sample.

Statistical Specification

To incorporate the effects of the unobserved stochastic process and the time-varying co-variates, we use a partial likelihood specification to estimate the influence of these factors on termination by acquisition among a sample of joint ventures. Partial likelihood estimates the influence of explanatory variables (or co-variates) on the hazard of termination without specifying a parametric form for the precise time to failure. Instead, it rank orders ventures in terms of the temporal sequence of terminations. For each event time, it specifies a likelihood that the observed terminated venture should have terminated, conditional on the co-variates of the ventures at risk:

$$L_i(t_i) = h_0(t_i)(\exp(BX_i + BX_i(t_i)/h_0(t_i)))[[\Sigma_j(\exp(BX_J + BX_J(t_i)))]].$$

(6)

For simplicity, the coefficients and co-variates are given as vectors B and X, respectively, with i indexing the venture which failed at time t_l, j indexing the ventures at risk at time t_l, $h_0(t_l)$ is the baseline hazard, and L is the likelihood for the ith event. The time-varying co-variates (*annual growth* and *residual error*) are indexed by the time of the event (t_l).

It should be noted that the partial likelihood is general in its specification. The parametric assumptions are the linearity imposed on the coefficients and the log-additivity of the baseline hazard and covariate terms. The distribution of the baseline hazard is nonparametric and entirely general. By leaving the baseline hazard unspecified, no bias is incurred by misspecifying the stochastic process by which unobserved variables influence the observed hazard rate. While efficiency is lost by ignoring the exact termination times, the estimates are consistent; the efficiency loss has been shown to be modest (Efron 1977; Kalbfleisch and Prentice 1980).

This generality is achieved by restricting the baseline hazard to be the same for all the ventures. By this assumption, $h_0(t_l)$ cancels out. As shown first by Cox (1972), this likelihood is equivalent to allowing only the conditional probabilities to contribute to the statistical inferences. No information on the precise timing of, or the elapsed time to termination is required; hence it provides a partial, rather than full maximum, likelihood estimate. Consequently, we do not need to know the functional form of the baseline hazard and, implicitly, the underlying process generating changes in the valuation of the venture or the boundary condition giving the point of exercise of the option.

The partial likelihood is calculated as the product of the individual likelihoods. Estimation proceeds by maximizing jointly the likelihoods that the ith venture should terminate conditionally on the characteristics of the other ventures at risk at the time of termination. We use the Newton–Raphson algorithm by which to estimate numerically the coefficients and standard errors. There is no constant or error term. A positive coefficient indicates that increases in the covariate tend to increase the likelihood of termination; a negative coefficient indicates the reverse.[14]

Statistical Results

The statistical results are given in Table 6.2. As can be seen from the Student T scores, the principal hypotheses are confirmed under a two-tail significance test. Concentration is significant at 0.002. In concentrated industries, joint ventures appear to be used as an intermediary step towards a complete acquisition. A complementary but more speculative interpretation is that joint ventures are also often part of the restructuring of mature industries, either due to new, and perhaps foreign, competition or to efforts to stabilize the degree of rivalry. By acquiring the assets, a shifting of ownership occurs without an increase in industry capacity.

Ventures with R&D activities or marketing and distribution activities are more likely to be acquired at 0.1 significance under a two-tail test and at 0.05 under a one-tail. The production variable is positive, though insignificant.

Table 6.2. Partial Likelihood Estimate of Covariates' Effects on Log Likelihood of Acquisition

Variable name	Full sample (1)	Without computer industry (2)	Without computer industry (3)	Without computer industry (4)
Concentration	0.26	0.02	0.03	0.02
	(3.16[a])	(2.84[a])	(3.08[a])	(2.59[b])
R&D	0.58	0.70	0.57	0.70
	(1.67[c])	(1.88[c])	(1.58)	(1.91[c])
Production	0.16	0.10	0.20	0.06
	(0.44)	(0.26)	(0.56)	(0.16)
Marketing/distribution	0.61	0.66	0.59	0.62
	(1.75[c])	(1.76[c])	(1.63)	(1.66[c])
Annual growth	0.03	0.22	0.03	—
	(2.25[b])	(1.28)	(1.89[c])	—
Residual error	0.0001	0.006	—	0.01
	(0.45)	(2.88[a])	—	(3.48[a])
N =	92	88	88	88

Notes: Significance under two-tail T-test: (T-statistics in parentheses); [a] $P < 0.01$; [b] $P < 0.05$; [c] $P < 0.10$.

The most interesting comparison is between the growth and residual error variables. The growth variable has a positive effect on acquisitions and is significant at 0.05. The residual error coefficient, on the other hand, is indistinguishable from a null effect.

Given the sample size, it is important to look at the effect of possible outliers. Large residuals might be generated by a poor fit of the linear trend line. The trend lines for ten industries (in which there are 12 ventures) have significance levels worse than 0.05. Of these 12 ventures, six terminated by acquisition. Their elimination from the sample changed the results only mildly.

A more direct way to identify outliers is to plot the residual errors and growth rates for each industry. The electronic computing machinery industry (SIC 3573) stands out dramatically from the rest. For 1986, for example, the residual error for computers was 30 times greater than the next highest industry. The remarkable trait of the industry is that since these growth rates have been sustained for two decades and more, negative residual errors are generated even when the growth rate is still substantially above the mean and median for the whole sample. As three of the four ventures in this industry terminated in an acquisition, the estimates are strongly affected.

Re-estimating the regression equation without these four ventures gives strikingly different results. Significance levels for the other variables stay largely the same. The most striking change is in the positions of the residual error and growth variable. Both are now positively signed, but the residual error variable is significant at 0.01. The coefficient on the growth variable is indistinguishable from the null hypothesis. These results are much kinder to the proposition that managers are sensitive to a long-term intra-industry base rate which serves as a standard by which to evaluate annual changes.

The decline in significance of the growth variable is partially the result of the collinearity with the measure of the residual error. Unusually high (low) growth is likely to result in larger (smaller) residual errors. The correlations for *annual growth* and *residual error* ranged as high as 0.85 for one year, though often were much lower. Since collinearity tends to raise the standard errors, the loss in significance for *annual growth* should be interpreted with some caution.

To address this confounding, *annual growth* and *residual error* were entered separately into the regression analysis. The results are given in equations (3) and (4) of Table 6.2. Whereas *annual growth* is only significant at 0.1, *residual error* is significant at 0.001. It is reasonable to conclude that the decision by managers whether to acquire or divest the joint venture is more significantly sensitive to annual departures from a long-term trend than to short-term indices of industry growth.[15]

Discussion of Market Signals

The above findings indicate that increases in excess of the long-term trend in shipment growth are significantly related to the timing of the acquisitions of ventures. Such a relationship suggests that managerial decisions are cued by market signals that the venture's value has increased. Because of the level of aggregation of our sample, the cue may be indirectly related, that is, there are intervening variables (e.g. revenues to the venture) between the variables we chose and the direct cues bearing on managerial choice.

In turn, it could be argued that the take-off in growth signals industry consolidation, thus forcing exits. Conceptually, this objection is weak, for a shake-out should occur when the market does poorer than its historical record. The relationship between *residual error* and the likelihood of acquisition suggests the opposite, namely, acquisitions tend to occur when the market does better than its historical record.

To test whether consolidation leads to divestment, we calculate a new variable *change in concentration* which indicates the percentage change in the four-firm concentration at the four-digit SIC level during the life of the venture.[16] The results given in equations (1) and (2) of Table 6.3 show no support that consolidation leads to an increase in acquisition.

Another interpretation of the findings is that managers are myopic and fail to consider that short-term deviations may be outliers. Frequently, this error is referred to as ignoring regression to the mean or the law of small numbers (Tversky and Kahneman 1971; Hogarth 1982). Incidences of annual

Table 6.3. Partial Likelihood Estimates of Covariates' Effects on Log Likelihood of Termination

Variable name	Acquisition		Dissolution	
	Full sample (1)	Without computer industry (2)	Full sample (3)	Without computer industry (4)
Concentration	0.03	0.03	0.01	0.01
	(3.14[a])	(2.90[a])	(1.16)	(1.16)
R&D	0.59	0.75	0.53	0.53
	(1.66[c])	(1.96[c])	(1.30)	(1.30)
Production	0.16	0.10	−0.18	−0.17
	(0.45)	(0.27)	(−0.43)	(−0.43)
Marketing/distribution	0.62	0.69	0.30	0.30
	(1.75[c])	(1.83[c])	(0.73)	(0.74)
Annual growth	0.03	0.02	−0.01	−0.01
	(2.23[b])	(1.22)	(−0.77)	(−0.77)
Residual error (0.39)	0.0001	0.007	0.003	0.003
	(0.39)	(2.93[a])	(0.72)	(0.72)
Change in concentration	0.143	0.59	—	—
	(0.14)	(0.60)	—	—
N =	92	88	92	88

Notes: Significance under two-tail T-test: (T-statistics in parentheses); [a] $P < 0.01$; [b] $P < 0.05$; [c] $P < 0.10$.

growth rates and residual errors, in other words, may reflect extreme values of a random process.

That managers do not simply react to any short-term change can also be addressed empirically. If short-term myopia leads to a divest and acquire decision, then it should lead to a dissolve decision when the market turns down. We can test this proposition by estimating the same model for the likelihood of termination by dissolution.

This test is especially important if the argument that joint ventures frequently serve as real options is correct. The nature of an option should be kept in mind. Once the capital is committed, the downside risk is low, especially if there is a market for the acquisition of the assets and operating costs are not high. The selling of the venture means that one firm puts a higher value on the assets; it does not mean the venture is unprofitable.

Though it should not be expected that the same co-variates should be theoretically related to dissolution, we include them in order to make the results comparable.[17] These results are given in columns 3 and 4 of Table 6.3. As can be seen, there is no significant relationship between dissolution and the growth and residual error measures.

The insignificance of the *annual growth* and *residual error* variables lends further support to the options argument. For if joint ventures are designed as options, then as long as the investment is sunk and the operating costs are moderate, downward movements should not lead to dissolution. Rather, it pays to wait and see if the process generates more favorable outcomes. The asymmetry in the acquisition and dissolution results supports strongly the interpretation that joint ventures are designed as options.

Conclusion

This article has investigated the proposition that joint ventures are designed as options that are exercised through a divestment and acquisition decision. The statistical investigation analyzes what factors increase the likelihood of an acquisition. These factors have been shown to be unexpected increases in the value of the venture and the degree of concentration in the industry.

There is a wider implication of this study for theories of organizational behavior. At least since Knight's ([1921]1971) observations, it has been widely claimed that risk reduction can be achieved through organizational mechanisms, or what Cyert and March (1963) labelled 'uncertainty reduction.' But firms, if not other organizations, may also profit from uncertainty.[18] Such profit taking might be achieved through a more flexible production process or organizational design, as described by Piore and Sabel (1984). It might also be achieved by investments in joint ventures which serve as platforms for possible future development. After decades of research on the mechanisms of reducing risk, a look focusing at the way which organizations benefit from uncertainty appears promising.[19]

Acknowledgments

The author would like to acknowledge the research assistance and suggestions of Kristiaan Helsen and the comments of Ned Bowman, Colin Camerer, Weijian Shan, Gordon Walker, and the anonymous referees. The research has been funded under a grant from AT&T under the auspices of the Reginald H. Jones Center.

☐ ENDNOTES

* This chapter is a revised version of B. Kogut (1991) 'Joint Ventures and the Option to Expand and Acquire,' *Management Science*, 37: 19–33.

1. See Myers (1984), for an interesting qualitative discussion of real options, and Mason and Merton (1985) for an extensive analytical treatment.

2. See Kester (1984) for an interesting tabulation of the option value of many large firms.

3. For a study of joint ventures in the oil industry, see Mead (1967). Note, however, that the decision whether to pump the oil can be viewed analytically as an option to wait. See McDonald and Siegel (1986).

4. See Contractor (1985) for an analysis of joint ventures with resulting side payments.

5. Variations on the waiting to invest option are given in McDonald and Siegel (1986); Majd and Pindyck (1987); and Pindyck (1988). Kulatilaka (1988) provides a general formulation, allowing for switching between active and wait modes.

6. This explanation is incomplete without a consideration why a joint venture is favored over alternatives. For a discussion, see Kogut (1988).

7. Ex ante, the value of the option is determined by not only by the known parameters, but also the stochastic process determining the value of the venture.

8. As the acquisition price is likely to be state dependent, it is important to note that McDonald and Siegel (1986) provide a solution for an option where the value of the underlying asset and exercise price are both stochastic.

9. The comments of one of the referees helped clarify the necessity of both conditions. See also Doz and Schuen (1988) for a discussion of negotiating problems stemming from different evaluations of the venture's growth potential.

10. See also Kunreuther (1969) and the analysis of similar 'bootstrapping' models in psychology by Camerer (1981).

11. See Tversky and Kahneman (1982) and the discussion in Hogarth (1982: 38–42).

12. In the sampling process, some of the joint ventures were reported as starting up later and, in a few cases, earlier than the initial time span.

13. The lag is motivated by pragmatic and design concerns. Since the shipment data ends in 1986, a lag would have been necessary for the ventures surviving to 1987. Also, as the ventures can terminate at any time during a given year and as the termination date usually follows by several months the decision, it is more conservative to take the lag value.

14. See Allison (1984) and Kalbfleisch and Prentice (1980) for the treatment of tied data.

15. Though the coefficient to *annual growth* is larger, they are not comparable due to the differences in their measurement.

16. As concentration is only published for every fourth year, we took the starting year closest to the year of birth of the venture and the closing year closest to the year of termination or censorship.

17. For an analysis of the dissolution of joint ventures, see Kogut (1989).

18. In some cases, they may even seek higher risk (Myers 1977; Bowman 1980).

19. One of the more interesting directions of population ecology is the comparison between strategies which differ by their ability to survive under varying conditions of risk. See, for example, Brittain and Freeman (1980).

7 Operating Flexibility, Global Manufacturing, and the Option Value of a Multinational Network*

with Nalin Kulatilaka

Introduction

The theory of the multinational corporation has traditionally sought to explain why a firm can successfully invest in overseas operations. As Hymer (1960) noted, a foreign company operates at a disadvantage relative to local firms; it must control the operations over longer distances and it is at a handicap in a foreign culture. Thus, he concluded, direct investment must be motivated by a competitive asset that provides the foreign firm with an advantage.

Around this central perspective, the work in both economics and management has developed a substantial and complementary body of research. In the field of the economics of the multinational corporation, considerable attention has been paid to the theoretical and empirical investigation of firm-level advantages and foreign direct investment. In the area of management, a principal line of inquiry regards the costs of managing foreign operations due to differences in culture, labor relations, and human resource practices. The management literature, in effect, has investigated in detail Hymer's supposition of the higher costs of managing in foreign countries.

This central perspective, however, loses considerable relevance for the investigation of the economic and competitive behavior of multinational corporations. There is a distinction between the economic and management aspects of a firm's first and subsequent investments in a foreign country. Nor is this distinction minor when it is considered that around 40 percent of US trade stems from the transfer of goods among affiliates within a corporation and that the predominant proportion of US direct investment is in the

Table 7.1. Destination of Shipments of US Manufacturing Affiliates Abroad (as percentage of total sales)

Area	Local sales (%)	Third country sales (%)	US sales (%)
Canada	61.9	3.4	34.8
Europe	60.2	34.2	5.6
Japan	83.3	7.8	8.9
Other Asia and Pacific	60.9	18.0	21.1
Latin America	78.6	23.0	13.6

Notes: Aggregation due to presentation of Original Data.

Source: Benchmark Survey of US Direct Foreign Investment Abroad (1989).

form of reinvested earnings in already existing subsidiaries.[1] An indication of the use of foreign subsidiaries as part of an internationally coordinated strategy is given in Table 7.1. This table shows the sales of affiliates within the corporation and to the outside. The degree of internal transfers is quite high, especially for the Asian region which provides a platform for global sourcing.

The coordination of a network of subsidiaries dispersed throughout the world provides an 'operating flexibility' that adds value to the firm. This operating flexibility is an advantage gained by being a multinational corporation. As developed below, it can be conceived as owning the option to respond to uncertain events, such as government policies, competitors' decisions, or the arrival of new technologies in some parts of the world.

The following article develops a formal model of the option value of multinationality. For purposes of illustration, we use the example of global manufacturing, where building plants in two countries is shown to generate additional value for the firm by shifting production depending on the real exchange rate. Using stochastic dynamic programming, simulations are generated by varying the volatility and speed by which the exchange rate returns to parity. We expand the across-country option of production shifting to include the creation of the within-country growth option.

In the last part of the article, we show that this model is more than normative but captures changes in the organization and information systems of multinational corporations. By examples from the recent management literature, the observed changes in internal accounting and pricing heuristics of the multinational corporation are argued to reflect the efforts to provide the correct information and incentives required for exercising operating flexibility. We show how the control system must be altered to support the transformation of a 'dyadic' relationship between headquarters and subsidiaries to a network structure.

In this sense, our treatment of the option value of a multinational corporation has a more general implication. The network structure of the multinational corporation provides the organizational capability to coordinate subsidiaries flexibly across borders. The economic merits of the international firm as a network are derived from the option value of multinational operating flexibility under the critical condition of uncertainty. The network structure of the multinational firm is an evolutionary response to the uncertainty of international markets.

Operating Flexibility and Multinational Options

Options are valuable due to three conditions: uncertainty, time dependence, and discretion. That flexibility is valuable only when there is uncertainty is obvious. Yet, often, the problem of understanding the source and properties of the uncertainty is substantial. A simple example is the difficulty of describing the probabilities attached to the arrival of new technologies.

A more subtle feature is time dependence. The application of option analysis to investments is important, because it captures the value in the dependence of decisions over time. To provide a counterexample, some investments, such as those characterized by easy entry and exit into perfectly competitive markets, can largely be analyzed independent of how today's decision influences future decisions.

These two conditions imply that the value of an option stems from the investment in the capability to respond profitably to future uncertain events. A critical issue is, then, the third condition, that is, that this capability is accompanied by the discretion to exercise the option. For example, the option to withdraw from a country is of little value, if the firm is encumbered by restrictions on laying-off workers or by the requirement to make burdensome severance payments.[2]

It is important to note that an investment in a foreign country generates two kinds of options. One kind is a 'within-country' growth option which, by establishing a brand label or simply knowledge of the market, provides a platform for the introduction of new products. This kind of option applies also to an investment by a domestic firm. The second kind is an 'across-country' option provided by operating flexibility.

Within-country options are significant in the international case because of the Hymer condition mentioned above, that is, the first international investments are made by firms which lack the organizational knowledge and supporting assets in the foreign market. The first investment carries, consequently, a large option value, as it opens the market for subsequent expansion. But the creation of these options is not itself an advantage of being international, but rather an aspect of the process by which the firm expands in a foreign country. In fact, as the firm grows in the foreign market, the value of these options to launch new products or to diversify within the country becomes the same as for a purely domestic corporation.[3]

The advantage of operating across borders relative to a purely domestic firm lies, then, not in being international, but in the ownership of options to coordinate flexibly *multinational* activities within a network. The option value of multinationality is different from that of the benefits of geographic diversification. The benefits of diversification are created by the reduction in variance of the overall portfolio of subsidiary results.[4] An option, on the other hand, is valuable because it gives *managerial discretion* to respond profitably to the realization of uncertain events.

In this sense, a real, as opposed to a financial, option differs in an important sense. (By real, it is meant an investment in operating activities rather than the purchase of financial instruments.) The exercising of a financial option is rarely impaired by institutional impediments; prices are easily available from markets and trading is relatively easy to carry out. But the exercise of a real option faces important impediments that cannot be ignored. A firm must be able to gather the appropriate information to know when the option should optimally be exercised; even when the information is known, exercise may be hindered by organizational features that obstruct flexibility.

We investigate these issues more formally by analyzing the problem of evaluating the value of manufacturing in two different countries. The source of uncertainty is the fluctuation in the real exchange rate; time dependence arises because the flexibility to shift production can only be realized by investing in two plants; managerial discretion is achieved by creating the proper accounting and organizational practices.

As our intention is not to model the extant manufacturing location problem, we focus only on the aspects of interest to our argument, that is, the increase in value gained through operating flexibility. We lay out first the formal model of the value of shifting production in response to exchange rates. We extend the results to consider a generalized global sourcing from more than two countries, hysteresis and growth options. Then, we turn to examining the accounting and pricing rules required to support the exercise of operating flexibility in a multinational network.

Global Manufacturing and Production Shifting

The literature on global manufacturing planning models has largely focused on the problem of plant location and scheduling in the absence of multiperiod flexibility. Recent advances have tried to embed the location and scheduling problem within the context of a network of production and distribution facilities (Cohen et al. 1989; Cohen and Lee 1989). Whereas these approaches have progressed considerably in analyzing cost minimization of multinational operations within a network, they do not incorporate the value of flexibility under uncertainty. The effect of uncertainty in a single-period model has been addressed in a mean-variance approach (Hodder and Jucker 1985a, b). This approach addresses uncertainty as a penalty to be minimized; multinationality, via diversification effects, is valuable only insofar as the variance of the portfolio of manufacturing sites decreases with geographical dispersion.

An attempt to capture the value of flexibility under uncertainty is provided in the one-period stochastic model of production shifting of de Meza and van der Ploeg (1987). A multiperiod stochastic model explicitly incorporating the option valuation of production shifting in a network is qualitatively described in Kogut (1983, 1985) and formally analyzed in Kogut and Kulatilaka (1988). It is this multiperiod stochastic formulation that is explored below.[5]

To analyze the value of multinational coordination of manufacturing, consider a firm with assets dispersed to various parts of the world. The decision facing the firm is to minimize total cost producing in a single location or switch flexibly between two sites located in different countries. Factor prices and final demand are given and known. Uncertainty arises through fluctuations in exchange rates. By treating prices and output as given, we are able to focus on the effect of location switching on value.[6]

Though a number of factors generate economic shocks which are likely to influence the value of investing in flexibility, fluctuations in exchange rates are certainly one of the more potent sources of disturbance. The variance in real exchange rates is illustrated in Figure 7.1 which shows the (trade weighted movement) of the Deutsche mark and dollar over the period 1976 to August

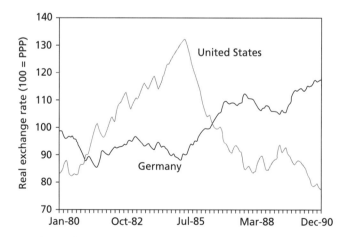

Figure 7.1. Trade weighted real exchange rates

1992. The monthly variance of these rates about the mean of 1.00 (i.e. if PPP holds true) is in the order of magnitude of 8 percent and the total band is given by the range (0.6, 1.4). These violations of PPP point to substantial disparities in prices in the real-goods markets. Clearly, in the absence of arbitrage between-goods markets—an assumption which is eminently reasonable for labor and for sticky energy pricing—there is a value in investing in the option of where to produce.

THE SIMPLE FORMULATION: COSTLESS SWITCHING

The principal elements of our argument can be most clearly examined by modeling a simple example. Consider a firm which is evaluating a project to invest in two manufacturing plants—one in the US and the other in Germany. The plants are identical in their technological characteristics and differ only in the prices (evaluated in dollars) of the local inputs. The firm carries redundant production capacity, so that total demand, which is known and nonstochastic, can be met with either plant. (This formulation also accommodates the case where only part of the production is shifted in response to changing exchange rates.) The product of the firm is priced in a world market, say in US dollars, and fluctuations of the DM/USD exchange rate do not affect the dollar market price.[7]

Suppose some input factors of production are also priced in the world market. Other inputs (e.g. labor) are priced in the local currency and their prices do not comply with the law of one price, due to institutional and government regulatory factors. Since short-term wage movements tend to be independent of short-term movements in exchange rates, the law of one price frequently is violated for the case of labor. Consequently, the wage rates in the two countries are equated not by the nominal exchange rate but by the *real* exchange rate:

$$w_\$ = \theta w_G \qquad (1)$$

where $w_\$$ is the wage rate in the US expressed in \$, $w_G = w_M S(\$/M)$ is the dollar value of wage rate in Germany, w_M is the German wage rate in Deutsche Marks, $S(\$/M)$ is the nominal exchange rate, and θ is the effective *real* exchange rate (i.e. deviation from the law of one price). In such a world, if the firm could shift its production between the two plants, the production location will be determined by the relative price of the locally sourced input. In addition, taxes (subsidies), tariffs, trade and financial barriers, and transportation costs can affect the dollar value of the locally sourced input.

MODELLING UNCERTAINTY

The option value to switch production can be affected by a number of sources of uncertainty, including labor unrest, government policies or threats, or local suppliers' demands. Clearly, however, one of the most important sources of uncertainty, as suggested by Figure 7.1, is the volatility of the exchange rate. For simplicity, we let uncertainty in the model only arise from the real exchange rate. It is important to note that this assumption eliminates other relevant uncertainties facing the firm, and, thus, under-estimates the total value of the option to switch.

In order to elucidate the insights of our model, we choose a discrete time specification for the real exchange rate which is affected by factors beyond the control of the firm.[8] Hence, the firm faces an exogenous stochastic process that affects its production decision. It is reasonable to assume that the stochastic process is one where θ tends to revert towards its equilibrium value, $\bar{\bar{\theta}}$. In this context, we can think of the mean reverting property of the real exchange rate as arising from the goods market equilibrium conditions that motivate purchasing power parity. In fact, models of overshooting exchange rates implicitly assume that the real exchange rate tends to revert back towards its long-term purchasing power parity, i.e., $\bar{\bar{\theta}} = 1$.[9]

With increasing volatility in the foreign exchange markets, the probability of deviating from equilibrium becomes greater. When the real exchange rate (θ) is greater than one, it is cheaper to produce in Germany. However, as discussed below, when switching is costly, the decision rule is not simply to switch when the threshold of $\bar{\bar{\theta}}$ is crossed.

The discrete-time mean reverting stochastic process for the real exchange rate can be written as:

$$\Delta\theta_t = \lambda(\bar{\bar{\theta}} - \theta_t)\Delta t + \sigma\theta_t\Delta Z_{\theta 0} \tag{2}$$

where ΔZ_θ are the increments of a discrete-time Wiener process and are normally distributed with mean 0 and variance Δt, $\sigma\theta_t$ is the standard deviation of θ per unit of time, and λ is the mean reverting parameter. Randomness is introduced via the ΔZ term. The parameter λ acts as an elastic force which serves to bring the price indices in the two countries towards parity. For example, when $\lambda = 1$, any random shock which affects the real exchange rate would be corrected (i.e. purchasing power parity is restored) within one period. For $\lambda < 1$, only partial adjustment will take place during that period.

It should be clear that the parameter values depend on the particular currency and must be scaled to adjust for the chosen length of the unit time period. For example, if the PPP disparities are corrected by 50 percent in one month, it will be corrected by 0.875 in three months. Since the variance of ΔZ_θ is linear in Δt, the estimated σ varies with the square root of the time interval.

THE RELATIVE COST FUNCTION

Under our assumption that the output price is set in the world market in dollars, the production decision will be based entirely on the lower cost alternative. Suppose the plant in the US is facing input prices $P_\$$ (a vector of input prices), the minimum cost of producing one unit of output within a time interval Δt is given by the unit *dollar* cost function $\psi^\$ = \psi(P_\$)$. Furthermore, since the technologies are identical, the unit *dollar* cost function of the plant in Germany must be $\psi^G = \psi(P_G \theta(\$/M))$, where P_G is input price vector faced by the German plant and is expressed in US dollars. Since by definition $\psi(\cdot)$ is homogeneous of degree 1 in prices, $\psi(P_G) = \psi(\theta P_\$) = \theta\psi(P_\$)$.

The advantage of focusing on cost functions is to isolate the relationship between the two relevant parameters (i.e. λ and σ) in our model, since, by assumption, other outputs are not affected by the real exchange rate and revenues are held constant. Notice that when $\theta < 1$, $\psi^\$ > \psi^G$, making the firm choose to produce in Germany; when $\theta > 1$, $\psi^\$ < \psi^G$ and the firm will produce in the US. Hence it is the relative cost of production that determines the production location choice.

Without loss of generality, we normalize the costs of the US plant as one: $\psi(P_\$) = 1$. If *all* input prices are locally determined then the dollar value of the German costs equals:

$$\psi^G(\theta) = \psi(\theta P_\$)/\psi(P_\$) = \theta.$$

In general, when only some of the input factors are locally priced the normalized cost function of German production can be expressed as $\psi^G(\theta)$.

Value of Flexibility

Given the above macro and micro economic description, the option value of flexibility can be solved as a dynamic program. To be evaluated are the stream of costs from the plants each with an economic life of T periods of length Δt. At the beginning of a period, the firm knows with certainty the realized values of all relevant variables, including the real exchange rate θ, for that period.

If switching between locations is costless, then the time T present value of the costs under the flexible production arrangement obtained by choosing the location with the minimum costs over the last time period is:

$$\Im(\theta_T) = \min[1, \psi^G(\theta_{T-1})]. \tag{3}$$

At any previous time t, the value of the project will be the sum of costs from the optimal operation in the period beginning at time t and the (minimized) value function at time $t + 1$. By this logic, we arrive at the following recursive equation for $F(\theta_t)$:

$$\Im(\theta_t) = \min[1, \psi^G(\theta_t)] + \rho E_t \Im(\theta_{t+1}), \quad t = 0, \ldots, T, \qquad (4)$$

where E_t is the expectations operator conditional on information at time t and ρ is the one-period risk-free discount factor.[10] This recursive system of equations states the fundamental proposition in our model. It expresses the value of the project as the discounted flow of a temporal series of options.[11]

WHEN SWITCHING IS COSTLY

In practice, it is costly to switch between plants due to costs associated with shutdowns and startups, labor contracting, and managerial time commitments. If the decision to switch production takes into account the costs of switching multiple times over the life of the plants, the switching decision becomes also a function of the current mode of operation. Compared to the costless case, cost differences must move sufficiently to justify switching production. We denote the cost to switch from location i to j, as k_{ij}. When the US is defined as location 1 and Germany as location 2, k_{12} is the cost of switching manufacturing from the US to Germany.

This problem is more complex than the previous one, as it involves solving a compound option where the value function depends on the operating location chosen during the previous period. For example, if the firm operated at location 1 during the period $t - 1$, then the value function at t is given by:

$$\Im(\theta_t, 1) = \left\{ \underbrace{\min\left\{[1 + \rho E_t \Im(\theta_{t+1}, 1)]\right.}_{\text{cost of using location 1}}, \underbrace{\left.[-\kappa_{12} + \psi^G(\theta_t) + \rho E_t F(\theta_{t+1}, 2)]\right\}}_{\text{cost if switch to location 2}} \right\}$$

$$(5)$$

where $F(\theta_t, l)$ is the value of the flexible project at time t (when θ_t is realized) when the location l was in operation during the period $t - 1$. The first argument of the minimum operator is the cost if the firm chooses to use location 1 for the period beginning at time t, and is computed in a manner similar to Equation (6). The second argument of the minimum operator gives the cost when the firm switches to employ location 2 and incurs a cost k_{12}.

Similarly, the value of the project when operating in location 2 during the previous period is:

$$\Im(\theta_t, 2) = \min \left\{ \underbrace{[1 + \kappa_{21}\rho E_t \Im(\theta_{t+1}, 1)]}_{\text{cost if switch to location 1}}, \quad \underbrace{[\psi^G(\theta_t) + \rho E_t \Im(\theta_{t+1}, 2)]}_{\text{cost of using location 2}} \right\} \quad (6)$$

Another way to think about the problem of coordinating two plants located in different countries is to consider what are the optimal exchange rates at which production is shifted. If switching costs are zero (i.e., $k_{12} = k_{21} = 0$), then the optimal exchange rate would be independent of the current operating mode. No matter, then, if Equation (5) or (6) were to govern the value of the project, the timing of switching between the two plants would occur at the same optimal exchange rate. At this threshold exchange rate, the value of the two cost functions are identical.[12] However, when costs are incurred, the boundary conditions are not the same. These costs cause the threshold exchange rates for shifting production to deviate from the break from the break-even rate for cost-less switching.

If it were not for switching costs, the solution to the optimization problem would be simple: choose in each period the location l that maximizes ψ^l (θ_t) in that period. However, switching costs make a forward-looking analysis necessary. A firm may decline to switch locations if the possibility of a reversal in the relative cost advantage due to subsequent exchange rate movements is high. The probability distribution of *future* real exchange rates affects the *current* choice of technology. This band of inaction is commonly called a *condition of hysteresis*. In Figure 7.2, we provide a stylized representation of hysteresis in production switching between two locations. Except for a few

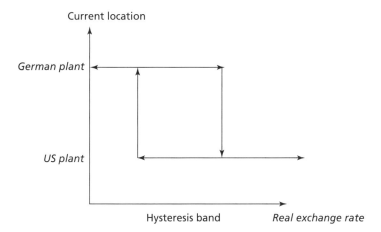

Figure 7.2. Hysteresis and real exchange rates

degenerate processes, this band widens with the degree of uncertainty and switching costs.[13]

GLOBAL SOURCING: THE GENERAL FORMULATION

In general, when there is a set $L = \{1, \ldots, L\}$ possible production locations with associated cost functions ψ^l, the valuation equations can be written as:

$$\Im(\theta_t, l) = \min_{m \in L}[-K_{l,m} + \psi^m(\theta_t) + \rho E_t \Im(\theta_{t+1}, m)], \quad l \in \pounds. \qquad (7)$$

Parenthetically, the model becomes intractable for multiple-exchange rate processes, but it should be recalled that since most currencies are pegged to the dollar, ECU, or yen, the model can be reduced to considering two exchange rates.[14] Neglecting transportation and factor cost differentials, the intuitive solution to this more generalized problem is to choose to locate a plant in a country whose exchange rate is the most volatile. Given plants in $n-1$ countries, the selection of a new site will be influenced by its correlation with the portfolio of current and potential operating locations as well as volatilities. The lower the correlation, the greater the contribution to overall volatility and to increasing the value of the underlying options. In this sense, correlations matter: pure volatility contributes directly to increase the project values.

Differences among firms in the covariance structure of the cost movements of their international plant locations will influence competitive interactions among multinational corporations in a nontrivial way. Much of the anecdotal discussion of the effects of exchange rates on Japanese and American competitors is a reflection of this influence. A more complete rendering of the influence of exchange rates on the competition among international firms requires a specification of pricing and production decisions as dependent on exchange rates and competitors' responses.[15] Other variations of this model include differences in the technology, uncertainty arising from more than one source, restrictions imposed by host governments on some factor use, transportation costs, and multiple-product manufacturing strategies. Each of these modifications complicates the implementation of the above model, but the fundamental results are conceptually similar to the simple version above.

A Numerical Example

Insight into the significance of the option value to switch can be gained by a numerical analysis. Through the numerical solutions, the magnitude of the value in across-border coordination is analyzed by varying the parameter values of the exchange rate variance and adjustment coefficient. The major issues in specifying the simulations is to characterize the technologies (cost functions), the nature of uncertainty, and the associated parameter values.

For the purpose of identifying the contribution of changes in exchange rate variance to the option value, we specify a linear cost function of the form ψ $(\theta) = -\alpha + \beta\theta$, where α and β are constant coefficients (i.e. Leontief functional form). More complex functional specifications, such as scale economies and carrying-costs of excess capacity, would give essentially the same results, though dampened in magnitude. (Some of the dampening effect is captured in our switching costs parametrization.) Since total demand is treated as constant, revenues are not affected by switching. Thus, the cost side is driving the location choice.

When we use a characterization of uncertainty such as the mean reverting process given by Equation (2) the expectations must be computed numerically. We do so by discreting the statespace.[16] Suppose at any time t, θ_t can only take one of M discrete values, $\theta^1, \theta^2, \ldots, \theta^M$ (say between 0.5 and 1.5). If we observe θ_t to be θ^1 (e.g., $\theta_t = 0.95$), then the probability $\theta_{t+1} = \theta^1$ (e.g. $\theta_{t+1} = 1.05$) is the transition probability from state i to j which we denote by p_{ij}.[17]

In this discrete state-space we can rewrite Equation (7) as:

$$\Im(\theta_t = \theta^l, l) = \min_{m \in L}\left[-\kappa_{l,m} + \psi^m(\theta^l) + \rho \sum_{i=1}^{M} \Im(\theta_{t+1} = \theta^l, m)p_{l,t}\right]. \quad (8)$$

The parameter values consist of five factors: time horizon, duration of the intervals during which switching is not possible, switching costs, variance of the real exchange rate (σ), and the adjustment coefficient (λ). The first three factors are fixed at 20 years, quarterly intervals, and 2.5 percent of mean (i.e. when $\theta = 1$) quarterly costs per switch for all the simulations.[18] Switching costs capture expenses associated with adjusting labor schedules, inventory, and start-up.

Because our central focus is on the effect of the real exchange rate variance and, though less so, the PPP adjustment coefficient, we vary σ and λ over simulations. In the initial runs, we set $\lambda = 0.05$, and let σ vary from 5 percent to 10 percent (base case) and 20 percent. These exchange rate variances are not substantially different from the estimated variances given by Figure 7.1. In the second set of simulations, we let the adjustment coefficient vary from 5 percent to 20 percent, with σ set to 10 percent.[19]

Table 7.2. Sensitivity of Value of Flexibility to Parameter Changes

	$\sigma = 0.05$	$\sigma = 0.10$	$\sigma = 0.20$
$\lambda = 0.05$	5.58%	11.09%	17.45%
$\lambda = 0.10$		8.34%	
$\lambda = 0.20$		5.99%	

DISCUSSION OF PRINCIPAL RESULTS

The simulations provide an opportunity to investigate the incremental profitability of production shifting to changes in the parameters, especially that of the real exchange rate variance. Figure 7.2 provides a graphical illustration of the values of flexibility for three values of volatility: $\sigma = 5$ percent, 10 percent, and 20 percent. (λ is held at 5 percent.) As is apparent, the incremental profitability is far from insignificant. Of particular interest is the relationship of the expected value of flexibility given the initial real exchange rate, with the greatest percent increase in profitability expected when θ is close to one.

The explanation of these peaks is transparent on reflection. Since the likelihood of a change in the real exchange rate crossing the boundary (of one) is greatest when the current rate is close to one, the value of the option must also reach a minimum at this boundary. To borrow from the terminology of financial option markets, the option to switch is deepest in the money when $\theta = 1$. Conversely, as the derivation from PPP increases (i.e. the real exchange rate moves away from 1), the likelihood of a boundary crossing is reduced.

A more precise illustration of the sensitivity of the value of the option to switch production is given in Table 7.2. The center column gives the numerical values of the percentage increase in profitability shown by Figure 7.3. At the mean exchange rate ($\theta = 1$), the value of flexibility increases from about 5.5 percent when $\sigma = 5$ percent to 17.5 percent when $\sigma = 20$ percent. Having the flexibility to move production to locations with lower input prices has the effect of insuring against detrimental movements of the real exchange rate. Increased exchange rate volatility will increase the upside benefits while the insurance feature of value derived from location flexibility is greater in periods of volatile exchange rates. The value of multinationality increases with greater volatility.

These numerical results give a simple static decision rule. The project, building the second plant, should be undertaken if the increased value due to flexibility is greater than the required initial investment.

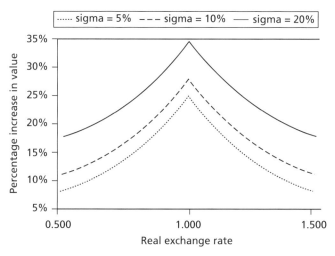

Figure 7.3. Value of flexibility

EXTENSION: HYSTERESIS AND WITHIN-COUNTRY OPTIONS

So far, we have analyzed the value of multinationality as arising from the across-country coordination of production. This development has been couched in the context of a *vertical* direct investment decision, that is, whether to build one or two plants. Clearly, there are also implications for the economics of the 'horizontal' direct investment whereby a plant is built in a country to support local sales in that market. The horizontal investment decision can be seen as part of a well-documented sequence by which a firm expands from exporting to investing in local production.[20] The sequence by which a firm expands from exports to local investment is, conceptually, a product of the exercise of a *within-country* option established by the investments made in country-specific goodwill and experience to support exports.

In this wider context, the band of inaction is generated by two components of hysteresis. We call the component associated with switching costs between plants in two locations 'production hysteresis.' (See the above discussion in 'When Switching is Costly'.) There is also a hysteresis effect resulting from the more fundamental decision whether or not to invest in goodwill (e.g. brand labels and sales force recruitment) to serve a market through exports; these effects have been discussed in Dixit (1989a), Baldwin and Krugman (1989), and Dumas (1988). We call this component 'export hysteresis.'

While the investment in goodwill leads to a condition of hysteresis, it leads to increase the likelihood that the initial export activity will eventually be followed by investments in manufacturing. These observations imply that any subsequent investment can benefit from the initial establishment of goodwill.

Table 7.3. Threshold Values of Real Exchange Rate

	Threshold θ
Naive investment	1.0
First entry (when entry can be delayed)	1.5
Subsequent switch to German plant	0.975
Exit from German market	0.575

The accumulation of goodwill generates what Myers (1977) first called a growth option, that is, it serves as a platform by which a firm expands in the future.

Growth options are not acquired per se by the establishment of multinational investments; they represent opportunities gained by investing in a current activity, no matter if this investment is made by a domestic or international firm. However, they are important in underscoring the likelihood that foreign investors will persist in a market once they have initially entered. As general experience and goodwill are gained, the cost of launching new products in the foreign market is reduced. The combination of hysteresis, along with the acquisition of growth options, underscore the argument that the initial entry into a country increases the likelihood of subsequent investments.

Some insight into this pattern can be gained from Table 7.3, which provides the threshold exchange rates for entry for the first time and subsequent entries. Assuming that later products can enjoy the initial investment in goodwill, then subsequent products can be introduced at a significantly lower critical exchange rate than the case when exporting began. (These values are estimated by assuming the same production function for the initial and subsequent products.) In this sense, the initial investment establishes a growth option for future product entries.

Heuristic Rules and Operating Procedures

An important objection to the above model is the of question whether labor can be treated as variable. However, the benefits of production shifting rely less on the feasibility of layoffs than on rules for labor flexibility. It is important to recall that direct labor costs are an increasingly insignificant proportion of total production costs (Johnson and Kaplan 1987). The main cost drivers are materials and energy, the prices of which are determined by domestic market forces and government regulations. A more general characterization is to treat W as a vector of those inputs that are priced locally in the country where the plant is located.

Along these lines, an alternative, and more appropriate, way to understand the above model is to treat the investment in two countries as the creation of excess capacity in the overall system. Plants are never closed. Rather, what is shifted is overtime production. Even if the value of production shifting is realized by savings from material and energy usage, labor policy still remains important in terms of creating flexible overtime.

These considerations raise the general question whether this operating flexibility is discretionary. One way to address this question is to consider whether the effect of costs of operating flexibility, for example establishing contracts for flexible overtime, on the hysteresis band eliminates the plausibility of switching.[21] But another way to understand this issue is by focusing on the often overlooked question of whether managers have the information and institutional flexibility to identify and exercise these options. It is this avenue we explore by analyzing internal accounting practices, and pricing.

Internal Accounting Practices

What should be the control system appropriate to the coordination of cross-border activities in response to fluctuating exchange rates? Because floating exchange rates only were introduced in the mid-1970s, it is possible by reviewing a few empirical and prescriptive studies to trace how evaluation systems have developed to provide information, and incentives, for across-border coordination. What is striking is how the heuristic rules of international accountability have changed to meet the environmental pressures of multinational competition and coordination.

The canonical problem in international performance evaluation of foreign subsidiaries is how to treat the effects of exchange rate movements on accounting variances. This problem can be most simply stated as the choice of exchange rate values by which to budget and to monitor performance. Between the time of budgeting and monitoring, exchange rates move. The control problem is what exchange rate should be applied and who should be held accountable for exchange rate effects. Clearly, if the control system removes the effect of exchange rates on operating decisions and results, there is no mechanism by which to trigger the shifting of production.

The seminal prescriptive analysis of this problem was given by Lessard and Lorange (1977). Figure 7.4, taken from their article, depicts the combinations of three exchange rates that can be used for control purposes: the spot exchange at the time of budgeting, the spot exchange rate at the time of tracking performance, or some kind of forward rate determined at the time of budgeting. Four cells are not permitted as they represent illogical combinations.

Rate used to track performance relative to budget	Actual at time of budget	Projected at time of budget	Actual at end of period
Rate used for determining budget			
Actual at time of budget	A-1	A-2	A-3
Projected at time of budget	P-1	P-2	P-3
Actual at end of period (through updating)	E-1	E-2	E-3

Figure 7.4. Possible combinations of exchange rates in the control process
Source: Lessard and Lorange (1977).

Each combination carries particular behavioral consequences. For example, for any combination where the same rate is used, the foreign subsidiary bears no risk for the effect of exchange rate movements. When the rates for budgeting and tracking differ, the local subsidiary bears the full risk of exchange rate movements. In this latter case, there is an incentive for the local subsidiary to hedge. Even if not permitted to do so by engaging in financial positions, it may do so by building up inventory or by insisting on local manufacture to support local sales.

The combination that Lessard and Lorange prescribed was the use of forward rates for budgeting and tracking. In this case, the subsidiary and the central controller's office have the incentive to establish accurate forward rates for purposes of budgeting, with the spot rate at the time of tracking or the forward used for evaluation. Empirical studies showed that one of these two combinations tended to prevail during the 1970s. (See, for example, Business International 1976.)

It is interesting to note the unstated assumptions of this approach. In the Lessard and Lorange formulation which represented best practice at the time, the control problem was headquarters assessing the performance of a subsidiary. In other words, the control problem was perceived as 'dyadic,' that is, involving only two players. The effect of the ability to coordinate production across borders is not built into the performance evaluation.

In addition, the competitive effects of exchange rates were largely neglected. This neglect is permissible as long as the international competition is American, and hence all competitors are exposed to the same exchange rate. However, as competition becomes more multinational in character, exchange rates carry implications for prices and quantities.[22]

But this innovation to use forward rates to budget and to track performance entails a number of assumptions that were not suited to the competitive environment of the 1980s. As documented initially by Doz (1978), the internationalization of markets began to lead to the rationalization of production into global plants. Similarly, Flaherty (1986) has described global sourcing policies as the standardization of manufacturing across geographically dispersed plants. In short, the coordination of global manufacturing has increasingly become part of the competitive strategy of the firm (Cohen et al. 1989).

The internal sourcing of production as part of a coordinated international strategy conflicts with the assumptions of the original Lessard/Lorange proposals. The evaluation problem is no longer the dyadic control by headquarters of each subsidiary. Rather, the transfers across subsidiaries require that the evaluation of performance be conceived in the context of a network with the flexibility to shift production in response to exchange rates. The decision to transfer production from one country will depress the operating results of that subsidiary, but to the gain of operations elsewhere. Sterilizing operating results from exchange rates removes the incentive to coordinate production multinationally.

Control within a network requires minimally two related changes, as recognized in the subsequent writings of Lessard. First, since the advantage of multinational shifting is to schedule production where real costs are minimized, the selection of the appropriate exchange rate is much more complicated. One possibility is to budget and track at the PPP rate (Stewart 1983). But while this rate will give a more accurate appraisal over longer periods of time, it fails to provide the incentives for operating flexibility.

The recommendation, made by Lessard and Sharp (1984) and Jacque and Lorange (1984), is to establish the PPP rate as the benchmark, but to work out the implications of deviations from these rates on operating results. Thus, the second change proposed by Lessard and Sharp is to develop, at least implicitly, a set of contingent budgets to be used for tracking depending on the actually realized exchange rate. These contingent budgets incorporate, for example, the expectation that production will be shifted contingent on the real exchange rate that prevailed during the period under evaluation. If operating flexibility is to be built on the exercise of discretionary options, then the control system must itself build in the flexibility in the choice of benchmarks by which to evaluate operating results.[23]

MARKET AND TRANSFER PRICING

Despite the substantial impact of exchange rates on operating performance, the diffusion of new evaluation techniques has been slow. Moreover, the internal performance evaluation methods clearly influence other decisions, such as pricing. If effects of exchange rates on comparing operating costs across subsidiaries are ignored, then the tendency will be to use accounting procedures and estimates based on the home market.

The relationship between control systems and pricing has been documented in a number of studies. In his field research, Sharp (1987) found that a number of American multinational operations continued to price by adding a mark-up to the American unit costs. While these practices made sense when the competition was American and all competitors were following similar pricing policies, the persistence of these pricing heuristics led, Sharp found, to poorer performance for the firms facing multinational competition.

These practices show up in a few popular MBA teaching cases. Caterpillar Tractor is described as using cost-plus pricing rules, with the cost estimates derived from US plant experiences.

Because the company used a uniform dollar pricing policy, dealers all over the world were billed in dollars, irrespective of the origin of the machines. The prices were often based on US manufacturing cost, and when the dollar was strong, the company had to engage in price-cutting (Harvard Business School 1985).

In the mid-1980s, it switched to competitive pricing, as Komatsu began to make severe inroads in the United States and elsewhere.

Matsushita, interestingly, seems to be following a similar pricing rule. 'In general,' it is noted in the case, 'the [Japanese] plant was expected to absorb the effect of any changes in its costs during the year, while the subsidiary was expected to deal with changes in market conditions *without modifying the transfer price*' (Matsushita Electric Industrial 1987). Where Japanese companies face foreign competition, prices tend to be set to the market; where they face only Japanese competitors, pricing tends to be set on the basis of Japanese costs, much like the earlier experience of American multinationals (Marston 1990). The pricing and control policies of Matsushita reflect their dominant position in their major market, VCRs, which is only challenged by other Japanese competitors. In this respect, these policies mirror American practices of the 1970s when world competition was more US-based.

In summary, the pricing rules and evaluation systems tend to reflect the degree of multinationality in the competitive environment and of the firm. As corporations establish foreign subsidiaries and as they face competition from competitors from many countries, the potential to gain an advantage through international coordination can be achieved only through the development of the appropriate systems of evaluation and operating heuristics. The ownership of the option to shift production is of little value if the managerial information is poor, if the incentives are tied to the wrong benchmarks, and if pricing rules do not capture the value of the flexibility to manufacture at the lowest cost site. It is not surprising, consequently, that a number of firms in a recent survey reported a break with traditional practice by denominating transfer prices in the source country currency (Business International 1990).

Conclusions

The above model has analyzed the benefits of multinationality as the ownership of dispersed international operations that provide valuable operating flexibility through multinational coordination. As an illustration, we have used the example of production shifting and global manufacturing. For this particular example of multinationality, there remains a number of areas requiring further work. One area is the important question of whether contracts can be designed to provide these benefits. It may well be possible, as appears in the case in the international apparel industry, to write short-term contracts that allow the buying firms to switch suppliers based upon changes in costs and exchange rates. Another area requiring development is a fuller comparison against other alternatives, such as flexible manufacturing systems, that might be used to change inputs or market segments in response to cost shocks.[24]

Despite the simplicity of the above model of production shifting, it captures the importance of the element of flexibility within a network of subsidiaries. It is this element of flexibility that underlies the recent management treatment of the multinational firm as consisting of the ability to exercise the option to coordinate and transfer resources internationally.[25] This ability is not one simply of insurance through the buffering of the firm against uncertainty. Rather, it is the expression of why multinationality, as a result of these options, can be a source of value due to uncertainty.

The formal model presented above allows an abstract and general format by which to frame the management discussion on the organization and practice of the multinational corporation. This framework of the option value of multinationality, we are aware, can be generalized to cover other applications, such as acquisitions, investments in new skills and knowledge, and platforms into new technologies. But the option application to multinationality is especially apt, because the high variance of international markets increases the value of operating flexibility and global coordination. Despite the popular notion of the riskiness of international markets, it is this uncertainty that drives the opportunities available to the firm that it is multinational, as opposed to only domestic, in its investments and operations.[26]

An Example: Production Location Choice Problem

Here we will show how the above general model can be used to evaluate a flexible project consisting of plants in the US and Germany. The relevant stochastic variable θ, is the real exchange rate which we assume follows the process in Equation (12).

Let $\psi(\theta_t)$ be the dollar value of the profit flow when producing in Germany and value of US and $\pi(\theta_t)$ be the dollar profit flow when producing in the US. The cost of switching from US to German production is k_1, and from German to US production is k_2. Since the only relevant stochastic variable is θ the value of both production locations will be governed by the partial differential equation (PDE) in Equation (13).

Suppose $V(\theta_t, t)$ and $W(\theta_t, t)$ are the values of the US and German production, respectively. Let $\bar{\theta}$ and $\underline{\theta}$ be the critical real exchange rates at which the firm switches from US to German plant and vice versa. At these free boundaries the firm will be indifferent between the continuing at the current operating mode and incurring the switching cost to change the production location, i.e.:

$$
\begin{aligned}
V(\bar{\theta}) &= -k_1 + W(\bar{\theta}), \\
V'(\bar{\theta}) &= W'(\bar{\theta}), \\
W(\underline{\theta}) &= -k_2| + V(\underline{\theta}), \\
W'(\underline{\theta}) &= V'(\underline{\theta}).
\end{aligned}
$$

Examining the limiting cases of $\theta \to 0$ and $\theta \to \infty$, we note that $V_\theta > 0$ and $W_\theta < 0$. Furthermore, since both V and W follows the PDE in (13), the solutions must be of the form:

$$
V(\theta_t, t) = \underbrace{\gamma_2 \theta^{\varepsilon_2}}_{\text{option to switch to US}} + \underbrace{\frac{\alpha_\pi}{r} + \frac{\beta_\pi}{r - \delta_\pi} \theta^{c_\pi,}}_{\text{value of fixed US production}}
$$

$$
W(\theta_t, t) = \underbrace{\gamma_1 \theta^{\varepsilon_1}}_{\text{option to switch to Germany}} + \underbrace{\frac{\alpha_\psi}{r} + \frac{\beta_\psi}{r - \delta_\psi} \theta^{c_\psi,}}_{\text{value of fixed German production}}
$$

where $\gamma_1, \gamma_2, \bar{\theta},$ and θ satisfy:

$$
\gamma_2 \bar{\theta}^{\varepsilon_2} + \frac{\alpha_\pi}{r} + \frac{\beta_\pi}{r - \delta_\pi} \bar{\theta}^{c_\pi} = -k_2 + \gamma_1 \bar{\theta}^{\varepsilon_1} + \frac{\alpha_\psi}{r} + \frac{\gamma\psi}{r - \delta_\psi} \bar{\theta}^{c_\psi},
$$

$$
\gamma_2 \varepsilon_2 \bar{\theta}^{\varepsilon_2 - 1} + \frac{\beta_\pi c_\pi}{r - \delta_\pi} \bar{\theta}^{c_\pi - 1} = \gamma_1 \varepsilon_1 \bar{\theta}^{\varepsilon_1 - 1} + \frac{\beta_\psi c_\psi}{r - \delta_\psi} \bar{\theta}^{c_\psi - 1},
$$

$$
\gamma_1 \underline{\theta}^{\varepsilon_1} + \frac{\theta_\psi}{r} + \frac{\beta_\psi}{r - \delta_\pi} \underline{\theta}^{c_\psi} = -k_1 + \gamma_2 \underline{\theta}^{\varepsilon_2} + \frac{\alpha_\pi}{r} + \frac{\beta_\pi}{r - \delta_\pi},
$$

$$
\gamma_1 \varepsilon_1 \underline{\theta}^{\varepsilon_1 - 1} + \frac{\beta_\psi c_\psi}{r - \delta_\psi} \underline{\theta}^{c_\psi - 1} = \gamma_2 \varepsilon_2 \underline{\theta}^{\varepsilon_2 - 1} + \frac{\beta_\pi c_\pi}{r - \delta_\pi} \underline{\theta}^{c_\pi - 1}. \tag{9}
$$

These equations are linear in ε_1 but nonlinear in $\underline{\theta}$ and $\bar{\theta}$.[27] The range $[\underline{\theta}, \bar{\theta}]$ forms the hysteresis band.

In search of analytical solutions we consider two special cases. First, consider the case when US profits are normalized to 1 and the German plant has linear profits, i.e. $\pi(\theta, t) = 1$ and $\psi(\theta, t) = \theta_t$. The above non-linear equations are now simply as follows:

$$\gamma_2 \bar{\theta}^{\varepsilon_2} + \frac{1}{r} = -k_2 + \gamma_1 \bar{\theta}^{\varepsilon_1} + \frac{\bar{\theta}}{r - \delta},$$

$$\gamma_2 \varepsilon_2 \bar{\theta}^{\varepsilon_2 - 1} = \gamma_1 \varepsilon_1 \bar{\theta}^{\varepsilon_1 - 1} + \frac{1}{r - \delta},$$

$$\gamma_1 \underline{\theta}^{\varepsilon_1} + \frac{\underline{\theta}}{r - \delta} = -k_1 + \gamma_2 \underline{\theta}^{\varepsilon_2} + \frac{1}{r},$$

$$\gamma_1 \varepsilon_1 \underline{\theta}^{\varepsilon_1 - 1} + \frac{1}{r - \delta} = \gamma_2 \varepsilon_2 \underline{\theta}^{\varepsilon_2 - 1}$$

Now we have a simpler set of nonlinear equations to solve for the γ_1's and the threshold exchange rates. However, even these equations can not, in general, be solved in closed form. In the very special case, when $k_1 = k_2 = 0$ and $\delta = 0$, we get the obvious solution $\underline{\theta} = \bar{\theta} = 1$ and $\gamma_1 = \gamma_2 = 1 / r (\varepsilon_1 - \varepsilon_2)$.

When $a_\psi = 0$ and $c_\psi = b_\psi = 1$, and $a_\pi = b_\pi = c_\pi = 0$, i.e., θ is the cash flow from the export operation, then we can solve the equations in closed form. This is similar to the problems handled by Dixit (1989a) and McDonald and Siegel (1986).

⬚ ENDNOTES

* This chapter is a revised version of B. Kogut and N. Kulatilaka (1995) 'Operating Flexibility, Global Manufacturing, and the Option Value of a Multinational Network,' *Management Science*, 40: 123–39.

1. See Kogut (1983) for a discussion.

2. For an interesting case illustrating these kind of restrictions, see Harvard Business School (1981).

3. Of course, they carry substantial implications. For example, the predominant means of entering a foreign country is by acquisition, which represents an immediate way to gain brand label and distribution platforms for other products.

4. This diversification, because shareholders can achieve it more efficiently through capital markets, has empirically been shown to be of minor value to the multinational corporation. See Jacquillat and Solnik (1978).

5. This model has been expanded to explore critical exchange rates at which optimal exercise occurs (Kulatilaka and Kogut 1990). Huchzermeier (1990) and Cohen and Huchzermeier (1991) have embedded this model in the context of a richer formalization of the logistical and distribution network.

6. In this formulation marginal costs do not equal price at each point in time: rather profits fluctuate with the exchange rate. This condition need not be a violation of perfect competition in a dynamic setting; see Dixit (1989b).

7. To use the terminology of Flood and Lessard (1986), the currency habitat of the output product price in US dollars.

8. In Appendix 7.2 we analyze the possibility of modeling uncertainty within a continuous-time framework. Analytic solutions can only be obtained for a very restrictive class of problems.

9. See, for example, Dornbusch (1976).

10. Cox et al. (1985), have shown that when θ is the price of a traded security or if does not contain systematic risk the appropriate discount rate is the risk-free rate. Furthermore, even when θ is not the price of a traded asset and when it contains systematic risk, a simple adjustment to the transition probabilities allows the use of risk-neutral discounting. See Hull (1989) for a good intuitive discussion of this point.

11. In order to solve this recursive system we must specify a stochastic process for θ, such as in Equation (2). Under certain very restrictive assumptions about the process we can obtain closed-form solutions for F. See Kulatilaka and Marcus (1988) where the option values are derived in closed form when θ follows geometric Brownian motion.

12. The equivalence of the two cost functions satisfies one of two boundary conditions; the other condition is smooth-pasting. See the Appendix 7.1 for a discussion.

13. See Baldwin (1989), Dixit (1989), and Baldwin and Krugman (1989). It is important to note that the magnitude of the hysteresis band is time invariant only when the horizon is infinite. In a finite-time horizon problem, as the firm approaches the terminal time the band widens since the firm has a shorter time period to recoup the switching costs.

14. See Baillie and Bollerslev (1989) for an analysis of the common root in multiple-exchange rate movements.

15. For an exploration, see Dornbusch (1987).

16. See Appendix 7.1 for details.

17. For stationary processes p_{ij} is time independent.

18. Quarterly intervals were suggested by discussions with plant managers and are longer, in fact, than those attributed to Japanese production planning. See Abegglen and Stalk (1985). We can very easily reduce the intervals and permit continuous switching. This situation can also be thought of as a way of endogenizing the switching intervals.

19. In the numerical simulations we restricted the possible range of θ values between 0.25 and 1.75. In order to avoid distortion from end-point approximations we only report the value of flexibility for the θ ranging from 0.5 to 1.5. Note that these bounds are close to those empirically estimated from Figure 7.1, as reported earlier.

20. See Davidson (1980).

21. See Kulatilaka and Kogut (1990) for an analysis.

22. See Dornbusch (1987) and Flood and Lessard (1986) for a discussion.

23. A recent Business International (1989) publication showed that the most common current policy is to sterilize operating results of exchange rate effects, though a number of firms were reported to calculate exchange rate variances to evaluate the responses of subsidiaries.

24. For work on production flexibility as an option, see Fine and Freund (1990) and Kulatilaka (1987).

25. See Bartlett and Ghoshal (1989), Prahalad and Doz (1987), and Hedlund (1986).

26. This research has been supported by a grant from the Reginald H. Jones Center and the Huntsman Center for Global Competitiveness at the Wharton School. We thank Bernard Dumas, Donald Lessard, and anonymous referees for their helpful comments.

27. Note that in general, we must solve this set of $2M$ non-linear equations using numerical techniques.

8 Strategy, Heuristics, and Real Options

with Nalin Kulatilaka

Looking Inward and Outward

Strategizing is the application of heuristic frames to analyze the world and to generate normative evaluations of potential avenues of implementation.[1] Yet, like many professional schools caught between academics and application, strategy research is often ambivalent about the implications of valuing the development of heuristics. Because a test of a good heuristic is its application, the relevant community by which to evaluate such contributions appears often to be the commercial world.

This tension is probably more functional than commonly realized. Professional schools of business share, as Simon noted, commonalties with schools of design, e.g. engineering or architecture. Strategy research reflects competing ideas about how the world looks, or what the world needs.[2] However, like their counterparts in engineering or architecture, strategy researchers distinguish themselves from practitioners by their attention to an articulation of theory and evidence.

One of the most important bodies of strategic ideas at large today are associated with the notions of capabilities or core competence. The book by Gary Hamel and C.K. Prahalad, *Competing for the Future*, has sold more copies than any other Harvard Business School book. The resource based theory of the firm, which has seized the intellectual agenda from industry analysis, views the unique capabilities of the firm as the cornerstone of sustainable rents.

Ned Bowman (Kogut and Bowman 1995) has made the distinction between strategies that look in the mirror and those that look through the looking glass. It is not surprising that during a time of restructuring and re-engineering, strategy researchers should shift the emphasis from industry analysis to the internal sources of competitive advantage. The international competition and the introduction of information technologies have, as the extensive literature on American competitiveness has documented, generated considerable competitive pressures on corporations.

This emphasis on looking in the mirror begs the question of how to choose among alternatives. Hamel and Prahalad (1994) essentially invert this framing by proposing the concept of white spaces in the topography of existing businesses to identify valuable avenues of exploration. This language is strongly reminiscent of the commonly made distinction between exploitation and exploration.[3]

We propose that the real options literature provides an appropriate theoretical foundation for the heuristic frames suggested as ways to identify and value capabilities. Since capabilities are platforms that create a generic set of resources, they represent investments in future opportunities. The distinction between exploitation and exploration has an exact correspondence in the difference between net present value and option valuation. The attractiveness of real option thinking is only superficially in the obvious characteristic of forcing managers to think about the value of flexibility in response to uncertain events. The more fundamental contribution is to require that the valuation placed upon a strategy is derived from dynamic equilibrium prices in the market. In effect, real option valuation marries the resource based view with industry positioning by disciplining the analysis of the value of capabilities by a market test.

We proceed by first characterizing what are heuristics and how real option theory and core competencies are related through the concept of capabilities. Capabilities reflect irreversible investments, because of the costliness of transforming the organizational knowledge in a firm. We illustrate these ideas through a stylized mathematical description of the problem of adopting radical change. This formalization clarifies that the benefit of a real options heuristic is the imposition of a market test to derive the valuation of capabilities.

Heuristics

A good heuristic has four qualities: it is easy to use, easy to communicate, provides a better direction than ones currently employed, and motivates people who have to implement the strategy. The Boston Consulting Group growth matrix is the canonical heuristic. It requires only two data inputs of market growth and relative position. The famed ideograph of stars, dogs, question mark, and the cash cow have an Orwellian Rosebud value, i.e. they are comprehensible and memorable.[4] The implementation leads to a clear motivation. As the CEO of General Electric stated, the objective of GE's business units is to be number 1 or 2 in world markets. However, the not-so-minor drawback is that the heuristic often gives the wrong direction.

Because heuristics are intended to be used, they have many qualities that upset the norms of academic research. The objections come from all quarters. Sociologists point out that such heuristics reflect prevailing norms of style or conceptions of control. Cognitive psychologists note that heuristics are prone to type 1 and 2 errors, that is, managers ignore evidence of misfit and overstate the possibility of success. Social scientists are quick to criticize the absence of formal theory and empirical evidence.[5] Ad hoc field research indicate that well-educated PhD business faculty frequently moan over the humiliation of teaching heuristic frames that are not clearly derived from their formal education.

Heuristics are useful because formal theory often does not suggest operational rules, or is not credible, for the problems decisions makers confront in actual conditions. Since they are intended to guide action, heuristics are designed to motivate. From a normative perspective, over-estimation is an evolutionary attractive property for assembling human effort; an emphasis on sober assessment screens out people who are most likely inclined to act.[6] Because they are meant to influence action, they are biased toward current conceptions of the world; they are also liable to be dispensed as these conceptions change.

Heuristics have the advantage of countering some cognitive biases, but at a cost. In a study on plant scheduling, Bowman (1963) found that managers would do better if they used linear estimates from their experience rather than tried to optimize in response to each situation. In real time, the search for optimal strategies can be too costly or liable to be influenced by recency effects (e.g. the arrival of new information). Kunreuther (1969) modified these findings that rules cued to selective environmental information improve actual decision-making.

One of the merits of a heuristic is its real-time utility. Studies on innovation show remarkable tradeoffs between costs and time for innovations (Scherer 1967; Mansfield 1985). Field research and experimental evidence show ample evidence that people rely upon rules of thumb and known routines in situations constrained by time, even for simple problems for which there exist optimal rules. Because decisions must be made, managers and firms often transfer these suboptimal rules to settings that are poorly suited to these proven heuristics.[7] The limits to the robustness of a heuristic are usually experiential, because the theory is rarely explicit or is ignored.

Heuristics and Strategizing

The history of strategic planning tools documents the applicability and limitations of heuristics. Following distinctions made in cognitive science, we separate a heuristic into its cognitive frame and the rules of search. A cognitive (or heuristic) frame refers to the 'representation' of the problem and solution

Table 8.1. Strategizing as Cognitive Frames

Cognitive frame	Theory	Initial data	Analysis	Implementation
Experience curve (BCG)	Scale and experience drivers	Attractive (growing) markets	Relative market position	Dominance by scale
Industry analysis	Industrial economics	Industry forces	Cost or differentiation strategies	Value-chain exploitation
Capability	(Real options)	Intended strategy	Core competence	Exploratory business strategies

space. The heuristic rules of search are the algorithms by which solutions are found in the represented solution space.[8]

Table 8.1 compares three cognitive frames for developing business strategies. The BCG cash flow matrix 'works' to the extent that the theory of scale and experience driving down cost is the proper characterization of value creation. From the initial data, it bootstraps from observations on market growth and relative positions to evaluate whether a firm can dominate a market. Though a fairly simple heuristic, it shared the common bias of its times that size drives success, as opposed to the more modest inference that size is the outcome of success.[9]

Porter (1980) developed his industry analysis in the immediate aftermath of the oil shock and during a period of depressed corporate profitability. Its theory is derived from an industrial economics that appears as antiquated by contemporary advancements, but reflects the preoccupations of a time when the historical peaking of oligopolistic measures of concentration suggested that industry structure deeply influenced corporate performance. It is, in many ways, an inevitable implication of the BCG analysis that a world in which a few firms grow to dominance should lead to a focus on how to attain the conditions of structural stability. The initial data on industry forces serves to inform (though the mapping is not clear) the choice between low-cost and differentiation strategies. The implementation proceeds through an evaluation of the value-chain, with the criterion being contribution to profit. Compared to the requirements of the BCG growth matrix, the methodology is intensive in the use of data.

The core competence concept arose in the late 1980s during the height of re-engineering propelled by acquisitions and new information technologies. It is a direct response to the reputed financial pressures from financial markets dominated for the first time by institutional investors.[10] The formulation by Hamel and Prahalad (1994) suggests that the initial data are in the spirit of understanding the intended strategy of the firm that should be grounded in a distinctive competence.[11] This competence is defined by three attributes: it should be 'extendable' to multiple markets, it should be hard to imitate, and it should satisfy a derived customer demand (Hamel and Prahalad 1994: 202–7).

The theoretical foundations to this view are several, from the reasoning on why knowledge is hard to imitate to the evolutionary theories of firm growth. From a decision theoretic perspective, the core competence framing lends itself readily to a real option interpretation. A real option is defined by an investment decision that is characterized by uncertainty, the provision of future managerial discretion to exercise timing, and irreversibility.

These three elements are jointly required for the application of a strategic options heuristic. An option has value only if there is uncertainty, though defining the relevant source of the uncertainty is not trivial. An operationally important element of design is the provision of discretion, such as the staging of an R&D project to correspond to discrete points of go–no-go decisions.

Irreversibility is an easily overlooked feature and signifies the inability to costlessly revisit an investment or decision. A classic example is the BCG categorization of the 'dog' product division which a firm should divest, assuming there is a market. However, the ability to divest a poorly performing division is, as Winter (1987) observes, rarely exercised without incurring a loss on the original investment. In this context, irreversibility is the inability to recover the investment costs already expended for the product division.

Capabilities as Strategic Options

This definition of a core competence as a strategic option is close to the argument put forth by Barney (1986) regarding the resource-based view of the firm. To Barney, the creation of entrepreneurial rents is fortuitous. If managers understood the value creation process, the knowledge through imitation would lead to the immediate erosion of these rents.[12] The presence of a strategic factor market serves to arbitrage the value of these assets to guarantee a competitive return. (We return to this observation later to motivate the explicit use of a traded security for valuation of a real option.)

The important difference between this early statement of the resource-based view of the firm and core competence is the latter's insistence on the value of a resource as derived from its future but uncertain use. In the sense that Barney relies on market valuations to back into his identification of unique assets, he is consistent with the view that the market values the use of these assets in reference to their potential use by firms bidding for their ownership. But he makes an incomplete inference, namely, that these firms must have differential information. An equally plausible insight is that firms differ in their opportunity set, inclusive of the organizational features that are costly and time consuming to acquire. Consequently, some firms will discover profitable projects, where the 'excess rents' are earned on their organizational, not physical capital, assets.

Real option theory bridges the positioning and core competence by dynamically deriving the value of capabilities simultaneously from two discrete operating states: their value as 'is' and as 'could be.'[13] The 'as is' evaluation is a net present valuation based upon an evaluation of the range of possible pay-offs to operations currently in place. The option value is derived from the discretion to alter these operations to take advantage of future opportunities. In this simultaneous valuation of both operating states (they are clearly dependent), the analysis derives the valuation by creating a shadow security based on the market value of the strategic factor.

It is the identification of the opportunity set, as established through market valuations, that should drive the identification and valuation of core competence. Some writers fail to make this observation altogether. For example, Teece, Pisano, and Shuen write:

We define those competences that define a firm's fundamental business as core. Core competences must accordingly be derived by looking across the range of a firm's (and its competitors) products and services...The degree to which a core competence is distinctive depends on how well endowed the firm is relative to its competitors, and how difficult it is for competitors to replicate its competences (Teece et al. 1997: 516).

This statement is, however, rather problematic. It derives a core competence from the description of a firm's businesses, and in comparison to competitors. Finally, it notes that distinctiveness depends on a firm's endowment and the difficulty for the assets to be copied.

The missing element in this analysis is, of course, value. A firm may be well endowed with patents making it difficult for competitors to imitate. However, the important question is whether these endowments, which we might also call more generically the knowledge of the firm, is useful not only to current, but also to future applications. This question is not answered by a notion of dynamic capabilities, or of combinative capabilities, unless the normative criterion is the identification and investment in core competences in reference to their potential uses. This objection is not petty, for it is easy to imagine that without market discipline on the analysis, the potential candidates for core competence quickly multiply.[14]

There is another way to think about this problem, suggested by Winter (1987), as a broader formulation along the lines of optimal control. Winter (1987: 180–1) states:

From evolutionary theory comes the idea that a state description may include organizational behavioral patterns or routines that are not amenable to rapid change, as well as...more conventionally defined assets. It is by this route that a variety of considerations that fall under the rubrics knowledge and competence may enter the strategic state description.[15]

This suggestion seems odd, for optimal control requires an excessive belief in the rationality and knowledge of decision-makers, a belief that Nelson and Winter (1982) have strongly criticized. However, it is not a bad heuristic frame (Winter uses this term) if some of the insights of a capabilities approach is properly specified. A conventional formulation is to describe the characteristics of the state description and allow the decision maker discretion over a few control variables, e.g. technologies or output. A transformed formulation deprives the decision maker of control over some variables and, in effect, captures the constraints and opportunities of capabilities through a richer description of the given state in a decision context.

Consider the example of flexibility through the installation of new automated equipment. A conventional approach assumes that this technology enters into the description of the state and provides the decision maker with the choice of whether to exercise flexibility. However, a new capability is not determined by the capital purchase but by the presence of an organizational system that identifies and supports such flexibility. Because technology can be bought, or peopled hired into a firm, it is the organizational constraints that are often the most binding. Robert Stempel, the former head of General Motors, noted:

We've tried automation without knowledgeable workers, and it doesn't work. We put a tremendous amount of automation and electronics into our Cadillac plant in Hamtranck. And we couldn't run it because our people didn't understand what we were asking them to do.[16]

The study by Ittner (1996) found that a major problem in the exercise of flexibility at General Motors was that the accounting system focused on unit labor cost variances; there was no measure for whether flexibility was under- or over-utilized.

This accounting problem is reflected also in the capital budgeting problem. Just like accounting variances do not measure flexibility properly, net present value techniques wrongly estimate the value of building capabilities.[17] The important insight into the failure at General Motor is that new technology and organization are complements. Even though technology can be purchased, the organizational complement requires a longer period of experimentation and gestation. In other words, the organizational value of capabilities depends upon the potential uses of flexibility in future but uncertain states.

It is, consequently, reasonable to think of a firm's technology and organization as forming a coherent and dynamic set of capabilities whose value is derived from their value in future and stochastic states of the world. Such capabilities as speed of production or the ability to produce a particular quality are created through the possession of a set of technologies and of organizing principles. Given these capabilities, the firm is endowed with the resources that may be exploited strategically in the market.

New Capabilities as Organizational Discontinuities

It is useful, before starting, to explain why investments in capabilities are irreversible because of the tight coupling of technology and organization. The close relationship between organizing principles and technology is apparent in standard definitions in the literature on innovations and organizational sociology. Scott (1993: 227) defines technology as including 'not only the hardware used in performing work but also the skills and knowledge of workers, and even the characteristics of the objects on which work is performed.' Scott's definition encompasses the standard economic distinction between new products and processes and the embodiment of human capital formation in better techniques and products.

By technology, then, we mean the physical and human capital stock; by organization, we mean the way physical capital and people are jointly coupled through organizational routines, processes, incentive schemes and governance structure. For example, a system of mass production consists of the serial placement of capital equipment coupled with an assembly line of workers performing standardized tasks and under staff supervision. The technology is embedded in the equipment; the organizational knowledge is the principle by which work is arranged and supervised in conjunction with the use of this technology.

An area of debate has been whether to treat major technological innovations as radical or incremental. The organizational literature, especially Tushman and Anderson (1986), has offered the resolution that these innovations can be characterized as radical or incremental depending upon whether they destroy or enhance a firm's competence. (See also Henderson 1993.) This resolution raises the more fundamental problem that a firm, by its ability to recruit new engineers and managers, should have the capacity to alter its technological competence. The costs of switching to a technology should, by this reasoning, consist of the costs of hiring new individuals trained in the new science or engineering technology. Yet, clearly, the difficulty of adopting new capabilities cannot be explained by the relatively open recourse to the labor market in most advanced capitalist countries.

This reasoning ultimately leads to the consideration that the radicalness of an innovation has less to do with the novelty of the technology than its conformity with existing knowledge of the firm, in other words, the ways by which work is organized and power is distributed. Since the way work is organized will vary by firms, then the radicalness of a technological innovation can not be determined independent of a particular organizational context. Switching, or adoption, costs are strongly contingent on the current organization of work.

If radicalness of a technological innovation is a question of the organization, it follows that the potentially most radical kinds of innovation are those which alter directly the method by which work is organized. New ways of doing things are often difficult to understand and implement. They also pose, by their very nature, threats to the existing agreement on the allocation of power.[18]

To draw out why, consider the very important literature in organizational behavior concerning the suitability of particular organizational and technological combinations. One of the most perplexing questions in organizational behavior is the failure to identify clear matches between technologies and organizational structures. Yet, the findings are rather ambiguous in this regard. The line of work begun by Woodward and later the Aston school that linked performance to particular technological and organizational combinations has not resulted in clear relationships. Indeed, the most robust finding appears to be between organizational size and output volume rather than between particular structural and technological configurations. Indeed, even the findings between size and authority relations have been found to be sensitive to contextual variables, such as culture.[19]

Dosi and Kogut (1992) proposed that the failure to find robust relationships has been due to the tendency to theorize element to element correspondance, such as high volume production with vertical hierarchy.[20] (See Figure 8.1(A).) The empirical results do not show that these are complements when other factors are controlled. Alternatively, the correspondence might be set to set, where a set of organizational practices maps onto a set of technologies. The data might not reveal that A and B exist as complements; all we observe is A and C, and D and B. Complementarities need not be unique between any given technology or organization, but they still should be relationally bounded. The recent findings by MacDuffie (1996) on 'bundles' of human resource practices in auto plants indicate that there is a logic that relates organizing practices to each other, and to technologies. (See Figure 8.1(B).) As suggested in the opening citation of Robert Stempel, the experience of General Motors and other car manufacturers, as confirmed in MacDuffie's study, is that adopting the new capabilities of flexibility and speed requires changes in automation and organization. Between these two sets, there are many functionally equivalent complements, but there are no unique element-to -element correspondences.[21]

This description captures also the idea of co-evolution of technology and organization through two key features. First, technology and organization do not represent random assignments, nor is their coupling simply at the discretion of managers. Rather, the matches of a technology and organizing principle are constrained to reasonable set-to-set correspondence. However, within these 'developmental' constraints (to borrow from biology), improvements in technology and organization are correlated through experiential learning. For example, the introduction of mechanical equipment to move the incomplete chassis from one line to the next required the organizational innovation to

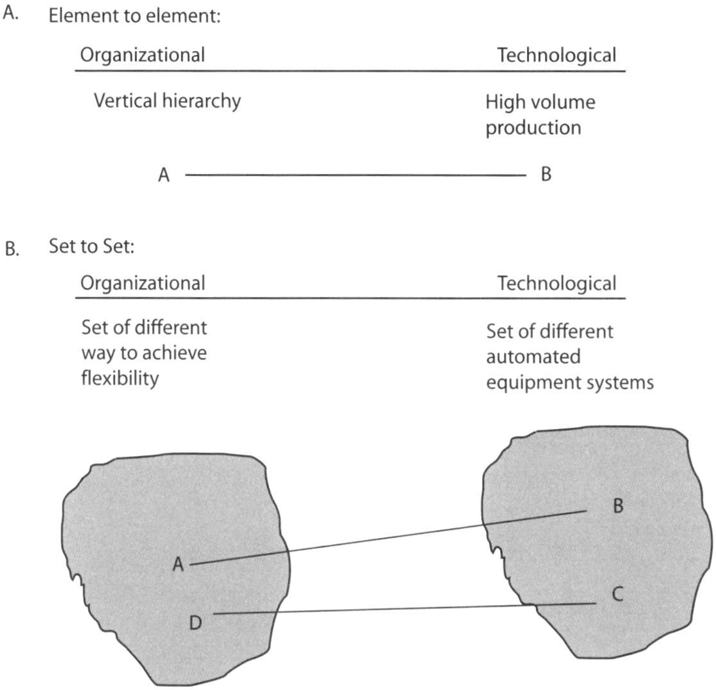

A.   Element to element:

Organizational	Technological
Vertical hierarchy	High volume production

A ———————————————— B

B.   Set to Set:

Organizational	Technological
Set of different way to achieve flexibility	Set of different automated equipment systems

Figure 8.1. Correspondence of technology and organization

increase the 'tightness' of the coupling of serial work processes in the factory. In other words, technology and organization are dynamically coupled in their evolution.

The tight coupling of technology and organization means that the costs of organizational change means that firms will persist in their old ways beyond the recommendation of the net present value. This persistence defines a range of inertia, or what we call a hysteresis band. Because organizational change is disruptive and hence discontinuous, managers hesitate to change radically their organizations, hoping perhaps that future states of the world would provide more appealing environments.

Figure 8.2 provides a simple illustration of this point. A firm can choose between two complementary systems, called low and high variety. The important issue is whether the relative value of gaining the capability of variety is enough to offset the costs of discontinuous change. The choice of capabilities is, as we depict it, derived from the market price placed on variety. Because of uncertainty over the evolution of the value of variety and the costs of adoption, managers rationally might choose to persist with inferior techniques before they are confident of future developments.

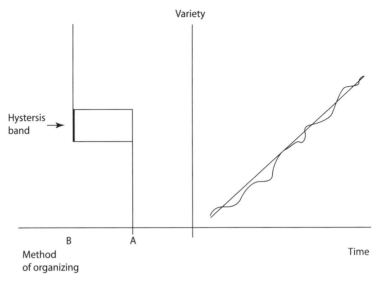

Figure 8.2. The implications of hysteresis on the choice of new techniques

Notes: A = Mass production; B = Toyotaism.

In the analysis below, we develop a modeling framework by which to examine this hysteresis band and the complementarity of organization and technology contingent upon a stochastic parameterization of the environment. The formal description explains how investments in organizational and technological capabilities are derived from their evaluation in the market. We suggest that knowledge accumulates in terms of two activities: competence in the use of particular technologies and in the organizational capability by which this technology is applied.

The problem facing the firm is to choose this set such that it tries to maximize its value in reference to its expectations on the evolution of prices and innovations in capabilities. In this formulation, the nature of the environment and strategy play an important role in shaping the capabilities of the firm. This problem is dynamically complex, as the firm must consider not only how its choice influences current profits, but also the learning of future capabilities.

This descriptive formulation clarifies two central claims. The current capability set and prevailing environment and market structure influence the choice and performance of a set of capabilities. The second claim is that there is a set to set correspondence between families of technology and organization that bound the feasible bundles of practices; but there is no unique element to element correspondence between a particular organizational practice and technology.

A FORMAL DESCRIPTION

The market price of a similar firm provides the most direct link between the performance of a capability set and prevailing market conditions. This market price is not the value of the core competence. Rather, it permits a valuation of the organizational capability by identifying a correlated asset in the relevant 'scarce factor' market. Value of a capability is then inferred (at times calculated) from the observed price dynamics that replicate the pay-off to the real option. This replication is the device through which market discipline is imposed on the identification and selection of core capabilities, thus imposing financial market discipline.

To elucidate the intuition, consider again the framing of a real options problem. The organizational assets of a firm provide an option to spend a fixed amount to procure a new capability by purchasing a physical asset at the end of one year. If the option is exercised, then the resulting project value has the risk characteristics of an existing traded firm. For example, a pharmaceutical firm is considering an entry into biotechnology. It currently has a strong capability in conventional drug development that provides an option to enter into biotechnology at an estimated cost. This cost is idiosyncratic to this firm. However, once it enters into the market, its new business carries a market risk similar to other biotechnology firms. This example illustrates why the price of other firms does not give the value of the core capability, since the cost of entry is idiosyncratic to each firm. However, the price dynamics of other firms provide information on the factors (e.g. risk) that drive the value of the option to enter in this market.

The value of a financial option depends on the current share. Black, Merton, and Scholes derived this value through an option pricing formula. The simple, but critical innovation, was their eventual recognition that by composing a replicated portfolio, the value of the option could be perfectly tracked by a levered position in the traded stock. Therefore, a risk-free portfolio can be constructed by holding a combination of the stock and options.[22] Hence, once the range of possible future stock prices is known (from its volatility), the market price of the option can be inferred by risklessly discounting the possible option pay-offs.

In many instances, there may not be a traded security whose price perfectly tracks the value of the resulting capability. In such cases, we can use one of two possible tracks to retain the market discipline. First, there maybe a bundle of pure assets (an index) that captures risk characteristics of the capability. For example, 'crack spread' on crude oil as a proxy for the gross operating margin of an oil refinery; the SOX/SXE equity index of semiconductor manufacturers serves as a proxy for the value of the production from a chip fabricating plant. Second, the value of the capability depends on the price of product or factor prices whose risk is spanned by traded assets in the economy. The value of the capability then is obtained by explicitly specifying the profit function using these prices as an argument.

A simple example is a microprocessor, whereby a quality-adjusted price can be expressed as the ratio of price to the processing speed (or 'mips' for millions of instructions per second). An increase in processing speed implies that the price for one 'mips' has declined. This quality-adjusted price of the output enters the profit function. Thus, the price dynamics of chips directly drives the expected cash flow from operating the 'as is' assets and from possibly exercising the option to exploit the 'could be' investment.

THE ECONOMIC ENVIRONMENT AND QUALITY ADJUSTED PRICES

Let's use this last example to specify, descriptively, the method by which the price dyanamics of the scarce factor is inferred through observations on a traded output. We then will take this description of the price dynamics to derive the profit function. Once we have this profit function, we then can describe the qualitative properties of how an investment in new organizational capabilities influences the definition of a core competence. The fundamental conclusion of this exercise is to motivate the definition of a core competence as the capabilities that provide the best response to prevailing market opportunities.

In order to identify and value a core competence, we must specify the evolution of the quality-adjusted price which we call θ. However, since θ is not a pure security but is the observed price of a scarce factor, its price characteristics need not necessarily evolve according to its equilibrium risk characteristics. Local supply and demand conditions and technological innovation determine the evolution of θ. In particular, the expected rate of appreciation of θ may be different from its risk-adjusted equilibrium rate of return. Hence, the risk-neutral dynamics of θ will depend not only on the risk-free rate of interest but also on the difference between the equilibrium and actual growth rates of θ.[23]

We assume θ to be exogenously determined and characterize its evolution by stochastic process:

$$\Delta\theta_t = \underbrace{\mu(\theta_t, t)\Delta t}_{\text{Deterministic Growth}} + \underbrace{\sigma(\theta_t, t)\Delta Z_t}_{\text{Smoothly evolving uncertainty}} + \underbrace{\kappa\,dq}_{\text{Discrete innovations}}$$

where μ is the expected growth rate of θ, σ is its instantaneous volatility, ΔZ_t is standard Normal distributed, dq is a Poisson process with intensity parameter λ and κ is the random percentage jump amplitude conditional on the Poisson event occurring.[24]

This discrete-time process captures the main features of the notion of a scarce factor market with technological innovation.[25] The drift term reflects the expectations regarding technological progress. For example, the performance of memory semiconductors follows a fairly predictable path, with performance improvements occurring every few years and prices declining subsequently.

Changes in the quality-adjusted price may also reflect unpredictable shifts in consumer preferences. For example, an increase in oil prices would lead consumers to prefer cars which save in fuel consumption. As long as these changes are fairly smooth, it seems reasonable to capture this uncertainty in volatility.

Other changes may be more radical, such as the arrival of new organizational innovations. These changes would appear as a sudden jump in price to a firm. Recall that these are quality-adjusted prices. The introduction of assembly line methods at Ford appeared to competitors as a sudden decrease in price. However, as Raff and Bresnahan (1997) show for the history of the automobile, part of the competitive effect of new techniques was accomplished through changes in quality, holding the nominal price the same. They estimate that quality-adjusted prices fell by 5 percent a year from 1906 to 1940; about 60 percent of this decline was to due to falling production costs and 40 percent to improved quality. We capture these impacts of innovative change by allowing price to evolve in response to quality and process innovations.

A market-traded proxy for the quality-adjusted price of computer chips can be constructed as the price index of chip making firms. Such an index will span the relevant risk characteristics. The rate of return on the index will proxy the equilibrium return. However, to the extent that the growth rate of the quality adjusted price deviates from the traded index, we correct the actual price process. This deviation will enter into the risk neutral representation of the option pricing model as a short-fall from equilibrium akin to a convenience yield.[26] Since the total risk characteristics of the quality adjusted price, θ, is similar to that of the proxy variable, the volatility can be estimated from the market for the chip company stock index. In fact, options contracts on such an index (SOX/SXE) is traded at the Philadelphia Stock Exchange. The implied volatility of these options provides a market source for information on the standard deviation (σ) given in the above equation.

Profit Functions

Having described the evolution of quality-adjusted prices, we can now turn to describing the relationship between capability sets of the firm and its profit function. Consider a firm that has the set of capabilities c, where $c \in C$ is the set of all feasible capabilities.[27] The firm faces exogenously determined 'quality adjusted prices', θ. The single-period profit obtained when operating under the set of capabilities c and facing prices θ_t is denoted $\Pi(\theta_t, c)$. This simple description captures the idea that firms are heterogeneous and their profits are determined both by the price of output and their organizational capabilities.

Given this set of capabilities and the realization of θ, we examine how the firm chooses its investment and production strategy. As an example, consider the case where C contains 'mass' and 'lean' production families with their associated organizational structures. Each family of production techniques can contain many distinct technologies. They are, however, coupled with the same organizational structure. Hence, a technology family refers to all technologies that can be operated within a single organization.[28]

Suppose the firm is currently employing technology in the 'mass' production family, i.e. $c_m^i \in c_m \in C$. The firm's problem is to decide what capabilities it should use in the current period. Specifically, its choices are (a) continue using c_m^i (b) continue in the same family but make incremental technological improvements by employing a better mass production technique, c_m^i, or (c) make discontinuous organizational switch and employ lean production technique, c_l^k. Choices a and b reflect 'as is' evaluations; only c involves a 'could be' alternative.

Furthermore, a capability provides a dynamic representation of the firm. A firm's capabilities not only serves to meet the current demands but also places it in a position to make further investments to launch new products to meet changing demand conditions. A capability endows the firm with an ability to change. A static profit function, therefore, can not be a complete description of a capability. The description of capability must capture the dynamics that determine the type, level, and timing of investment needed transform capabilities over time.

In other words, we must consider explicitly the costs of switching from one capability to another, be it from mass into lean, or conventional pharmaceutics to biotechnology, from a current capability such as mass production to a technique in the lean production family. Switching from one capability to another incurs large costs due to reorganization.[29] We denote these large organizational costs of switching as Δ_{ij}. For example, the cost of switching from c_n (mass production) to c_l (lean production) can be denoted as Δ_{ml}.

Within an organizational capability, however, switching costs are small, but not insignificant. At the same time, continuing within the same family enables the firm to capitalize on local learning effects. If the firm continues in c_m^i or moves to a better mass technique c_m^j then it will subsequently learn by doing. However, switching from the ith to the jth technology may still incur

Table 8.2. T_{ij} and Ω_{lm} Switching Cost Pairs

		c_m		c_l
		c_m^1	c_m^2	c_l^3
c_m				
	c_m^1	[− −]	[+ −]	[+ +]
	c_m^2	[+−]	[−−]	[++]
c_l				
	c_l^3	[++]	[++]	[−−]

technological costs. We define the local learning benefits in mass production as $-o_{mm}$ and technological switching costs δ_{ii}.

To summarize the magnitude of switching costs between all combinations of capabilities and technologies, we denote the cost of switching from c_m^i capability to c_l^j will be:

$$\delta_{ml}^{ij} = \underbrace{T_{ij}}_{\text{Technological change}} + \underbrace{\Omega_{ml}}_{\text{Organizational learning}}$$

where

$$T_{ij} = \begin{cases} \overbrace{\delta_{ij}}^{\text{technological cost}} & \text{if } i \neq j \\ \underbrace{-\delta_{ii}}_{\text{technological learning}} & \text{if } i = j \end{cases} \qquad \Omega_{ij} = \begin{cases} \overbrace{o_{ml}}^{\text{organizational cost}} & \text{if } m \neq l \\ \underbrace{-o_{mm}}_{\text{organizational learning}} & \text{if } m = l \end{cases}$$

Consider a special example where mass production family c_m contains two technology modes c_m^1 and c_m^2 and lean production family c_l contains a single technology mode c_l^3. Table 8.2 presents the switching matrix containing the technological and organizational cost pairs. A negative entry indicates learning value from continuing to use the same technology or organization. A larger sign reflects a larger value.

More generally, the diagonal elements in the switching cost matrix will contain negative entries indicating the learning value.

We can now write down the firm's maximization problem. Each set of capabilities c_m^i has an accompanying profit function that is obtained by solving the usual profit maximization problem:

$$\Pi\left(\theta, c_m^i\right) = \max_{y \in c_m^i} \theta . y$$

where θ is a vector of quality adjusted input and output prices and y is the vector of input and output levels that are determined by the capability set. This simple expression indicates that the firm's ability to choose the best strategy is contingent on its organizational resources.

Critical Capability Set

STATIC PROFIT MAXIMIZATION WHEN THERE ARE NO SWITCHING COSTS

To fix ideas, let us first consider the static case where the firm maximizes its single-period profits. Suppose the firm can costlessly obtain any feasible capability in C. Then we can define a static capability c^* as:

$$c^*(\theta) = \operatorname*{argmax}_{c \subseteq C} \left[\Pi(\theta, c) \right]$$

(Argmax simply picks the capability that achieves the optimal response for a given θ.) In our simple example, c^* picks an element from either mass or lean families depending on the respective profit functions and the particular realization of θ.

STATIC PROFIT MAXIMIZATION WITH SWITCHING COSTS

Consider now the case where switching between capabilities involves costs, e.g. corporate or business re-organization. The critical capability set depends not only on θ and the characteristics of the various profit functions, but also on the currently employed capability set. For instance if the firm is currently using c_m^i, the optimal single-period profit maximizing capability set is given by the solution to the following problem:

$$\Pi\left(\theta_t, c_m^i\right) = \max_{c_l^j \in C} \left[\Pi\left(\theta_t, c_l^j\right) - \delta_{ml}^{ij} \right]$$

Figure 8.3 illustrates this choice in the special case where mass and lean families each contain only a single technique. In a costless world, the lean technique dominates globally the mass technique. However, with switching costs, the relevant comparison is between the profit function of the currently employed mass technique and the profits of the lean technique net of switching costs. When θ falls below the intersection point θ^*, the static decision rule calls for switching families.

DYNAMIC VALUE MAXIMIZATION

The static analysis ignores the impact of the current capability choice on future choices. When future values of θ evolve stochastically, the current decision influences all future decisions as well. The decision by a mass producer of cars to invest in flexible manufacturing using lean production runs the risk that

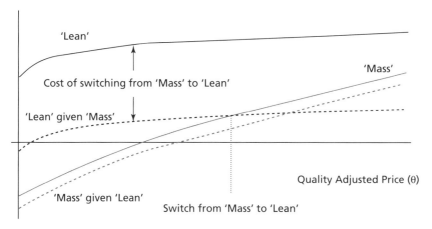

Figure 8.3. Choice of capability set 'static case'

the American market suddenly decides to buy large recreational vehicles made best by standard mass production techniques. But now they face the problem that they are invested in lean manufacturing, and cannot easily switch back. The tight coupling of organization and technology is essential to understanding why capabilities radically changes the understanding of strategy as not only market competition, but as the selection of competence.

The way to incorporate the implications of future switching is to write out explicitly the problem over time. To do this, we no longer work directly with profit functions, but instead with a value function. While technically this problem is often hard to solve, its formulation is both intuitive and insightful. At a point in time (t), this formulation treats the present value of all future benefits given optimal future behavior, as represented by the value function $V(\theta_t, c_m^i)$. The value function is the solution of the well-known Bellman equation:

$$V\left(\theta_t, c_m^i\right) = \max_{c_l^j}\left[\left(\Pi\left(\theta_t, c_l^j\right) - \delta_{ml}^{ij}\right) + \rho E_t\left[V\left(\theta_{t+1}, c_l^j\right)\right]\right]$$

where c_m^i, is the current capability pair (consisting of technology i and organization m) and j and l are chosen from the set of feasible technologies and organizations at time $t+1$.

The Bellman Equation indicates that in each period the producer contemplates switching into a new capability. If it chooses capability c_l^j, it realizes benefits of $\Pi(\theta_t, c_l^j)$, but pays switching costs of δ_{ml}^{ij}, and then arrives at the following period with value function $V(\theta_{t+1}, c_m^j)$. This value depends on the capability chosen, c_l^j, as well as on the value of the state variable next period, θ_{t+1}. Because still θ_{t+1} unknown at time t, we take expectations; we also discount at rate ρ.

In each period, the producer chooses the capability c_l^j that maximizes the value of the project. This can be interpreted as the *dynamic capability*. More formally, we define the dynamic capability as:

$$c^{**} = \underset{c_l^j}{\operatorname{argmax}} \left[\left(\Pi\left(\theta_t, c_l^j\right) - \delta_{ml}^{ij} \right) + \rho E_t \left[V\left(\theta_{t+1}, c_l^j\right) \right] \right]^{30}$$

In the absence of switching costs, the solution to this optimization problem is simple: choose in each period the capability c_l^j that maximizes $\Pi(\theta_t, c_l^j)$ in that period. This is the static critical capability discussed earlier. However, the presence of switching costs makes a forward-looking analysis necessary. The probability distribution of future prices affects the current choice of technology and organization.

This definition of a dynamic capability defines our reinterpretation of a 'core competence'. Core competence is the capability set (i.e. combination of organization and technology elements) that permits the firm to choose the optimal response for a given price realization of the strategic factor.

Hysteresis and Costly Switching

With the above concepts, we can now analyze more fully the hysteresis band first given in Figure 8.2. If a firm is unable to choose the optimal response, these conditions lead to a competency trap that is expressed by a hysteresis band. In Figure 8.4, the profit functions for two capability sets and the resulting hysteresis band is graphed. Since the dynamic analysis takes into account the impact of a current switching decision on all future switching decisions the hysteresis band is wider than in a static analysis.

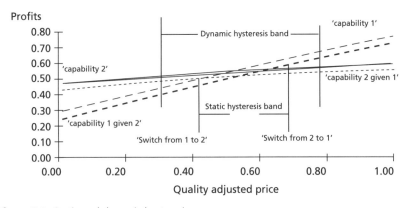

Figure 8.4. Static and dynamic hysteresis

For the costless switching case, the switch occurs exactly at where the two functions cross. The presence of switching costs has two effects: static and hysteretic. The static costs results in the switch occurring at the value of θ where profits associated with the new mode justify the costs of adopting new organizational capabilities of lean production. θ would have to decline past this point of switching in order to justify the switching costs back to mass production.

The band between the switching costs is underestimated by looking only at static costs. Because of the possibility that θ may revert back to previous values (e.g. due to a sudden drop in oil prices favoring gas-guzzling cars), the firm persists in its current mode and waits to see how prices evolve in the future. At some point, however, θ takes on values that justify not only the one-time switching costs but also the probability-weighted costs attached to switching back. The range of inaction associated between switching in and out of a capability set is what is defined as the 'dynamic hysteresis band' depicted in Figure 8.4.[31]

Competency Traps and Learning to Learn

Due the benefits of learning by doing, the firm's capabilities improve dynamically. In effect, the profit function can be described as shifting outward over time. By staying in its current activities, the firm becomes increasingly more competent. Techniques of mass production are expressed in well-understood routines that couple technology and people through known organizing principles of work.

The danger remains, of course, that θ will suddenly jump to a range or cross a critical threshold in which the firm's competence is no longer profitable. In a sense, its accumulated learning in the old techniques is a 'competency trap.' By improving in mass production, it is less attractive to change organizational capabilities. Hence a firm might rationally preserve its way of doing things, because it has become so good at doing the (now) wrong thing. Dougherty (1995) has labeled this 'core incompetence.' Exploitation of current knowledge drives learning by doing; the pitfall is that this learning increases the rigidity of the firm.

To speed its transition to new techniques, the firm may decide proactively to allocate funding to exploration by experimenting with new techniques. This diversion of resources slows down its accumulation of learning with the current technology. At the same time, it increases the value of the option to switch to new capabilities by lowering the costs of switching. To characterize this wider menu of choices, Figure 8.5 depicts the decision of a firm that has accumulated a particular breadth of knowledge in the current production

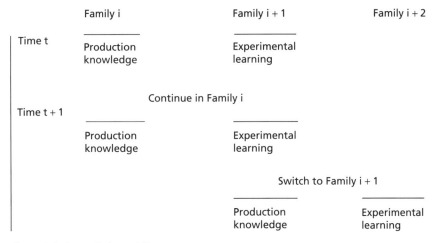

Figure 8.5. Expanded capability sets

techniques, as well as in learning derived from experiments with new methods. (We can think of these experiments as 'joint ventures,' such as the Nummi venture between General Motors and Toyota.)

The net effects of learning are ambiguous and depend upon the rate by which new knowledge is gained through learning by doing relative to experimentation. In Figure 8.6, this comparison is graphed by showing the upward change in profit functions over time due to these two learning effects. By construction, we show the gains to experimentation dominating learning by doing.

We can expect that the attractiveness of experimentation increases with time for two reasons. First, the drift of prices leads to the expectation that over time, the old techniques should be scrapped. Second, it is reasonable to think of the gains to learning as marked by eventual declining

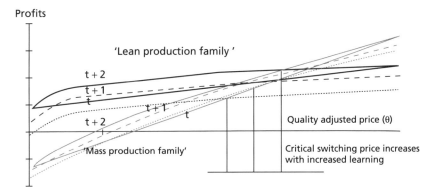

Figure 8.6. Effects of learning

returns. As the '*technological opportunities*' of the current capabilities are exhausted, the attractiveness of exploring in the new set of techniques should increase.

We expect, therefore, that investments in learning should follow a cyclical pattern. Indeed, the historical record suggests that the early experiments in mass production gradually dwindled. It would be consistent with this view to expect that the investments in incremental learning so often attributed to Japanese firms should also decline over time, as these opportunities are exhausted. It is not necessary to stipulate that for cultural reasons, Japanese firms are better learners than American firms are. Rather, a particular cross-section of time, Toyota had *more* to learn about how to expand its capabilities than Ford, which had after 60 years explored most of the terrain of how to organize mass production of standardized products. When there are few gains to exploration, allocation to exploitation of current capabilities dominate investments in incremental learning.

Combinative Capabilities

Our portrayal of exploitative learning by doing as a process of discovering better matches between organizational and technological elements suggests a dynamic by which knowledge accumulates through recombination. This characterization of learning implies that the capabilities of firms can improve by a modular design. In this case, there is a higher order strategy rested upon the combinative capabilities of a firm to dynamically re-adjust its knowledge (Kogut and Zander 1992).

We can make this similarity more transparent by analyzing in more detail the dynamic by which learning accumulates through recombination. This point is implicit in the argument of Baldwin and Clark (1991, 2000) that the benefits of modularity are realized through exercising the embedded options to ratchet up improvement. They note that modularity allows for a better process of 'mix and match' through an improved understanding of subsystems.

An intuitive way to understand their model is to compare two kinds of strategies of throwing dice.[32] Let the score on each die indicate performance. The first strategy is to toss both dice, and then to accept or reject the total. The second is to toss each separately, and apply the same decision rule to each die separately. The first strategy reflects an *integrated* design, the second, a *modular* design. The modular design allows for the possibility that one die scores a 5, while the other only a 2. In this case, the designer may decide only to toss the second die. By this process of mix and match, improves in design evolve through re-combination.

These benefits are derived through the strong assumption that performance is the sum of independent draws, i.e. the outcome of tossing a die. There are two important implications from dropping independence of the draws. The first is that the benefits falls, because the experiments are correlated. Behaviorally, correlation in experiments captures realistically the limitations of any firm in designing independent projects; statistical correlation reflects the bias of managers in the projects they are willing to support.

The second implication is that interdependence makes the design problem more difficult. For by fixing one of the die, the performance contribution of the second module is dependent not simply on its own efficiency, but also on its interaction with the first module. As a consequence, the optimization of a given set of modules does not guarantee that this evolutionary process can ever arrive at a 'best' system. However, the notion of correlation also expresses tightly the idea that irreversibility is derived from the rigidity of competence in managing a particular set of interdependent organizational and technological elements.

This insight of correlated performance underscores why exploratory search is required. Implicit in any modular design is a system constraint. If the overall system performance is inferior to competing systems (e.g. lean production), then evolutionary learning through recombination within a given capability set leads to a competency trap. It is this evolutionary characterization of the learning process that provides the behavioral basis to the concept set-to-set correspondence as defining a capability set.

How Good a Heuristic?

Strategic option theory is obviously a complex heuristic to apply. However, much like the BCG growth matrix does not need to measure costs, a core competence heuristic does not (always) need to value the option. Instead, through identifying the value of the competence as derived from market price of correlated assets, strategic option theory disciplines the core competence analysis to understand valuation as sensitive to competitive forces. These forces tend to limit the potential exploitation of a competence through a consideration of the effects on price and competition.

There are, however, several important complications to a strategic option heuristic. These complications provide important insight into the use of strategic options, and they also suggest the suboptimal transfer of the heuristic to inappropriate settings. For illustration, we consider three problem areas.

COMPETITIVE INTERACTIONS

The valuation of a strategic option requires an identification of a market price by which to derive the replicate the underlying asset. In financial markets, this price is easily given by stock or future prices. An important, and reasonable asssumption, is that exercising the option does not influence the value of the replicating portfolio.

This assumption does not hold always for strategic options for two reasons. First, by exercising an option to enter a market, a firm often influences prices through increasing supply. Second, by entering (or exiting) a market, competitors will alter their behavior. As a result, the market price is endogenous to the decision whether to exercise the option.

This problem is partly resolved by recognizing that the value of theta reflects the assessment on entry.[33] But this assumption hardly provides insight into the identity of possible entrants and their strategic behavior. A structural approach is explicit regarding the nature of future competition. Kulatilaka and Perotti (1998) follow this approach by evaluating the decision to launch a new technology in the context of different conjectures about market structure. This solution marries the industry structure analysis to core competence, but through the stipulation that the analysis is forward-looking rather than focused on current market structure.

WHY NOT SWITCH NOW?

The hysteresis band, we have suggested above, is influenced by the extent to which a firm has locked into a tightly coupled system. Another explanation seeks to explore a question—often under-theorized in strategy research—concerning who gains from a decision to switch. Baldwin (1982) showed, for example, that owners would maintain inefficient plants in a bargaining setting to threaten workers from seeking higher wages.

Kulatilaka and Marks (1988) analyzed why owners might choose to persist in an older, non-flexible technology as a way to signal a credible commitment to workers over wages. Both of the above papers suggest that bargaining strategies increase the value of maintaining older technologies and hence widen the hysteresis band.

A related issue is the difference between innovators and imitators. In the case of innovation, the profit windfall means that the bargaining problem is dividing a larger pie; Ford could win acceptance by increasing wages to USD5 a day. (See Raff 1988.) For imitators, adoption is in the midst of declining revenues; there is less to redistribute and hence bargaining is more of a zero-sum game for some parties. The situation facing imitators is more of an endgame, where bankruptcy is a credible outcome. In this context, switching to new practices is more an issue of survival than improving fitness relative to rivals. These concerns form the central debate in the strategic thinking in Europe and elsewhere on whether firms should insist on flexible labor markets as a policy to respond to international competition.

STOCK OPTIONS AS COMPENSATION

This notion of flexibility in employment is often also extended to flexibility in compensation. There is a frequent belief that a large firm could be more flexible to seize opportunities if employees' compensation was contingent on outcomes. There are, however, two major problems to such an argument. Putting in option-like compensation clauses results in high variance of compensation for managers in comparable positions. As almost all studies on compensation show, pay and performance are not closely linked because it is demoralizing; employees do not believe that differentials reflect ability and they find the social comparison to be unfair. The implications for promoting what should be the source of gain to a firm—namely, sustained coordinated and cooperative behavior—are invidious.

Second, compensation by options does not encourage flexibility. As Lambert et al. (1991) found, managers treat options that are in the money as wealth, and they consequently do not want to take decisions that eradicate their value. Unless a compensation scheme can be designed so that every decision is linked to a contingent payment, compensation by options is a disincentive for flexibility. Excessive incorporation of options in compensation is a heuristic, while appealing in its financial language in an age of institutional investors, whose application is detrimental.

Conclusions

Real option analysis provides the theoretical foundations to heuristics derived core competence. It offers the improvement by conditioning an understanding of competence in relation to a market test (e.g. Barney's notion of a strategic factor market) and by putting the organizational dilemma in central stage as the leading explanation for the irreversibility of investments in capabilities. In a narrow sense, it denigrates discounted cash flow analysis as the principal tool of understanding the value of a firm. But more profoundly, the recognition that the coupling of people and technology is a source of considerable option value challenges simplistic notions of firms as 'pure asset plays.'

It is reasonable to also ask whether the formal theory itself is liable to be implemented through a more usable heuristic framing. Reducing the mathematical formulation to linear approximations, for example the proposal by Bowman and Moskowitz (1997), makes this framing more plausible to the manager. However, the larger challenge remains whether the rigor of using an assessment of market valuation of options leads to heuristic frames that improve the quality of strategizing.

Through the link to the value of the embedded knowledge in organizational assets, the treatment of capabilities as strategic options deflects, ironically, a purely financial evaluation of the firm. Because organizations consist of coupled systems, the value of the firm is not reflected in the present value of its constituent parts, but in the combinative potential (i.e. the option value) of deploying these capabilities for innovation in existing markets or for addressing new markets.

The implications of modularity as maintaining the option to recombine capabilities has an intuitive appeal to current trends in flat and flexible organizations.[34] It suggests that firms are dynamic systems consisting of the complex coupling of technology and people through organizational design. The ironic conclusion to the sustained application of financial modeling to firms is that in the end, the fundamental basis of the value of the firm is its organizational capability to exploit current and explore future opportunities.

Acknowledgments

We would like to thank Carliss Baldwin for many helpful comments, and managers of Lucent for a reality check on some ideas.

⬚ ENDNOTES

1. This chapter is based on Kogut and Kulatilaka (1992, revised 1994); the published version B. Kogut and N. Kulatilaka (2001) 'Strategy, Heuristics, and Real Options,' in D. Faulkner and A. Campbell (eds.) *Handbook on Strategy*. Oxford: Oxford University Press. Considers organizational theories in more depth.

2. Mintzberg (1990) suggests there are no less than ten schools of strategic planning.

3. See Hedlund and Rolander (1990) and March (1991).

4. This aspect of communicability has been under-estimated. However, in an increasingly more integrated 'community of practitioners,' the importance of ideographic and metaphoric communication is critical to the success of information technology implementation and performance.

5. For overestimation bias, see (Kahneman and Lovallo 1993); for a discussion of a lack of theory, see Simon's (1992) discussion of the professional school.

6. An interesting set of statistics are MBA entrance data. Whereas Wharton MBA's score at the top of the GMAT percentiles, their GPAs are usually around B+. These are smart people who do not like to study too much.

7. See Allison (1971) on frames; psychology experiments of Bartlett (1958) and Cohen and Bacdayan (1995) for evidence on schemata and suboptimal transfer.

8. See Minsky (1985: 74, 243–53) for an example. The definition of heuristic search is discussed in Bowman and Moskowitz (1997).

9. For examples of this bias, see Chandler (1962) and Servan-Schreiber (1967). Only in light of this backdrop is it possible to understand the contribution of Piore's and Sabel's (1984) counter-revolution in thinking about size and performance.

10. See Useem (1996a).

11. Selznick (1957) was one of the first to develop the idea of distinctive competence, which was absorbed into the language of the early business policy literature, as well as of writings on the value-added chain.

12. The inimitable observations in Barney are more fully explicated in a related literature on knowledge of the firm. See Zander and Kogut (1995) and Szulanski (1997) for empirical studies that measure inimitability, or tacitness.

13. See Dixit and Pindyck (1994) and Amram and Kulatilaka (1999) for extensive discussions on the application of real options.

14. One of the authors visited an optical fiber business unit of a large company. In response to a question about core competence, the factory and business managers identified the capability to quickly code the fibre in color packaging.

15. Winter continues to recommend present value evaluation as adequate. However, when uncertainty is added, present value has to be adjusted, as shown later, to account for expectations.

16. Fortune (1992), cited in Bernard Wolf and Steven Globerman (1992), 'Strategic Alliances in the Automotive Industry,' mimeo, York University. See also the discussion in Ittner and Kogut (1995).

17. Winter (1987) suggests net present value as a measure, which is appropriate for the case without uncertainty. Most surveys on the use of capital budgeting techniques show that almost all large corporate firms use net present value calculations for investment decisions. See Kogut and Kulatilaka (1992) and Baldwin and Clark (1992, 1994) for a discussion on why investment in capabilities is not a net present value of cash flows but a real option valuation.

18. Nelson and Winter (1982) consequently refer to organizational routines as 'truces'.

19. See the review given in Dosi and Kogut (1992) and the summary of the work comparing US and Japanese organizations (Lincoln 1993).

20. This point is implicit in the lattice formulation of Milgrom and Roberts (1990), where a firm's choice is constrained by technical complementarities. It is, however, difficult to see the implications from their formulation for the many studies on organizational performance.

21. A good example of the linking of capability and technology is modular design, in which modularity provides an option to improve a product by component; however, the product design has to be backed by an organizational structure to allow specialization. See Baldwin and Clark (1992).

22. As the stock price fluctuates, the portfolio weights to reflect the changing sensitivity of the value of the option to the stock price.

23. This is analagous to a dividend on a stock or convenience value derived from a commodity. See Hall (1997: ch. 13), for a general model on valuing derivative securities. More extensive treatments can be found in Dixit and Pindyck (1994) and Amram and Kulatilaka (1999).

24. More generally, we could define this process in vector form over a set of Wiener processes. See Merton (1976).

25. For reasons of exposition, we work in discrete time.

26. See McDonald and Siegel (1984); an application of adjusting for the shortfall can be found in Kogut and Kulatilaka (1994).

27. C will include technological and organizational characteristics as well learning opportunities.

28. For now we assume that families do not overlap, in that each technology can only belong to a single family. This assumption can be easily relaxed.

29. For simplicity we are assuming that switching across organizations only incur organizational costs. In effect, we assume that switching from any mass technology to any lean technology incurs the same cost. This can easily be generalized to include both technological and organizational costs.

30. For present purposes we ignore issues of risk. See Pindyck (1991) and Kulatilaka and Marcus (1991) for a treatment of the systematic risk in θ.

31. For an analysis of hysteresis effects of foreign direct investment under fluctuating exchange rates, see Kogut and Kulatilaka (1994).

32. This exposition is due to Per-Goeran Persson's remarkable student paper written for a course on organizational design at the Stockholm School of Economics. His Monte Carlo simulation of the following description is available on request.

33. This endogeneity is similar to the work done on currency rate dynamics when traders form expectations on central bank policy. See the essays in Krugman and Miller (1992).

34. Baldwin and Clark (1992) provide an interesting discussion and model of the value of modularity as options under the assumption of independence among the modules or development projects. An issue that cannot be pursued here is the observation that the value of the firm rests in managing the dependence among these modules; otherwise, a policy of outsourcing, e.g., a Toyota production system can equally manage independent modules for eventual downstream assembly.

Part III

Practices and Institutions: Their Diffusion and Geography

9 National Systems, Organizational Practices, and Institutions*

The importance of national institutions and context has been an enduring, if not always obtrusive, element in the study of the character and performance of organizations. The factor of national origins is explicit in studies on the relationship between network governance and firm capabilities (Gerlach 1992), the comparative analysis of the degree of adoption of quality circles by three countries (Cole 1985), or the behavior of individual workers depending upon their ethnic origins and the national ownership of their place of work (Lincoln 1985; Lincoln 1993). The national dimension is implicit in the more recent work on institutions and organizational performance, such as in the studies on Israeli kibbutzim (Simons and Ingram 1997).

The interest in national factors is clearly also associated with the immediate economic fortunes of countries. The performance of the United States over the past decade, for example, inspired dozens of books, theses, and articles in the United States, not to mention the musings in other countries and languages. They analyze the role of venture capital, the Silicon Valley, and corporate governance as factors for American growth.[1] The structural adjustments in the older industries of steel, textile, and mining having been made in the 1980s and 1990s, US productivity growth boomed in the new information sectors, especially in computers.[2] Why the US should lead in the developed world economy in these new technologies is a question that is not at all well explained by the usual aggregates of labor and physical and human capital. It is not surprising, therefore, that the discussion of the sources of American growth has led to a search for the institutions, rather than factors of production, that foster high productivity and technological leadership. The American resurgence is, far more so than in the 1960s, understood to be an institutional challenge.

This attention on the US resurgence strikes a familiar note sounded in the celebrated book of the late 1960s by Jean-Jacques Servan Schreiber (1967). Yet, the comparison is also misleading. He proposed that American economic dominance stemmed from the operating efficiency of large multinational corporations. He cited above all that American strengths derived from efficient practices that the large multinational corporation brought to Europe. The most radical insight of this book—which is still sorely neglected in current discussions on the US resurgence—is that organizing principles, not technologies, drove the success of the American company.

In the minds of many commentators, these practices were linked to the institution of the large corporation that diffused by the national missions of productivity sent by France, among other countries, to the United States following the conclusion of the Second World War (Boltanski 1982; Djelic 1998). Later, American consulting firms sold the organizational principle of divisionalization to Europe (Kipping 1999; McKenna 1999). Only in the regard of the positive relationship between the state and the large firm did American practices constitute an institutional challenge. In fact, for many contemporaneous with Servan-Schreiber, the post-war period presented the increasing powers of the state and economic planning across all industrial countries. If there were to be an equifinality towards which all countries converge, it would be the powerful Keynesian State that regulated and managed the economy.[3]

This belief in the large firm and state appears anachronistic, and yet this is perhaps the enduring lesson. It is this ambiguity in the efficacy of institutions and practices that is the outstanding feature of the diffusion of economic knowledge. The new American challenge poses concretely this problem of identifying complex causality and competing explanations. At the core of these issues is the question of why better institutions or practices do not simply diffuse across national borders. What is causally responsible for differences in national performances?

To address this complexity, a body of literature called 'national systems' developed over the past decade.[4] This literature has migrated from explaining why one country is richer to why many countries are rich and yet are institutionally different. This is an important distinction. The former emphasis implies that there is a best configuration of institutions and practices. The second approach attempts to explain the variety of institutional configurations that support particular innovatory and productive capabilities.

The varieties of national systems approach is able to reconcile—sometimes by a felicity all too flexible—why rich countries show such wide differences in institutions, such as financial markets or the size distribution of firms. However, it also poses another set of issues. Given different national systems, is diffusion between systems possible? Can practices diffuse without institutional diffusion? More concretely, must France adopt American institutions in order to enjoy higher productivity and technological leadership?

These are frequently posed questions that beg a more fundamental issue: how tightly coupled are institutions and practices? The transfer of best practice literature has generally avoided this question by allowing for 'hybridization,' that is, for the recombining of elements of two different systems.[5] In itself, as will become clearer, recombination poses filtering out bad experiments from good ones. Thus, even at the level of practice, there are good and bad configurations. Not all hybridizations are good ones.

Hybridization is distinct from the more penetrating issue regarding the coupling of practice and institutions. The soft underbelly of the national system literature is the problem of institutional change. If such systems are composed of coupled 'complements,' then one element cannot be removed without affecting the whole system. Yet if individual practices are anchored in institutional systems, then adopting better practices or new technologies confronts the rigid and yet fragile institutional balance.

Clearly, this static portrayal of national systems and diffusion does not conform to the wide evidence that practices diffuse, even if subject to cultural reinterpretation.[6] There is a theoretical difficulty in coupling diffusion with complementarities. For elements that are parts of complementary systems, the diffusion of single elements can decay performance rather than help. The idea of co-evolution of organizations and technology has played the theoretical role of resolving this conflict between diffusion and complements (Dosi and Kogut 1993). By allowing elements to find each other by experimentation and imitation, co-evolution permits 'coupled change' to proceed by identifying some avenues for adaptation while ruling out others.

The co-evolution of new practices and technologies can be the occasion for a re-working of national institutions. Florida and Kenney (1991) argue this point at the regional level by noting that Japanese transplants succeeded in creating new institutional spaces inside the United States. In their comparative study of the evolution of corporate enterprise, Whittington and Mayer (2000) similarly note that European countries experienced the international diffusion of corporate governance and management systems, but in the context of their national debates. The more radical implication of their observations is that diffusion itself contributed to institutional change; national systems are not static entities.

These ideas have been adumbrated in many literatures and yet not satisfactorily developed in regard to two related sets of issues. The first is that the adoption of new practices can be institutionally neutral and does not require a re-coupling of institutions and practices. In this case, the search for better practice is often a cognitive problem, albeit one rooted in salient work identities and in the local politics of careers and power. The second set of issues concerns the case when the adoption of practices requires institutional change.

In this case, the impediment to change is often not only cognitive, but also entails national political struggles. Change is possible, but is achieved through the political strategies of powerful interests (Fligstein 1990).

These are indeed complex issues that are deserving of simplicity in analysis. I propose to simplify this discussion by presenting a Boolean description that indicate different modalities by which practices and institutions interact. This description places the ideas of complements within the tradition of experimental designs and comparative institutional analysis. To a surprising extent, the varieties of national system approaches return to an older body of ideas associated with functionalism. Boolean analysis renders explicit the ambiguity inherent in deciphering causal effects. Even in the case of bootstrapping from what is known, many possible evolutions are feasible. Ideology is part and parcel of the political struggle to stabilize national institutions into believed coherent systems. Adaptation is possible exactly because these systems are coupled not by technological givens, but by nominal beliefs about acceptable practices and institutions.

I illustrate this approach by considering three illustrative examples of the diffusion of practices, institutions, and people. The United States stands out as a particularly unusual national configuration of institutions, because it represents an 'open system' that serves as a source for world innovation, while being deficient in some of its own institutions. The cautionary note in the analysis is that rich countries, by evidence of their success, represent multiple configurations by which economic performance is causally explained. There is unlikely to be a single 'bullet' institutional factor that explains the contextual causes for organizational success, and indeed no factor may be even be necessary for all successful cases. The more subtle implication is that institutions and practices are always molded by different national experiences, and they also influence the subsequent acceptance of new ideas of work and organization.

A Boolean Primer on Institutions and Practices

The literature on the varieties of capitalism varies widely in approach. A good example of this latter approach is the work of David Soskice on Germany. Soskice (1990) proposes that the institutions of labor, enterprise hierarchies, banking, and business associations characterize Germany as an ideal type of 'corporatist' solution to social cooperation. Each of these institutions are represented by formal institutions or dominant actors (the Central Bank and governments also play a role). These institutional actors bargain to create a 'high equilibrium' that supports the coordination of work to produce quality export-oriented products.

Thus, the national systems approach poses a theory that explains the composition of institutions and their relation to economic performance. These theories are often fitted to rich country cases and suggest that the observed institutions are complements, that is, the bundling of specific institutions are sufficient for explaining the economic performance.

To validate such claims, some comparative studies try to isolate an effect by quasi-experimental design. For example, Bendix (1956) in his study on the relationship of authority systems to national development chose Russia, the UK, Germany, and the United States as four countries, each which occupied a single cell in his two-dimensional framework. Since he had two causes and four countries, he effectively created a 2 by 2 factorial design.

The construction of experimental design using a small number of cases is a common template used in comparative research. Charles Ragin (1987) offers the most rigorous treatment of this approach that can serve as a canonical model in comparative business research. Ragin formalizes and extends the comparative method of John Stewart Mills by using rules of Boolean algebra. Weber implicitly uses this approach in his comparative investigation of why capitalism developed in the West, and in more recent studies, such as Guillen's (1994) study of managerial ideologies.

Consider the argument of Masahiko Aoki (1990) that the strength of the Japanese firm relies upon three duality principles that can be summarized as the joint presence of the main banking system, vertical ranks for promotion, and horizontal control among workers and suppliers. He argues that when these three elements are present, they produce a truth condition of a high performing economy. We can represent this by the following claim:

Main Bank	Vertical Rank	Horizontal Control	Truth Condition: Performance
1	1	1	1

The ones indicate that these conditions are present. Aoki proposes in other words a 3-way factorial design. To consider all the possible cases (i.e. combinations), we would need to look at 2^3 or 8 combinations. Of course, Aoki does not engage in this comparison and is content to propose his theory as 'fitting' the Japanese case. Most of the studies conducted in relation to his theory have looked at variations within Japan, especially between firms that belong and do not belong to business groups. Of course, these studies run into a selection bias (they are already chosen to be members or not prior to looking at performance). Nor do they test at all adequately the claim that all three principles must be present in order to achieve high performance. Yet these studies are reasonable first approaches to look at how institutions influence performance within a country.

The extrapolation of these findings to other countries is stymied by four problems. The first one is easily treated and is an example of spurious causality as delineated by Simon (1957). This problem is easily treated by Ragin's comparative Boolean methodology. In particular, we will utilize the following Boolean rule. A cause A can be present (denoted as A) or absent (denoted as 'a'). In one case AB are two factors that are both present and are associated with a truth condition of high performance. In a second case, factor A is still present but factor B is not, and yet the outcome is still high performance. By Boolean algebra, given that the truth condition is the same, $AB + Ab = A$. In other words, only cause A is causally related to the outcome of high performance. Indeed, for this comparison, A is sufficient to cause high performance. In the absence of other causes, A also appears as a necessary factor.

Let us reconsider the Aoki formulation more carefully. Using now our binary symbols of 1 and 0 rather than upper and lower case letters, we can represent Aoki's claim, as we saw, as mapping the combination of {1 1 1} to the condition of high performance. What if we found a second country, say Korea, that had only two of these conditions but still had high performance? Comparing the two cases, we have

Japan: 1 1 1
Korea: 1 0 1

We can now conclude that only the first and third causes are causal; Boolean algebra eliminates condition three.

The second problem falls under the label of functional equivalence, as first analyzed and studied by Merton (1949). To illustrate this problem, consider a case where we compare Korea to a third country, say France, both of which are high performing (if it seems unfair to compare rich France to moderately rich Korea, keep in mind that there are much poorer countries than Korea.) By assumption, these two countries have the following configurations:

Korea: 1 0 1
France: 0 1 0

We cannot reduce these expressions further. They represent functionally equivalent institutional configurations to achieve high performance.

Now this conclusion might be troubling to our penchant for matters to be more precise, such as there is one configuration that dominates all others. But as we have learned from the literature on the varieties of capitalism (e.g. Berger and Dore 1996), there are many ways by which countries can achieve similar performance outcomes despite different institutional configurations. In the parlance of game theoretical approaches to national systems, there are multiple equilibria that represent a variety of national system solutions to achieving high economic performance.

The problems of spuriousness and functional equivalence are easily dispatched by the application of a Boolean methodology. However, our third and fourth problems are not fully resolvable. The third is the problem of insufficient variety in the empirical data. As noted earlier, Aoki's 3-way factorial design implies 8 distinct configurations. These are {0 0 0} {1 0 0} {1 1 0} {0 1 0} {0 0 1} {1 0 1} {0 1 1} {1 1 1}. What if history does not provide all these experiments? Or what if the research design did not generate a fully saturated model by its sampling methodology?

It is easy to see that we can make an error. Consider the case in which we have sampled Japan and Korea as before in the first two rows and then subsequently consider the case of a third rich country called the US:

Japan: 1 1 1
Korea: 1 0 1
US: 0 1 0

Clearly, we can no longer decide to eliminate the second cause. In fact, this second cause appears as sufficient, but not necessary in order to have a rich outcome. We have now two configurations that are suggested by Boolean reduction. This analysis reduced the complexity of the three cases to two configurations.

The last problem is the related issue of omitted variables. It is always the case in empirical research (and in theorizing) that we have neglected variables that not only matter but also interact with the variables we have chosen. In econometrics, there are statistical treatments to eliminate unobserved heterogeneity, but these treatments are themselves guesses about the distribution of the unobserved error; they do not handle issues of complex interactions.

The effect of the problem of complexity is easily represented by Ragin's Boolean approach. Consider a comparison of Japan and Chad; Chad looks the same as Korea but is poor. We could conclude that the absence of the second factor is causally responsible for poverty by analyzing the following configuration.

Japan: 1 1 1
Chad: 1 0 1

We already know that Korea has the same configuration as Chad and it is relatively rich. The contradiction indicates that there is a problem due to an omitted variable and an incomplete theory. If we add in a fourth condition, we might have:

Japan: 1 1 1 1
Korea: 1 0 1 1
Chad: 1 0 1 0

Now we see that the fourth variable is causally responsible. But we discovered this only because there was a logical contradiction, and because we expanded our theory to look at a variable in which Japan and Korea agree but Chad differs. It almost looks as if we cooked the books. Theorizing country differences that do not permit testing is indeed an exercise in exotic and imaginary cuisines. Yet theorizing is indisputably required in order to guide the choice of variables and to prevent the list-like presentation of country differences that is often in the literature.

Boolean algebra does not eliminate all inherent complexity in causal relationships. It does provide, however, a methodology by which to sample countries (i.e. saturate the design) and to characterize the factorial combinations as necessary, sufficient, or causally unrelated. This approach has always been implicit in country comparisons, but yet rarely explicit as a template for conducting comparative research.

Boolean Algebra of Diffusion

The national system literature presents countries as independent experiments, sometimes precariously balanced in an equilibrium in which all actors must continue to agree to perform. However, it is also clear that practices and institutions diffuse across borders. How can we understand the study of Eleanor Westney (1987) on the importation of organizational forms into Japan if we contend that organizational effectiveness is contingent upon rigid institutional configurations? Similarly, the work of John Paul MacDuffie (1993), discussed above, indicates that American factories can adopt Japanese practices (in configurations) and achieve high performance productivity in the US despite different institutions?

Diffusion presents thorny issues to comparative work. Called the Galton paradox, this objection states that if the national systems are not independent trials, the comparisons are contaminated by diffusion. In fact, Tilly (1984) raises this paradox when he objects that globalization prevents the utility of national comparisons. Similarly, Ragin (1987) objects to Skocpol (1979) for choosing Russia of two different years as independent cases; clearly the more recent case is not independent from the earlier one.

The problem posed by diffusion highlights the failure in theory and method of national system comparisons at two levels. The first is to separate the effects of genesis from diffusion. It is perhaps true that certain institutional configurations gave rise to particular practices; this is historical causality. But once such practices are known, they may diffuse to other institutional conditions.

The second level is a failure to understand that actors are far more adaptive than implied by these comparisons and that these practices themselves undergo radical re-interpretations. Within the corporatist balance of

Germany, practices at the firm or factory level may change, sometimes by diffusion, but in the context of a discursive search among actors to adapt these practices. It is surely more complex to adapt when practices challenge existing categorizations of work encoded in an existing division of labor, such as skill categories that are tied to prestige and to wages. Yet even here, the political balance among corporatist actors at the macroeconomic level need not be tightly coupled with the changes in work practice adaptations at the micro level of work and industrial organization.

As a first pass at these issues, consider the case of the adoption of a practice by a French firm that is institutionally neutral. In this case, the problem is largely cognitive, for the adopting firm needs now only to understand the right causal combination and to adopt the various elements. The French firm is organized as a hierarchy, with banking investors, and internal recruitment of top managers. We can characterize this system then by the following summary:

Hierarchy	Internal Recruiting	Truth Values:	Productivity	Quality
1	0		1	0

Consider now an American firm that has a different organizational structure of

$$0 \quad 0 : 1 \quad 1$$

In other words, the American firm produces at the same level of efficiency as the French firm but at better quality. What can the French firm do? It has control, subject to its negotiations with its managers, over the degree of hierarchy and its internal recruitment (indeed, the 1980s revolution in American corporate life resulted in flatter hierarchies and more external recruiting (Useem, 1996)). Given this, the French firm can make three changes.[7]

Hierarchy	Internal Recruiting	Truth Values:	Productivity	Quality
0	1		?	?
1	1		?	?
0	*0*		?	?

It becomes transparent right away that there are multiple experiments to run, as each configuration can take on four different combinations of truth values. This is complicated, so we can make our lives easy by assuming that productivity does not decline.

The first two cases represent hybridization, very much in the sense of Boyer (1998), by recombining American and French practices. These two recombinations represent feasible paths from the French system. It is possible, of course, that these hybrids are superior to the American configuration, in which case there might be reverse diffusion. The third case (in italics) is Americanization, with the wholesale adoption of the American configuration. If the two first cases both lead to high quality and high productivity, then they are functionally equivalent. If neither works, then the firm is constrained to choose the American configuration.

It should be clear that even in this easy case, finding the right solution is not simple. We have restricted the choice to two factors. Of course, there might be more elements. In addition, a firm might be unable to run all these experiments. As a consequence, it might observe other firms that have experimented, or it might hire consultants (Haunschild and Miner 1997). Of course, even then, borrowing might be too inclusive and practices might be borrowed that have little to do with performance. They are like the hitchhiking genes in genetics, bits of practices that have no clear causal outcome.

INSTITUTIONAL INFLUENCES

Even in the third case, the new configuration may not do well because of interactions with French institutions. This is the problem of omitted variables discussed above. In this case, the initial configuration might have to include the influence of institutions, e.g. the type of external financial market. In effect, we are now combining practices with institutions and are considering two levels of analysis. In this wider consideration, the initial configuration is the following:

Hierarchy	Internal Recruit	Bank Finance	Truth Values:	Productivity	Quality
1	1	1		1	0

Here, a value of 0 for bank finance means that the firm relies upon equity markets. If the external financial institution is a fixed constraint, there are three possibilities:

1. How a firm is financed does not affect performance.
2. Source of financing matters in conjunction with some configurations but not all.
3. How a firm is financed is a necessary condition (with equity finance required in order to achieve quality).

The first possibility represents a null hypothesis. The second possibility suggests that French firms can adopt hybrid forms that suit the national conditions. For different countries, there will be different configurations of practices that generate both high productivity and high quality. An obvious point is that there is not a single best set of practices. But the more important point is that what gets diffused, or should be diffused, from a source country (e.g. the US) varies from country to country. In Italy, given its small firm structure, the adoption of American corporate organization might well decrease productivity. At the same time, external recruiting of managers might help performance.

The idea of core practices is, then, possibly wrong, for it presumes that there are necessary and sufficient practices. As we have seen, diffusion of practices from one country to the next can be compatible with multiple configurations. In other words, there is no set of best practices, once we admit the choice of practices can depend upon the institutional setting.

The last possibility poses the problem of institutional change. For if French firms wish to achieve both quality and productivity, then there will have to be changes in financial markets. Institutional change is different than adopting practices, for it concerns the social and political agreements among diverse actors. In this wider consideration, not only cognition is a problem (that is, do managers and workers recognize the evidence for a better practice) along with the internal politics of the firm, but also the credible commitments made by various parties to institutions.

Institutional change poses, then, particular problems for diffusion of practices. Of course, the example of superior American quality might seem anachronistic—if it was ever valid. But if we switch the truth value to radical innovation, and the financial system under consideration to be venture capital (or its absence), we have indeed posed precisely the contentions in the popular press that Silicon Valley markets are critical for the new economy success of the United States. In fact, France, Germany, and other countries have introduced new stock markets to provide incentives (through initial public offerings) for venture capitalists.

Yet even the simple idea of introducing a stock market for small firms can pose complex institutional interactions. We have not, therefore, entirely treated the problem of institutional change. For the problem is rarely simply altering a single institution, but rather the consideration of a change in the ensemble of interacting institutions.

Again, an illustration might help. If we return to Soskice's description of Germany, the corporatist economy is a fragile balance between competing interests. German financial institutions interact with central bank powers and with national and sectoral unions that bargain for wages. The logic of adopting new practices might require changes in an institution. However, changing a given institution might itself cause national agreements to decay.

Thus, it is not simply an issue of whether a firm should finance, by equity and stocks, but how the choice of stronger shareholder will affect the strategic behaviors of other economic actors.[8] The external shareholder representatives of American financial institutions still must sit on supervisory boards consisting of 50 percent worker and managerial delegates (see Juergens et al. (2000) for a discussion). Whether such piece-wise institutional changes are possible have yet to be fully observed. Clearly, such proposals are rejoined with an active debate among the institutional actors.

There is an important caveat to be made. Our earlier example considered two outcomes of quality and productivity, both of which were desirable; hence achieving both is better than achieving just one. Of course, national configurations might lead to different kinds of outcomes that are substitutes reflecting their comparative advantage. For example, the Japanese system has long been hypothesized to be consistent with incremental innovation because of its educational and labor market features; the American system, because of its star system of differential pay and labor mobility, leads to radical system (Westney 1993). A priori, we would not want to rank order them. In fact, these differences in performance will be more or less desirable depending upon the industry and its life cycle.

Of course, in a larger sense, we can say that even if the industrial outcomes are substitutes, we can still rank countries in terms of overall macroeconomic performance, such as per capita incomes. This ranking is probably more complex than suggested by the tables in a World Bank development report; countries indeed may have different national macroeconomic objectives. But the more practical implication is that countries may differ in their comparative advantages and the sectors in which they specialize and in the competences they create because of their institutions and their social preferences (e.g. the amount of public and social goods provided). It seems silly to praise one country for a high average incomes and condemn another for lower average incomes without considering the distribution of income, the quality of life, and other social indicators. After all, institutions are not simply supposed to be inputs (e.g. capital and labor) to the production of material outputs, but to represent wider understandings and conflicts regarding the nature of society.

COMPLEMENTS AS 'TASTE'

This scenario of the crisis of institutions is a common feature to the current debates in many countries regarding the impact of globalization and the new economy. In part, this debate is about power; and in part it is about persuading each other what needs to be adopted and changed. Given the causal complexity, these debates will be decided not on the technical proof of what matters, but by the power of ideas in politicized contexts.

However, the characterization of national systems as complementary institutions that support production and innovation within a political equilibrium begs the underlying question of when practices and institutions are complements. It is obvious that there are sometimes technical complements. An example is the integer problem in production planning: if a steel blast furnace works optimally at four million tons capacity and the iron foundry at three million tons, then the optimal configuration is three blast furnaces and four foundries. Of course, technical complements do not seem to cover many of the practices discussed in the work practice literature. Hence, complements are sometimes seen as sociotechnical (MacDuffie 1993) or cultural such as in payment systems (Ichinowski, Shaw and Prennushi 1997). Game theory thinks of complements in terms of strategies, or in the commitments required to render credible a course of action.[9] Clearly, the term is more flexible than that suggested by the national systems literature or our Boolean algebra.

In this regard, it is important to remember that complements are often issues of tastes in the sense of aesthetics or proper behavior. This consideration may seem to stretch the meaning, but it is critical to understanding the potential for adaptability. In cuisine, we clearly accept that complements are cultural. White wine is not drunk with most cheeses in France, but it is in California; corned beef and mayonnaise is possible in the US Midwest, but not in New York.

Similarly, debates on the virtues of paying stock options are often couched in arguments regarding complements (e.g. to motivate our managers in decentralized hierarchies we have to pay them options—the italics indicate the complements). Yet the opposition to stock options often argues that they are tasteless or unfair.

Accordingly, in this complex space of culture, technologies, and strategies, there are far more possibilities for adaptation within national systems than presumed. For surely the attitudes towards money and other economic transactions have changed over the centuries. See the wonderful study by Zelitzer (1978) regarding life insurance policies in the late nineteenth century America.

Boltanski and Chiapello (1999) are right to stress the importance of the transformations in the artistic and social critiques of capitalism for understanding the adaptive potential of capitalist economies and their national varieties. They argue that capitalism succeeds only insofar as it borrows its cultural justification from other social domains. To a large extent, adopting complementary capitalist practices is a matter of making culturally acceptable what had been anathema before. Issues such as cultural preferences for certain social outcomes (e.g. equity in income distribution) influence what countries tend to view as acceptable or unacceptable complements. The thesis of Douglass North is that institutions change if the costs of maintaining them are too large relative to the benefits of change. For example, feudalism collapsed when the plague decimated the labor supply, bidding wages up and encouraging workers to break their feudal bonds (North and Thomas 1973). Sometimes change happens by micro steps, in which institutions corrode by the many decisions of individuals. Thus, feudalism did not collapse by revolution in most cases, but by the increased power of labor to negotiate its liberation during a period of labor shortage. The description of economic change in China by Nee (1992) essentially reflects this theoretical belief that institutions change endogenously in response to opportunity costs. Yet, even in these works on the economic logic of institutional change, institutional change occurs through the ideological reconstitution of coalitional support, as the later North (1990) recognized. It is not surprising, then, that institutional change is often motivated by ideological challenges to notions of what is best and right.

EMPIRICAL ILLUSTRATIONS OF DIFFUSION

The national systems models provide the starting-point for understanding diffusion within varying institutional contexts but understate the adaptive potential of economic and political actors to re-interpret practices and institutions. The relationship between institutions and practices is fundamental to understanding the diffusion between the United States and Europe. In this exchange of knowledge between the continents, the diffusion of practices and institutions are often but not always linked. When they are linked, the diffusion of practices not only may be impeded; their adoption may lead to effects quite different than the home country.

To illustrate this interaction, we analyze below three cases: diffusion of the practice of divisionalization; of an institution of privatization; and of a global institution of immigration policies. A Boolean reasoning indicates that the causal claims in many studies and polemics are not justified. More positively, such reasoning suggests the potential explanatory candidates that might be contingently important in the context of ongoing national debates and adaptive behaviors by institutional actors.

Diffusion of Practices: The Multidivisional Structure

An excellent illustration for the diffusion of a practice and its relations to institutions is the diffusion of the multidivisional structure. The history of the diffusion of this organizational structure reflects precisely Servan-Schreiber's observations that the American firm is more productive because it is better organized. The multidivisional structure was invented in the United States just after the First World War by Dupont and quickly spread throughout the American economy. The initial diffusion showed a strong sectoral pattern, and imitation effects strongly characterized its diffusion (Kogut and Parkinson 1998); this pattern also holds for studies of latter periods (Palmer et al. 1987, 1993). Teece (1981) showed that its diffusion resulted in increased profitability for early adopters. Armour and Teece (1978)

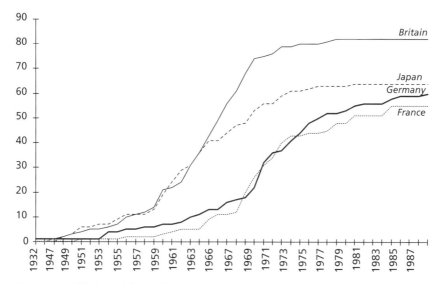

Figure 9.1. Diffusion of the multidivisional structure in Europe and Japan

calculated that early adoption in the oil industry led to over a 2 percent increase in return on assets, a sizeable profit for the capital-intensive oil companies.

As is well known now, the multidivisional structure was taken to Europe not only by American multinational companies but also by the active agency of consulting companies, especially McKinsey (Channon 1973; Kipping 1999; McKenna 1999). Moreover, there had been some early experimentation with this form in the UK and in France prior to the Second World War. In the case of Japan, interestingly, the multidivisional form was discovered by indigenous efforts and its diffusion was quite rapid (Suzuki 1991).

Figure 9.1 shows the diffusion of the multidivisional structure in some European countries and in Japan[10] (the chart is normalized for differences in sample sizes among the countries; exact numbers should not be taken seriously). There are two observations to be made from this chart. The first is the more rapid diffusion of the form in the UK and in Japan. One might hypothesize that the differential adoption of the multidivisional structure reflected the larger size and greater diversification of companies in the leading countries. However, the lack of national patterns in diversification cannot support a thesis of common factors in adoption. Differences in foreign adoption speed do not seem to be related to the factors found to be important in the US (Kogut and Parkinson 1998).

The second, and more interesting observation, is that by the 1980s, this form had diffused widely in all of these countries (Whittington and Mayer 2000). Why had this form diffused so widely? This variance in speed of the adoption of the divisional form, especially when compared against the adoption of other practices such as Taylorism, suggest that diffusion was strongly conditioned by different national experiences (Kogut and Parkinson 1993). Clearly, an important possibility is that the adoption of the multidivisional structure was largely institutionally neutral. It did not challenge the institutional balance in the adopting countries. Often, divisionalization did not even lead to restructuring of assets, merely reflecting changes in the hierarchical relationships and accounting rules inside the firm. Indeed, in countries such as Germany, the liquidation of companies and their reintegration into the firm not only posed tax liability issues but also removed labor from supervision over the absorbed companies. Thus, it is not surprising that German divisionalization often maintained the fiscal and juridical identity of the companies, while assigning them to reporting lines within the divisionalized holding structure.

Of course, the other possibility is that the introduction of the multidivisional form often reflected a 'paper' change rather than deep restructuring. There is no question of an element of superficial changes. And there was also an element of cultural preference, as revealed by a British executive who thought the linking of pay to results was 'rather tasteless' (cited in Channon 1973). Yet the historical record of many of these firms shows consistent efforts to reorganize their companies through rather strenuous efforts. In all, the multidivisional structure diffused because it was a practice that was institutionally neutral in these countries. Where it posed problems—such as in Germany—local adaptations sufficed to render it politically harmless.

It is, however, a different issue to ask whether the multidivisional structure was causally responsible for better performance. Whereas the US studies are fairly clear in showing increased profits to adoption, the European studies are ambiguous at best. The most intriguing study is that of Cable and Dirrheimer (1983) that showed no effect on profits for German firms that adopted. To put this into Boolean terms, we have a contradictory result regarding the adoption of the divisional structure. The theory appears to be multidivisional structure, diversified firms, and large enterprises lead to better performance. If we label this, following Ragin's notation, as M D L for these three causal factors, respectively, we have the contradiction that in the US, they lead to high performance and in Germany to no clear effect.

Is it possible that German firms spent fortunes on restructuring and consultancy with little effect on improved performance? This conclusion reflects the possibility that divisionalization had little meaning in the institutional context of Germany. With extensive crossholdings among firms and banks, divisionalization surely did not play the same role as in the US in increasing transparency for the shareholder or in increasing shareholders' representation in corporate decisions. The many studies on divisionalization in the US never identified the source of the increased profitability. Was it improved accounting, better incentives, or better governance? In Germany, perhaps *institutional* factors, such as relationships with banks that served as auditors, *substituted* for the *practice* of divisionalization. (For evidence on the one-time positive benefit of bank ownership, see Gorton and Schmid 1996.) With such blurred causality, it would not be surprising that the adoption of the divisional structure should have ambiguous results that depend upon the national institutions of the adopting firm.

There is a cautionary inference from this analysis. It is hard to isolate a causal factor in the success of another country that, if moved by itself, would have the expected consequences; there are rarely sufficient causes. The diffusion of the multidivisional form suggests, even when a practice appears institutionally neutral, it is not sufficient by itself to cause the desired change. Moreover, it may not even be necessary. Thus the conglomerate form appears to be successful in many countries without the divisional form found in the West (Khanna and Palepu 1999). Causal complexity is almost always a feature of the diffusion of practices across borders.

The diffusion of divisionalization as a practice was, in other words, only partly institutionally neutral. It could be found in a number of countries, some of which developed it indigenously as in the case of Japan. Yet, the evidence for its efficacy is only persuasive for the United States and suggestive for the UK. For some countries, the consequences appear as neutral. It could be argued that Germany lacks other complementary practices, or the appropriate institutions. Or it could be that the studies were not powerful enough in their data and methods. But it is exactly this uncertainty that is fundamental to detection of causality under conditions of complex interactions among potential complements. Whereas some, such as Whittington and Mayer (2000), conclude by inference from their diffusion that the large firm and its divisionalization are linked to higher efficiency, an off-the-cuff Boolean analysis indicates that the evidence does not support the conclusion that adopting divisionalization is beneficial in all institutional contexts.

Diffusion of Institutions: Privatization of State-Owned Enterprises

The diffusion of practices is a permanent feature of the world economy. With the spread of multinational corporations and their domination of world trade and investment, the diffusion of practices travels these international arteries more quickly. Whereas their adoption always confronts problems of re-interpretation and re-combination with existing practices, diffusion is surely better facilitated today by the increased economic integration.

Institutions, however, do not travel easily by the arteries of multinational corporations. They reflect patterns of behavior that are inscribed in legal code and in political and economic relationships. Outside the power of any one actor to change, institutions are social agreements that guide and coordinate the interdependent acts of economic actors in a country.

One of the most important sea changes in the post-war period has been the waxing and waning of the power of the state in national economies. In the first decades after the Second World War, the state grew in power and authority in all European countries, as well as in the United States. This growth was due partly to the military tension of the post-war period that called for large defense budgets, as well as to meet the demands of social benefits.[11]

The role of the state varied, however, dramatically by country. State ownership of key enterprises has been an important influence in France, somewhat less in the United Kingdom, and even less so in Germany and Japan. With little prior history of government ownership, France experienced two waves of nationalization, just after the war and with the ascendancy of Mitterand to the presidency. The UK experimented for 30 years with direct ownership of steel companies as well as public utilities, before reversing the policy in the 1980s. The German government owned large industrial enterprises inherited from the Nazi period, principally Volkswagen and Salzgitter, as well as public utilities, such as the Bundespost or Lufthansa. Influenced by the American model, Japan did not nationalize enterprises after the war, and has also privatized many of its utilities.

Given these different traditions, it is not surprising that countries differed dramatically in the participation of the government in the ownership of companies. Shephard (1976) estimates the shares of public ownership in major economic sectors to show Germany at 9 percent in 1950; Japan at 10 percent in 1960; the US at 15 percent in 1960; France at 17 percent in 1954; and the UK at 25 percent in 1962. Thus, despite different regulatory regimes, the State took substantial positions in all of these countries.

This role has been greatly curtailed in the past 15 years. Figures 9.2 and 9.3 show that privatization started in the United Kingdom but quickly diffused to other countries. Thus, in this case, transatlantic change started in the UK, even if the ideology has a distinctive American flavor.[12] Of course, the value of privatizations reflects how much the State had to sell, as well as the type of assets being sold. Yet the picture shows fairly clearly that privatization diffused widely in Europe in the 1980s. It has not been a prominent feature of the US, where deregulation has been the dominant policy to remove the State from economic influence.

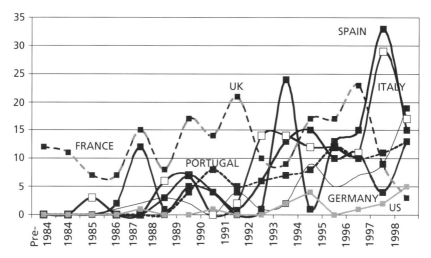

Figure 9.2. Number of privatizations in Europe and the US

The effects of these institutional policies have been quite different across countries. The case of France is instructive, because state ownership has had two consequences. The first is the impact on the career paths of the elites. French government policy has been implemented not only through indicative planning and fiscal incentives but also through close personal ties. In 1990, 45 percent of the CEOs of the 200 largest French corporations began their careers inside the government, many of them with degrees from the elite schools (Fridenson 1997).[13] (See also the sociometric study of Kadushin (1995) that confirms the importance of top school diplomas on subsequent friendship among financial elites.) As a consequence of the privatizations, the career paths of the French elite are less certain now that they have been since the end of the Second World War.

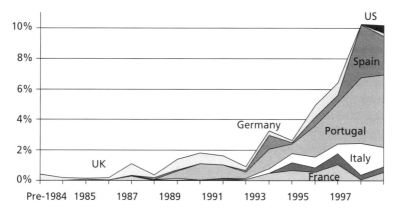

Figure 9.3. Value of privatizations in Europe and the US

The second consequence of the nationalizations and privatizations has been to upset the financial ties between French firms. While the Balladur privatization policy of allocating 'noyaux durs' shares to French companies insured a core of French ownership, French ownership links has dissolved in the past ten years. The deux étoiles of Paribas and Suez no longer are important in French ownership patterns. In France, loss of bank control and penetration of foreign and institutional equity capital are the highest of the major European countries (Ponssard 2000). In Germany, the dense intercorporate structures have facilitated a German resistance to the inroads by foreign equity investments (Kogut and Walker 2001). Even if these inroads are under threat as well, Germany consists of many redundant ties among firms and banks that have developed organically over the past century. It is with these organic ties the successive policies of nationalization and privatization broke in the French setting (Windolf 2001).

Thus, changes in the French institution of state ownership disequilibrated a national system. With decreasing state influence, ownership patterns, career paths and educational training lack a critical complement to their institutional logic. The growing importance of equity investment has opened the door to the discussion of new 'complementary' practices, for example pay for performance, stock options, that have yet to be re-interpreted in the French context or to be proven for their efficacy. Indeed, the debate in France is centered upon the cultural acceptability of breaking such policies as the solidarity wage and taxes that have sought, at least in word, to mitigate large economic differences among citizens.

Again, it is instructive to note that studies on the economic benefits of privatization are inconclusive (see Coffee 1999). Compared to public firms, state-owned enterprises adopt with the same propensity divisional structures and corporate strategies (Whittington and Mayer 2000). In Boolean terms, privatization is not a sufficient cause for improved performance; it is not clearly a necessary one. Possibly, deregulation is the sufficient practice, with privatization being a secondary and redundant element of this reform package. Or other complementary practices might be required, such as appropriate tax regimes, the support of unions, or social solidarity regarding capitalist practices.

No wonder that the arguments for such practices are deeply cultural and political in the tenure of their debate (Boltanski and Chiapello 1999). The changes in institutions have altered the allocation of power among indigenous actors. In doing so, these actors seek to argue that certain 'practices' are better, knowing as well that their adoption also influence the distribution of income and wealth. Thus, the cultural discourse of debate is closely linked to political mobilization. Institutional change of privatization, followed by American pension fund holdings, has instigated a discussion of new governance procedures and managerial incentives. The causality of any of these practices is far from established in the French context. But they reflect an attempt to change the acceptable 'complementarities' in France by coupling believed high performance practices to higher pay for managers. The sorting of ideology and power from true complementarities is not possible, because the right 'bundle' is itself a question of cultural transition in France regarding what is 'tasteful.'[14]

The complex interaction of new institutional and existing national systems is, of course, paradigmatically illustrated by the transformation of the former communist countries. Thus, Stark (1996) discusses the recombinative process in Hungary by which elements of the previous system are re-assembled with new pieces. Because the socialist countries differ, this recombination looks different in other nations despite the recommendations of international agencies to adopt the same reforms. The emergent bundle does not reflect the economically best package, but the negotiated and adaptive outcome of powerful groups operating in distinctive cultural and political settings (Haryi and McDermott 1998; Stark and Bruszt 1998). No wonder privatization policies have achieved such a mixed record in Central Europe and the former Soviet Republics. They are not sufficient, or even clearly necessary causes, to successful economic transformation.

Global Systems: Skilled Labor and the American Model

The instability caused by institutional change confirms the bias of the national systems approach that these systems are tightly coupled systems. Yet the histories of the importation of foreign practices and institutions show a large plasticity in the ability of countries to adapt. However, sometimes adaptation is difficult and blocked. Then what happens?

One of the most important adjustments made in blocked systems is the exodus of people to other better performing systems or systems that offer these type of individuals better opportunities. The United States is, in this regard, a predatory system. Lacking the corporatist institutions of Europe, the United States under performs in many areas, especially in the education of sufficient numbers of skilled technicians and engineers. However, as an open system, it provides a career path for the educated world elite and arguably constitutes a system that innovates for the benefit of the world economy. Predatory behavior and innovation are the two sides of the American system.

There are two important elements to this system. The first are the very close ties between universities, research centers, and business, often at a regional level. In a comparative study of the French and American biotechnology industries, Michelle Gittelman (1999) found that France and the United States did not differ widely in the quality of their basic science. Both French and American start-up companies showed similar innovatory records; these companies performed better in both countries than incumbent pharmaceutical firms. The better American record of commercializing science results from the difference in entrepreneurial activity; there are very few French start-up companies and many more American ones. The French scientific system created institutions for science, but not for radical technological innovations.

These results are not unique to biotechnology, because they point to institutional factors that transcend sectors. A candidate institutional factor in understanding the US innovative performance is the market for skilled labor, as by the mobility of engineers in diffusing knowledge in the semiconductor industry in the Silicon Valley (Angel 1989; Almeida and Kogut 1999). The institutional capability that permits human capital to migrate to its more effective use (and to high remuneration) is a feature absent in many countries. In some cases, such mobility is discouraged on the demand side by the excessive costs for firms to lay off workers. Or it is discouraged on the supply side by cultural norms regarding the value of employment loyalty. In Europe, the stickiness in labor markets is often believed to be a deficit in creating high technology industries (Weil 2000).

Yet, the American system conflicts with Soskice's German description that such job stability is critical to reward firms to invest in the training of workers. Absent such inhibitions, nice firms pay for the education and bad firms poach on these investments. With lower training costs, the latter are able to offer higher salaries and be more competitive. The system is unstable.

In fact, the US has failed to train sufficient numbers of engineers for most of the past few decades and relies heavily on immigrant engineers; this proportion has remained steady over the past few years partly due to visa restrictions. This shortage of skilled labor is due, it is widely believed, to the poor quality of education in many geographical areas. The second important element to the open systems of the United States is, then, its immigration policy. In 1995, 15 percent of scientists and 17 percent of engineers were foreign-born in the United States, compared to 10 percent foreign-born in the overall employed population (Burton and Wang 1999). Immigration policy works through two mechanisms. The first is the important role played by higher education in attracting the best students from around the world, then providing them with work visas to stay in the US for high skill jobs. As a consequence, foreign-born engineers are better educated on average than their US counterparts; 53 percent of them have an advanced graduate degree compared to 29 percent of the US-born engineering labor force (Burton and Wang 1999). The second mechanism is the special visas allowed for accepting highly skilled labor into

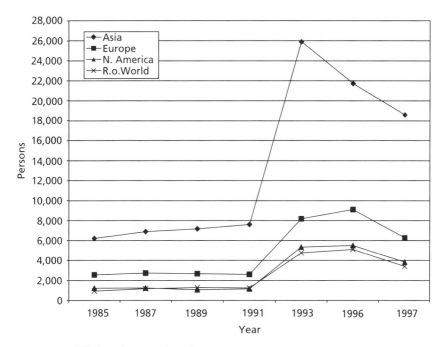

Figure 9.4. Skilled worker entry into the US

the US, either for university or for industrial positions. In recent years, this type of visa has been fully subscribed, with educational institutions complaining that they are unable to fill academic posts with the best candidates in the world as a consequence.[15] In effect, the American university plays the role of the immigration bureau for the US for admitting promising candidates already endowed with substantial human capital from their national origins. Given the information that applying students must release for admittance, it is a curiously efficient system.

Figures 9.4 and 9.5 graph the number of skilled labor immigrants into the US for the past few decades. Because of a change in law, the numbers change in the early 1990s, as do the reporting by individual countries. Clearly, we see a rise in Asian migrants, but we also see political considerations, such as the number of Polish and Irish immigrants—both politically sensitive ethnicities in the US.

But the important point of this chart is the long tradition of the US in accepting highly skilled labor into its economy as part of its technological strategy. As Saxenian has shown in her recent studies, expatriate labor head over 25 percent of new start-ups in the Silicon Valley (Saxenian 1999). The US national system is global in its premeditated design to attract the best educated and able, a design particularly attractive given the high variance of primary and secondary education.

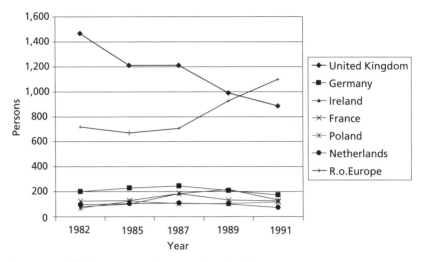

Figure 9.5. Skilled European worker entry into the US

In this regard, the US succeeds not because it imports practices more efficiently than other countries or because its institutions create the high skill
domestic equilibrium that Soskice claims is the German achievement. The US
system succeeds because it identifies the human capital held by individuals to
be the asset that it wishes to import from the global economy. The United
States is not a national system; it is a global one.

To be more precise in Boolean terms, the claim is that specialized immigration policies (I) are a substitute for adequate investments in training
native engineers (T); either 'It' or 'IT' can achieve high performance, where
lower case means the absence of these institutions. Countries without such
immigration policies, such as Germany, must invest in training programs to
maintain the skills of their workers. To return to our earlier discussion on
high skill countries, immigration policies are probably a central component
in explaining why low(er) skill educational systems can be innovative. Yet, we
should also caution that specialized immigration policies may not be enough,
as witnessed in the relatively modest innovative record of such countries as
Kuwait that imports its labor. There are obviously other systemic factors that
are involved.

Since educational investments are expensive and skilled labor cheap, it is
tempting for other countries to imitate this behavior. Germany has in fact
enacted a law to permit the restricted immigration of more than 50,000 skilled
workers despite still rather steep national unemployment. It may well be
hard for other countries, given their institutionalized educational and labor
markets—not to mention the frequent cultural outbursts against immigrant
populations—to replicate this aspect of the US system. There is, clearly, a
collective action problem, insofar as the United States can be seen as predatory

and free-riding on the human capital investments of other countries. The resulting 'brain drain' appears to be a peculiarly unfair tax on the educational investments of developing countries.

Yet it can also be argued that this drain has led to innovations that, though originating in the US, drive the innovative frontier of the world economy through diffusion and higher productivity. The historical evidence for this trend is mixed, as shown in studies done on patent histories (Cantwell 1989; Tidd et al. 2001). Yet, data on royalty payments drawn from international balances, as reported by the IMF, clearly indicate that the US has maintained the highest ratio of foreign inflows over outflows of any country. Moreover, the growth of communications has increased the ability of firms to source human capital *in situ*, such as the software houses in Bangalore. In effect, the US labor model is itself increasingly global in its reach with far-reaching consequences for local labor markets (Sassen 1998). In these complex spaces consisting of global and local labor markets, we clearly see the pertinence of Tilly's (1984) objection that global institutions lessen the validity of the notion of independent national experiments.

Conclusions

These short illustrations of the diffusion and co-evolution of practices and institutions across borders point to the importance of the political economy and cultural context of national systems. Given the high ambiguity in causal relations among practices and institutions, the adoption of new ways of doing things is rarely determined by transparent efficiency. Rather, adoptions of institutions or practices that impinge upon institutions are accompanied by an ideological and cultural re-configuration among economic and political actors.

The usual explanation for the observation of diverse and yet rich national systems is that there are multiple equilibria that represent successful national resolutions to the reconciliation of labor and capital in producing wealth. We have sought to outline a more challenging thesis. By observing the diffusion of practices and institutions, an alternative, though compatible, perspective suggests that complements themselves are not technically determined nor inscribed in socio-technical rules of social systems. Complements are endogenous features of the political and cultural landscapes of a country and, consequently, they serve as the occasion for the re-working of national institutions. This observation does not mean that law-like conclusions cannot be drawn. Rather it implies that convergence towards a single global configuration, or even multiple configurations, of best institutions and best practices is not predetermined by exogenous socio-technical factors. Multiple configurations of institutions and practices reflect the joint effects of technology, existing national institutions, and social preferences in shifting political landscapes.

It is not surprising that discourse will matter to this debate, as parties seek to convince each other of the desirability of change. Surely, international actors, such as consultants, international agencies, and multinational enterprises, are implicated in these discourses that are still played out in national settings (Meyer et al. 1997). The idea of convergence to a particular configuration, for example the Anglo-Saxon, is part of the ideological debate among interested parties who naively, or cunningly, shape the evolution of acceptable institutions and practices in a country. It is exactly in this micro dynamic by which economic actors seek to decouple and recouple institutions that national systems change, but rarely in the direction that any actor expected.

☐ ENDNOTES

* This chapter is a revised version of B. Kogut (2001) 'Le Nouvea défi,' *Notes de L'Ifri*, 26: 52.

1. For two recent scholarly treatments of the Silicon Valley success, see Kenney (2000) and Lee et. al. (2000)

2. See Robert Gordon at: http://faculty-web.at.northwestern.edu/economics/gordon

3. See Hall (1989), on international Keynesianism and Piore and Sabel (1984) on the broad acceptance of the large firm, despite inhospitable national experiences.

4. For representative works, see Hamilton and Biggart (1988); Soskice (1990); Kogut (1993); Nelson (1993); Berger and Dore (1996); and Boyer (1996); Hollingsworth and Boyer (1997).

5. See Boyer (1998) for an insightful analysis of hybridization and work systems.

6. Westney (1987); Kogut (1993); Brannen et al. (1998); Zeitlin and Herrigel (2000).

7. With two elements to perturb, there are four possible configurations; the firm's current configuration occupies one possibility.

8. The Eichel Plan to forgive taxing German companies for restructuring their holding companies has the appearance of creating more American capital market pressure on firms.

9. See the outstanding book by Topkis (1999).

10. The European data were collected from archives using the studies of Channon, Dyas and Thanheiser. The Japanese data were provided by Professor Suzuki, drawn from his own study; as I cannot check these data to assure comparability, the Japanese data are only indicative.

11. This literature is too immense to consider to cite. For an incisive study that reflects the bias of its time, see Shonfeld (1969).

12. Yergin and Stanislaw (1998) provide an engaging history of the ideological origins of privatization during the Thatcher administration in the UK.

13. This pattern of movement from government to industry is known as 'pantouflage,' referring to house slippers: one need not put on shoes to make the transition. It is interesting to compare this pattern to the Japanese. Schaede (1995) finds that the Japanese practice for bureaucrats to descend into private firms plays a similar role. More than 50 percent of the bureaucrats hired by the ministries graduate from the law school of the University of Tokyo. In 1991, of the 177 former government bureaucrats that were directors in the 100 largest Japanese firms, 40 percent were either CEO, chairman, or executive director; 5 percent of all directors were former bureaucrats.

14. See Manière (1999) for a representative popular statement of the stockholders revolution in France.

15. Other countries, especially Germany but also Singapore, have adopted similar policies in recent years.

10 Prototypes and Strategy: Assigning Causal Credit Using Fuzzy Sets*

with John Paul MacDuffie and Charles Ragin

Long-term strategy is the choice of capabilities that result in a bundle of attributes embodied in a product or service that allows a firm to position itself via other firms favorably in a market. This characterization suggests then two stages, the first involving the development of capabilities, and the second the exploitation of these capabilities to achieve a particular positioning in the market. The dynamic problem is then the development of capabilities that permits the firm to position competitively in markets for its products and services (Kogut and Kulatilaka 2001).

The complicating feature of this choice is that these capabilities are embedded in human–machine relationships that are not additive in their effects. In the parlance of recent body of economics, these interactions define complementary practices whose efficacy depends upon the presence of the joint composition (Milgrom and Roberts 1990). A classic example is the achievement of high performance work systems (MacDuffie 1995). Such a work system consists of a bundle of practices that improves the productivity and quality of production. Candidate practices are work systems that use human resource policies that dictate incentives and training levels. Since the effective use of one practice is contingent upon the adoption of another practice, there are inherent interactions among these elements.

However, the lists of factors that can compose these systems are many, and the number of experiments is limited. Hence, the task of sorting out these interactions into configurations, or complements, of practices poses a problem of complex dimensionality. If we think of practices as taking on high or low values (e.g. present or absent), then the analysis of two practices suggests looking at a 2^k combinatorial problem. Because dimensionality enters as the exponent, the combinatorial space rapidly expands with the increase in practices. The interdisciplinary interest in this problem is an indication, in fact, that dimensions are likely to be many. The choice of bundles is influenced by the economics of production, by the internal policies of a firm, and by institutional factors (e.g. unions or regulation). As a consequence, the statistical analysis to identify bundles and measure their effects is itself quite complex.

Recent attempts to sort out this problem have relied upon case descriptions and upon simulations. A case description cannot sort out complex causality and is incapable to determining bundles unless considerable controlled experimentation is permitted. We refer below to the problem of complexity as 'assigning causal credit.' Simulations can be useful. However, they often avoid the principal points of interest by stipulating a fixed technological landscape and dimensionality, assuming all combinations can be visited, and being unable to confront empirical data.[1] In a more philosophical perspective, complexity poses not only the intriguing problem of the contingency of what is knowable, but also the human construction of what is believed to be contingent. Hence, we would like a method that searches for causality but in recognition of its contingent knowability and its human construction. The method we propose to identify 'bundles' under these conditions is fuzzy set methodology.

It is often missed in the literature on the transfer of best practices that there must first be agreement on what are the best practices. Because of the complexity of this assignment of causality, it is not surprising that we deal linguistically with such complexity by the use of fuzzy *prototype* categories that reduces multiple dimensions to discrete categories. For example, the strategy of divisionalization was often defined in reference to General Motors. The literature on high performance work practices in the auto industry has stressed the importance of the Toyota model of production as a point of emulation. The terms 'Toyotaism' or 'Ohnoism' (after an influential production engineer at Toyota) populate the academic discussion (Coriat 1991), while the popular discussion has centered on 'lean production' as the generic characterization of the Toyota model (Womack et al. 1990). The Toyota Production System serves, in effect, as a prototype in the sense of Rosch (1978). Few firms, or plants, conform precisely to the typified Toyota operation, but approximate this idealized type through some degree of possession of the attributes that constitute membership in this category.

Evolving strategies often reflect this competition to migrate toward prototypical configurations that act as poles of attraction guiding the search for better practices. Behind this search is a set of recurring questions: do these prototypic configurations lead to better outcomes? Did a firm that claims to have adopted 'lean production' actually do it and if so, to what extent and to what effect? Is a firm that adopts only new work teams a better example of high performance work systems than a firm that adopts performance-based pay and extensive training? Or are they both examples of transitional systems, or variations of traditional work practice configurations? How do patterns of work practices interact with changes in production practices, such as the implementation of lean inventory buffers? And how much are the combined socio-technical innovations required to affect performance? In short, the inferential problem of assigning causal credit is easily overwhelmed by the *limited diversity* that the world offers as experiments, as well as the fundamental difficulty of categorizing these data into primary units of analysis.

Earlier work has sort to identify bundles by statistical analysis of data, often collected at the plant level.[2] For example, MacDuffie (1995) collected questionnaire observations from auto plants—the data used in this article—and developed constructs based on bundles of practices to test their interactive effects on performance, that is, to identify configurations. Similar efforts have been made by Ichniowski et al. (1997) in their analysis of steel plants. These efforts persistently face the difficulty of omitted influences and the risk of misspecification of the functional form. Comparative work, for example, has found that the adoption of work practices (e.g. mass production or quality circles) is strongly contingent upon the institutional context of a country (Piore and Sabel 1984; Cole 1985). The interaction of contextual factors with work practices creates a high-level problem of dimensionality. As a result, it is very hard to sort out the influence of unobserved contextual factors from the proper specification and identification of the relationship among work practices. Because of the high order of dimensionality in the problem, research into complementarities among elements is often forced to apply *simplifying assumptions* about the interactions that are guided by these prototype understandings.

We seek to provide a grounded method for discovering configurations by applying an inductive fuzzy logic methodology.[3] Fuzzy logic is a classifier methodology that 'assigns credit' to specific combinations of traits for achieving an outcome. The problem of credit assignment, to use Holland's (1992) phrasing, arises in the context of genetic algorithms that search for the string of genes responsible for particular phenotypic outcomes. Managerial practices are usually many elements strung together, with opaque clarity as to their causal implications. Unlike biological genes, practices are rarely crisply manifested, but rather are characterized by a fuzzy membership in prototype categories that are cognitively understood. Fuzzy logic, as developed in Ragin (2000), begins with the recognition that categorization is not unique and crisp and that diversity is limited. Based on a fuzzy categorization of membership, it identifies sufficient and necessary configurations, or complements, that explain a given outcome but in reference to simplifying assumptions. In this way, it assigns credit to the combination of elements that are causally responsible for the observed outcomes, with the caveat that this credit is assigned in the context of limited diversity—the world cannot generate all experiments—and of explicit logical assumptions made by the analyst.

After explaining the methodology, we analyze MacDuffie's (1995) data on high performance systems in the world auto industry. MacDuffie collected data on 70 auto assembly plants throughout the world. He formed three constructs from multiple questionnaire items to measure lean buffers, new work systems, and human resource practices. While controlling for other factors, he found that each of these constructs positively influenced productivity and quality in separate regressions. He also tested for their two-way and three-way interactions, using both multiplicative and log-additive specifications. The results showed that the interactions also were correlated with better performance, suggesting that there were complementarities in their joint interaction. Not all the interactions were positive, and there was modest indication of a lack of robustness in the analysis of quality.[4]

Strategies consist, of course, of more than just the choice of production elements and include such positioning factors as pricing or market choice. In Figure 8.1 given in Chapter 8, we depicted the formulation of strategy as consisting of the state variables that describe a firm's resources and hence its capabilities (one the left hand side) and the choice of markets, prices, and other positioning choice variables (on the right hand side). In our analysis, we hold positioning variables constant by focusing on auto plants that are producing cars for a similar mass market with considerable cross-country shipment of product. By this choice, we analyze for a cross-section in time a sample of plants to determine the configuration of practices and technologies—what can be called production strategies—that are complements for achieving high performance. We define high performance as the joint achievement of high productivity and quality. Through iteration between the fuzzy configurations and the qualitative data (see also MacDuffie 1996, 1997), we seek to provide a rich analysis of high performance cases that lends itself to generalization.

Motivation

The vast debate over the definition of Japanese production methods reveals a history of a discursive search for better practices amid a time of heightened competition and yet create uncertainty over the complex causality in regard to performance. Many academics played important roles in defining and diffusing understandings regarding Japanese practices. For example, Ouchi's (1981) Theory Z analysis pointed to the importance of managerial techniques as the source of competitive gain for Japanese enterprises. In a strikingly precocious study, Schonberger (1982) discussed the combination of practices required to achieve Japanese high quality and high performance in manufacturing plants. Studies were made that rebutted the claim that the source of cost advantage is lower capital costs (see, for example, Flaherty 1984). By 1985, a major study on the world automobile industry concluded that the Japanese approach to production organization established a new standard of best practices (Altschuler et al. 1984: 161). At the same time, some union studies took a skeptical attitude towards such initiatives as quality circles (Parker 1985). In addition, there was considerable skepticism over lean production techniques that unions saw as methods to 'speed up' the line.[5]

In the studies focused on a single sector, such as automobiles, the growing body of field observations and data suggested a number of practices that might explain a perceived Japanese cost advantage. Yet, there was disagreement over how to categorize these practices and over the variation in Japan that posed the question of what exemplified 'Japanese' manufacturing. This debate continues in more recent studies, such as the overview offered by Liker et al. (1999) that concludes that the Japanese Management System, in their terminology, cannot be reduced to a prototypical configuration exemplified by Toyota.

This debate around best examples, or the ideal type, suggests that the discourse at this time was around category formation (what constitutes new practices) and around prototypes by which to anchor these understandings. (See, for example, Rosch 1978 and the early statement by Lakoff 1973.) In Lakoff's (1987) analysis of prototype categorization, people hold category concepts that are characterized by central members, or objects. Members more distant from these central prototypes are peripheral; hence categories are radial, with central and peripheral membership. A classic example of a prototype illustration is the category of birds (Lakoff 1987: 44–5). Though most people would agree that a robin is an excellent member of the category of birds, an ostrich or penguin are more distant members. Scientifically, their membership may be satisfied by a definition of the required genetic makeup of a bird. However, cognitively, people hold a prototypical image of a bird, and membership to this class is characterized by a radial property in which some birds are attributed a higher degree of membership than others. In fact, members to the same category may hold no feature in common, and yet the implicit categorization may link them through a 'category chaining.' For example, a penguin and ostrich may have no common defining characteristic of 'birdness,' and yet belong to the same category due to their sharing different traits in common with the central trait.

Fuzzy sets are, as discussed below, exactly these polythetic categories that classify membership by a type of chaining rule. The methodology classifies cases by membership, treating them as characterized by configurations of attributes. It infers causality by testing all combinations against their membership value in the set of outcomes (e.g. productivity) and, thereby, assigns credit to the individual factors that are logically identified as explanatory, either separately or as discrete combinations. It then returns to the field observations by analyzing the prototypical cases. It is this iteration between formal classification and qualitative assessment that distinguishes fuzzy set methodology from more statistical approaches.

Yet all of these studies collect data on somewhat different variables, propose different bundles or clusters of practices, and suffer from the problems of unobserved effects and the difficulty of estimating the full set of interactions among practices, as noted above. In the language of an inductive analysis, these results diverge because of a disagreement about the size of the dimensional space, the variables that define this space, and the specification of the complexity of these variables. Logical analysis resolves these issues by conceding them. The determination of a configuration of variables that are causally related to a given outcome (e.g. high performance) is sensitive to dimensionality and limited diversity. This problem is not eliminated by complex distributional assumptions regarding unobserved effects. To the contrary, the problem (which manifests itself in the Boolean logic as contradictions, or as unexplored diversity) is an invitation to return to the cases, informed by an inductive empiricism combined with explicit theoretical suppositions.

In the academic discussion, the eventual evidence pointed to the claim that best practices could be represented by a prototype drawn from the Japanese examples that consisted of advanced automation and three *sets of practices*: work, inventory management, and human resources. Ichinowski et al. (1997) determined that these factors were the complements that were suitable for steel plants producing for an environment marked by an increasing combination of cost and quality considerations. Similarly, MacDuffie (1995) argued that these three practices, while controlling for technology and scale, produced jointly high performance, as measured by quality and productivity. In the work below, we propose this prototype as the working theory: plants that are characterized by all three of these practices dominate those that characterized by two or, even more so, by one or none. It is possible, in fact, that in the absence of one or two of these practices, the best choice would be *not* to choose the third practice. Thus, we would like to have a method that relates polythetic categories to performance outcomes. We propose a fuzzy set methodology for this purpose.

Ideal type profile analysis, as proposed by a reviewer of this chapter, assumes that all elements of the ideal type be considering when examining the fit of each case to this type. In the fuzzy set analysis, the goal is to examine the different configurations of features derived from a prototype (or ideal type if preferred) that are linked to specific outcomes. In effect, fuzzy set analysis disassembles the ideal type and then reassembles them systematically through testing their causal relation to an outcome. This method is not atheoretical; it starts with a prototype and then provides a more exhaustive inferential engine to identify multiple conjunctural causation. If, by ideal type analysis, it should be meant the testing of all possible configurations for their causal claims, it then indeed converges to the Boolean (or fuzzy set) methodology. However, ideal type or contingency theory has not produced any adequate alternative methodology, because of a failure to understand the conceptual challenges, and opportunities, to exploring causal complexity.

Boolean Crisp Sets

Given this complexity, a natural approach is to turn to non-parametric methodologies that rely upon rankings and that engage the researcher in trying to identify the causality. One approach is to identify logically the possible interactions as bundles of complements that define a configuration. The analysis of configurations confronts the difficulty of trying to understand 'configurations' whose elements share an unspecified and unknown relationship among themselves in reference to an observed outcome. In crisp Boolean logic, these elements are coded 0 or 1, and their observed effect is also coded as 0 or 1. Each configuration indicates, consequently, a truth statement that pairs a particular configuration of elements to a binary outcome.

Qualitative comparative analysis uses Boolean logic to identify the minimal list of configurations that determine the truth condition of the observed cases (Ragin 1987). It proceeds by inductively coding the configuration and truth condition of each case, and then applying a 'logic' algorithm developed for electronic circuit design to find robust causal (or functional) relationships that reduce the observed truth table to a minimal number of logical statements.

To return to the example of the auto industry, it is often posited that new work practices (e.g. work teams plus job rotation plus off-line problem-solving groups) and certain human resource practices (e.g. extensive training, performance-based pay) are required to achieve a high performance system. We would code the two causal factors as 0 if absent in a given factory, and as 1 if present; similarly, we code high performance as absent, 0, or present, 1. Since any causal element can take two values, there are then 2^k, or 4, possible configurations: {0,0}, {0,1}, {1,0}, {1,1}. Let's make the critical assumption— to which we will return later—that we empirically observe each of these configurations, and each configuration has a corresponding truth value of low performance (0) or high performance (1).

We want to pose the question what is the minimal 'covering' logic to which we can reduce the four possible configurations. This reduction is both an empirical and logical question, that is, we need to know the empirical truth values in order to make the logical reduction. Consider, for example, two configurations where the first two columns refer to work teams and training, respectively, and the third column gives the truth value for high performance.

Case 1: 1 0: 1
Case 2: 1 1: 1

In this case, the second factor is clearly redundant and the presence of work teams is *sufficient* to cause high performance. Our two-dimensional box collapses to a line whose end points [0,1] sufficiently determine the truth condition. By sufficiency, we mean the logical inference that an effect is present whenever a given cause is also present. We can also say that a configuration is sufficient if, whenever the member factors are jointly present, they always generate a given effect.

To illustrate necessity, consider an effect that has three potential causes. To continue our example, we can add, to work teams and training, the third causal condition (column 3 below) of whether a factory is lean (1 for low inventory buffers) or not lean (0 for high buffers). Three factories have the following configuration and associated truth values:

Case 1:   101: 1
Case 2:   111: 1
Case 3:   100: 0

For these configurations, we no longer can claim that work teams (column 1 entries) are sufficient, for they are present in case 3 and yet the effect of high performance was not observed. A comparison of cases 1 and 2 eliminates training as a causal factor and implies that high performance is caused by the joint presence of work teams and low buffers. Case 3 indicates, though, that work teams are not sufficient to cause high performance in the absence of low buffers; such practices are necessary but not sufficient. Work teams were present in every configuration associated with high performance. Thus we can infer that they are a necessary condition; if they are not present, high performance is not observed.

The logic of necessary and sufficiency conditions is essentially, then, a statement about the set-theoretic relationships between cause (X) and effect (Y). A necessary condition always subsumes the set of outcomes. There are cases in which a necessary cause is present but there is no effect, but there is never a case in which the effect is present but the necessary cause is not. In other words, there is no case in which Y but not X. (We relax this statement below to hold true statistically, but not absolutely.) Sufficiency implies that the outcome also includes the set of sufficient causes. There may be cases where high performance exists but a sufficient cause is missing, but a sufficient cause cannot be present without the presence of high performance. In other words, there is no case in which X but not Y.

Thus a cause (X) that is sufficient or necessary for a given effect (Y) implies the following relationships:

$$X \text{ is a necessary condition: } Y \subseteq X \text{ if } Y \Rightarrow X$$
$$X \text{ is a sufficient condition: } Y \supseteq X \text{ if } Y \Leftarrow X$$

In the case that Y and X are subsets of each other, then we can infer that X is a necessary and sufficient cause of Y.

Of course, causes need not be individually sufficient or necessary and the logical reduction of cases may result in a complex array of causal configurations. Boolean comparative analysis essentially is an inductive logic to find the minimal set of configurations that explains the truth condition. A configuration is itself the intersection of factors whose conjunction causes an outcome. To say that the combination of lean buffers and new work practices cause high performance through their joint presence is logically equivalent to stating that their intersection is causally associated with a particular truth condition. By intersection, we mean that lean buffers 'AND' new work practices causes high performance.

These simple definitions formalize some of the discussion on universality, contingency, and configuration. A sufficient condition is universal; a necessary condition—when not also sufficient—is contingent, or perhaps better said, all causal combinations are contingent on its presence (see Delery and Doty 1996). For social science, it is common to find that a given effect is associated with multiple configurations. Multiple conjunctural causation is characterized by the condition of an effect being produced by different combinations of factors. A listing of these causal combinations is expressed logically as the union of the configurations. Union means, for example, that lean buffers 'OR' new work practices causes high performance. (In this example, we would conclude that either condition is sufficient.)

Boolean minimization relies upon two principal operations:

$$\text{Absorption: } A + AB = A$$
$$\text{Reduction: } AB + Ab = A(B + b) = A(1) = A$$

The second operation is derived directly from the distributive and complement laws of Boolean algebra.[6] The first operation derives from the laws of subset. If AB is the intersection of the sets A and B, then this intersection must be equal to, or be a subset of, A.

How many possible logical configurations are there? In the degenerate case of no variance in the truth condition, each configuration is causally associated with the outcome and, consequently, there is no possible reduction in the configurations. With variance in truth conditions, the application of Boolean logic reduces configurations to simpler causal statements.

In the earlier example, we skipped by an important point that a factor might be causal in its presence or absence, or be redundant. The 2^k calculation, illustrated above, assumes that each factor is causal. As we saw, the application of Boolean logic seeks to reduce these configurations to more robust and general relationships, and some factors might drop out as redundant. For example, lean buffers might cause high performance; not-lean buffers might also cause high performance (perhaps in conjunction with high volume); lean or not-lean buffers may have no effect at all. Let's demarcate the presence of 'lean buffers' by a big B, 'not-lean buffers' by lower case b, and its absence of any effect by eliminating it from the causal configuration, denoted by '$-$'. We have then three possible states that lean buffers might take—present (B), absent (b), no causal effect ($-$). Similarly, we use 'T,' 't,' and '$-$' to denote teams, not teams, and no causal effect of teams. Consequently, if n (the number of possible causal factors) is 2, we have $3^n - 1$, or 8, possible causal combinations: $\{b, t\}$, $\{B, t\}$, $\{b, T\}$, $\{B, T\}$, $\{B, -\}$, $\{b, -\}$, $\{-, T\}$, $\{-, t\}$.

If the number of cases is large, the probabilistic significance of each observed configuration can be tested against a benchmark proportion, called p^*, that represents an analogue to the researcher's prior of the mean success of a 'very good' theoretical prediction. The realized success of a configuration in correctly predicting a truth value can be compared against this benchmark, and this deviation—along with the sample size and estimate of the sample variance—can be used to calculate a Z-score as a measure of probabilistic significance:[7]

$$\frac{(P - P^*) - {}^1\!/2N}{\sqrt{pq/N}} \geq z$$

Obviously, if the number of cases is small, it will be difficult to reach significance.

This latter observation raises the important issue that some configurations will not be observed. This problem of *limited diversity* is distinct from the issue of specification error through omitted variables. Of the possible interpretations, two are particularly important. The first is that limited diversity reflects a weakness in the research design to sample cases for all experimental combinations. An analogue would be a study of the effects of smoking on mortality of men and women that failed to include any observations on smoking women. But another possibility is that nature does not run all experiments. This possibility raises the question of what should be the inference from missing configurations. The Boolean approach forces the researcher to analyze the implications of unobserved logical combinations. This contrasts sharply with conventional statistical analysis, where regions of the vector space that lack cases are included in the results by implication, with no thoughtful consideration of these regions. Through an examination of limited diversity directly, the researcher is invited to explore existing and *possible* worlds.

FUZZINESS

It is an obvious objection that the world rarely conforms to a binary, or crisp, characterization. A rich person is different than very rich. Sexual membership as male or female is, biologically, relatively crisp in some respects, but less so in others. It is clearly not crisp if the question is sexual preference or sexual identification. It is common in social science research to rely on categories to offer discrete approximations of a continuum. For example, rich countries have per capita income in excess of USD 15,000, middle income is less than USD 15,000 but more than USD 5,000, and the income of poor countries is less than USD 5000. It is possible to code each of these discrete categories as three binary variables. The logical complexity increases dramatically through this method, since the number of configurations increases exponentially by 2^n.

However, there is a more fundamental issue than logical complexity concerning the way people categorize and describe phenomena. It was noted early that individual often classify on the basis of prototypes. Prototypes are best examples of members belonging to the same category. The usage of prototypes implies, therefore, that the degree of membership is a gradient, with more distant members holding lower degrees of membership.[8] Using this concept, we define membership in a fuzzy set of a given member x in the fuzzy set of A as:

$$m_A(x) = Degree\,(x \in A)$$

Degree of membership can be geometrically portrayed by a hypercube in which a set is no longer constrained to be located at one of the 'crisp' vertices. The simple case is a straight line:

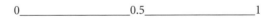

The two end points are the crisp values of 1 or 0, in or out of the set. Values in between identify fuzzy membership, e.g. fairly rich countries or not very rich countries (Klir and Yuan 1995). The mid-point, 0.5, is of interest, for it defines maximal fuzziness (or what Kosko (1993) refers to as maximal entropy) and it represents a natural cognitive anchor.

A prevailing practice in statistical work is to combine like-items into a scale by imposing a functional transformation. For example, the data can be factor analyzed, or transformed into z-scores while testing for their inter-item discrimination. Membership values in a fuzzy set can also be subjected to scaling. The caveat to scaling is that since the causal analysis (as described below) relies upon greater than, or less than, relations (rather than correlations), the results are very sensitive to the data values.

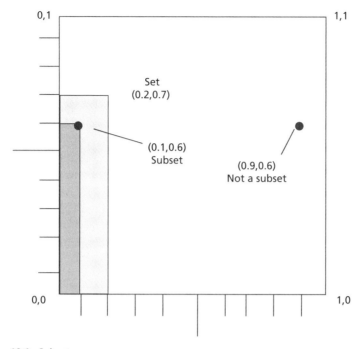

Figure 10.1. Subsets

Partially as a consequence of this sensitivity, the assignment of membership can be strongly influenced by linguistic hedges (Klir and Yuan 1995: 230–1). Zadeh (1972) proposed that such a hedge as 'very' signifies that membership values should be squared (what he called concentration). The hedge 'fairly' is naturally captured by taking the square root of membership (or what he referred to as 'dilation'). These transformations have a common sense property. Clearly, an apple that has a membership value of .5 in the set of red apples should have a lower membership value in the set of very red apples.

The above example relies intuitively upon a notion of subsets. An important property upon which we rely heavily in the analysis below is that membership of x in a subset of A is less than or equal to membership in the set of A:

$$m_{B \leq A}(x) \leq m_A(x)$$

Figure 10.1 provides a graphical illustration that membership of X in the subset of A, defined by a two-dimensional space, lies in the domain of the set of A.

FUZZY SET LOGIC

The categorization of entities by their degree of membership means that categories are not exclusive. This property has the attractive feature of conforming to commonsense notions of categories: people can be somewhat religious or somewhat moral. Manufacturing plants similarly have high membership in new work practices, but low membership in team organization. This property of membership, however, poses the question of how should we define the intersection and union of fuzzy sets. What is the membership value of a plant in the intersection of new work practices and work organization?

Because membership values are binary, logical operations on fuzzy sets are more complicated than crisp operations, though fairly simple. The key difference is that membership values in a fuzzy set lies in the interval of $[0,1]$. As a result, the operations of negation, union, and intersection must heed the membership values.

Negation

In crisp logic, the set of A has the complement of the set of not-A. (See Klir and Yuan 1995: 50). This operation applies also to fuzzy sets. Consider the set A whose element X has a fuzzy membership denoted by a point along the unit interval. Then, negation is simply:

$$m_{\bar{A}}(x) = 1 - m_A(x)$$

This definition is technically intuitive, and yet deserves a note of caution. For while the complement of rich is not rich, we would not want to say that the complement of rich is poor. We may view Portugal as holding a membership value of 0.4 in the set of rich countries, and hence the value of 0.6 in the set of not rich countries. Yet, we may assess its membership in the set of poor countries as considerably less than 0.6. Language matters in understanding fuzzy sets, and the use of a predicate logic does not eradicate the ambiguity in linguistic terms and quantifiers.

Union

The union of two sets is logically denoted as an 'or' operation. The union of A and B implies that x belongs to A or B. However, this denotation is complicated in the context of fuzzy logic, because the membership of x in A or B can take on any value between, and including, 0 and 1. Fuzzy logic applies the union operator by taking the maximum of the membership value of X in each of the two sets:

$$m_{A \cup B}(x) = \max(m_A(x), m_B(x))$$

If X is short and smart with membership values of 0.5 and 0.8 respectively, in these two sets, X has then a membership value of 0.8 in the set of people who are short or smart. This definition corresponds intuitively with the implication of an 'or' operation. That is, x is a member of set A or set B with degree of membership equal to its maximum membership in each set.

Intersection

Fuzzy logic defines the intersection operator as the minimum of the membership degree of X in each of the two sets:

$$m_{A \cap B}(x) = \min(m_A(x), m_B(x))$$

The intersection of two sets is logically denoted as an 'and' operation. To belong to two sets means that X is member of both set A and set B. If X is not jointly a member, then it does not belong to the intersection. Again, we see a complication that X is likely to have different membership degrees in the two sets. It is unappealing that X's membership in the intersection should be greater than its membership in either of the individual sets.

The application of the minimum operator makes intuitive sense and is consistent with a prototype theory of membership. Consider the adjectives of big and furry to describe dogs. A given dog can be furry and very small, and it has membership values of 0.9 and 0.10 in the respective sets of furry and big. To average these membership values would give the misleading impression that furry can linearly compensate for being small. It might be surprising, having purchased a dog by the Internet without a photo and who bore only the characterization as 'a more or less' member in the set of big and furry dogs, to open a big box containing a Pekinese. To most, a Pekinese has a low degree membership in the club of dogs who are both furry and big.[9] The minimum operator also makes formal sense. Recall the earlier definition of complementarities as supermodular. Since the value of doing two things together is higher than when they are apart, it makes sense to guarantee that the arguments to the function are all increasing. Taking the maximum would neglect the inferior argument. The minimum indexes increases in the joint presence of two variables by the least value. This permits a direct test of whether the minimum of doing two (or three or more) is associated with increases in performance.

FUZZY CAUSAL INFERENCE

Assigning membership values to all possible combinations constitutes the first step in the analysis. The second step is to derive those combinations, or

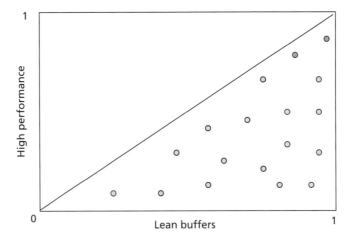

Figure 10.2. Plot of fuzzy relationship of necessary condition and causal effect

complements, that explain the causality of observed outcomes. Causality in fuzzy logic shares some of the intuitive properties commonly confronted in statistical work. In linear specifications, we ask how does y vary with more of x. Fuzzy causal inference relies upon the set-theoretic definitions of necessity and sufficiency to identify factors that satisfy the subset axioms (Ragin 2000). For necessity, the outcome is a subset of the causal factor. Necessity implies, then, that the membership degree of a case in a causal factor should be associated with a *smaller* membership value in an outcome. For sufficiency, the causal factor is a subset of the outcome. Sufficiency implies, then, that the membership degree of a case in the causal factor should be associated with a *larger* membership value in an outcome.

A graphical illustration of determining necessary and sufficient conditions can be given by graphing the degree of membership in a hypercube in which a set is no longer constrained to be located at one of the 'crisp' vertices. Figure 10.2 shows a hypothetical relationship between lean buffers and the causal outcome of high performance. Lean buffers satisfies the axiomatic definition of a necessary condition, because all cases have larger membership degrees in it than in the causal outcome.

Figure 10.3(a) portrays the analysis of sufficiency. Since the membership value in work teams uniformly is less than the membership degree in the causal outcome for all cases, we conclude that lean buffers is sufficient. Figure 10.3(b) illustrates the same analysis for a configuration of two factors (lean buffers and work teams). Since we are looking at their joint effect (or intersection), we take the minimum of each case's membership value in these two factors. The minimum effectively moves the distribution of dots to the left, except for the unlikely case that the membership values in the two causal factors are the same.

(a) Single sufficient cause

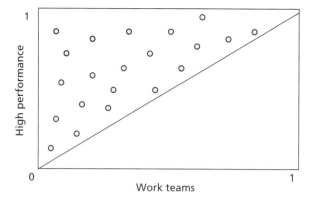

(b) Two sufficient causes

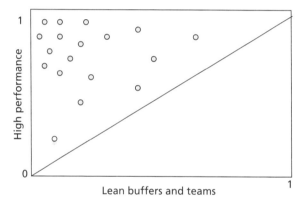

Figure 10.3. Plot of fuzzy relationship of sufficient condition and causal effect

It is obvious that a given factor cannot be both sufficient and necessary, except for the cases when the causal factor and causal outcome share the same membership values. Empirically, we expect that a causal factor or configuration will not be found only above or below the diagonal. The statistical formula to calculate the z-score, as given above, permits an assessment of the statistical significance of necessity and sufficiency. Moreover, since, for fuzzy set logic, every case has a membership value in a configuration, the problems of small sample size are much less severe than for crisp logic.

The calculation of the z-score requires the researcher to state a benchmark. Here the linguistic hedge suggests the choice of the benchmark proportionality. To ask, for example, if the observed proportion is significantly greater than 'usually necessary' indicates a benchmark of 0.65. A benchmark of 'very necessary' implies a value slightly greater than 0.7 benchmark. (The linguistic hedge of 'very' is mathematically equivalent to squaring the membership value, as discussed earlier; the square of 0.71 is approximately 0.5, the cognitive anchor where a member is maximally more or less a member of the set of 'very necessary' causes. We use the value of 0.65 in the following analysis.) Whereas these benchmarks may seem arbitrary (but no more arbitrary than the conventions governing questionnaire scaling such as a Cronbach alpha or significance tests), sensitivity analysis around the benchmark easily provides a way to assess robustness. In addition, sensitivity of measurement error can be examined by adjusting the diagonal to accept errors that differ by a stated percentage off the diagonal.

The determination of fuzzy sets proceeds, then, by statistically identifying necessary causes. Cases that reveal zero membership in the necessary causes are eliminated (by definition, they cannot satisfy the logical condition of necessity). Sufficient causes are then found by identifying causal configurations that statistically satisfy the requirement that their membership values are less than the causal outcome.[10] This analysis generates then a listing, or union, of sufficient configurations, conditioned on the initial identification of necessary causes. To achieve a global assessment of the statistical strength of the analysis, a membership score in the sufficient configurations for each case can be calculated. The comparison of this membership degree against the observed membership in the causal outcome serves to generate a test statistic to determine the significance of the classification success of the method.

Any cause that is individually sufficient is also sufficient jointly. (See Appendix.) Necessity of one cause does not mean, however, that two necessary causes are jointly necessary. However, any jointly necessary conditions are also individually necessary. It is thus justified to apply rules of Boolean absorption to fuzzy sets. Since the configuration Ab is a subset of the configuration of A (i.e. Ab is an intersection and hence a subset of A), the union of two configurations Ab and A logically implies that x will have a membership value equal to its membership value in A. Thus, $Ab + A$ logically reduces to A.

For example, the statement that tall men must shave can be absorbed into the statement men must shave. To a great extent, this rule captures the meaning of a radial category. Peripheral members are absorbed into more basic representations of the category.

However, the rule of Boolean reduction does not apply. Since $(B + b)$ equals $\max(B, b)$ and not 1—as in crisp logic, the crisp law of complements does not hold and $Ab + AB$ does not reduce further. Fuzzy set analysis consequently loses some of the logical sharpness of the crisp method, since configurations do not easily reduce to more general and simpler causal factors.

This loss of sharpness is compensated partly by the statistical analysis that tests each configuration for significance. Since all cases (e.g. auto plants) are members *to some degree* in each configuration, each configuration has a sample size equal to the number of all plants in the sample.[11] This property greatly facilitates the application of statistical methods, as described above. The configurations that pass significance can then be minimized by the absorption rule that applies to both crisp and fuzzy sets.

The final step of the analysis then assigns cases to configurations by choosing the maximum membership value of that case in the minimized configurations. For example, an analysis of auto plant productivity might find that technology and human resource management constitute one configuration and technology and high scale form another. A given plant has a membership score of 0.4 in the first and 0.7 in the second (each score is derived by taking the intersection, or minimum, of the two practices constituting that configuration). The assignment rule would then assign this plant to the second configuration.

This reduction can obviously assign plants that are bad examples of a particular configuration. It makes little sense, for example, to claim that a given plant is characterized by high performance work practices when it belongs weakly to every attribute set that defines this configuration. This possibility conforms with a prototype theory of classifications whereby an ostrich is bad example of a bird. It also reflects a methodological weakness in fuzzy sets insofar as operations of intersections can assign members to classes that are not commonsensical. Lazarfeld (1937) offers, as noted before, a proposed solution to this type of problem by ruling out implausible combinations. (This intervention is broadly standard in statistical methodologies, such as in confirmatory factor analysis or model specification.)

In a similar fashion, we propose to allow for the use of commonsense and theoretical intervention in two forms. First, in the interpretation of the configurations, we look at the 'better' prototypical examples, that is, those cases that score 0.5 or more in a configuration. Second, to reduce the overall solution space, we check the *simplifying assumptions* that eliminate configurations that grossly violate theoretical and commonsensical relationships. As in the case of Boolean comparative analysis, the fuzzy set methodology faces the problem of limited diversity. Consider Figure 10.1 that provides a two dimensional representation of operations on fuzzy sets. Imagine that the graph is divided into four quadrants from each of the midpoints at 0.5. The corners represent the crisp sets, and in this way, each quadrant is associated with a given crisp configuration. Limited diversity arises when there is no case in a quadrant. For Boolean analysis, limited diversity is obvious, as no case will show the configuration.

For fuzzy sets, since all cases have membership in all configurations, it is necessary to be especially careful to check that a causal configuration is not derived from an assumption that is not strongly justified by the empirical data.

This verification is conducted by enumerating all the crisp sets and identifying those that have no cases with membership values greater than 0.5. This list can be used to isolate the combinations of factors for which there is little empirical evidence. This then poses the question if these combinations, that Ragin (2000) labels simplifying assumptions, are justified to play a role in deriving the minimized configurations. To check robustness, the researcher can check if these assumptions have been incorporated into the results of the sufficiency analysis. If this is the case, the researcher can either eliminate the simplifying assumption, which may change the results, or decide for theoretical reasons that the assumption should be retained. Both of these strategies have analogues in other methods. Econometrics often infers from the absence of a condition that decision makers did not choose this configuration because it was not profit maximizing. This provides information and can be used in the estimations (see Athey and Stern 1999 for an example). The second strategy is more common and arises in multiple variable regressions when one factor is not significant, but contributes to the overall estimation. An advantage with the Boolean and fuzzy set methodologies is that the researcher can explicitly identify the simplifying assumptions used in the minimization and decide, based on theory or field knowledge, if they should be eliminated or retained.

SAMPLE AND VARIABLES

We apply the technique of fuzzy sets to identify bundles, or complementary practices, among technical and organizational factors affecting manufacturing performance in the world auto industry. The International Assembly Plant Study was sponsored by the International Motor Vehicle Program (IMVP) at M.I.T. Ninety assembly plants were contacted, representing 24 producers in 16 countries, and approximately 60 percent of total assembly plant capacity worldwide. Survey responses were received from 70 plants during 1989 and early 1990. These plants were divided into 'volume' and 'luxury' categories (the latter defined as plants producing automobiles with a 1989 US base price of over USD 23,000), on the assumption that the production systems for these product types might differ substantially. This paper includes data from the 62 volume plants, whose surveys were more complete; because of missing data, only 57 plants are used for productivity and 45 for quality. The actual samples used in the logical analysis are 56 and 44, respectively, as the analysis assigns one plant in each sample a zero membership in the outcome and consequently eliminates it from the analysis.

Table 10.1 lists the distribution of the 62 volume plants by regional category. The proportion of plants in different regions corresponds closely to the

Table 10.1. Composition of Volume Assembly Plant Sample

Regional category	*n*
Japan (J/J)	8
Japanese-parent plants in North America (J/NA)	4
US-parent plants in North America (US/NA)	14
Europe (All/E)	19
New Entrants, including East Asia, Mexico Brazil (All/NE)	11
Australia (All/Aus)	6
Total	**62**

Source: International Assembly Plant Study, MacDuffie (1995).

proportion of worldwide production volume associated with those regions, with a slight under-representation of Japanese plants in Japan and overrepresentation of New Entrant and Australian plants, whose volume is low. Plants were chosen to achieve a balanced distribution across regions and companies, and to reflect a range of performance within each participating company, minimizing the potential for selectivity bias.

QUESTIONNAIRE ADMINISTRATION AND DATA COLLECTION

Questionnaires were sent to a contact person, often the plant manager, who distributed different sections to the appropriate departmental manager or staff group. Plants and companies were guaranteed complete confidentiality and, in return for their participation, received a feedback report comparing their responses with mean scores for different regions. All 90 plants that were contacted were visited by one of the researchers between 1987 and 1990. Early visits provided the field observations that became the foundation of the assembly plant questionnaire. Some of these plants were used to pilot the questionnaire as well. For the 70 plants that returned a questionnaire, the visit often followed receipt of the questionnaire, providing an opportunity to fill in missing data, clarify responses that were unclear or not internally consistent, and carry out interviews to aid the later interpretation of data analyzes. When the visit preceded receipt of a questionnaire, this same follow-up process to improve data accuracy was carried out via phone and fax. We calculate membership degrees for both productivity and quality measures from the sample of plants for which there are usable outcome data. Some cases eliminated later due to missing data for the independent variables anchored the performance scaling at these extreme values; thus the ultimate membership scores for performance do not necessarily vary from 0 to 1.

As the measures are described in detailed in MacDuffie (1995), we supply only brief descriptions here.

MEASURES: DEPENDENT VARIABLES

Productivity

Productivity is defined as the hours of actual working effort required to build a vehicle at a given assembly plant, adjusted for comparability across plants by a methodology developed by Krafcik (1988). The productivity methodology focuses on a set of standard activities that are common across all plants in the survey, to control for differences in vertical integration. Since a large vehicle requires more effort to assemble than a small vehicle, adjustments are made to standardize for vehicle size. Adjustments are also made to standardize for the number of welds, which differs across designs and therefore affects headcount in the body shop.

This scale was fit to a [0,1] interval. Then, because high labor hours per vehicle indicates low productivity, we took the complement (i.e. subtracted the membership degree from 1) to create a reverse scale that indicates monotonic increases in productivity.

Quality

The quality measure is derived from the 1989 survey of new car buyers in the US, carried out by J.D. Power. The variable measures the number of defects per 100 vehicles. It is adjusted to reflect only those defects that an assembly plant can affect, in other words omitting defects related to the engine or transmission, while emphasizing defects related to the fit and finish of body panels, paint quality, and the integrity of electrical connections (Krafcik 1988). As with productivity, by taking the complement, we reverse scaled this measure.

MEASURES: INDEPENDENT VARIABLES[12]

Production Organization Measures

To measure the organizational logic of lean vs. mass production systems, three component indices were constructed—use of buffers, work systems, and HRM policies. The variables included in these indices reflect choices, based on fieldwork, about what items to include in the assembly plant questionnaire as well as statistical tests aimed at boosting the internal reliability of each index. Reliability tests are reported in MacDuffie (1995).

Each of the three component indices is composed of multiple variables, described below. All variables are standardized by conversion to z-scores before being additively combined to form indices. Each variable in an index receives equal weight, because there was no clear conceptual basis for assigning differential weights. For ease of interpretation, a linear transformation is applied to the summed z-scores for each component index, such that 0 is the plant with the lowest score in the sample and 100 is the plant with the highest score. The validation of these indices is described in the next section.

1. *Use of buffers*: This index measures a set of production practices that are indicative of overall production philosophy with respect to buffers (e.g. incoming and work-in-process inventory). A high score on this index signifies a minimal buffer 'lean production' approach, and a low score, a large buffer 'mass production' approach. It consists of three items.

2. *Work systems*: This index captures how work is organized, in terms of both formal work structures and the allocation of work responsibilities, and the participation of employees in production-related problem-solving activity. A low score for this variable indicates a work system with a narrow division of labor that is 'specializing' in orientation, and a high score indicates a 'multiskilling' orientation.

3. *HRM policies*: This index measures a set of policies that affects the 'psychological contract' between the employee and the organization, and hence employee motivation and commitment. A low score for this variable indicates a 'low commitment' set of HRM policies and a high score indicates 'high commitment' policies.

CONTROL VARIABLES

The idea of control variables is standard in regression analysis to eliminate potential influences in non-experimental settings. For Boolean or fuzzy set analysis, they pose added dimensionality that can quickly complicate the logical inferences, especially for small data sets. We chose, therefore, to work with three control variables to capture technology, scale, and model age; to explore robustness, we also added part complexity.

Technology (Automation)

The main technology variable, the automated percentage of direct production steps, captures the level of both flexible and fixed automation. For each functional area, a proxy measure for direct production activities was developed; see MacDuffie (1995) for details. Then a weighted average level of automation for the plant was calculated, based on the amount of direct labor each functional area requires in an average unautomated plant.

Table 10.2. Descriptive Statistics

Variable	Mean	Standard deviation	Pearson correlation						
			PROD	SCALE	WORK	BUFF	HRM	AGE	TECH
PROD	0.5512	0.2208	1.000	0.306*	0.587**	0.502**	0.529**	0.558**	0.685**
SCALE	0.2289	0.1841	0.306*	1.000	0.222	0.238	0.188	0.137	0.514**
WORK	0.2202	0.2712	0.587**	0.222	1.000	0.651**	0.652**	0.304*	0.292*
BUFF	0.4698	0.2655	0.502**	0.238	0.651**	1.000	0.586**	0.542**	0.382**
HRM	0.3388	0.3192	0.529**	0.188	0.652**	0.586**	1.000	0.350**	0.461**
AGE	0.7293	0.2108	0.558**	0.137	0.304*	0.542**	0.350**	1.000	0.525**
TECH	0.6626	0.2008	0.685**	0.514**	0.292*	0.382**	0.461**	0.525**	1.000

Notes: * Correlation is significant at the 0.05 level ($p < 0.05$); ** Correlation is significant at the 0.01 level ($p < 0.01$). As Quality reduces the size of the data set, we do not include the descriptive statistics for it here. They are available on request from the authors.

Scale

This is defined as the average number of vehicles built during a standard, non-overtime day, adjusted for capacity utilization. Overtime is not included in either production levels or hours worked, which adjusts for overcapacity situations.

Model Design Age

This is defined as the weighted average number of years since a major model change introduction for each of the products currently being built at each plant. This measure is a partial proxy for manufacturability in the assembly area, under the assumption that products designed more recently are more likely than older products to have been conceived with ease of assembly in mind. While older designs, by moving down the learning curve, could be associated with fewer hours per car, most evidence suggests that the benefits of more manufacturable designs outweigh learning curve gains (Womack et al. 1990).

Parts Complexity

This measure is compiled from two subgroups of variables: parts or component variation and factors influencing the logistics of material and parts flow and the administrative/coordination requirements for dealing with suppliers. All these variables are scored on a 1–6 scale, where 1 is the lowest and 6 the highest complexity level. They are additively combined and the resulting index is rescaled from 0 to 100, as above.

Table 10.2 contains descriptive statistics for the variables used here. Means are based on the rescaling of each variable from 0 to 1, as required by fuzzy set analysis. The mean for productivity as transformed is roughly centered in the middle of this distribution. The control variable means reflect that the predominance of plants have relatively high levels of automation and relatively young product designs. The mean for scale is relatively low because the largest plant, scored as 1, is an extreme outlier in terms of size; we discuss the effects of this outlier on the analysis below. Finally, means for the indices linked to lean production reveal that the use of lean buffers is most common in this sample, with a mean near 0.5, while the means for both the HRM and work systems indices are considerably lower.

As Table 10.2 also shows, both the variables capturing lean production (WORK, BUFF, HRM) and the control variables (SCALE, AGE, TECH) are significantly correlated with productivity. Indeed, the weakest correlation is with scale, suggesting that economies of scale are not such a dominant influence on labor productivity in this setting as it commonly supposed. Correlations among the three indices of lean production are also quite high, as the conceptualization of this overall production system would suggest. While plants with high scores for lean practices also tend to be highly automated and have younger products, they are not necessarily large; the correlations between the three production organization indices and scale are not significant. Scale and technology are strongly correlated, however, as both capture different aspects of capital investment at a given plant.

ANALYSIS OF CASES

Fuzzy set methodology is a classifier technique that combines logic with the researchers' knowledge of the terrain. The search for the fuzzy sets of complementary activities involves first an analysis of necessity, then of sufficiency. If the analysis reveals any necessary conditions, this condition then appears in all configurations that pass the sufficiency test. We first calculate all $3^n - 1$ combinations for the variables. These variables include the controls (i.e., scale, technology, model age) and the organizational factors (i.e. new work practices, advanced human resource management practices, and lean buffers.) There are consequently 728 causal combinations to test. The test statistic for sufficiency compares the proportion of the times that the minimal value of a configuration (defined by the intersection operator) is less the value of the outcome (productivity or quality) against some benchmark. We use .65 as the threshold for sufficiency, as this hurdle resulted in the most parsimonious results. The causal combinations that pass this test are then submitted to an 'absorption' algorithm to derive the minimal configuration.

We made two decisions to arrive at robust solutions. First, we squared the measures for productivity and quality. Squaring serves to accentuate the hedge 'very,' as noted earlier, and served to dissipate the bunching of outcome

Table 10.3. Fuzzy-Set Analysis of Complements: Results for Productivity (Number of cases: 56)

Variable	N cause outcome	Observed proportion	z	p
(a) Necessary Cause Analysis				
scale	48	0.86	3.11	0.001*
SCALE	6	0.11		
work	43	0.77	1.71	0.004
WORK	7	0.13		
buffers	31	0.55		
BUFFERS	31	0.55		
hrm	40	0.71	0.87	0.193
HRM	18	0.32		
age	12	0.021		
AGE	50	0.89	3.67	0.000*
technology	20	0.36		
TECHNOLOGY	49	0.88	3.39	0.000*
(b) Sufficient Cause Analysis*				
scale, HRM, AGE, TECHNOLOGY +				
scale, WORK, BUFFERS, AGE, TECHNOLOGY +				
scale, BUFFERS, hrm, AGE, TECHNOLOGY				
Fit Measure: 0.822				

Notes: *(Exclusion of simplifying assumptions: scale, WORK, buffers, hrm, AGE, TECHNOLOGY); test proportion: 0.65; significance level: < 0.01; fuzzy adjustment: 0.05.

variables. A plant with a high productivity score is 'very' productive. Second, we were sensitive to the potential that the inferential engine by which all permutations are taken and then tested for necessity and sufficiency might lead to outcomes that have low empirical and theoretical support. Thus, for a configuration evaluated as sufficient, we would like to verify that the conclusion was not reached by an inference from assuming a configuration to be empirically valid when the actual support is low. This error arises from the problem of limited diversity discussed earlier. We made then the following decision rule: for all simplifying assumptions (configurations for which the empirical support is weak), if two out of three production organization indices (WORK, HRM, BUFFERS,) were in a not-condition, we rejected this simplifying assumption and did not allow it to contribute to logical absorption. This decision rule resulted in a more parsimonious and robust set of solutions. We discuss the applications of this rule below.

Productivity Analysis

Table 10.3 provides the baseline test for productivity-squared that includes the indices of buffers, work practices, and HRM practices as well as controls for scale of production, level of automation, and average age of the models being assembled. Recall that intersection is represented by multiplication (AB), whereas union is represented by $(A + B)$. The necessary cause analysis indicates three necessary conditions ($p < 0.01$): not-scale, a low (young) product age, and a high level of automation. (The statistical test is one-tail, as we do not care about cases that fall below the benchmark.) While this result was as expected for product age and automation, it seemed unusual to find not-scale, in other words a relatively low level of daily production, to be associated with higher labor productivity, i.e. fewer hours per vehicle. After all, the auto industry is generally regarded as the prototypical example of economies of scale.

Upon investigation, we found that the division of the sample into scale and not-scale categories was heavily influenced by the presence of a single outlier case. This plant, the largest in the world at that point in time, had a daily level of production more than four times the sample mean and 30 percent more than the second highest volume plant. This plant was also relatively inefficient, particularly in relation to its supposed scale advantage; it can in many ways be viewed as a prime example of the diseconomies of scale. Because of this outlier, the classification procedure is assigning membership in the set of 'extremely large' and 'not extremely large' plants. 'Not-scale' as a necessary condition contains nearly 90 percent of the sample, all plants with scores above 0.5 in this set of 'not extremely large' plants. Besides the outlier plant, five other plants have scores of above 0.5 in the 'extremely large plant' category and hence don't meet the necessary condition of 'not scale.' It is worth noting that many plants in the 'not-scale' subset are well above any threshold of minimum efficient scale, and operate with a production volume well above the world average; these are not low-volume plants, they are simply not 'extremely large.'

Exploring Complexity

We have emphasized that a primary advantage of Boolean or fuzzy analysis is the exploration of the effects of missing combinations, or combinations of low probability. We examined the simplifying assumptions involved in the sufficiency analysis. One such assumption included 'not' conditions for two of the three indices of production organization, specifically not-buffers and not-HRM. According to this assumption, highly productive plants were associated neither with low levels of buffers (or inventory, repair space, utility workers) nor with high levels of commitment-inducing human resource management practices. Based on prior analyzes of this data set and extensive fieldwork at these plants, we concluded that this particular assumption (and following our decision rule, any assumption that negated two or more of the production organization indices) was implausible, and we excluded it. After this exclusion, the sufficiency analysis for productivity generates three causal combinations.

The second configuration (not-scale, WORK, BUFF, AGE, TECHNOL-OGY) contains six plants, five of which surpass the threshold value of 0.5. These plants are all located in Japan and most closely resemble the lean production ideal type. While their highest sufficiency score is in this configuration, four of the five plants also have a sufficiency score greater than 0.5 in the previous configuration. This suggests that all three of the production indices (HRM, WORK, and BUFF) are identified as sufficiency conditions for being a high productive plant in this grouping, beyond the necessary conditions of high automation levels and low product age. These results are very supportive of the consensual understanding of Japanese high performance work systems.

The third configuration (not-scale, BUFF, hrm, AGE, TECHNOLOGY) contains 33 plants and is the most geographically diverse group, ranging from the US and Europe to Australia to Brazil, Taiwan, and Korea; it includes no Japanese plants or transplants. Only six of these plants surpass the 0.5 threshold. What characterizes these six plants is that they have pursued productivity through a different adaptation of the lean production model, namely a heavy emphasis on the reduction of buffers and a minimal emphasis on 'high commitment' HRM practices or new work practices. The other plants in this category have low scores on various of these variables. Some have very low levels of automation, others build very old product designs, and many have very large buffers of inventory (which generates a low score on BUFF). Any of these could be the primary reason that these 27 cases are not identified in the set of 'very productive' plants. These non-productive characteristics also frequently overlap; many of the plants in new entrant countries have low automation, old product designs, and a production system reliant on large buffers.

The national diversity of these grouping also suggests two interpretations. The first is that the historical point in time when these surveys were collected reflected an incomplete diffusion. This interpretation is in line with the finding of the predominance of Japanese plants in the first and second configurations that satisfy the 0.5 hurdle. The second, and related interpretation, is that plants in other countries were still experimenting in the context of different national environments. Practices such as those related to teams were anathema to nations, as they challenged both union and firm control over the workplace. It is not surprising in this light that the third group shows a groping for new combinations that did not lead, however, to high productivity.

We undertook one sensitivity analysis to test the effect of choosing a 0.5 threshold for membership in a causal configuration. Changing the threshold to 0.4 adds two plants to the first configuration, no plants to the second configuration, and nine plants to the third configuration. These plants did not alter the substantive interpretation of the categories. The difference between applying a membership threshold of 0.4 versus 0.5 appears to be a matter of degree and not of kind. Plants with sufficiency scores above 0.5 are simply stronger members of the set of very productive plants. Therefore, we continue, in subsequent analyzes, to apply 0.5 as the threshold for membership in a configuration.

Table 10.4. Robustness Test for Productivity by Varying N (Number of Cases: 43)

Sufficient cause analysis shown only:*

scale, HRM, AGE, TECHNOLOGY +
scale, WORK, BUFFERS, AGE, TECHNOLOGY +
scale, BUFFERS, hrm, AGE, TECHNOLOGY

Fit Measure: 0822

Notes: *(Exclusion of simplifying assumptions: scale, WORK, buffers, hrm, AGE, TECHNOLOGY); test proportion: 0.65; significance level: < 0.01; fuzzy adjustment: 0.05.

QUALITY ANALYSIS

In order to identify high performance plants (defined as plants that are highly productive and have high quality), we turn next to the analysis of quality. Because we have only data on quality for 43 plants, we report in Table 10.4 the productivity analysis for this smaller subset to test for robustness. The necessary and sufficient conditions are unchanged; indeed, the fit measure is identical. This smaller sample is used for the remaining analyzes.

The results for the necessary conditions—which are not reported here—are the same as for productivity, although the significance level for the technology variable is somewhat weaker ($p < 0.05$ rather than $p < 0.01$). This is consistent with earlier analyzes (MacDuffie 1995) which found automation level was not strongly correlated with quality—even though most high quality plants were highly automated, many high automation plants had quite poor quality. We thus treat scale as a necessary condition, and let technology be determined by the sufficiency tests.

Table 10.5. Results for High Performance Systems: Fuzzy-Set Analysis of Quality and Performance (Number of cases: 43)

Sufficient cause analysis shown only*:

scale, WORK, BUFFERS, AGE +
scale, WORK, HRM, AGE +
scale, BUFFERS, HRM, AGE +
scale, work, HRM, AGE, TECHNOLOGY +
scale, buffers, HRM, AGE, TECHNOLOGY

Fit measure: 0.772

Notes: *(Exclusion of simplifying assumptions: scale, WORK, buffers, hrm, AGE, TECHNOLOGY; scale, work, buffers, HRM, AGE, TECHNOLOGY; scale, WORK, buffers, hrm, AGE, TECHNOLOGY); test proportion: 0.65; significance level: < 0.01; fuzzy adjustment: 0.05.

Exploring Complexity

For the sufficiency analysis given in Table 10.5, we excluded three simplifying assumptions, following our decision rule regarding the infeasibility of any such assumption in which two out of three production organization indices (WORK, HRM, BUFFERS,) were in a not-condition. Five causal configurations result from this analysis. The first configuration consists of a combination of lean buffers and work-related practices, such as problem solving. The next two configurations each contain two organization indices combined in different ways (WORK BUFFERS, WORK HRM, and BUFFERS HRM) along with the necessary conditions. The final two configurations both contain HRM; 'not-work' is also included in the fourth configuration and 'not buffers' in the fifth configuration. As with productivity, this analysis reveals differences in the extent to which plants with strong membership in the category of high-performing plants have implemented certain of the production organization policies of lean production. Whereas for productivity, plants with minimal buffers but more traditional HRM policies achieved respectable performance, the pattern for quality differs. Here it is high-commitment HRM policies that are most consistently associated with high level of quality performance; HRM appears in four of the five configurations. It is not a necessary condition because one configuration exists for plants for which WORK and BUFFERS are sufficient to predict quality without HRM being causally relevant.

HIGH PERFORMANCE ANALYSIS

We defined earlier high performance plants as those producing quality autos at high levels of efficiency. We took therefore the intersection (i.e. the minimum) of productivity and quality to form a single outcome called high performance. In Table 10.6, we examine plants that achieve high performance in both productivity and quality, that is, the 'high-performance system' plants. The same three necessary conditions hold, with a significance level of $p < 0.01$ for TECHNOLOGY once again. We exclude only one simplifying assumption here, the same assumption identified in the productivity analysis.

This analysis identifies four causal configurations in the sample of 43 plants for which we have both productivity and quality data. Using the threshold of 0.5, we find only 12 plants are strong members of this category of high-performance plants. There are two plants in the first configuration, six plants in the second configuration, four plants in the third configuration, and none in the fourth configuration. This reduction in the number of plants is not surprising. Many plants are able to maximize either productivity or quality by trading off against the other outcome, but only the highest performing plants are able to achieve both productivity and quality simultaneously.

Table 10.6. Robustness Results for High Performance Systems by Varying Excluding Assumptions (Number of cases: 43)

Sufficient cause analysis shown only:*

scale, WORK, BUFFERS, AGE, TECHNOLOGY +
scale, work, HRM, AGE, TECHNOLOGY +
scale, WORK, HRM, AGE, TECHNOLOGY +
scale, buffers, HRM, AGE, TECHNOLOGY

Fit Measure: 0.766

Notes: *(Exclusion of simplifying assumptions: scale, WORK, buffers, hrm, AGE, TECHNOLOGY); test proportion: 0.65; significance level: < 0.01; fuzzy adjustment: 0.05.

There is not a high level of differentiation in performance among the configurations in this analysis. Some plants have identical membership scores in two of the three configurations; we treat these plants are members of both configurations in the performance analyzes below. Still other plants have their highest membership score in one configuration, but have a membership score above the 0.5 threshold in another configuration, indicating a strong overlap in the influence of the sufficient conditions across these configurations.

The first configuration (not-scale, WORK, BUFFERS, AGE, TECHNOLOGY) contains six plants located in Japan. Four of these plants have identical scores for the third configuration (not-scale, WORK, HRM, AGE, TECHNOLOGY), and the other two also have strong membership (score > 0.5) in the third configuration. The first four plants confirm quite closely to the lean production ideal type. Their identical scores across these configurations reinforces the conceptual argument about mutual interdependence across the three aspects of production organization measured here, and the positive consequences of this interdependence for simultaneous achievement of high productivity and high quality. In contrast, the latter two plants are distinguished by a somewhat lower adherence to commitment-inducing HRM policies in relation to plants in the other two configurations.

The second configuration (not-scale, work, HRM, AGE, TECHNOLOGY) contains six plants that were all included in the first configuration of the productivity analysis (see Table 10.3). Four of these plants are Japanese transplants located in North America, and the other two are located in Mexico and Korea; the latter two also manufacture autos of Japanese design. In relation to the other two configurations, these plants have very high scores on HRM but lower scores on WORK and BUFFERS because they had only partially implemented on-line/off-line work team activities and just-in-time inventory policies at this point in time. For the Japanese transplants, these scores reflect not only the relatively young age of these plants but also the decision to make small group activities more voluntary than in Japan, and the necessity of stocking higher levels of inventory given the much greater geographical dispersion of the supply chain in the US.

Table 10.7. Performance Means for Productivity Configurations

Configuration	Productivity (hours per vehicle)
Group 1 (scale, HRM, AGE, TECH) threshold = 0.5	26.5
Group 2 (scale, WORK, BUFF, AGE, TECH) threshold = 0.5	17.5
Group 3 (scale, BUFF, hrm, AGE, TECH) threshold = 0.5	31.4

The presence of plants in Mexico and Korea in this category of 'high performance' plants suggests that product design may play some role in a plant's performance level, since superior design-for-manufacturability can make assembly both more efficient and less vulnerable to defects. But it also suggests that many of the production organization policies can be transferred successfully to settings in emerging economies, where automation levels are typically quite low. In such plants, high levels of worker training and high levels of selectivity for jobs viewed as quite desirable, in terms of pay, benefits, and job security, helps compensate for the generally lower level of education among the workforce.

The third configuration (not-scale, WORK, HRM, AGE, TECHNOLOGY), as mentioned above, contains four Japanese plants that are also members (with identical scores) of the first configuration. In contrast, the fourth configuration (not-scale, not-buffers, HRM, AGE, TECHNOLOGY) contains no plants with scores above 0.5, suggesting that plants with relatively large buffer stocks and only modest adoption of flexible work practices are not capable of achieving membership in the category of 'high performance system' plants, even if their use of commitment-inducing HRM policies is extremely high.

In Figure 10.4, we graph the relationship between the observed (actual) high performance of a plant and the maximum value the plant takes in any of the four configurations. Given the classification system that seeks to align configurations and performance, it is not surprising the scores lie along the diagonal. The interesting aspect of the figure is the identification of how few plants and their associated best configuration are prototypes of high performance.

Tables 10.7 and 10.8 examine the performance means for the causal configurations identified in the productivity (Table 10.3) and 'high performance system' (Table 10.6) analyzes. For productivity, the second configuration (not-scale, WORK, BUFFERS, AGE, TECHNOLOGY) has the best average labor hours per vehicle (17.5); plants in the other configurations require 51 percent and 80 percent more hours per vehicle, on average. The combined analysis of 'high performance systems' given in Table 10.8 (which corresponds to Table 10.6 and to Figure 10.4), there is much less difference across the

(a) Actual versus predicted productivity

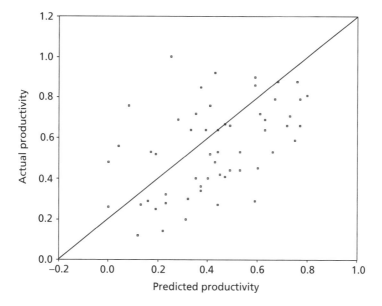

(b) Actual versus estimated high performance

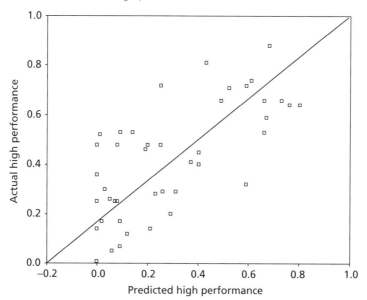

Figure 10.4. Scatter plot of actual and predicted maximum membership value

Table 10.8. Performance Means for 'High Performance' (Productivity *and* Quality) Configurations

Configuration	Productivity (hours per vehicle)	Quality (defects per 100 vehicles)
Group 1 (scale, WORK, BUFF, AGE, TECH) threshold = 0.5	18.9	53.5
Group 2 (scale, work, HRM, AGE, TECH) threshold = 0.5	24.4	43.2
Group 3 (scale, WORK, HRM, AGE, TECH) threshold = 0.5	19.1	44.1

configurations. The four Japanese plants that possess membership in configurations one and three have the best combined performance, at an average of 19.1 hours per vehicle and 44 defects per 100 vehicles; by virtue of this combined membership, we know that they have high scores on WORK, HRM, and BUFFERS. Consistent with the earlier analyzes, the configuration with the best quality performance (#2, at 43.2 defects per 100 vehicles) features high scores on HRM, while the configuration with the best productivity performance (#1, at 18.9 hours per vehicle) features high scores on WORK and BUFFERS.

Thus while there is no one single configuration of production characteristics associated with 'high performance systems,' lean production achieves performance advantages through the complementary interactions across two of three key areas of production organization: the management of buffers, the organization of work, and the human resource. These policies yield high levels of skill and flexibility in the workforce and induce high levels of performance. However, these results do not confirm the three-way interaction associated with the prototype of complementarities among all three dimensions of a production organization.

Discussion

The above results present a cross-section in the diffusion of practices that began in Japan.[13] High performance systems are generally associated with Japanese plants located in Japan or outside. We did not find that all three work practices were complements associated with high performance, but we did find that two configurations of two of these three practices were complementary. The diffusion interpretation is further suggested by the plants outside of Japan that evidenced a greater variability in the degree to which they implemented these practices. Generally, higher performance plants were those that more successfully emulated 'Toyotaism,' that is the complementary implementation of these practices.

Comparing these results to MacDuffie (1995), we can identify a few important differences in methodological treatments and conclusions. Like the MacDuffie analysis, the fuzzy set methodology rejects a three-way interaction (though the latter approach induces this result simultaneously for productivity and quality). The set theoretic treatment of the cases allows configurations to be identified rather than a subset tested for the statistical significant of multiplicative interactions; see Ichinowski et al. (1997). Thus, we can see more clearly why, for example, that MacDuffie's tests of complementarities to achieve high quality were more problematic; clearly the interactions among practices are highly complex. We are also easily able to define high performance as the intersection of high productivity and high quality, and avoid separate tests for each. Finally, the analysis allows for an exploration of assumptions and the exploration of combinations (even if membership may be weak).

That a few combinations of practices can be assigned causality for the achievement of high performance systems across many countries suggests a transition period of experimentation, whereby diversity in configurations— whether planned or not—permitted an exploration of practices, to decouple old practices and recouple new ones. It is an important question, which these single cross-section data cannot answer, whether this transition lead to a convergence in a single set of best practice or in competing prototypes. We did identify one 'universalistic' element of small scale as a necessary condition (see earlier discussion regarding the topology of Delery and Doty 1996); it is possible that in times of transition, smaller factories provide better experimental conditions. For this cross-section, we did not however find a single configuration, but several associated with high performance. In large part, these findings of multiple paths to a similar outcome restate the idea of 'equifinality' proposed by Miles and Snow (1978). It will take a time series to sort out whether this multiple conjunctural causation is the product of multiple equilibria, multiple environments, or a snapshot in a historical process yet to converge to a best configuration.

Conclusion

The methodological treatment of complexity by fuzzy inference permits a cautious assignment of causal credit. In our application, we analyze an example where performance itself is two-dimensional (productivity and quality). We provide a method—the intersection of the two solutions—to show how causal assignment to configurations is still possible. This analysis is directly primarily at the understanding of the choice of capabilities, as we held the product market constant across the plants. Obviously, the full combination of capabilities and product market positioning requires a fuller treatment of a firm's strategic decisions.

The world does not generate enough experimentation to sort through all causal claims; the attribution of strategies or any entity to particular categories can only be made with fuzzy membership claims. Fuzzy set logic expresses this fundamental limitation on possible inferences. For even if we had full substantive understandings of the correct choice of strategy in particular environments, the complex interactions observed in practice poses two related problems of assigning membership and causality. The membership problem is, as we have seen, how to identify correctly the match between strategy and noisy environments. The causal credit problem is how do we know causality when observed or unobserved factors outside the model influence the strategy choice.

Our proposal is to recognize the inherent complexity facing researchers and decision makers and to develop inferential methods of exploration that render explicit the challenge of assigning membership and assigning causal credit. Rather than control for unobserved sources of variation, or lack of variation itself, we propose a systematic treatment of, one, how people (researchers and managers) think about the world through prototypes and, two, how causal relationships can be inferred through reduction and exploration of assumptions. The conclusions to this exercise reflect informed thought experiments about possible worlds through exploratory data analysis. It is this avenue of analyzing worlds that may exist that is the most intriguing aspect of the application of logic to empirical cases. This perspective broadens the analysis from induction for the purpose of asserting general claims towards the disciplined examination of worlds logically possible but empirically and historically unobserved.

☐ APPENDIX 10.1

Define sufficiency as a causal condition that satisfies $\frac{(P-P^*)-^1/_2 N}{\sqrt{pq/N}} \geq z$ where z is distributed by the standard normal distribution.

Proposition

If A and B are individually sufficient causes of Y, then $A \cap B$ is also a sufficient cause.

Proof

Let $\{a^*, y^*\}$ denote the ordered pairs where $a_i = y_i$ for all i pairs. Similarly, $\{b^*, y^*\}$ denotes the pairs where $b_i = y_i$ for all i. These pairs form the diagonal of the two-dimensional space in $R \times R$, as depicted in Figure 10.2. By assumption, both A and

B are sufficient causes for Y. This assumption implies that the proportion of ordered pairs lie above the diagonal satisfies the sufficiency test defined above. To calculate this proportion, we ask whether $\{a_i, y_i\} \geq \{a^*, y^*\}$ and $\{b_i, y_i\} \geq \{b^*, y^*\}$.

Consider the intersection of A and B given by $\{\min(a, b), y\}$.

CASE 1

All ordered pairs $\{a, y\}$ and $\{b, y\}$ lie above the diagonal. If $b < a$, then $\{\min(a, b), y\} = \{b, y\}$. But, since $\{b, y\}$ lies to the left of the diagonal, clearly then $\{a, b\}$ also lies to the left. This argument holds symmetrically for $b > a$, where $\{\min(a, b), y\} = \{a, b\}$. Therefore, all intersections of causes that individually lie to the left of the diagonal also lie jointly to the left.

CASE 2

Similarly, all cases when both a and b lie to the right of the diagonal individually also lie jointly to the right; neither cause is sufficient, nor are they jointly sufficient.

CASE 3

Consequently, the only interesting case is when $a_i > y_i$ and $b_i < y_i$, or $b_i > y_i$ and $a_i < y_i$. As the arguments are symmetrical, arbitrarily let $a_i < y_i$ and $b_i > y_i$. But since $\{\min(a_i^*, b_i), y\} = \{a_i^*, y_i\}$, the intersection $a \cap b$ for any i pairing also lies to the left of the diagonal.

Thus, if we define P_a and P_b as the proportion for the two sufficient causes A and B, it must be true that the intersection $A \cap B$ generates a proportion that is no worse than $\min(P_a, P_b)$, each of which individually satisfies sufficiency.

Note: This logic does not hold symmetrically for necessity. Necessity is defined as ordered pairs that lie below the diagonal in a proportion that satisfies the condition above. Again, only case 3 is interesting. Clearly, if $\{a, y\} < \{a^*, y^*\}$ when $\{b, y\} > \{b^*, y^*\}$, then $\{\min(a, b), y\}$ also fails. It is thus possible that the proportion of $P_{a \cap b}$ can fail to pass the necessity test, even though both P_a and P_b satisfy necessity. However, it can be easily seen that two causes that are jointly necessary are also individually necessary.

Acknowledgments

We would like to acknowledge the financial support of the Reginald H. Jones Center, and to thank the anonymous referees and editor, Mark Fitchman, John Lafkas, Anca Metiu, Richard Nelson, Michael Trick, Arie Schinnar, and participants in seminars at Carnegie Mellon, Columbia University, Ohio State University, Stockholm School of Economics, and the University of Chicago for their comments. Kriss Drass provided critical programming support and we thank him in memoriam for his work on our behalf.

⬚ ENDNOTES

* This chapter is a revised version of B. Kogut, J. P. MacDuffie, and C. Ragin (2004) *European Management Review*, 1: 114–31.

1. Activity analysis in operations research had long noted the problem of complements and the problem posed to optimization. A literature that addressed this type of questioning is 'contingency theory'; see Miller (1996), and Ferguson and Ketchen (1999) for recent statements. (We thank a referee for these suggestions.) Recent articles using case or simulations are Levinthal (1997); Rivkin (2000); and Siggelkow (2001).

2. An excellent review is given in Pfeffer (1998) and in Ichinowski and Shaw (2003).

3. This analysis was reported in the working paper Kogut et al. (1999).

4. Hunter and Lafkas (1998) also show a link to wages from the adoption of high perfor- mance systems. See Pil and MacDuffie (1996) for a more recent discussion of bundles and diffusion in the auto industry.

5. Adler (1993) provides an incisive examination of this debate by looking at the General Motors–Toyota joint venture; Sengenberger (1992) reviews some of the reactions of unions in several countries.

6. In Boolean (and fuzzy) algebra, union (logical OR) is indicated with a plus sign (e.g. $A + B$), while intersection (logical AND) is indicated through multiplication (e.g. AB).

7. For $n < 30$, a binomial probability test can be used.

8. We flag that there is a debate regarding prototype theory and fuzzy logic. For example, Lakoff (1973) sees fuzzy logic as insufficient for fully accounting for observed categoriza- tion heuristics.

9. Hampton (1997) summarizes some of the objections from cognitive psychology to fuzzy set definitions of prototypes. Part of these objections consists of problems of taking intersections among nested sets, a classic paradox in set theory. We empirically avoid these operations below.

10. Theoretically, if enough cases lie exactly on the diagonal, a cause can be found to be both sufficient and necessary. For the analysis of necessity, we lose cases whose outcome values are 0.

11. We choose to work with scaled measures rather than each item; obviously, dimensionality would explode otherwise. It is possible to work out fuzzy ways to reduce these items; we relied upon our case knowledge to evaluate the scales.

12. One of the referees asked for the use of firm dummy variables. Treating firm membership would, obviously, explode the dimensionality that we treat. More importantly, as all our data are the plant level and we are holding constant the product market, we prefer to look at firm effects by looking at the membership of the plants in each configuration and then identifying firm, or nationality, effects.

13. As Quality reduces the size of the data set, we do not include the descriptive statistics for it here. They are available on request from the authors.

11 Localization of Knowledge and the Mobility of Engineers in Regional Networks*

with Paul Almeida

Ideas, because they have no material content, should be the least spatially bounded of all economic activities. Being weightless, their transport is limited only by the quality and availability of communication. Since ideas serve both as the inputs and outputs in their own production, their location need be constrained neither by the happenstance of the spatial distribution of raw materials, energy, and labor, nor by that of demand and markets.

Yet, there is good reason to believe that the production of ideas may be, contrary to its economics, prescribed within spatial boundaries. In his comparative analysis of nations, published in *Industry and Trade* (1920), Alfred Marshall noted that economic activity was drawn to regions rich in the 'atmosphere' of ideas. Vibrant regions are those that produce knowledge externalities that denote the spillover of ideas from innovating firms to other firms.[1] The existence of these stable regions implies that these externalities are also localized; that is, they do not spill perfectly over spatial borders.

Yet, the economic treatment of externalities largely assumes them to be 'there'—such as embodied in capital goods—rather than a property that itself deserves to be explained. Knowledge externalities, however, are not simply generated by a given technology. The relationship among firms, universities, star scientists, and engineers strongly conditions the extent by which knowledge spills over.[2]

The importance of regions in economic development has been a persistent, though often lost, theme in economic sociology. Jane Jacobs (1969) put forth an argument that the growth of cities is based on a positive cycle of linkages among industries; the social and economic linkages among diverse activities generate and sustain growth. In a seminal study, Annalee Saxenian

(1994) carried out an ethnography of engineers in Silicon Valley (south of San Francisco) and Route 128 (which rings Boston), and attributed the success of the former to a more robust exchange of ideas among firms.

The relationship between social networks and the spatial localization of knowledge is usually neglected in economic studies on externalities. In an important exception, Jaffe et al. (1993) analyzed patent citation data pertaining to domestic university and corporate patents to test the extent of localization of knowledge spillovers. At three different geographic levels (country, state, and SMSA), they found evidence that patents citations tend to belong to the same geographic area as the originating patent (the patent they cite), even after controlling for the existing concentration of patenting activity. Their findings indicated that knowledge localization exists in the aggregate. Because they did not analyze the variation of localization by region or technology, they left open the issue of whether the properties of technology and institutions determine knowledge externalities.

We hypothesize that variations in regions influence the spatial character of knowledge externalities. This study applies the methodology of Jaffe et al. (1993) to investigate if and why a particular kind of knowledge (i.e. the design of semiconductor devices) is localized to particular geographic communities and *not* to others. A consideration of the sociology of localization addresses two questions previously left on the table, namely: is there variation across economic regions? Does this variation occur because of differences in the sociology of the local labor networks and relations among firms?

Our analysis consists of two stages. In the first stage, we find that the localization of patentable knowledge varies across regions. Semiconductor knowledge in the Silicon Valley and, less so, New York triangle and Southern California tends to be localized but this is not true for other regions. We show through several diagnostic tests that these results are robust.

The second stage of research seeks to show how ideas are transferred through labor markets. By an examination of the mobility paths of patent-holders, we trace the effect of inter-firm mobility on the pattern of patent citations. We show that ideas are spread, in part, by the mobility of patent-holders. This pattern suggests, along the lines of Jacob's (1969) argument, that localized knowledge builds upon cumulative ideas within regional boundaries. We offer the speculation that a driving force for local externalities in semiconductor design is the mobility of people.

Research Setting

The interdependence of technological accumulation and regions has marked the development of the semiconductor industry from its origins. The industry originated from the invention of the first solid state transistor at the laboratories of AT&T (Bell Labs) in New Jersey in 1947. Over the next five decades process and product technology in the semiconductor industry has advanced at a rapid pace while the industry has grown increasingly international.

Within the United States, inter-firm linkages between domestic companies are common. Most firms, including Intel, Advanced Micro Devices, National Semiconductors, and Texas Instruments, have a history of alliances of various types with other semiconductor firms. Of the over 1,800 recorded alliances in the industry between 1961 and 1989, nearly 1,200 involved US firms (Kogut and Kim 1992). Formal technology transfer arrangements have also helped to diffuse technology internationally. Japanese and European firms have both benefited from extensive strategic alliances with US firms.

In addition to the formal transfer of technology, there is also impressive ethnographic evidence of the spread of knowledge through more informal channels that may differ by region. Since its inception, the American semiconductor industry has been characterized by interfirm mobility of scientists and engineers. Rival firms actively courted key engineers leading to extensive interfirm mobility of personnel (Rogers and Larsen 1984). Entrepreneurship has been another significant characteristic of the American industry. Ever since William Shockley left Bell Labs to start Shockley Semiconductors in Palo Alto, California, start-ups have played an important role in the diffusion of knowledge and the evolution of the industry (Moore 1986). Several of Shockley's assistants left his firm and formed Fairchild Semiconductors in 1957. The origins of almost every firm in Silicon Valley can be traced back to Fairchild. In addition to the role of the pioneering firms, universities played an important role. The area boasts two frontier universities in electrical engineering, University of California at Berkeley and Stanford University, which proactively pursued the diffusion of knowledge to the region (Leslie and Kargan 1996). The significance of university research for local diffusion is confirmed in several studies, notably Jaffe et al. (1993) and Zucker et al. (1994).

Regional Differences

Saxenian's (1994) study presents a compelling and yet puzzling comparison of two of America's best-known regions of innovation in the electronics industry. These regions had similar histories, yet they face different futures—Silicon Valley is flourishing while Route 128 has stagnated in recent years. Saxenian argues that while Silicon Valley developed a system of collaboration and learning among small specialist companies, Route 128, dominated by a few large corporations, was slow to adjust to changes in markets and technologies. In effect, Saxenian puts forth the argument that the higher externalities among relatively smaller networked firms in the Silicon Valley leads dynamically to higher rates of innovation and productivity in the region. Angel (1991) conducted a survey of personnel at 67 semiconductor firms and found that those located in the Silicon Valley tended to hire more labor with substantial experience, suggesting a dynamic by which experience accumulates broadly in the region.

An important difference between the Silicon Valley and other regions, and the US and other countries, is the role played by start-ups. Of the 176 start-ups founded in the world semiconductor industry between 1977 and 1989, 88 percent were located in the United States, and 55 percent were located in Silicon Valley (Dataquest 1990). The study by Eisenhardt and Schoonhoven (1990) on regions and start-ups in semiconductors showed that survival rates of new firms in the Silicon Valley, despite its high density of activity, was not significantly different from other regions. In investigating why, they found that entrepreneurs in Silicon Valley were more closely networked with venture capitalists and, to a lesser but still significant extent, with other firms.

Knowledge and Regional Networks

The ethnography of Saxenian poses the important question: why should there be variation in the dynamic trajectory of these two regions? The two regions, Route 128 and Silicon Valley have the same industry (i.e. semiconductors), the same 'cluster' (i.e. computers), and yet the dynamics by which innovations are created differ dramatically. In fact, by any standard economic logic, Silicon Valley appears disadvantaged for two reasons. First, the inability of a firm to establish property rights over knowledge should lead to a decrease in its willingness in invest in R&D. The possibility that free-riders will benefit from the investment of other firms should lead to a vicious cycle that erodes the innovative investment of the region. Second, if inventive knowledge leaks across firms, it should leak across the boundaries of a region. In short, why should the spatial borders of a region be less permeable than the proprietary borders of a firm?

One obvious reason for why knowledge should be regional is that it is held tacitly by skilled engineers who remain within the region. Studies on innovation point clearly to the importance of their comprehensibility, as Rogers (1983) and Winter (1987) argued, as a factor in their diffusion. The degree to which knowledge is not codifiable and is tacitly held by individuals have been found to be important determinants in the speed by which major innovations are transferred within and among firms (Kogut and Zander 1994; Zander and Kogut 1995).

An important aspect of diffusion is not only the inherent qualities of knowledge (i.e. whether it is tacit or easily imitated), but also whether there is a regional labor market for the engineers, scientists, and workers. Some regions appear as remarkable in this regard. In a memorable quotation, an engineer from the Silicon Valley observes that 'people change jobs out here without changing car pools.' Saxenian (1994) cites an engineer who claims that:

Here in Silicon Valley there's far greater loyalty to one's craft than to one's company. A company is just a vehicle which allows you to work. If you're a circuit designer, it's most important for you to do excellent work. If you can't succeed in one firm, you'll move on to another one.

The observations that innovative knowledge is held by individuals and that there are active labor market networks in some locations are critical components to explaining why the localization of ideas may vary by region. The central engine of this argument is the necessary conditions that the knowledge held by design engineers has a tacit quality and that these same engineers are mobile among firms *within* the spatial boundaries of a region. Parenthetically, differences in intellectual property law do not appear to explain differential mobility of engineers, and thereby the creation of externalities. Neither Silicon Valley nor other American regions differ in the common law treatment that the firm owns an employee's knowledge (Hyde 1997).

We test the assertion that mobility influences the creation of localized spillovers through two steps. First, we show that there are regional variations in the localization of knowledge. Second, we test whether the mobility of engineers holding major patents leaves a trace in the patent citation records and whether mobility varies by region. By tracking individual engineers, we link the stronger presence of externalities in the Silicon Valley to the movement of individual patent holders who remain within the region.

Data and Methods

For the following statistical analysis, we use patent citation analysis of important semiconductor innovations and apply a case-control methodology and regression analysis to test for the localization of knowledge.[3]

Patent Data and Citations

Patent documents provide data on the inventor and his or her location at the time of the invention, the owner (assignee) of the patent (usually a firm), the time of the invention and also the technology of the invention. In addition, through patent citations, we are able to infer the technological influences on a particular invention.

The patent citations contained in a patent document have two possible sources: (a) the inventor and the patent lawyer; and (b) the patent examiner. The patent applicant is obliged by law to specify in the application any and all of 'the prior art' of which he or she is aware. Interviews with patent reviewers reveal that the examiner undertakes a thorough search of files to determine the patent's relationship to existing patents. In the final list, some citations represent direct technological influences on a particular innovation, while other citations may only represent indirect technological influences (since the patent examiner added them). Several studies (Carpenter et al. 1981; Narin et al. 1987; Albert et al. 1991) have shown that patent citation counts are a good indicator of the technological importance of an invention. Further, Trajtenberg (1990) in his study of CT scanners, showed that the number of citations to a patent serves as an indicator of social and economic value of the innovation as well. We therefore analyze only highly cited patents that tend to be of both technological and economic importance.[4]

Establishing the Regions

Major regions of semiconductor activity in the United States were identified by plotting actual plant locations of over 750 facilities and demarcating the corresponding regional clusters. (See Appendix 11.1 for data sources.) The location of semiconductor plant clusters was confirmed through the use of county level establishment and employee data from County Business Patterns (corresponding to SIC 3674). Regions were demarcated around contiguous counties having two or more semiconductor establishments. The analysis reveals 18 regional clusters. We analyzed patents belonging to the top 12 regions. These 12 regions accounted for more than 95 percent of the highly cited patents.

Identification of Major Patents

We first isolated patents related to semiconductor design with the help of experts in the Patent and Trademark Office. These patents belonged to two time periods—those patents filed in 1980 and those filed in 1985. For every patent in these two panels, we counted the total number of subsequent patents

Table 11.1. Descriptive Statistics

(a) Full Panels

Panel	Number of major patents	Number of citations	Mean citations	% Self citations
1980	131	2,371	18.1	10.5
1985	172	2,722	15.8	17.9

(b) Distribution of Major Patents by Region

Region	1980 Citations			1985 Citations		
	Number of major patents	Number	Mean	Number of major patents	Number	Mean
NY–NJ–PA	20	601	30.5	20	510	25.5
AZ	4	40	10	11	107	9.7
CO	7	126	18	5	47	9.4
FL	3	32	10.7	5	59	11.8
MA–CT	10	99	9.9	10	156	15.6
VT	11	145	13.2	9	109	12.1
OR–WA	4	31	7.8	12	126	10.5
NORTH CA	20	478	23.9	20	468	23.4
SOUTH CA	20	323	16.2	20	233	11.7
TX–DALLAS	20	324	16.2	20	334	16.7
TX–AUSTIN	6	64	10.7	20	280	14
TX–HOUSTON	6	108	18	20	293	14.7

(up to 1995) that cited them. For each region and for each time period, we selected the top 25 percent most highly cited patents. Since this method generated an extraordinarily large number of patents for large regions, we took the 20 most highly cited patents as our sample. For some regions, the top 25 percent consisted of less than 20 patents. As a result, the samples for some regions had less than 20 major patents by which to generate the citations. To the degree that more highly cited patents are more or less geographically localized than less highly cited patents, this procedure potentially opens the possibility of a sample selection bias. We show below that our results are robust to this concern.

Descriptive Statistics of Major Patents

Table 11.1(a) displays descriptive statistics of the panels of major patents analyzed. Since not every region had 20 highly cited patents, the total number of major patents were 131 for the 1980 panel and 172 for the 1985 panel. Table 11.1(b) gives the distribution of major patents and the number of citations to these patents by US region. While the larger regions had at least 20 highly cited patents, some regions such as Arizona and Florida had fewer.

Citations and Controls

Localization is the use of knowledge created by others in the same region. Operationally, it is defined by the joint condition that the citing patent and the major innovation belong to the same geographic region. To measure the frequency of localization, we geographically matched each major patent with the citing patents.

Clearly, the observed frequency of geographic coincidence of the major patent and the citing patents may also reflect the distribution of patenting activity (rather than the localization of spillovers). Silicon Valley has a lot of semiconductor firms, they patent a lot, and hence they cite each other a lot because the region dominates the overall patent count. To adjust for any bias due to this existing distribution of technological activity, we followed Jaffe et al. (1993) in the construction of a control sample. For each citing patent, we identified a corresponding control patent. This patent was identified such that the patent (technology) class was identical to that of the citing patent and the application date was as near as possible to the citing patent. Since the control patent does not cite the major patent, the frequency of a geographic match between the two reflects the existing concentration of patenting activity for a particular region. This frequency of geographic matches between the major patent and the control patent sets the baseline against which we compare the frequency of major patentciting patent matches. This research design is very conservative. By use of controls, we isolate spillovers 'above and beyond' agglomeration effects. Certain regions are unusually rich in their innovative activities, and this richness is itself suggestive of an externality. The controls capture this baseline agglomeration effect.

Statistical Test for Localization of Spillovers

Let P_{cit} be the probability that the major patent and citing patent are geographically matched, and P_{con} be the corresponding probability for the major patent-control patent match. Assuming binomial distributions, the null hypothesis is:

$$H_0 : P_{cit} = P_{con},$$

and the alternate hypothesis is:

$$H_a : P_{cit} > P_{con}.$$

The t statistic is calculated as:

$$t = (P_{cit} - P_{con})/[(P_{cit}(1 - P_{cit}) + P_{con}(1 - P_{con}))/n]^{0.5}.$$

The 't' statistic tests the difference between two independently drawn binomial proportions. We calculated the statistic for each of the 12 regions in each panel.

The case comparison controls for the effect of technology. By matching patents by their technological relatedness, we control for the differential degree of spillovers across a broad technological space. Podolny and Shepherd (1996) show that the evidence for spillovers is stronger among technologically dissimilar patents. By matching a control to the citing patent by technology class, our method conservatively eliminates the effects of technological distance and isolates the geographic dimension to diffusion.

Differences in Regional Localization

One of the major goals of this paper is to establish that externalities simply do not exist, but vary systematically by region. To demonstrate that these variations are statistically significant, we also test for differences in the extent of localization between regions.[5] For Region A, P_A represents the degree of localization of knowledge and is given by $P_A = P_{Acit} - P_{Acon}$.

For Region B, P_B represents the degree of localization of knowledge. We call P_B a baseline region for comparison. We test the hypothesis H_o : $P_A = P_B$ against the alternate hypothesis H_a : $P_A > P_B$. The t statistic is calculated as:

$$t = (P_A - P_B)/[(P_A(1 - P_A)/n_A + P_B(1 - P_B)/n_B]^{0.5}.$$

Testing for Regional Variations in Localization

The main results of the case-control tests for both the samples are given in Table 11.2a. The 'number of citations' corresponds to the total number of cites for the major patents. 'A' and 'B' are the percentage of citations and controls, respectively, that belong to the same geographic region as the major patent. The t-statistic tests the equality of the control and citing proportions as described previously.

For the overall samples, there are significantly higher proportions of citation matches than control matches indicating localization effects. (Results significant at the 0.05 level or better are given in bold.) These results confirm the principal findings of Jaffe et al. (1993). The results indicate quite strongly that knowledge is localized at the regional level. Silicon Valley shows the strongest localization effects, while the results for the Southern California,

Table 11.2. Test of Localization of Knowledge in US Regions (Significant Results at 0.05%
in Bold)

Region	Number of citations		A = Citation matching (%)		B = Control matching (%)		T-statistic	
	1980	1985	1980	1985	1980	1985	1980	1985
(a) Results with All Cites								
NY–NJ–PA	601	510	22	29	13	8	**4.51**	**8.81**
AZ	40	107	5	7	0	1	1.45	**2.19**
COLORADO	126	47	6	11	2	2	1.55	1.71
FLORIDA	32	59	3	2	0	0	1.02	1.01
MA–CT	99	156	7	12	5	4	0.60	**2.74**
VT	145	109	13	14	1	1	**3.95**	**3.75**
OR–WA	31	126	10	5	0	2	1.82	1.02
NORTH CA	478	468	27	45	9	17	**7.56**	**9.89**
SOUTH CA	323	233	16	16	4	4	**4.93**	**4.35**
TX–DALLAS	324	334	10	19	5	8	**2.84**	**4.19**
TX–AUSTIN	64	280	11	10	0	4	**2.80**	**2.91**
TX–HOUSTON	108	293	13	20	3	2	**2.83**	**7.08**
TOTAL	2,371	2,722	17	22	7	7	**11.31**	**16.32**
(b) Results Without Self-cites								
NY–NJ–PA	502	385	12	12	11	5	0.30	**3.11**
AZ	37	96	0	3	0	0	0.00	1.76
COLORADO	115	46	1	9	1	2	0.00	1.39
FLORIDA	32	54	3	0	0	0	1.02	0.00
MA–CT	92	127	1	2	5	2	−1.67	−0.45
VT	103	74	0	0	0	0	0.00	0.00
OR–WA	26	112	0	1	0	0	0.00	1.00
NORTH CA	448	431	24	43	8	16	**6.71**	**9.09**
SOUTH CA	307	209	11	8	4	4	**3.34**	1.45
TX–DALLAS	303	235	7	3	3	3	1.88	0.00
TX–AUSTIN	57	242	4	4	0	2	1.44	0.79
TX–HOUSTON	78	166	0	1	0	1	0.00	0.00
TOTAL	2,100	2,177	11	12	6	5	**5.96**	**8.36**

New York–New Jersey–Pennsylvania, Vermont, and all three Texas regions are
also significant.

An examination of the underlying data reveals that localization may often
be driven by self-citations (when the major patent and the citing patent have
the same owner). Often the citations belonged to the same plant (not just
firm) and thus these citations did not represent cross-border knowledge flows.
Further, several firms (especially Texas Instruments, IBM, and AT&T) have
shown a strong propensity to cite their own patents, contributing to a strong
(but perhaps misleading) localization effect.

We, therefore, run the analysis without including self-cites (Table 11.2(b)).[6]
We find that only Silicon Valley exhibits strong localization effects and indeed
contributes significantly to the overall localization findings. NY–NJ–PA and
Southern California are each significant in one panel. The evidence qualifies
the interpretation of the results of Jaffe et al. (1993). As with the earlier study,

Table 11.3. Test of Localization of Knowledge: Regional Differences

Region B	Results of *t*-Tests					
	Region A					
	NY–NJ–PA		North CA		South CA	
	1980	1985	1980	1985	1980	1985
NY–NJ–PA		**8.75**	**8.39**	**4.35**	−1.65	
AZ	1.74	1.44	**9.26**	**8.56**	**4.87**	0.10
COLORADO	1.74	−0.07	**9.26**	**4.83**	**4.87**	−0.82
FLORIDA	−0.82	**5.06**	**3.67**	**12.60**	1.19	**2.69**
MA–CT	—	**7.43**	—	**13.96**	—	**4.30**
VT	1.74	**5.06**	**9.26**	**12.60**	**4.87**	**2.69**
OR–WA	1.74	**3.52**	**9.26**	**11.25**	**4.87**	1.61
NORTH CA	−8.75	−8.39			−3.91	−9.53
SOUTH CA	−4.35	1.65	**3.91**	**9.53**		
TX–DALLAS	−2.50	**5.06**	**6.33**	**12.60**	**2.15**	**2.69**
TX–AUSTIN	−1.18	**3.51**	**4.20**	**11.40**	**1.28**	1.47
TX–HOUSTON	1.74	**5.06**	**9.26**	**12.60**	**4.87**	**2.69**

Notes: All figures are *t*-statistics for differences in regional localization; bold indicates significance at 0.05% or lower.

the above analysis indicates that, in the aggregate, patent citations tend to be localized. However, localization of knowledge is not a universal phenomenon. Geographic regions reveal different patterns in the local diffusion of knowledge externalities.

In Table 11.3 we test whether the degree of knowledge localization is significantly different across regions. Because three regions (i.e., Northern California, Southern California, and the New York–New Jersey–Pennsylvania) evidence significant degrees of localization (see Table 11.2), we use them to compare differences in localization across regions. The results show that knowledge is significantly more localized in Silicon Valley than in any other region (though the other two regions also evidence considerable localization).

Tests for Sample Bias

It is interesting to note that the three regions showing significant localization are ones for which we have 20 patents. These three regions could be exhibiting localization because highly cited patents are more localized than less cited patents. We therefore test whether the localization findings are an artifact of the sampling procedure by comparing two samples of patents from Northern California (Silicon Valley) for the 1980 time period.

Our first sample consisted of the 20 highly cited patents for Northern California for the 1980 panel considered previously. We matched every patent from our 'highly cited' sample with another randomly selected patent controlling for the region (Northern California), time period (1980 panel) and technology (same technology class). We thus had a second sample of 'other' patents that represent less highly cited patents. We then compared the frequency of regional citation matches between the two samples and tested to see whether the 'highly cited' sample was more localized than the 'other' sample.

The results of the test, available on request, indicate that the 'Other' sample has, as expected, fewer citations but the frequency of local citation matches does not differ significantly across the samples. The result holds whether or not we include self-cites. These findings indicate that highly cited patents are not significantly more localized than less cited patents and therefore the sampling scheme used here does not introduce any bias.

Tracing Diffusion by Tracing Patent-Holders in the Network

We hypothesized earlier that regions that are marked by spatially defined labor markets should evidence higher rates of localization. For semiconductor design technologies, skilled engineers, some of whom hold major patents, hold significant knowledge. By compiling deeper data on patent holders and through interviews, we collected information on the importance of individuals in the localization of knowledge. To measure the interfirm mobility patterns of semiconductor engineers, we developed a database of the career paths of semiconductor engineers with patenting records. For all the 438 individuals who hold major patents being analyzed, the career paths from 1974 to 1994 were traced through the records of their patenting activity. There were a total of 174 intraregional moves observed and 181 interregional moves. While some information on job changes is undoubtedly missed, the data are surprisingly revealing.

Table 11.4 shows the mobility patterns of these engineers at the regional level. The first column, 'total years,' is the summation of the number of years for which we counted moves for all the patent holders in our sample for the particular region. (For instance, if we observed 20 patent holders on average for ten years each within Region A, the 'total years' would be 200.) Moves are defined as the number of times that a major patent holder changes firms, as revealed in an analysis of all semiconductor patents. Thus for NY–NJ–PA we observed 48 moves by the patent holders. Of these 48 moves, 17 were within the region and 31 were from NY–NJ–PA to other regions. Next, to make comparisons across regions we standardized the moves by calculating the 'moves per 100 years.' The last column provides the most important data. It represents

Table 11.4. Regional Mobility of Major Patent Holders

Region	Total Years	Moves		Moves per 100 Years		Net
		Intra	Inter	Intra	Inter	
NY–NJ–PA	920	17	31	1.85	3.37	−1.52
AZ	181	1	5	0.55	2.76	−2.21
CO	101	5	7	4.95	6.93	−1.98
FL	82	1	4	1.22	4.88	−3.66
MA–CT	240	9	7	3.75	2.92	0.83
VT	304	2	5	0.66	1.64	−0.99
OR–WA	156	4	10	2.56	6.41	−3.85
NORTH CA	**750**	**76**	**23**	**10.13**	**3.07**	**7.07**
SOUTH CA	568	21	16	3.70	2.82	0.88
TX–DALLAS	475	13	19	2.74	4.00	−1.26
TX–AUSTIN	297	9	7	3.03	2.36	0.67
TX–HOUSTON	243	1	15	0.41	6.17	−5.76

the net intraregional moves of all major patent holders, standardized across regions.

The Silicon Valley is clearly unique in terms of inter-firm mobility. The level of intraregional mobility is very high, while extent of interregional moves is much smaller. Only MA–CT, Southern California and Texas–Austin show more intraregional movement than interregional movement, though to a much lesser extent than Silicon Valley. The table demonstrates considerably that regions differ to a considerable degree in the extent to which they facilitate interfirm job transfer through mobility.

Regression Analysis

The simplicity of the means tests runs the objection that unobserved factors influence these results. In fact, the slight differences between the results for the two time periods suggest that changes in structural parameters (e.g. regional and institutional variables) over time influence the degree of localization. An alternative strategy is to test directly for the institutional effects on the generation of regional externalities. We investigate the factors influencing the localization of knowledge through a logistic regression analysis. (Variable definitions and data sources are given in Appendix 11.1; descriptive statistics and correlation tables are available on request.)

Agglomeration and size effects are measured through the number of establishments in the region and the density of design establishments per square mile in the county with the largest number of establishments.[7] We also included two mobility measures, defined to capture the intraregional turnover and the interregional turnover among the patent holders. In addition, a variable for the number of startups over the period in the region was added, since startups recruit, by definition, new engineers and managers. By controlling for start-ups, we can observe directly the effect of mobility independent of the opportunities for new employment.

To sort out possible period effects, we created dummies for the panels, plus added a time term for years lapsed since the original major patent. We control also for whether a university held the major or citing patent. The logit odds are coded 1 if the citing and major patent are from the same region; 0 if otherwise.

In Table 11.5, we report the results from this logit specification by estimating four models. The first model gives the results for regional variables alone, plus the control (patent) variable, plus the temporal and university variables. (There is no change in the results when the model is reestimated absent the temporal and university effects.) It is important to keep in mind that the control patent variable already incorporates many of the unobserved variables to the regression. In all the regressions, the control variable is significant, as to be expected; it covaries with the localization of the dependent variable. The interesting issue is what can be explained above and beyond the baseline expectation for localization.

The results of the specified models in Table 11.5 point quite clearly to the significant role played by agglomeration economies, mobility, and start-up activity. (To check for potential multicolinearity, we also estimated the model without start-ups; there is no change in the significance levels of the other variables.) The most interesting result is that the coefficient to intraregional mobility is positive but that to interregional mobility is negative. The institutional variables of universities were not significant. Clearly, the degree of mobility at the regional level is associated with the degree of localization.

To pinpoint more concretely the relationship of mobility to localization, we created an additional variable called 'inventor intraregional mobility.' This variable is a dummy that indicates if the inventor of the original patent subsequently moved within the region. As shown in the second regression, this variable is positive and significant at the 0.05 level. The parameters to the other mobility variables remain significant, indicating that the localization of knowledge is generally related to the mobility of top inventors within and between regions.

Diagnostic Tests for the Regressions

In the last two models given in Table 11.5, we report two diagnostic regressions to test the robustness of the results by including a dummy for Northern

Table 11.5. Logistic Analysis: Localization of Knowledge

Variables	Model 1 (without self-cites)	Model 2 (without self-cites)	Model 3 (without self-cites)	Model 4 (all cites)
Intercept	−4.2233**	−4.1801***	−4.1817***	−2.1679***
	0.3983	0.3991	0.4717	0.2576
Control	0.8374***	0.8398***	0.8372***	0.7692***
	0.1562	0.1561	0.1563	0.1221
Regional variables				
Density of establishments	0.6022***	0.5862***	0.5969***	0.3818***
	0.0982	0.0984	0.1032	0.0543
Intra-regional mobility	0.1535***	0.1463***	0.1414	−0.1979***
	0.0269	0.0273	0.0791	0.0427
Inter-regional mobility	−0.2204**	−0.2298**	−0.2193**	−0.0044
	0.0805	0.0802	0.0806	0.0409
Start-ups	−0.2160**	−0.2110**	−0.2151**	−0.0582
	0.0666	0.0667	0.0667	0.0477
North California			0.1012	1.9525***
			0.6218	0.324
Temporal variables lag	0.0619***	0.0639***	0.0619***	0.0196
	0.0181	0.0181	0.0181	0.0132
Period 1980	−0.0831	−0.1377	−0.0938	−0.3876***
	0.1511	0.1539	0.1515	0.0878
Universities major patent	0.3442		0.3469	0.4642
	0.2617		0.2624	0.2457
Citing patent	−0.3369		−0.3357	−1.0561
	0.5441		0.5441	0.5299
Individual variable inventor intraregional		0.2240*		
Mobility		0.1143		
Maximum likelihood	1294.91	1293.99	1294.90	2374.96
Number of observations	4,357	4,357	4,357	5,093

Notes: * = Significance level of 0.05; ** = 0.01; *** = 0.001. Standard errors in italics.

California (principally the Silicon Valley) and using self cites. Given the high correlation of 0.94 between the dummy for Silicon Valley and intraregional mobility, it is not surprising that the variables are not significant. A common test for whether an additional collinear variable adds explanatory power is to compare the likelihood scores with and without this new variable. Comparing the likelihoods of Models 1 and 2 shows no significant improvement. This test implies that intraregional mobility is equivalent to the Silicon Valley effect. Interesting enough, the coefficient to interregional mobility remains negative and significant, indicating that this variable captures a source for the loss of localization.

The last regression includes self-cites. Self-citing is especially prominent among the larger firms, such as Texas Instruments and IBM, that populate the Texas and New York area regions. The results are very intuitive. Interregional mobility, though still negative, is no longer significant. We infer from this result that the larger firms, such as Texas Instruments, Intel, and IBM that have plants in several regions and account for most of the self-citations, build upon their own knowledge across regions, leading to the weaker negative coefficient result for interregional mobility. In this expanded data set, both the Silicon Valley and intraregional mobility variables are positive and significant. A particularly interesting change is the loss of significance for the time lag. In effect, large firms appear to build more rapidly upon their knowledge, as suggested in a shorter time to citation of their major patents. (The mean time to citation for the sample with self cites is 5.4 years; for a cite by another firm, the mean is 5.9 years.) Intraregional mobility generates local diffusion, but the process is less rapid than intrafirm diffusion.

In results not reported here, final diagnostics split the sample between cases in which the controls reveal localization and those that do not. By estimating the regressions on the split samples, we check for important interaction effects between the specified variables and the unobserved sources of localization embedded in the control variable. The results do not reveal any important interactions.

These results indicate clearly what is meant by the 'above and beyond' effect of mobility on the localization of knowledge. Even after controlling for agglomeration and unobserved localization captured through the control variable, mobility still has a significant and positive effect on the probability that a patent will build upon a major patent from the same region. The implications suggest that the ability to build upon semiconductor design knowledge is tied significantly to the career paths of innovative individuals. The lower intraregional mobility of engineers appears to be related to the presence of large firms that build upon their knowledge in-house. However, these regions also show higher rates of departure of innovative engineers to other locations. These observations suggest that engineers in larger firms face a choice between building careers within the internal labor markets or entering the external labor market, often by departing for other regions and carrying their innovative knowledge to new firms in new sites. A corollary to this speculation is that the entrepreneurial and high intraregional mobility through local labor markets is a factor behind the localized nature of the diffusion of innovation among firms confined to the Silicon Valley region.

Conclusions

One of the most important trends in the economics of research has been the diminishing role of the individual in patenting. This trend, long noted since Schmookler (1966), disguises the persisting importance of individuals in research. Across the landscape populated by laboratories and organized research, individuals appear as active agents in the creation and spatial diffusion of knowledge.

Ultimately, some appeal to institutions and the structure of relations is required to explain why certain regions show a higher degree of localization and in the ability to absorb and build upon previous knowledge. The many studies on technology transfer indicate the importance of social capability, prior experience, and access to the absorption of knowledge and its creation.[8] But these observations are fairly sterile unless understood in the context of the economic sociology of these regions or nations.

Externalities play a central role in economic theory, and yet are rarely studied. On examination, externalities are reflections of the nature of the knowledge held by individuals or groups in the context of specific social networks. To the mobile engineers of the Silicon Valley, the transfer of their knowledge and abilities is made through a partially visible network. Our results offer the speculation that externalities are the outcome of actions of skilled labor in spatially defined markets.[9]

Because these markets differ geographically, regions also evince large differences in their social structures and stimulation for innovation. The ethnographies of Saxenian (1994) and Rogers and Larsen (1984), and the statistical results derived from patent citations, indicate that externalities are not created uniformly across all regions, nor are they natural by-products of particular technologies. Rather, externalities are created through the existence of broader social institutions that support a viable flow of ideas within the spatial confines of regional economies.[10]

☐ APPENDIX 11.1: VARIABLE DEFINITIONS AND DATA SOURCES

The definition and sources of data used in the logit regression are given below:

1. Dependent variable: regional match/no match between major patent and citing patent.
2. Control variable: regional match/no match between control patent and major patent.
3. Density of establishments: number of semiconductor plants per square mile in the largest county (in terms of establishments) in each region.
4. Intraregional mobility: number of intraregional inter-firm moves per 100 years by patent holders. Inter-regional mobility: number of inter-regional, inter-firm moves per 100 years by patent holders. Inventor intra-regional mobility: dummy variable coded 1, if major patent holder moved across firms within the region.
5. Start-ups: log of total number of regional start-ups between 1975 and 1990.
6. Lag: citation lag (filed date of citing patent—filed date of major patent).

7. Period 1980 and period 1985: dummy variables for 1980 and 1985 samples.

8. Universities: major patent and citing patent: dummy for university patents.

9. Northern California: dummy variable, coded 1 if major patent is from Northern California.

Data Sources

1. Patent data were obtained through the on-line patent database available on LEXUS-NEXUS and through CHI Research, a private research firm.
2. Plant locations were obtained from company reports and Dataquest (1990).
3. Establishment and employee data were obtained from County Business Patterns (1975–90), a US Department of Commerce publication.
4. Data on start-up firms were obtained from Dataquest (1990).

☐ ENDNOTES

* This chapter is a revised version of P. Almeida and B. Kogut (1999) 'Localization of knowledge and the mobility of Engineers in Regional Networks,' *Management Science*, 45: 905–17.

1. We use externalities and knowledge spillovers interchangeably to denote the benefit of knowledge to people, or to firms, not responsible for the original investment in the creation of this knowledge.

2. See Allison and Long (1987) for evidence that institutional affiliation provides a significant spur to productivity; also Crane (1965) on invisible colleges, and Brown and Duguid (1991) on communities of practice.

3. A patent is the grant of a property right to an inventor for an invention conferred by the government. A US patent is granted for an invention which is 'useful,' 'novel,' and 'nonobvious to a person of ordinary skill in the art' (US Department of Commerce 1992).

4. We later show that the use of highly cited patents (as opposed to less cited patents) does not bias our study towards finding regional localization.

5. We would like to thank a referee and Rebecca Henderson for encouraging us to augment our original sampling methodology by collecting sufficient original patents from each region in order to conduct these tests.

6. In order to treat the citing and control samples evenly, when the assignee of the control patent was the same as that of the major patent, the record was also considered a self-cite and excluded from the final sample.

7. We took the density of the county with the most establishments due to the problem of comparing regions that differ widely in size, populated areas, etc.

8. See Pack and Westphal (1986) and Rosenberg (1987).

9. However, for some kinds of technologies, mobility does not seem to be important; see Argote et al. (1990) who found that learning by doing among shipyard workers did not transfer by rotation to other yards.

10. The authors are grateful to Peter Farkas, Patrick Abouchalache, Berlin Lai, and Jason Shrednick for their research assistance. They gratefully acknowledge the contribution of Mike Albert of CHI Research and thank Paul Allison, Tony Frost, Rebecca Henderson, Adam Jaffe, Paul Rosenbaum, Naren Udayagiri, and Sid Winter for comments and suggestions. Financial support for this project has been provided by the Huntsman Center for Global Competition and Innovation and the Reginald H. Jones Center at the Wharton School, and the Capital Markets Research Center, at the McDonough School of Business at Georgetown University.

12 Open-Source Software Development and Distributed Innovation*

with Anca Metiu

Introduction

The central economic question posed by the Internet is how commercial investments can appropriate value from a public good called information. Information can be transported and replicated at essentially zero marginal cost and its use by one party does not preclude use by another. Since information is digitally encoded, its provision is the service that is facilitated by the Internet. Internet companies seek to collect fees and payment on information services. The difficulty in finding mechanisms to extract payments on the provision of a public good explains, to a large extent, the high death rate among Internet ventures.

There is, however, another side to the consequences of the economics of information. The public-good quality of information on the Internet favours the voluntary provision by users. In some cases, this provision is sustained on a long-term and ongoing basis. We can describe the participating members as forming a community to which they share allegiance and loyalty. These communities are economically interesting when they constitute not only social exchange, but also a work organization that relies upon a distributed division of labor.

A simple example of a distributed division of labor is an intranet that supports communication and work among employees in a corporation. Work can be sent back and forth, even across time zones. Teams can be physically dispersed. There are still two important background aspects to this exchange. The first is that the corporation pays the workers. The second is that the firm has the standard property rights to the product of their cooperation.

From an economic perspective, the startling aspect of open-source development of software is that people cooperate in the absence of direct pay and property right claims. Software is quintessentially an information good insofar as it can be entirely digitally encoded. In addition, its demand is influenced by its dissemination. The utility to the consumer of a given software program frequently increases with the number of users. This network externality offers, consequently, the potential for a firm to earn sustainable rents by gaining a dominant position in the market that could impede entry. However, the critical institutional feature to maintain this model is the efficacy by which intellectual property claims are upheld.

Open source means that the intellectual property rights to software code are deposited in the public domain, and hence the code can be used and changed without requiring a user fee, such as the purchase of a licence. There are thus two dimensions to open-source development: public ownership of the intellectual property and a production model by which programming work is accomplished in a distributed and dispersed community.

The recent literature on open source has focused on the economic paradox of why people contribute to a public good. Of course, this paradox is not unique to open source. Experimental economics routinely finds that people contribute more to the provision of public goods than can be predicted by self-interest (Frey and Oberholzer-Gee 1997). The natural resolutions to this paradox are to tie provision to intrinsic rewards or to supplementary extrinsic rewards. An intrinsic reward is the satisfaction of 'helping out' as a form of gift-giving. In this view, people are altruistic because they share membership in communities that sustain reciprocity and identity. Extrinsic rewards would be the positive effect of a contribution on the reputation of a programer, thus signalling his or her merit in a competitive job market.

These resolutions surely have a bearing upon explaining the motivations of participants, but the focus on the paradox of the provision of public goods distracts from a more far-reaching observation. The rapid growth of open-source development suggests that the traditional methods of software development are often inefficient, and these inefficiencies are permitted only due to the imposition of legal institutions to enforce intellectual property right claims. That is, firms enforce intellectual property by achieving secrecy through the organization of software production within their own organizational boundaries. Open-source development exists because, once property rights are removed from consideration, in-house production is often revealed as less efficient.

There are, then, two related hypotheses that explain open-source software:

Hypothesis One: secrecy and intellectual property create incentives that lead to behaviors that render economic activity less efficient.

These behaviors include excessive patent claims, litigation as deterrence, and the lack of access to ideas by those without ownership claims. This hypothesis is the standard assumption in economics, but is usually believed to offer the second-best solution to market failure: innovators will not innovate if they do not have patent protection. Open source challenges this theory of the second best.

Hypothesis Two: the production model of open source is more efficient than in-house hierarchical models.

The central observation that leads to hypothesis two is that the concurrence in design and testing of software modules utilizes more efficiently the distributed resources connected by the Internet.

Our claim is that concerns over intellectual property create additional inefficiencies, plus prevent the deployment of more efficient production models. Once this is recognized, the interesting inquiry is to compare different open-source development models regarding their productivity and their effects on product design. We turn to this comparison after considering first the sociological background to open source.

Communities of Practice

The Internet is a technological system that relies upon a communication backbone consisting largely of fibre optics and packet switching and a set of software protocols that allow for inter-operability between distributed machines and operating systems.

The other side to the Internet is its utility as a means of communication and collaborative work that predates the commercial explosion. The Internet was developed first by the US military, and then by federal programs to create a communication network among research sites. From the start, then, the Internet was conceived as a communication mechanism for the dissemination of ideas and as a means to support distributed collaboration. The diffusion of the fundamental protocols (e.g. Transmission Control Protocol/Internet Protocol (TCP/IP), Hypertext Transfer Protocol (HTTP), Hypertext Markup Language (HTML)) arose out of research laboratories, such as CERN in Geneva. Tim Berners-Lee, who contributed the basic hypertext protocols that support the World Wide Web, noted that the Internet arose through 'webs of people' tied together through participation in research consortia (Berners-Lee and Fischetti 1999). In other words, the Internet is not only a technology, it is also a community of developers.

The World Wide Web is an open-source software program. The property rights to these protocols lie in the public domain and anyone can access the code, that is, the written program itself. An open-source document is much like a physics experiment to which hundreds of researchers contribute.

Open-source software appears as less puzzling when its production is compared to the production of research in an academic community. Science has often been described as a conspiracy constructed to provide incentives to researchers to invest their time in the production and public dissemination of their knowledge (Dasgupta and David 1994). To support these efforts, there are strong norms regarding the public ownership of knowledge and the importance of public validation of scientific results. Scientists are rewarded by status and prestige that can only be gained by the public dissemination of their research. In effect, the norms regarding research and its publication are aimed at rendering scientific results into a public good that can be accessed by one party without diminishing its consumption by another.

This model of scientific research conflicts strongly with the commercial interests of private enterprise to create innovations that are protected by strong intellectual property rights or by secrecy. The argument for the protection of intellectual property relies traditionally upon the theory of the second best. Society would be better off with the dissemination of innovations, but then inventors would lack the incentives to innovate. This argument is clearly at odds with the insistence in the scientific community on public access and validation of research. There is, then, a stark division between the norms that insist upon the public quality of scientific research that prevail in universities and research institutions and the concern of private enterprise to secure property rights to ideas and innovations.

Yet, many of the important contributors to the Internet and to open source were located in private enterprises. This blurring of the public and private is not unique to the Internet, but is to be found in the close networks of scientists working for biotechnology and pharmaceutical companies and other industrial research laboratories that depend upon the production of basic research. It is also to be found in the community of software developers, many of whom were employed by industrial laboratories that originally placed their software in the public domain. This clash between the private and public spheres is what makes the creation of the Internet such an interesting blend of economic incentives against a sociological landscape. However, there is a deeper issue involved than simply understanding these two dimensions to the historical development of the Internet. Commercial firms' insistence on private property is not only at odds with the norms of the scientific community which built the Internet, but is also at odds with an emergent model of distributed production that, for some tasks, appears far more efficient than historical alternatives.

There is, then, an important sociological aspect to understanding the origins of open-source development. Private claims to intellectual property are often seen as morally offensive owing to their distributional consequences and the fact that excluded groups are deprived of the benefits. It is fundamental in understanding the origins of open source to acknowledge the deep hostility of programers to the privatization of software. Early software, because it was developed by monopolies such as telecommunication companies, was created in open-source environments and freely disseminated. The creators of these programs were well known in the software community. They wrote manuals, appeared at conferences, and offered help.

Earlier, we noted that the open-source community shares many of the properties of science. It is also similar to the internal labor markets that now are part of the standard economic textbook description. In their seminal analysis of internal labor markets, Doeringer and Piore (1971) noted that work was not simply the conjunction of impersonal supply and demand curves, but usually found through a matching process conducted within an organization. Critical to this matching process was the notion of skill or 'practice' by which workers gain experience specific to the firm and specific to their task. Apprenticeship often took the form of on-the-job training. The specificity of these skills drove a wedge between external and internal markets.

An operating system such as UNIX was developed in a community that spanned the boundaries of firms. To drive the wedge between the internal and external markets, AT&T chose eventually to exercise proprietary claims on its use and development. However, unlike the experience dynamic that supports internal labor markets, the expertise to develop many software programs exists in a community of practice that is wider than the boundaries of a given firm. In fact, apprenticeship in the software community consists often of learning by 'legitimate peripheral participation'. In the case of open-source software, this learning rides upon the efforts of hackers to access software code for their own use and development.[1] It is not surprising that, given this wide diversity of skills, UNIX subsequently 'forked' into a number of competing versions.

There is, then, a conflict between the external production process of software within a community and the legal governance structure that restricts development to those owning the property rights. Open source does not dissolve this distinction between the production process and the governance structure. In all open-source communities there is an explicit governance structure. The contribution made by open source is to transfer this governance structure from the firm to a non-profit body that does not own the software.

Table 12.1. Open-Source Projects

Name	Definition/description
Zope	Enables teams to collaborate in the creation and management of dynamic web-based business applications such as intranets and portals.
Sendmail	The most important and widely used email transport software on the Internet.
Mozilla	Netscape-based, open-source browser.
MySQL	Open-source database.
Scripting languages:	
Perl	The most popular web programming language.
Python	An interpreted, interactive, object-oriented programming language.
PHP	A server-side HTML embedded scripting language.
Other:	
BIND	Provides the domain-name service for the entire Internet.

Descriptions of Two Open-Source Models

There are many software programs that are designed in open-source communities. Table 12.1 lists a sample of open-source projects other than Linux and Apache that we will discuss indepth. The world of open-source software is making inroads into areas beyond operating systems, Internet and desktop applications, graphical user interfaces, and scripting languages. For example, it is also making inroads in Electronic Design Automation for Hardware Description Languages (*Linux Journal*, February 2001: 162). Moreover, there are now many projects designed to make open-source products more user-friendly (see Table 12.2).

The commercial potential of open source rests not in the ability to charge licence fees, but in demand for consulting, support, and quality-verification services. RedHat, which sells one version of Linux, competes on the basis of customer service, and not on the basis of ownership of the intellectual property. Another example is Covalent, which is the leader in products and services for Apache, and the only source of full commercial support for the Apache Web server.[2]

Linux and Apache are two of the most successful open-source software communities (the World Wide Web is obviously a third.) To understand better

Table 12.2. Open-Source Projects Designed to Make Open-Source Products More User-Friendly

Name	Definition/description
KDE	Graphical desk-top environment for UNIX work-stations.
GIMP	The GNU Image Manipulation Program: tasks such as photo retouching, image composition, and image authoring.
GNOME	Desk-top environment.

how open source works, and how the various communities differ, we provide a short description of both.

LINUX

Linux is a UNIX operating system that was developed by Linus Torvalds and a loosely knit community of programers across the Internet. The name Linux comes from Linus's UNIX. In 1991, Linus Torvalds, a Finnish computer science student, wrote the first version of a UNIX kernel for his own use. Instead of securing property rights to his invention, he posted the code on the Internet with a request to other programers to help upgrade it into a working system. The response was overwhelming. What began as a student's pet project rapidly developed into a non-trivial, operating-system kernel. This accomplishment was possible because, at the time, there already existed a large community of UNIX developers who were disenchanted by the fact that vendors had taken over UNIX development. They also were unhappy with the growing reliance on Microsoft's proprietary server software.

The Linux development model is built around Torvalds's authority, described by some as 'benevolently' exercised.[3] Legally, anyone can build an alternative community to develop other versions of Linux. In practice, the development process is *centralized*, being distributed but subject to hierarchical control. New code is submitted to Torvalds, who decides whether or not to accept it, or request modifications before adding it to the Linux kernel. In this sense, Torvalds is the undisputed leader of the project, but there is no official organization that institutionalizes this role. As Linux grew in popularity and size, Torvalds became overwhelmed with the amount of code submitted to the kernel. As Linux members noticed, 'Linus doesn't scale.' Therefore, Torvalds delegated large components to several of his trusted 'lieutenants' who further delegated to a handful of 'area' owners. Nowadays, several developers have more-or-less control over their particular subsections. There is a networking chief, a driver chief, and so forth. While Torvalds has ultimate authority, he seldom rejects a decision made by one of these subadministrators.

Torvalds accumulates the patches received, and then releases a new monolithic kernel incorporating them. For software that does not go into the kernel, Torvalds does not prevent others from adding specialized features. These patches allow even greater customization without risking the integrity of the operating system for the vast majority. Sometimes optimizing for one kind of hardware damages the efficiency for other hardware. Some users require 'paranoid security' that, by definition, cannot be useful if disseminated;

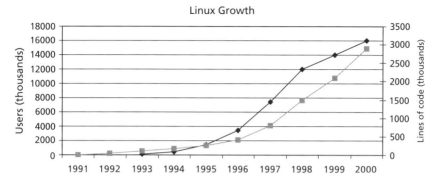

Figure 12.1. Growth of Linux: number of users and number of lines of code
Sources: RedHat Software, Inc. and *Forbes*, 10 August 1998.

or, some incremental innovations are too experimental to inflict on everyone.

The number of contributors also grew dramatically over the years, from Linus Torvalds in 1991 to 10,000 developers in 1998 (*Forbes*, 10 August 1998). Figure 12.1 portrays the remarkable growth in the number of Linux users (16 million in 2000) and in the product's lines of code (2.9 million in 2000). In terms of server operating systems shipped, Linux's market share was 24 percent in 1999. According to International Data Corporation, over the next four years, Linux shipments will grow at a rate of 28 percent, from 1.3m in 1999 to 4.7m in 2004.[4]

APACHE

The Apache HTTP server project is a web server originally based on the open-source server from the National Center for Supercomputing Applications (NCSA). A web server is a program that serves the files that form web pages to web users (whose computers contain HTTP clients that forward their requests). Web servers use the client/server model and the World Wide Web's Hypertext Transfer Protocol. Every computer on the Internet that contains a web site must have a web server program. The name reflects the practice of university-laboratory software being 'patched' with new features and fixes ('a patchy server').

The project was started in 1995 to fix an NCSA program. For most of its existence, there have been fewer than two dozen people seriously working on the software at any one time. The original group included eight people who later became known as webmasters, and many who went on to start open-source projects at commercial enterprises. Several of the original members came from the University of Illinois, which also spawned the web browser that became Netscape. The original group constituted the Apache core, and is responsible for the primary development of the Apache HTTP server.

The development for the Apache model is *federal*, based upon a meritocratic selection process. While access to the source code and the history information of changes is available to anyone, the ability to make changes is reserved for the Apache board, comprised of people that have been chosen because of proven ability and past contributions. Other contributors to Apache can join three different groups. The developer email list consists of technical discussions, proposed changes, and automatic notification about code changes, and can consist of several hundred messages a day. The Current Version Control archive consists of modification requests that resulted in a change to code or documentation. There is also the problem-reporting database in the form of a Usenet that is the most accessible list, consisting of messages reporting problems and seeking help.

The coordination of the development process is achieved via two types of rules. The initial rule, called 'review-then-commit' (RTC), was used during 1996 and 1997. It states that in order for a change to master sources to be made, a submitted patch would first need to be tested by other developers who would apply it to their systems. This rule leads to a time-consuming process, and it does not encourage innovation. Therefore, in 1998 a new process was introduced, the 'commit-then-review' (CTR). CTR speeds up development while exercising quality control. However, it demands vigilance on the part of the development team. Controversial changes need first to be discussed on the mailing list.

Mailing list discussions typically achieve consensus on changes that are submitted. However, particularly controversial topics may call for a vote. Because Apache is a meritocracy, even though all mailing-list subscribers can express an opinion by voting, their actions may be ignored unless they are recognized as serious contributors.

New versions of Apache are released when developers achieve consensus that it is 'ready,' and not by set calendar dates. Someone volunteers to be the release manager, who then receives 'code ownership' (Mockus et al. 2000). The developer has the responsibility for getting agreement on the release schedule, ensuring that new commits are not too controversial, contacting the testers' mailing lists, and building the release. Once a release is out, people start hacking on it.

Apache has a 62 percent share of the Internet server market (see www.netcraft.co.uk/survey/). Figure 12.2 graphs Apache's steadily increasing market share, beating out proprietary products such as Netscape's and Microsoft's server suites. Apache is now an umbrella for a suite of projects such as XML and Java projects.

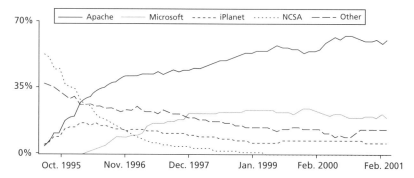

Figure 12.2. Growth of Apache
Source: Netcraft Survey.

Intellectual Property and Licences

The various open-source licences share the fundamental trait that the property rights to their use are placed in the public domain. They differ in the extent to which they allow public domain property to be mixed with private property rights. The historical trends have been to tolerate a hybrid of both. As noted earlier, these issues are similar to the conflicts surrounding public and private property claims to the results of basic research funded by public research institutions.

The first open-source licence was Richard Stallman's General Public License (GPL) created for the protection of the GNU operating system.[5] It was the decision of AT&T to issue proprietary control over UNIX that led Stallman to start the GNU Project in 1984 to develop a complete UNIX-like operating system as free software. Stallman started the Free Software Foundation (FSF) to carry out this project, and called his licence 'copyleft' because it preserves the users' right to copy the software.[6]

As commercial enterprises started to take note of open-source software, some members of the community thought they needed to sustain this interest by toning down the free software rhetoric. On the basis of the licence for the Debian GNU/Linux distribution developed by Bruce Perens in 1997, the Open Source Definition (OSD) was born.[7] This licence differs from the GPL. The GPL forces every program that contains a free software component to be released in its entirety as free software. In this sense, it forces 'viral' compliance. The OSD only requires that a free/open-source licence allow distribution in source code as well as compiled form.

The licence may not require a royalty or other fee for such a sale. Consistent with the requirements of the OSD, the Berkeley System Distribution (BSD) and Apache licences allow programers to take their modifications private, in other words to sell versions of the program without distributing the source code of the modifications.

The boundaries between the public and private segments of the software developed by the open-source community are thus not distinct. Even under the GPL, which allows double licensing, it is possible to make money on the commercial version. An author can release the source code of a project under an open-source licence, while at the same time selling the same product under a commercial licence. It is also possible to make money by developing proprietary applications for open-source infrastructure. Applications that operate independently (e.g. leaf notes in the software tree) can be proprietary, but the infrastructure should be open source.

The open-source licences conflict with most, but not all, interpretations of the functioning of a patent system. Mazzoleni and Nelson (1998) note recently that patent law serves several competing functions.

The first function is the resolution of market failure to reward innovators. Since inventions can be copied, the inventor requires an enforceable property claim in order to have a temporary monopoly to extract an economic return. But patents also serve other functions. They place in the public domain the knowledge of the invention and they establish property rights to important 'gateway technologies' that permit the further development of derived inventions in an orderly way. The critical feature of these arguments is the observation that research is an input and a product. By protecting the product, the danger is to slow progress by restricting the use of the innovation as an input into subsequent efforts.

The modern economics and law tradition in property rights has argued that patents are a solution to the 'tragedy of the commons' problem. In a seminal article, Hardin (1968) argued that public goods are prone to be overused when too many owners have the right to use them, and no owner has the right to exclude another. Hardin's explanation has also fuelled the policy of privatizing commons property either through private arrangements (Ostrom 1990) or the patenting of scientific discoveries.

More recent legal writings have, however, questioned this tradition. Heller and Eisenberg (1998) have pointed out that public goods are prone to underuse in a 'tragedy of the anticommons' when too many individuals have rights of exclusion of a scarce resource. An example of under-use of a scarce source is the fragmentation of rights in biomedical research in the US. The need to access multiple patented inputs may deter a user from developing a useful product.

In recent years, there has been considerable attention paid to the cost of excessively strong property regimes by which to reward innovation. In particular, the recent expansion of the legal protection of software from copyright to patents has been decried as a threat to innovation and to the sharing of knowledge in fast-paced industries. David (2000) has noted the dangers of this type of encroachment in the commons of academic research. Similar problems arise in other industries. Lerner (1995), for example, found that patents by large firms in bio-technology have effectively deterred smaller firms from innovating in these areas. In other words, the shortcomings of the patent-awarding process defeat the stated purpose of the patent system to provide incentives to innovate. Because firms use the legal system strategically, the second-best argument for patent protection becomes less clear. The implication is that no protection might, in some cases, dominate the policy of providing monopoly rights to the exercise of a patent.

American law has permitted the violation of private property if the loss of public access is considered to be excessive. Merges (1999a) cites the case of litigation over the right to built a new bridge over the Charles River in Boston. In 1837, the courts ruled in favour of the right of public access and against a company that had secured an exclusive franchise to operate bridges over the Charles River. Similarly, courts have rarely upheld the claims of companies to deter former employees from exploiting an idea. Hyde's (1998) study of the Silicon Valley shows that the 'law in action' in the region encourages rapid diffusion of information by protecting start-ups and employee departures.

Various solutions to the fragmentation of rights have been proposed in recognition of the fact that ownership and control of the cornerstone pieces on which the digital economy is built are crucial issues for economic policy. To meet the need of inter-operability among standards, Merges proposed patent pools as solutions that reduce the volume of licensing and lead to greater technological integration (Merges 1999b). Recently approved pools, such as the MPEG-2 pool that brings together complementary inputs in the form of 27 patents from nine firms, could serve as a guide to for other industries. The pool was an institutional expression of the creation of the MPEG-2 video compression technology standard. Patent-holders license their MPEG-2 patents to a central administrative entity that administers the pool on behalf of its members. The pool includes only essential patents, in other words those patents required to implement a widely accepted technological standard. Patent pools suffer, however, from a number of problems, the most important one being the potential for a hold-up by one of the parties.

A general patent licence avoids this potential by a 'viral' quality to enforce compliance. The GPL is unique in its provision that does not allow programers to take modifications private. This 'viral' clause results in all software that incorporates GPL-ed programs becoming open source as well. As noted above, patents serve two different functions: to incite innovation and to encourage incremental exploration. Public licences, such as the GPL, permit this additional function to operate, while obviating the negative consequences of a second-best policy. Since anyone has the right to use and modify an open-source software program, these licences provide maximum freedom for the exploitation of incremental innovations.

It is, however, the more pragmatic licences that support Apache that pose a danger to the incentives to form open-source projects. The licences that permit a blending of open and proprietary code put at risk the ideals on which the community has been built. For open-source contributors and advocates, intellectual property is a commons that needs to be protected from enclosure.[8] As such, open source provides an answer to the fragmentation of protected— patented or copyrighted—knowledge. Moreover, the open-source licences allow the community to protect the code it produces and to induce compliance with the philosophy expressed in these licences. It is these licences that keep the code in the commons, and they protect the generalized reciprocity that characterizes the community culture.

GOVERNANCE STRUCTURE

However, the licences may not be enough by themselves. The question then is whether there are in place governance structures that will prevent fragmentation of code into proprietary islands. Lawrence Lessig (1999) made an important argument that software code contains the constitutional rules by which participants behave in virtual communities, such as chat rooms. For open-source development, the causality runs the other way. The different governance structures influence the development of the code in at least two important ways. The first is that every open-source software program runs the danger of 'forking,' as seen in the case of UNIX or in Java. The second is that the organization by which work is delegated influences the product design.

Neither Linux nor Apache has forked into competing versions. The Apache governance structure has the advantage of being coalitional. The coalition itself can change, as participating developers can migrate to more important roles depending upon their contribution. It is thus easier to organize a response to potential efforts to 'fork' the code. The Linux community is also hierarchical, as we saw, but highly centralized on Torvalds. If Torvalds himself should play a less central role and hence the role of the charismatic leader (in Weber's sense) fades, then the methods by which disputes would be resolved are not at all obvious.

There is the interesting issue of whether the design of the product itself can force compliance. For example, initially Torvalds wrote the kernel as an integral unit, contrary to academic opinion. However, over time, it too became more modular. Apache, by virtue of its coalitional structure, from the start was very modular. There is thus convergence in product design, though the initial structure of the products reflected the differences in the governance structures of the two communities. A question, largely unexplored, is whether the vestiges of the Linux design force agreement on the interfaces between the modules and the kernel and core modules. In this case, the choice of technological design might force compliance to a standard. However, as this possibility is not compelling, it is unsurprising that Linux should be protected under a GPL that requires all code to be non-proprietary. In this way, if the code should be balkanized, it will not at least be proprietary. The Apache licence does not prevent proprietary code from being mixed with open source, but it also has a stronger governance structure to respond to defectors.

In conclusion, the open-source licences generally have the advantage of forcing the code into the public domain. They thereby favor a dynamic by which incremental innovations can be rapidly contributed to improve the code and to add functions. The danger of open-source development is the potential for fragmenting the design into competing versions. Governance structures offer some potential for preventing 'forking', as well as technological choices that might force compliance.

The Software Production Process

The second argument for open-source software is that it offers a better model for development. There is an active debate in the software literature regarding how much software development is 'craft' and how much is 'routinized.' The craft nature of software development was strained by the demand for 'integral' programs that required thousands of engineers. Brooks (1975) documented the difficulties posed by the creation of the operating system for the IBM 360 large-frame computer. A major problem for the design of sophisticated software programs has been reducing the complexity in the development process.

In traditional software production processes, two fundamental contributions have sought to reduce this complexity. The first is the use of 'hidden knowledge' incorporated in a module, with team managers focusing on interfaces to optimize overall functionality. The second contribution has been the partitioning of software development into discrete steps that can be conducted sequentially or concurrently. Both of these principles are used in open-source development.

While similar principles of design are used, open source benefits from two sources of efficiency gain. The first is the efficiency of implementing production in a distributed community of practice that permits frontier users also to be contributors. This gain is especially striking in light of von Hippel's finding that many innovations originate with users, not producers (von Hippel 1988). The second source is concurrent debugging and design. Whereas it is standard practice for software houses to release beta versions of their products, the release of open-source code permits a 'tweaking' of the code on a decentralized basis that can then be incorporated into official releases. It would be helpful to look at both of these sources of efficiency gains in more detail.

USER MOTIVATION

The critical question posed by an open-source licence is whether there are sufficient incentives for developers to contribute effort to innovation. One claim is that developers contribute out of a sense of 'altruism.' Indeed, there is considerable evidence in economic behavior that people ignore economic calculations in their decisions. For example, the experiments by Kahneman et al. (1986) and Bies et al. (1993) pointed to the role of fairness, by which people share a fixed reward. People also defect less than the prediction on prisoner-dilemma games. Defection falls dramatically with communication and with very simple screening devices (Frank 1988; Ostrom et al. 1992). The importance of reciprocity in the exchanges among members of the open-source community has been recently documented by Lakhani and von Hippel (2000). Their study of the support groups for the Apache web server shows that the most important reason for people posting answers on Usenet groups is the desire to help because they have been helped by others, or because they expect to need others' expertise in the future.

Lerner and Tirole (2000) propose an explanation that does not rely upon altruism, or identity. They argue that contribution to an open-source project is much like a tournament that signals merit. Contributors enjoy improved prospects in the labor market by signalling their merit.

These two perspectives of gift-giving and labor-market signalling reflect two different views of motivation. Gift-giving reflects an 'intrinsic' motivation, whereby the individual finds reward in the public validation of his or her value. Labor-market signalling is an 'extrinsic' motivation that ties contribution to pecuniary reward. Both motives may in fact be operating, though it would seem that communities with mixed motivations often dissolve owing to obvious free-rider problems. Indeed, many labor-supply models have noted the problem of signalling false quality. An efficient wage is one of many devices suggested to attain effort and quality from workers when defection is probabilistic.

The importance of distinguishing between these two motivations is central to the classic study on gift-giving in which Titmuss (1971) found that the extrinsic reward of paying for blood expands the supply but also makes voluntary contributions less intrinsically rewarding. The consequence is, ironically, the potential destruction of the market for blood by increasing uncertainty over quality.[9] These much-discussed results have two implications. The first is that the donors themselves have the best knowledge of the likely quality of their blood. Given the existing technologies and this information asymmetry, it makes sense to reduce potentially the blood supply but gain a 'free' filter to be imposed by the donor that leads to an overall higher quality supply. The second is that the donor is also a potential recipient. In other words, a voluntary policy provides a highly motivated donor.

There is little evidence that open-source participants are more motivated. Indeed, this conclusion would appear to be hard to defend on the existing evidence, especially if effort must be acquired for less interesting projects. However, the more relevant deduction is that the open-source model relies upon knowledgeable users to contribute as developers. It is not the average motivation that may matter, but rather the attraction of highly motivated and capable talent to the project. In this sense, open source more effectively exploits the intelligence in the distributed system.

CONCURRENCE OF DEBUGGING AND CODE-WRITING

We claim that open source exploits the intelligence in the distributed system. The development of complex software products poses severe engineering and managerial difficulties. To meet the challenge of reducing the costs of producing complex software, many companies adopted structured approaches to software development. Cusumano's study of the 'software factory' documents how software design moved from art to routinized tasks manipulating standardized modules (Cusumano 1991). This approach culminated in an attempt to rationalize the entire cycle of software production, installation, and maintenance through the establishment of factory-like procedures and processes.

The factory production process is not, however, well suited to all software design processes. Glass (1995) views software as a creative enterprise that cannot be fully routinized. Methodologies to convert design into a disciplined activity are not suited to addressing new problems to be solved (1995: 41). At the same time, writing of code involves solving the detail-level problems left unsolved in an inevitably incomplete design.

The factory approach to software development applies the Babbage principle of the mental division of labor. In this model, intelligent work is specialized to the design group, code writing is given to a less skilled group, and debugging and maintenance to an even less skilled group. *A reasonable production function for this kind of process is a 'weak link' chain, where the least productive element in the process determines the output* (see Becker and Murphy (1992) for an example).

The interactive approach suggests a production function in which value is maximized, subject to the constraints of threshold quality and time to market. This process will be less structured than a 'waterfall' sequence, where the design stage precedes coding and testing, but will allow for concurrent design and implementation. *This model suggests that the software production is as good as its most productive member.* It is in this sense that open source exploits the intelligence in the community; it provides a matching between competence and task.

Open-source development permits this resolution of complexity by consistently applying the principles of modular design. The modularization of software evolves through a series of complex adaptations. Open source has several traits in common with the description by Baldwin and Clark (2000) of the recombinative evolution of the assembly of component modules of computers. By relying upon an external market that proposes incremental module improvements, computer assemblers benefit from the distributed intelligence of competing suppliers. It is not surprising that some have taken this to be the key element to open-source development. For example, Axelrod and Cohen (2000) explicitly treat Linux as an example of a complex adaptive system. The open-source licences permit distributed and uncoordinated developers to propose variants to the existing program. These variants are then submitted to a selection process that chooses the better performing program.

The complex-adaptive-system approach captures the advantage of using system testing in a distributed community. However, the community is far more hierarchically organized for the actual development of software code than suggested by the metaphor of a population of interacting agents. For the contribution of large modules, Apache and Linux both assign these tasks to developers who manage the project.

It is not surprising that, in spite of the large number of participants in open-source communities, the actual number of constant contributors is small. We analyzed the 'Changes' files to Apache between March 1995 and February 2000. These files list the new patches included in each new version of Apache, as well as their author. The analysis reveals that a small number of developers are responsible for the majority of contributions. While there were 326 people who contributed patches during the analyzed period, most of these individuals—232 to be precise—only contributed one patch per person, and 36 only two patches per person. In contrast, the top five contributors each made between 20 and 30 changes, and another 14 individuals each made between ten and 19 changes. Other researchers have obtained similar results. Mockus et al. (2000) found that the top 15 Apache developers contributed more than 83 percent of the basic changes, and that the changes done by core developers are substantially larger than those done by the non-core group. The role of system tester is the function reserved primarily for the wide community

Table 12.3. Contributions to Linux and Apache

Contributions/person	Linux contributors	Apache contributors
1	1,866	232
2	355	36
3	110	16
4	44	9
5	17	5
6	12	2
7	2	5
8	5	
9	5	2
10–19	9	14
20–30	4	5
Total	2,429	326

Source: Our analyzes of Apache, and Dempsey et al.'s (1999) study of a subset of the Linux community.

of Apache users. The same pattern of contributions also holds in the Linux community. Table 12.3 shows the frequency count of the changes from Apache and from a study on a subset of the Linux community (see Dempsey et al. 1999).

Hence, it is not modularity that gives open source a distinctive source of advantage, because it too relies on hierarchical development. Rather the source of its advantage lies in concurrence of development and debugging. In spite of its unglamorous nature, maintenance alone can represent anywhere between 50 and 80 percent of the average software budget (Yourdon 1996). The largest part of the developer community is not involved with code writing, but with code debugging.

Raymond (1998) has eloquently summarized the efficiency of the open-source model in debugging code: 'given enough eyeballs, all bugs are shallow.' Such claims have been substantiated by researchers who compared the performance of commercial and open projects in terms of the speed of debugging. Kuan (2000) found that open-source projects ranked higher on the debugging dimension than closed-source projects. Also, Mockus et al. (2000: 6) found that the productivity of Apache development is very high compared to commercial projects, with lean code and lower defect density even before system test.

The efficiency of the open-source development model is indirectly established by software firms' efforts to emulate it, without even realizing it. Cusumano and Selby (1995) explain that in order to encourage exchange of ideas, Microsoft builds software teams and cultivates developer networks within the company. In this sense, Microsoft creates an internal community to appraise and debug the innovations of software teams. Yourdon (1996) also notes the company's practice of instituting the 'push back method' whereby people challenge each other's ideas.

Yet, this simulated 'open-source' environment differs not only in size, but also in separating final users from the process. One of the most important contributions by open source is, by releasing the code, to let users themselves fix the bugs. As often noted, no one knows the number of bugs in a Microsoft product because the software is proprietary. By placing the code in the public domain, open-source development corrects bugs concurrently with design and implementation. Users participate usually by posting questions and complaints through 'usenets.' This activity is separate from the design activity that, as explained above, remains hierarchically organized.

WHEN WILL WE NOT SEE OPEN SOURCE

Of course, not all software projects are amenable to open-source development. An operating system, because it is long lasting and widespread, can benefit from a system that provides rapid improvement and has a low catastrophic risk; but for example, a software system that is tailored to supporting trading activity on a specific stock market is an unlikely candidate for open sourcing; the code is too specific and hence not re-usable and the catastrophic risk is too high.

A product that is not modular would also not be appropriate for open-source development. A molecule, for example, is not modular; changing atoms drastically alters its pharmaceutical properties. Modularity can be achieved by breaking up the discovery and trial sequence into many steps. But such steps cannot be done concurrently, so there is no gain to open-source debugging.

Thus the range of modular to integral will greatly influence the application of open-source development, as well as the speed of the development cycle. For products that are modular and for which development times are short, community development by open source offers clear advantages. The important issue is whether the weak appropriability of open-source development swings the choice towards less efficient proprietary models of development that have strong intellectual property mechanisms by which to appropriate rents to innovation.

Conclusions on its Economics Potential

As a back of the envelope exercise, it is interesting to ask whether open source might make any material impact on developing countries. Developing countries present two central features. They have, in aggregate, the bulk of the world population and, hence, of the world's brain power. Yet, they have a minuscule share of world technological innovation. This disequilibrium has surely been a potent force in explaining the migration of educated individuals from poor to rich countries.

Can open source provide an alternative model whereby innovation can occur on a more distributed basis? Over the past ten years, the Indian software industry has grown at annual rates of over 50 percent. The industry's revenue in the fiscal year 1999/2000 was USD5.7 billion. The most prominent centre of software development in India is Bangalore, which accounted for over a quarter of India's total software exports in 1999/2000. In 1991, the government lowered tariffs on foreign goods and loosened investment restrictions. The Indian success in capitalizing on this liberalization is aided by the large and highly educated workforce of engineers. India produces about 70,000–85,000 software engineers annually, along with about 45,000 other IT graduates. The government plans to double the intake of IT graduates for the 2001/2002 academic year.

The Indian industry is not large relative to total GNP or to total employment. As low value-added links in the global software production chain, it would take rather improbable multipliers on the domestic economy to lead to the expectation that they could be engines for growth. Yet, if the value added in their software contribution should increase, then a more dynamic scenario is feasible. The critical question is whether Indian companies can move from 'body-shop' services to high value-added innovations. Can a developing country join the frontier of innovation or is it trapped in the seesaw of low value-added exports of products and high value-added exports of human capital to developed countries?

In this regard, open source poses policy questions that are familiar to economists and policy-makers regarding competition regulation and intellectual property rights. The traditional dilemma for anti-trust regulation and law is the balance between providing incentives for innovation by allowing for monopoly profits and yet avoiding the foreclosure of access to intellectual property that serves as a complement to other innovative endeavours. The doctrine of essential facility has sought to address this dilemma.[10] Software operating systems, such as Microsoft's Windows, are examples of such essential facilities. The regulatory and legal solution to treating essential facilities has been to respect the monopoly profits associated with the primary market, but to seek to require access for the purpose of entry into new markets. However, this solution is cumbersome and expensive; it addresses the issue of intellectual property rights without acknowledging that it would not permit the operation of the production model of open source.

The primary policy implication of open source is to emphasize that excessive intellectual property regimes prevent the implementation of production models that the Internet makes far more feasible today than previously. As we noted earlier, the open-source community shares many properties with the conduct of research by scientists. It is ironic that the trend in intellectual property of research content has been towards privatization of the commons, such as in the commercialization of data services and interference with 'fair use' under copyright law through digital signatures (see David 2000). However, the loss to the academic community is not simply the exclusion due to limited financial resources to purchase these data. The loss is also the erosion of communal values that undergird an open production model for research that is impressively efficient in creating incentives for individuals to invest in research *and* its dissemination.

The Internet is itself the outcome of a combination of public and private incentives. Since its utility is the provision of information goods that are both outputs and inputs for further innovation and research, the dissemination of information is desirable. Consequently, the Internet is bound to be marked by deep conflicts over the intellectual property as a right granted by legal discretion versus entitlement. The experience of open source poses a fundamental challenge to the traditional concerns over the effects of weak intellectual property 'rights' on innovation by representing an endogenous mechanism of global innovation that offers an efficient production model. In a time of deepening disparities in world incomes and massive migration flows of educated people from poor to rich countries, this alternative model deserves close attention in changing the tone of the debate. Open source represents the emergence of a production model ideally suited for the properties of information that can be digitally coded and distributed. The test of a contest of intellectual property over information goods must consider the economic loss of impeding the organization and production of distributed knowledge on a global basis.

Acknowledgments

We would like to thank the Reginald H. Jones Center, the Wharton-SMU Research Center at the Singapore Management University, and the Carnegie Bosch Institute for financing of the research. We would also like to thank Chuck Murcko, Paul David, Andrew Glyn, an anonymous referee, and participants in the *Oxford Review*'s seminar on the Internet.

☐ ENDNOTES

* This chapter is a revised version of B. Kogut and A. Metiu (2001) 'Open-Source Software Development and Distributed Intelligence,' *Oxford Review of Economic Policy*, 17: 248–64.

1. See Lave and Wenger (1991) for their discussion of 'legitimate peripheral participation'.

2. For a more comprehensive list of companies, see Krueger in *Wired* magazine, 7 May 1999, available at: www.wired.com/wired/archive/7.05/tour.html

3. See an interview with Brian Behlendorf, available at: www.linux-mag.com/2000-04/ behlendorf_01.html. Even Torvalds views himself as governing by his acknowledged software expertise and skills as a project manager (see appendix to DiBona et al. 1999).

4. See IDC report at: www.idc.com/itforecaster/itf20000808.stm

5. GNU is a recursive acronym for 'GNU's Not UNIX's', and it is pronounced 'guh-NEW'.

6. For these efforts, Stallman was called 'the last hacker' in a book on the beginnings of the computer (Levy 1984).

7. For more details see: www.debian.org/social_contract.html#guidelines

8. See interview with Tim O'Reilly in the *Linux Journal*, February 2001.

9. The findings that monetary rewards can have a negative effect on motivation are not new—see Lepper and Greene (1978) and, more recently, Gneezy and Rustichini (2000).

10. We thank a referee for this discussion.

Part IV
Looking Forward

13 The Network as Knowledge: Generative Rules and the Emergence of Structure

Introduction

The imputation problem is how to account for the sources of the value of the firm. I propose that part of the value of the firm derives from its participation in a network that emerges from the operation of generative rules that instruct the decision to cooperate. Whereas the value of firm-level capabilities is coincidental with the firm as the unit of accrual, ownership claims to the value of coordination in a network pit firms potentially in opposition with one another. We analyze the work on network structure to suggest two types of mechanisms by which rents are distributed.

The thesis of this chapter is that a structure of a network is an emergent outcome generated by rules that guide the cooperative decisions of firms in specific competitive markets. The observed differences in the patterns of cooperation across industries are not happenstance. They reflect rather the implicit operation of these cooperative rules and the competing visions that come to shape a network. The emergence of the structural pattern of cooperation is not the result of an abstract and static choice between market or firm, or market versus hybrid cooperative forms of governance. Structure is emergent in the initial conditions of a specific industry.

The structure of an industry is interesting, because it represents capabilities of coordination among firms, as well as claims on the property rights to profits to cooperation. The conventional emphasis on the opposition of market, contract and firm represents largely a static view of the boundary choice facing a firm. The common proposition that a viable firm is worth at least the sum of its parts rests on the supposition that internal organized coordination is a source of economic value. Winter (1987) has insightfully coined this problem of valuation as a question of imputation. In his formulation, a firm is the unit of account to which rents accrue. Imputation is, then, the assignment of a firm's value to its constituent parts, e.g. patents, people, and machines. The determination of a firm's value is the result of the uniqueness of these factors, their transferability, and their resistance to imitation by competitors. If these factors, and the knowledge of how to coordinate them, were imitable, then there would be no rent to impute. These conditions are equivalent to concluding that there are no rents to public knowledge.

This reasoning quickly points to the boundary of the firm as representing more than a legal definition of the firm as the *unit of accrual*, but also as signifying a qualitative barrier between the knowledge held privately and the knowledge that is public. Yet, this barrier has often been exaggerated, for knowledge even when shared among two firms may not be a public good in the conventional sense of this term, that is, information that is accessible to other parties at zero marginal cost. For coordination among firms itself entails principles of organization that can be idiosyncratic to their relationship and that code for particular kinds of capabilities, such as speed of product development or minimizing inventories.

The accounting for knowledge stumbles, consequently, on an important problem: how do we impute the knowledge external to the firm that nevertheless contributes to its profitability? This puzzle is related to the interpretation of 'total factor productivity' in macroeconomic growth accounting studies. After accounting for the contribution of inputs to economy-wide growth, the residual is attributed to exogenous technical change, institutional factors, or externalities. Alternatively, it is possible to specify explicitly the 'imputed' source of productivity gains:

$$y_i = a_i + \gamma a_m + \sum a_i X_i + R$$

where y_i is output of firm i, a_t is a shift parameter, $a_i X_i$ are weighted inputs (such as the value of capital and labor), R is a residual, and γa_m is the weighted value imputed to the fixed effect of membership in a network (all terms are in logs). This formulation proposes that 'network capability' is a source of imputed value to the productivity of a firm.

The most tangible expression of the direct value of external knowledge to the firm is the compelling evidence that rapid product development depends on the reliance on outside suppliers. Both Clark et al. (1987) and Mansfield (1988) found that time to market was speeded through a policy of outsourcing to suppliers. The capability to commercialize products can in this case be seen to rest on the successful exploitation of the knowledge of other firms. In this sense, the competitive capabilities of a firm rest not only on its own knowledge or on its knowledge of the network. The capabilities of the firm, rather, are dependent upon the principles by which cooperation among firms is coordinated and supported in the network.[1]

This view of the network as knowledge confronts four analytical challenges:

1. What is meant by network capabilities?
2. How do we understand the generative rules that drive the emergent structure of the network?
3. How does structure influence the competing claims to rents among members to a network?
4. If structure encodes emergent knowledge, how is the network transformed into intentional replication of this knowledge through time?

The contribution of this chapter is to understand networks as arising out of generative rules that guide the formation of relationships and code for organizing principles of coordination. These rules are 'sorting' provisions that indicate the match between firms and the nature of their cooperation. The rules code for principles (e.g. 'share research' or 'supply just on time') and in turn lead to network capabilities that are not specific to a firm, but represent joint gains to coordination and learning. We explain that the structural patterns that emerge in a network define two kinds of rents, one that accrues to a broker, the other more broadly to the members of a closed group. Because these capabilities are quasi-public goods to members and yet firms are the units of accrual—not the network, a central issue is how the rents to this coordination are made both exclusionary and sustainable in the face of potential defection.

Our reasoning rests upon three central ideas of what define a firm: unit of accrual, governance structure to resolve agency problems through residual claims, and a repository of coordinating capabilities and social identity. While these three ideas are operative in the analysis below, we stress, in particular, the latter property of the firm in order to analyze how capabilities are generated by network coordination. To shift the understanding of networks as simply a resolution to agency conflicts, or as access to information, to their capabilities in promoting variety and yet coordination in specific industry settings is a primary ambition of this chapter.

Specialization and Variety in Market and Networks

A definition of an economic network is the pattern of relationships among firms and institutions. In this definition, an idealized market is a polar case of a network in which firms transact at spot prices and are fully connected in potential transactional relations but are disconnected through their absence of cooperative agreements. Few markets exist of this type. Rather, most markets consist of sub-sets of firms and institutions (e.g. universities) that interact more intensely with each on a long-term basis. These patterns of interactions encode the structural relationships that represent the network.

This definition fails to convey the observation that the structure of a network implies principles of coordination that not only enhance the individual capabilities of member firms, but themselves lead to capabilities that are not isolated to any one firm. It is important to the following argument to distinguish between information and coordination (or what is also called knowhow). At a minimum, the ability of a firm to access information in a network constitutes an advantage, for example the effect of accessing the technology of a research center on its subsequent innovations. Of course, this access is most likely the outcome of a bargain, in which the two parties arrive at an understanding of contribution and compensation. This sort of access, stressed by Powell (1990) among others, exemplifies the informational benefits of enhancing a firm's capabilties through relationships.[2]

Cooperation, however, can also engender capabilities in the relationship itself, such that the parties develop principles of coordination that improve their joint performance.[3] Such principles might be rules by how supplies are delivered, such as by just in time or mass production. Or they might involve more complex rules governing the process by which innovations are collectively produced and shared. In this sense, the network is itself knowledge, not in the sense of providing access to distributed information and capabilities, but in representing a form of coordination guided by enduring principles of organization.

The proposition that part of the value of a firm can be imputed to the capability of its embedded network is implicit in the treatment of the division of labor as handled by Smith through Stigler. The now classic question in the analysis of the boundaries between markets and firms can be rephrased as the following: if networks are structured by organizing principles of coordination through a division of labor among firms, then why are these firms not organized within a single common governance structure?

Networks offer the benefit of both specialization and variety generation. The superior abilities of markets to generate variety is a commonplace belief that is, nevertheless, problematic. The converse of this statement is that firms are superior vehicles for the accumulation of specialized learning. To understand variety, we must also understand why specialization and variety are antithetical within the firm, but define complements within a network.

Smith's famous essay recognized the power of the market to achieve variety through specialization in the division of labor (Smith 1965). Smithian efficiencies in specialization were due to the inherent learning by doing by completing repetitive tasks, as well as the reduction in loss time due to changing tools and tasks. At the heart of Smithian efficiencies is the implication that learning by doing, despite the initial endowments of equal competence among individuals, accumulates to lower the costs of subsequent production.

Smith saw the division of labor as derived from the dynamic learning through specialization. He posited that people were largely similar in their a priori talents; differentiation into specialized competence was the outcome, not the precursor, to the division of labor. In other words, specialization through a division of labor is the driver of the acquisition of competence and, consequently, of knowledge.

The perspective of the firm as a repository of knowledge embraces Smith's observation on experience-derived learning through a division of labor as posing both a static coordination problem as well as determining dynamic paths of knowledge acquisition. Firms are social communities that permit the specialization in the creation and replication of partly tacit, partly explicit organizing principles of work.

But why are firms required to provide this coordination? The behavioral sciences provide an important insight. (See Kogut and Zander (1996) for a review.) Boundaries to a firm represent more than the legal unit of accrual; they provide the cognitive representation of what constitutes the object of membership, that is, of identity. Through identity, individuals anchor their perceptions of self and other and attach meaning to membership in a firm, as well as in the categories of skill that define a division of labor (e.g. 'worker' or 'accountant'). By this anchoring, they employ focal rules by which action is coordinated and intention communicated through common categorization of self and other. More importantly, through identification to occupation and firm, individuals are guided and motivated along coordinated paths of joint learning. Boundaries matter, because within the cusp of these social membranes, identities are circumscribed. The behavioral foundations to why the knowledge of the firm is bounded are to be found in the basic human motivation of belonging and membership.

If benefits of identity are to lower the costs of communication and coordination, they come at a cost. For identities represent a norm which indicates avenues of exploration; by implication, they also prohibit certain paths. Organization by firm is variety reducing. The great power of the market is not only its information properties, but also its function as a generator of variety in innovations and capabilities that are subject to selection. The 'market,' as an assemblage of firms pursuing different visions and organized by distinct identities, generates a variety that individual firms cannot manufacture internally without decrement to division of labor and the salience of focal rules, in other words to the organizing principles (inclusive of compensation and incentive schemes), by which work is coordinated.

In effect, a rent arises out of the scarcity value not only of land or technology, but also of behavioral coordination within the firm. Yet, at the same time, networks also provide capabilities to coordinate behavior among firms. This dynamic between the capability of the firm and market lies at the heart of Stigler's argument that a firm moves from vertical integration to disintegration of its activities according to the process by which a market 'learns' to supply inputs at a lower cost than it can itself (Stigler 1951).

These observations are important because they force a recasting of the received wisdom on the relative merits of markets—which we have indicated is a network—and firms. Curiously, the initial statement of Coase is compatible with the view that the structure of external relationships influences boundary between firm and market. Coase ([1937] 1995) posited that this boundary is determined by the internal costs of production and management relative to the costs of market search and procurement.

Coase, however, left unexamined the issue how structure reduces the costs of search and coordination. Just as Stigler pointed to learning in the market, Chandler's (1962) early contribution was to explore how higher order organizing principles of divisionalization could reduce the costs of internal complexity. His history of the innovation in internal hierarchy pointed to the role that structure plays in reducing the costs of coordination and authority. More importantly, divisionalization increased the internal variety of the firm by separating potentially competing visions into relatively contained units.

Figure 13.1 presents a diagram of the Coasian firm as the base case. Since Coase acknowledged market search and management costs, it is reasonable to think of these costs as increasing as the variety of products are produced internally or sourced externally. We index these costs as increasing in relation to a set of products that reflect the identity of the firm. At low variety, a firm

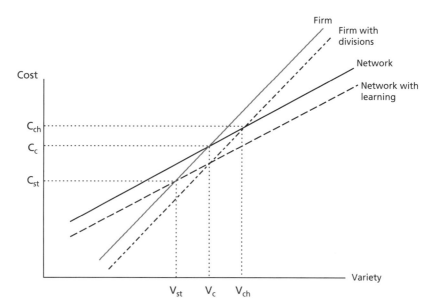

Figure 13.1. Static costs of sourcing variety with organizational and institutional learning

Notes: Subscripts-Stigler (st), Coase (c), Chandler (ch).

produces at lower cost than purchasing from other firms; this condition is simply to guarantee the existence of the firm. At some point, the internal management of increasing variety becomes more expensive than sourcing variety from the external network known as the market.

It is then straightforward to diagram the effect of a Chandlerian innovation; it increases internal variety at given levels of cost. Similarly, we can think of Stigler's life cycle notion of integration and de-integration as implying an improvement in the capability of the network. Just as a firm learns, so does the network insofar as suppliers come to substitute for internal production. In effect, the variety of the firm decreases as the knowledge diffuses to the market. Figure 13.1 illustrates this idea by showing how improvement in the efficiency of the market reduces the internal variety of the firm. As the market learns, the need to integrate vertically dampens. It is, in fact, exactly the increased knowledge in the supplier network, as realized through the innovations in the Toyota system, that has forced a radical disintegration of American auto assemblers. Gulati and Lawrence's (1999) observations on the extension of coordination to the external value chain are drawn from the historical diffusion of these innovations in the auto industry.

Simple Rules and Emergent Networks

A network is then a collection of firms, each ensconced in an identity that supports specialization and a dynamic of learning and exploration. But the network, unlike the firm, does not consist of an authority relationship that can enforce an organizational structure on its members. In Chandler's history, an entrepreneur imposes an innovation on the firm with the support of top management. How does a network learn to coordinate in the absence of authority?

The seeds of the answer to this question lie in Hayek's contention that the market is the engine of variety (Hayek 1988). Hayek's contribution is often credited for his observation that markets are superior to hierarchies for embedding information in prices. But Hayek, even in his heralded 1945 article on information, meant something more. Knowledge is held tacitly, raising the problem of how central planners could ever know as much as decentralized firms. Specialization is self-preserving, even if markets generate information as to their valuation and accessibility, because prices can be communicated, but not competencies. The dynamic advantage of the market is the generation of variety through an 'extended order' that supports coordination among specialized firms.

Hayek's notion of the extended order begs the question what generates the structure of this order, or what we would label the network. Obviously, markets differ from each other. The extended order supporting variety is hardly homogeneous across industries. Is the emergence of these network structures random or do they reflect the operation of operating principles that act as genetic rules?

Our claim is that the structure of a network arises from inherent characteristics of technologies that populate an industry, as well as social norms and institutional factors that favor the operation of particular rules. Technologies of mass production, which characterize some industries in some countries, influence the choices that firms make to cooperate or not. Industries characterized by science-based technologies tend toward rules that promote cooperation between research centers and firms. As these rules generate the structure of a network, the structure itself influences subsequent behavior.

For clarity, consider the simple example of the tit-for-tat rule as analyzed by Axelrod and Hamilton (1981). By analyzing the convergence properties in a population in which agents use different rules for cooperating and defecting, they found that particular rules, especially one that rewards for cooperation and sanctions for defections on the next round, tend to dominate. Convergence, however, is frequency dependent and thus vulnerable to tipping in either direction. The implication of this analysis is that structure that isolates 'cooperators' tends toward self-organizing communities of cooperation.[5] There is no authority, and yet the network self-organizes—that is, converges—toward the dominance of rule (e.g. tit-for-tat) over the other. Once achieved, the resultant structure supports a general capability of cooperation without even enacting the rule itself.

There are many studies whose results imply the operation of rules generating a dynamic of self-organization. These rules need not be technological in origin, but can also reflect institutional and cultural norms. They are also deeply embedded in the social identity of the actors. They may seem 'irrational' from a perspective of economic optimization. But what is critical to understand, as we will explain later, is that rules generate structure that dissuades rule-breaking behavior.

That identities underline the preference for particular rules is central to White's argument that networks are manifestations of the physics of identity and control (White 1992). This claim is implicit in White's early work on the structural implications of kinship rules (White 1963). (This analogy is not far fetched in light of the penchant for using familial descriptions in the alliance literature, such as 'parent' company or joint venture as a 'child.') Societies differ in their rules by which kinship encourages and prohibits marriage. As a consequence, kinship rules generate distinctive trees. Rules that permit marriage between first cousins generate radically different societal patterns of kinship than those that forbid marriage only between paternal cousins. The identity of what constitutes family is the foundation to the origins of the rules that govern familial replication.

In traditional societies, identity and family determined the economic and social networks. The study by Padgett and Ansell (1993) infers the rule, based on the analysis of the marriage and economic networks of Florentine families in the fifteenth century, that aristocratic families did not interact socially or economically with the new families. These families were situated in a fairly simple economic and social network determined by economic and marital rules. By mild violations of the rule forbidding economic ties, the Medici family influenced the structure such that they were two times more central in the network than the next family (Wasserman and Faust 1994).

The rules of kinship and social prestige have clear analogues in the implication of identity within the social community of industrial and financial firms. For example, the results observed in the study by Podolny and Stuart (1995) on cooperation are based on the rule that high status firms do not ally with low status firms. As a consequence, there is a sorting behavior by which prestigious firms are grouped by strong ties (cohesive ties with no intermediaries) and engage in weaker ties to less prestigious firms, sometimes as a form of endorsement (Stuart et al. 1999).

Despite our emphasis on the neglected social influences on cooperative rules, technological factors are obviously critical to understanding network in modern economies. The study by Axelrod et al. (1995) on standard setting for the Unix operating system assumes that because of technological complementarities, firms are encouraged to cooperate. Competitive pressures suggest a mating rule in which firms prefer to ally with distant rivals (see note 4, this chapter). In this case, a sorting rule is derived from competitive rivalry: avoid cooperation with near rivals. From this simple rule, they show that individual cooperative decisions among 'agents' (i.e. firms) generate a distinctive structure over time, with two groups formed around competing standards. The results of their simulation, using empirical data for parameter values, underscore how identities correspond strategically to competing visions of the future (e.g. distributed versus cenral computation, cable versus satellite transmission).

The tendency of some industries to converge toward what Gomes-Casseres (1994) calls competing constellations varies widely across industries. The emergence of structure in a network is sensitive to specific industry settings. Competing around standards is not, for example, a feature in the pharmaceutical industry. As a consequence, the network structure in pharmaceuticals does not conform to the Axelrod et al. prediction. The rule in the American biotechnology industry was the following: start-up firms should form alliances with established companies. The origin of the rules lies principally in the lack of financial resources and marketing and distribution capabilities of the start-up companies. Venture capitalists, concerned by the 'burn rate' of the initial capital provisions to these companies, required relationships to avoid costly expenditures and to signal the quality of the drug portfolio.

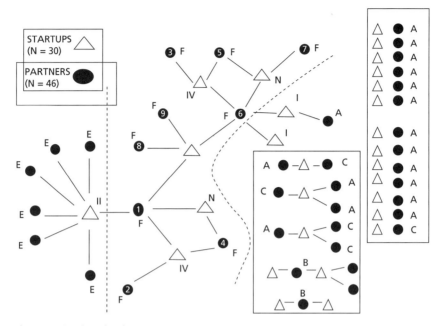

Figure 13.2. Biotechnology

The outcome of these rules is a pattern of alliances that as early as 1983, as shown in Figure 13.2, are marked by the creation of several fragmented star and hub subgraphs that reveal an emergent structure. (The structure is generated on the basis of the block-model data in table 3 of Walker et al. 1997.)[6] Sometimes established companies are relatively central; in a few instances, a new biotechnology company emerges as central. Overall, the network structure is very sparse, and yet there is an identifiable structure.

The rules in the biotechnology industry that generate the relational structure are themselves products of the non-random distribution of capabilities that distinguish start-ups and pharmaceutical companies. Start-ups, consisting of molecular biologists, lacked certain capabilities. But by implication, pharmaceutical companies were unable to integrate the new science, built upon particular professional identities, with their traditional research endeavors. Identification limited, at least initially, the internal variety of pharmaceutical companies (see Zucker and Darby 1995). Specialized by differentiated capabilities, their mutual need suggested a rule of relationship formation that generated distinctive patterns in the structuration of a cooperative network.

For this reason, the emergence of structure in biotechnology industries outside the United States followed a different trajectory. Here we see the importance of understanding the conjunction of technological and social influences. Because scientists in France identify professionally with national scientific laboratories, small firms were impaired in attracting the critical scientific talent (Gittelman 1999). In this network, laboratories have remained critical nodes in the network, with dense ties formed with national laboratories. Thus, different ideas of professional prestige in conjunction with the technological properties of genetic engineering research resulted in a dramatically different network structure in France, one built around laboratories and large firms.

This dynamic between internal capabilities, ensconced in specific identities and organizational structures, and the external knowledge in the market drives a co-evolution between the emergent properties in the firm and network. Even though markets and firms are organized by different principles, there is nevertheless a correspondence in their structure and properties. We return here to Smith's and Stigler's arguments that differentiation in the knowledge of the firm and market influence boundary decisions.

The findings of Gittelman suggest the grounded speculation that the dialectic between specific markets and individual firm competence drives a co-evolution that enjoys a reflection in the structure of the network. An example serves to illustrate this correspondence. The excellent study by Annalee Saxenian (1994) compares the structure of semiconductor and computer industry networks in the Silicon Valley and Route 128. She found that the two regions had very different network structures, even though the technologies and industries were the same. In Figure 13.3, we graph her

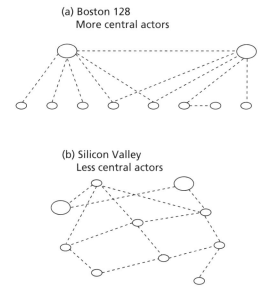

Figure 13.3. Saxenian's ethnographic description

ethnography. The top panel shows a hierarchical structure in Route 128; a few large firms dominate smaller companies. The Silicon Valley shows a decentralized network. Is it a coincidence that the internal structure of the Silicon Valley is described as flat and that of the Route 128 firm as hierarchical? Why should the internal structure correspond to the external structure?

In the case of the Silicon Valley, there is an institutional foundation that supports the flow of information and matches engineer to project and firm. Obviously, it is rarely in the interest of the current employer to see proven research talents exit their firm, and it is in their interest to discourage voluntary exits. The evolution of a labor market for talent counters potential negative sanctions by the current employer. That is, there are a sufficient number of job opportunities so that in the event the engineer exits in the future (because the hiring firm dies or the new project opportunity ends), subsequent sanctions by former employers are unlikely to be effective. A market consisting of many small networked firms cannot generate effective sanctions on the mobility of engineers. There is, as a consequence of high mobility, less motivation to build a vertical hierarchy by which to promise future rewards.

A labor market that is dominated by a few large firms permits sanctions through refusal of these firms to rehire the engineer or through their signals to other client firms in the area. These sanctions need be no more than the loss of relative ranking in the internal hierarchies of these dominant firms. (Note that the internal labor markets of Silicon Valley are characterized as flat; tall hierarchical ranks are not viable if labor market mobility is high and work is organized by projects.)[7] If a regional market does not support labor mobility, then individual engineers are likely to seek internal advancement, or—and it is important to stress this implication—to migrate from the region. (See Almeida and Kogut (1999) for evidence.)

The theoretical link between internal and external structure begins from the recognition that firms and markets are jointly emergent phenomena embedded in spatially defined labor networks. Their structure reflects the emergent properties that influence information and incentives, as well as the know-how and coordination, that inform firm and individual strategies. The structural opportunities through labor market has a powerful effect on differentiating the orientation of professional identities. In the hierarchical network of Route 128, engineers identify themselves with internal labor markets; the Silicon Valley encourages identification along professional competence in projects.

The comparison between the Silicon Valley and Route 128 raises the important distinction between emergence and intentionality in network structure. Networks are rarely formed by design, but rather they emerge initially in response to the institutional and technological opportunities of an industry or field. During this process of formation, relationships develop out of *informational* properties that drive a matching process among firms. However, over time, knowledge that is initially information gradually becomes encoded in persisting structures that influence subsequent behavior in two distinct ways: as a conduit of information and as the basis of *coordinated action*.

Structure in a network is thus not determined just by exogenous factors, but is an expression of competing and evolving rules that guide the behaviors of interacting entities. Sometimes, inherent technological characteristics favor the emergence of particular rules. A technology that enjoys scale economies tends to generate large firms; another technology, such as microprocessors (see below), tends toward network externalities. These characteristics influence size distributions and the structure of a network. Similarly, institutional contexts (e.g. socialist or capitalist, German or American legal environments, etc.) influence the origins and formation of networks. Institutions, such as governments, sometimes dictate rules. A rule that establishes monopolies compared to another that regulates prices has dramatic implications for the emergence of industry structure and organizing principles of coordination and competition. The effects of government discretion generated widely different industrial and relational structures among countries (Hughes 1983). Because markets and firms are not simply given constructs, but arise from varied institutional origins and technological influences, there are no generic rules that are exogenous and known a priori. Rather, the systemic interaction of technological, social, and institutional factors influence the evolution of network structure.

Capabilities and Rents

In an economic network, a firm is legally constituted as the unit of accrual. Hence, cooperation and coordination in a network pose the questions whether there are rents in networks and to whom do they accrue. Answers to these questions requires an understanding of the location advantages to both information access in a network and to membership in a coordinated network. In other words, we are interested in understanding the conditions by which certain network structures generate value that is captured differentially by participating firms through their coordination.

Call the first type of advantage a Burt rent. Burt describes the generation of network structure as the outcome of the competitive struggle among egos motivated by envy and self-interest. The key construct for Burt is the notion of 'non-redundant' ties. A tie is non-redundant if it represents the only path between two nodes as constituted by individuals, firms, or even industries. Entities that have multiple unique (i.e. non-redundant) ties with other nodes who are not connected occupy powerful brokerage positions called 'structural holes.' Burt has argued that firms that are positioned in structural holes are more powerful because they arbitrate the information flows between groupings of firms who have loose ties with each other. Such networks have a hierarchical structure, even if there are many hierarchies. In this network, the rent accrues to the firm bridging the structural hole.

The second type of advantage can be called a Coleman rent. Coleman (1990) stressed that redundant ties among firms (or actors) result in a resolution to collective action problems. Coordination is improved through repeated exchange among stable members to the group. This network tends to be flatter. In this case, depending upon the quality of the interaction, the rent accrues to membership in the group, with the actual allocation to individual members determined by rules of adjudication and relative bargaining power.

For example, Uzzi (1996) describes networks in the textile industry as characterized by problem solving, communication, and trust; Uzzi's description of a network is, in many ways, identical to the advantages of a firm, as listed above, regarding coordination, learning, and communication. The advantage of a textile network is, however, the flexibility to explore new relationships and opportunities, but within a relatively closed clique that supports long-term trust among members.

Though Burt and Coleman networks are distinct, they both generate potentially a rent to coordination, though with very different implications. The Burt rent accrues to the entrepreneurial broker located in a structural hole. This is an efficient network insofar as *information* flows throughout the network at the cost of maintaining a minimal number of relationships. Brokers, thus, increase the efficiency of the overall network and capture, as a result, a rent for this service. Just as in studies of monopoly, the calculation of whether the net welfare gain to the system is positive or negative depends upon the conjunction of the incentives for the broker to act in alignment with collective interests.

Studies by Burt (1997) indicate significant rents to brokers, but do not assess the global welfare benefits. (The term 'social capital' suggests a resource that improves collective welfare by fostering cooperation.) For example, his study on promotion and remuneration of American managers indicates that occupying a structural hole increases the size of bonuses (holding the rest constant) for senior offices increased by USD291,000. It could be that individuals who fill structural holes are scarce entrepreneurs who improve internal coordination through control over scarce resources and hence the performance of the system. (Burt's analysis of their attributes is ambiguous to these effects.) In this case, the role of a broker can be welfare improving for everyone since a service for the network is rendered to everyone's advantage.

However, in some kinds of networks, one party's gain is another's loss. A zero-sum implication is inherent, in fact, exactly in rank tournaments for promotion that serve as Burt's example. If we view promotion as a problem of mobility chains, then one person's promotion is indeed another's disappointment. In this case, local rent is at best a distributional transfer, ignoring the possibility for dysfunctional consequences and inviting strategic behavior on the part of dominated individuals or firms. A zero-sum (if not negative sum) game does not comply with most definitions of social capital. Clearly, redistribution is implied in the studies on the structure of input–output activities that indicate some industries occupy structural holes (Burt 1992).

A Coleman rent is associated with the benefits of trust supporting *coordination* in long-term relationships. This rent is not due to informational efficiency, for as Burt forcefully notes, a redundant network is not a minimal communication tree. However, dense relationships have the attribute of supporting monitoring and coordination by matching incentives to contribution. One could also argue that dense networks also foster a sense of collective identity that supports coordinated exchange.

Coleman (1990) distinguishes between independent and global viability in associations. The former consists of contributions of individuals to an organization (or closed network) with a proportional reward. Global viability, which Coleman believes cannot sustain an organization over time, rewards people at their reservation price of persistence in the club, while allowing for intraorganizational payments to members in an amount that violates rules of proportionality.[8] Whereas Burt implies that this group rent flows to the broker, a Coleman network claims that the gains to superior coordination must be distributed in ways to assure participation. Thus, different notions of viability are a critical distinction between Coleman and Burt networks.

The importance of understanding viability is implicit in the examples discussed earlier. For example, the study by Axelrod et al. (1995) relied upon Nash equilibrium. A coalition is only viable to the extent there is no improvement for any firm to defect to the other coalition. For a Saxenian network to function, individuals in a hierarchy must view this as more rewarding than defecting to a start-up. A hierarchical firm is not viable in Silicon Valley, because individuals will choose to switch jobs in that institutional setting.

The study by Walker et al. (1997) explored both Burt and Coleman types of networks. The early history of this industry revealed a network that was relatively unstructured and more like a market. Certainly, while entrepreneurs had important affiliations to sources of ideas (e.g. universities) or finance, horizontal ties among firms were weak.[9] In this type of network, market-like relationships emerge through firms communicating information regarding e.g. prices and specifications. Coordination in this instance happens through transactions governed by price signals. Learning takes place through the revelation of cooperative or dishonest reputations.

Over time, a more complex network emerges. Figure 13.2, shown earlier, represents a relational structure that reveals both structural holes and Coleman-type networks. The pharmaceutical company marked II is an isolate that has non-redundant ties with six start-up firms; it clearly occupies a structural hole. However, some firms, such as those in group IV, engaged in more dense transactions that are suggestive of formative type of Coleman networks. The analysis of subsequent relationships revealed that Coleman network based on coordination, inclusive of mutual know-how exchange, emerged. Because of this social capital, firms belonging to the same groups tended to cooperate with each other subsequent to their initial cooperation. Network structure began to replicate itself in stable patterns of enduring cooperation. It is not simply that biotechnology relationships are enduring across years that explains this persistence. It is rather that these formative groups formed progressively more closed cliques; the flow of new relationships was influenced by Coleman-type incentives for cooperating firms to deepen their cooperation. This pattern is also implied in the findings of Gulati (1995) who shows that partners tend to ally with those close to them in the network and with whom they have previously allied. (See Kogut, 1989, for the similar finding that previous relationships dampen the hazard of terminating the venture.)

The emergent properties of networks ride on self-organizing processes that tend to freeze the structure among firms over time into stable patterns of interactions. The Walker et al. (1997) study noted that a danger to a Coleman network is that it limits search and can reduce variety. Uzzi proposes that the optimal network structure in the textile industry has a high density of relationships among firms, yet while allowing new entrants and the possibility of further exploration. Since the advantage of the market is the generation of variety, too much structure reduces innovation. Of course, to the extent firms who defect from cooperation are eliminated, this reduction is desirable. On the other hand, the constraints on individual experimentation increase due to requirements to orchestrate coordination with other actors. The more networks take on the properties of firm organization, coordination deprives individual firms of potential avenues of exploration. Thus, neither Burt, nor Coleman structures can be ranked a priori for their welfare merits; additional structure to the analysis is first required.[10]

It may help to analyze this line of debate by anchoring the discussion in a few empirical facts. The primary observation is that alliance networks are exceedingly sparse. If there are 100 firms in a network and if we only count ties as non-directional (we ignore who sends and who receives), then we expect there to be 4950 potential ties. (We code a tie as 0 or 1, regardless of how many agreements two firms may have with each other). If we think about these ties as forming different coalitions of players, then we have a 2 to the n problem defining the solution space for potential membership in 2 coalitions—2 because a firm can choose to join or not join.) For a 100 firm network, there are then 2^{100} possible combinations in membership. Despite the combinatorial richness in potential alliances, empirically, we see networks that are sparse (i.e. the actual ties are far below the maximum) and that engage in rather limited experimentation over time regarding the changing identity of coalition partners.[11]

It would seem that sparse networks favor a Burt-like description of many structural holes. But another way to think about the strategic implications of stability in what appears to be self-organizing patterns of cooperation is to ask how sensitive are these groupings to defection of partners. (In the theory of graphs, this exercise is akin to asking how robust is structure when x of k edges are re-assigned randomly among n vertices.) After all, where there are rents, there are bound to be strategies to alter the structure by new alliances. An important test for the likelihood of success of a strategy is to compare Coleman-type structures (i.e. dense ties among few actors) and Burt-type structures (broker firms with few redundant ties among its satellites) for robustness.

The recognition that the results of this comparison are easy to predict reflects the stability of structure *despite* very sparse networks. Social networks are fairly stable to random perturbations (at moderate probability) because structures tend to be clustered into small worlds.[12] This statistical result is strengthened if we admit ties are not randomly assigned, but follow generative rules that encourage cooperation among firms already cooperating. After all, the advantage of membership in a local club promotes further cooperation among members. There is, in other words, considerable order despite rather low density of cooperation and the potential for a multitude of alliance structures. It is not surprising, then, that industries (or any community) vary in their structures, and yet share the property of tending toward self-replicating patterns of cooperation.

Yet, despite the tendency of a Coleman network to generate incentives for replication even in sparse networks, we are unlikely to arrive at a robust finding regarding global or group welfare. In one industry, the advantages of standard setting suggest that one rule for determining the decision to cooperate is to join a big coalition (Axelrod et al. 1995). Following this rule, for example, in Uzzi's textile industry butts up against a more appropriate rule to sort by prestige among low and high quality designers. It is not surprising that empirical results seem contradictory, when they reflect differences in the properties of given networks.

Similarly, caution is required to assume that Burt networks are not stable and converge over time to a market network. (Burt (1999) views structural holes as dynamically unstable.) It is important to avoid the logical fallacy of attributing persistence to genesis. Once structures are created, we need to ask what sustains them. Because action is constrained in emergent networks, the late recognition of how defection can benefit an individual firm may be inconsequential; that is, the firm cannot act upon it. Partners may not be available and may be unwilling to defect; switching may be costly and promise only uncertain advantages. Again, the notion of viability is critical. Defection may be prohibited because of sanctions imposed by the group. Or, for Padgett's and Ansell's medieval Florence or for Poldony's and Stuart's semiconductor firms, defection is deterred because the identities of membership in a group dissuade alliances with less prestigious families or firms. For either motive—economic or social sanctioning, the preferred strategy may be one of local replication, such as imitating the supplier strategy of a competitor, than creating shortcuts in the hope of destabilizing a fairly immobile structure. In theory, there is no clear reason to believe that structural holes are not sustainable.

Property Rights and Network Centrality

Of course, another way in which the emergence of structure is not only influenced, but also sustained, is through property rights. A basic property right is the ownership by an individual of the use of natural endowments, such as skill. Of course, if human capital were alienable from the person, it too would flow like a resource through a network, diminishing its value. It is, however, the stickiness of human capital that influences a person's eligibility to play a brokering role. The tacitness of firm knowledge similarly makes a firm less susceptible to the competitive imitation of its claim to broker.

This confounding of position in a network and attributes that makes one firm more central than another poses an econometric problems of endogeneity and of selection bias. Rents may accrue to 'quality' people or firms who therefore occupy structural holes.

In this regard, ownership of an innovation that is property right protected is an attribute that influences the generation and appropriation of rents independent of network effects. Yet, even here, the causality behind the generation of rents is complex, and the structure of the network becomes an endogenous feature in competition among innovators. It is important to emphasize that cooperative agreements are frequently concessions that permit the utilization of one firm's knowledge by another. Examples are the licensing of technology or the decision to cooperate in a joint venture in which firms contribute knowhow. It is a common feature that such agreements prohibit the selling of the technological rights to other firms, thus preventing undesired strategic shortcuts.

Property rights can particularly have a powerful effect on networks if the resource is scarce insofar as it constitutes a 'bottleneck' technology, such as an operating system standard for software, or an electrical grid, or the telecommunication 'pipe' to a residence. Possession of rights to a bottleneck resource can lead clearly to a monopoly position. However, it may also lead to isolation, rather than centrality, if a firm decides to exploit its position without cooperation. Hence cooperation is critical.

Cooperation is likely to result when a firm owns a scarce resource, and yet is competing against other firms who offer alternatives. These property rights to a bottleneck resource are especially valuable when coupled with 'network externalities.' These externalities arise when the consumption or use of a good by one person or firm makes it attractive to another to do the same—the classic example being a computer operating system. In these joint conditions of externalities in competitive environments, cooperation is encouraged.

Such externalities, for example, exist in microprocessors. Since software is written for microprocessor standards and people want to use the same software, there exist externalities that favor the dominance of one standard over another. For a microprocessor firm, the logical strategy is to grab the largest size of the market. Somewhat counter-intuitively, it would want to induce entry into its market as long as these entrants agreed to license its technology and standards. In fact, cooperation exploded in the microprocessor industry until Motorola and Intel achieved dominance; National Semiconductor did not achieve the same penetration and, interestingly, maintained a higher level of alliance activity. Because all entrants were required basically to cooperate on the standards, these three firms were each centered in the middle of a star of relationships. Centrality thus was the outcome of network externalities coupled with a strong property right regime.[13] Thus, in this case, the strategy to appropriate rents through technology licensing generated the structure, rather than structure simply determining the rents to a broker or Coleman group.

It is proverbially axiomatic that in a hub and spoke structure, such as associated with the dominance of Intel in microprocessor licensing, the central firm is in the better position to reap the rents in the network. (Think of this prediction as identical to the measure of market power by sales concentration.) Certainly, any bottleneck position should be associated with differential market power. The bottleneck could be property rights to the limited number of gates at an airport (which clearly is reflected in a 'hub and spoke' transportation pattern), the communications pipeline to the home, water reservoirs in a desert, etc. All of these bottlenecks produce structural holes with the gains to the broker.

In many industries, property rights to bottlenecks are not a characteristic of the competitive landscape. Firms would certainly benefit from trying to replicate the rent capture imposed through hierarchical dominance. And yet, the claim of Uzzi and others is that rent generation can be superior in a dense clique with thick ties among the players because of improved coordination and problem-solving. In such cases, the preservation of cooperation is maintained because exclusion to the club deprives the defecting member from sharing the

Table 13.1. Competing Rules and Structural Predictions (Ignoring Social Rules)

Regulatory	Technological	Feasible structure	Industry example	Competing rules
1. Strong property rights.	Bottleneck resource.	Central players with no isolates.	Microprocessors, software operating systems.	Induce entry by licensing v. dominate by superior technology.
2. Strong property rights.	No bottleneck resource.	Weak hierarchies with many isolates.	Pharmaceuticals.	Cooperate for finance v. dominate by superior technology.
3. Weak property rights.	Bottleneck resource.	Many closed hierarchies with no isolates.	Autos.	Source widely while switching often v. build competence in few single-source suppliers.
4. Weak property rights.	No bottleneck resource.	Decentralized relational networks.	Information and financial markets.	Seek new information v. rely on existing relationships.

group rents. (This sanctioning possibility is the basis of the Nash comparisons behind the Axelrod, et al. (1995), simulation discussed earlier.) In other words, rents to coordination again provide self-organizing incentives to members to maintain the network structure.

Table 13.1 summarizes the discussion of the relationship of network structure and property rights to bottleneck resources. The consequences for rent generation and distribution depend on the assessment of the viability of competing rules for cooperation. The empirical studies of various industries indicate that certain rules came to dominate, but in the context of particular historical and institutional settings. Thus, the rule for cooperation that appears to have proliferated in microprocessors is to share technology, while not giving up control to the bottleneck resource itself. In some industries where property rights are strong, but there is no bottleneck technology (e.g. in pharmaceuticals), the emergent structure does not consist of competition among a few hubs, but reveals a complex structure with many central firms and also many isolates. One surmises that in this industry, centrality might reflect the 'quality' of a firm rather than its control over a brokerage position. This may be the reverse in the financial industry, where in fact the position in an information flow results in the capture of rents. Quality is an attribute of the position. While trading relationships are still embedded in structure (Baker 1984), the incentives to cooperate are attentive to positions of prestige and rank. Here indeed we have Burt rents accruing to structural holes.

An interesting case is where property rights to a given scarce resource are not strong, but there still exists discernible structure among competing hubs. Automobile assembly is a good example, whereby assemblers have some power over access to distribution channels and customer loyalty but they do not have property right control over unique assembly skills. Indeed, entry by new companies has been an important element in the history of this industry.

Conclusions

We began with the observation that value is not a mystical entity. The source of its imputation is not always clear, as witnessed in the lack of consensus over the interpretation of a residual, called total factor productivity. In recent years, we have come to understand better that an important source of value for a firm lies in the capabilities supported by organizing principles of work. These principles constitute what is meant as the knowledge of the firm.

The study of networks as knowledge understands capabilities achieved through coordinated action at multiple levels of analysis. At one level, knowledge is the principles defining coordination in a division of labor that anchor identities of individuals and groups within firms. At another level, the boundary of firm and network are malleable definitions determined by shifting identities and their co-evolving capabilities. Operating upon these levels is the domain of generative rules of cooperation and competition.

The network generated by rules of cooperation differentiates firms by their structural positions. Since firms but not networks are units of accrual and selection, there exists, therefore, a potential divergence between the distribution of these rents and the contribution of individual firms. Sometimes, this divergence is mitigated through the coincidence of structural position and property right claims. However, in situations in which knowledge is diffuse among a group of firms, coordination can become prey to concerns over cooperation. Embedding a monitoring and sanction mechanism into a cycle of positive returns attached to technology transfer drove the particular success of the supplier system of the Toyota Production System. And by devising credible rules that guaranteed independent viability, Toyota could, by intention, replicate the network (even if particular members changed) in new locations.

Networks are more than just relationships that govern the diffusion of innovations and norms, or explain the variability of access to information across competing firms. Because they are the outcome of generative rules of coordination, networks constitute capabilities that augment the value of firms. These capabilities, e.g., speed to market, generate rents that are subject to private appropriation. It is through an understanding of networks as knowledge encoding coordination within and between specialized firms in specific cooperative and competitive structures that the 'missing' sources of value can be found.

Acknowledgments

This chapter is supported through the Reginald H. Jones Center of the Wharton School. I would like to thank Gordon Walker for many helpful discussions, Udo Zander who contributed substantially to parts of this paper, and the anonymous reviewers.

☐ ENDNOTES

1. Most, if not all studies of networks treat knowledge as the question of knowing who has knowledge and the access of this knowledge through cooperative relationships. (See Powell, 1990, for example.

2. See Gulati (1998) for a discussion of information and network formation and Palmer, Jennings and Zhou, 1993, for cohesion studies on innovative diffusions. Early studies on the idea of competition among alliance networks are Nohria and Garcia-Pont, 1991, and Gomes-Casseres, 1994. The intriguing idea of 'communities of practice' is also akin to this perspective, in which 'connectivity'—rather than position in a network—is a source of advantage. See Brown and Duguid (1991).

3. Studies on the capabilities of networks are explored in many studies on Italian and German networks, e.g., Lorenzoni and Baden Fuller (1995), Lipparini and Lomi (1996), Herrigel (1993) and Piore and Sabel (1994).

4. Note the study of Baum, Calabrese and Silverman (2000) has the contrary assumption that distance provides the benefits of new information, a weak tie argument. As we note throughout this paper, both assumptions (or rules) can be right, depending upon the industry context (e.g. standard setting versus competence seeking).

5. For an insightful analysis of how structure influences diffusion (e.g. cooperation) by agents, see Boorman 1974. The parallel between the proposal to understand structure as emergent and rule-based shares obvious affinities to the literature on complex adaptive systems; see Axelrod and Cohen (2000) for a treatment. The genetic algorithms in the vein of Holland (1992) are an appropriate research strategy by which to think about rules appropriate for stylized industry conditions. Empirically the identification of rules may be fairly simple, as I try to illustrate in the subsequent examples in this article.

6. I thank Jon Brookfield for suggesting this graph.

7. This line of argumentation comes closest to Coleman (1990: 439ff.), who assumes that external labor markets are competitive markets. He thus does not consider the relationship between the type of external and internal labor markets and its effects on the location of innovation. For an analysis of a related problem, see Anton and Yao (1994).

8. This description is similar to the theory of clubs (and to Olson-type of selective incentives among small groups). There are many rules by which individuals can be rewarded that satisfy their reservation price (i.e. minimum for staying a member). See Cornes and Sandler (1996) for a summary.

9. See Powell, Koput and Smith-Doerr (1996) on ties.

10. See the discussion in Walker et al. (1997) on the potential for dense relationships to drown out experimentation and learning. Rowley, Behrens, and Krackhardt (2000) provide an excellent review of the relationship of strong and weak ties to exploration, with

evidence indicating the importance of industry context in evaluating the relationship of structure to individual firm performance. See also the discussion by Walker (1998) on the search models indicating that weak ties proliferate from the objective of maximizing information access. This notion of the proliferation of weak ties is similar to Khanna, Gulati, and Nohria's (1994) notion of alliance scope. See also Baum et al. (2000), and the comparison by Zaheer and Zaheer (1997) of structural holes and weak tie arguments.

11. See Kogut and Walker, 1999, for a discussion of some examples; working paper later published as Kogut and Walker, 2001.

12. For simulations of the robustness of local structure (that is, small worlds) in sparse networks, see Watts and Strogatz (1998); for one of the first simulations using empirical data and analyzing robustness, see Kogut and Walker, 2001.

13. This analysis is given in Kogut, Walter, and Kim (1996).

REFERENCES

Abbott, Andrew (2001) *Chaos of Disciplines*. Chicago: University of Chicago Press.

Abegglen, James C. and George, Stalk (1985) *Kaisha: The Japanese Corporation*. New York: Free Press.

Abernathy, W. and J. Utterback (1975) 'A Dynamic Model of Product and Process Innovation,' *Omega 3*, 6: 639–56.

Acemoglu, Daron, Simon Johnson, and James Robinson (2001) 'Colonia Origins of Comparative Development: An Empirical Investigation,' *American Economic Review*, 91: 1369–401.

Adler, Paul A. (1993) 'Time-and-Motion Regained,' *Harvard Business Review* (January–February): 97–108.

Akerlof, George and Rachel Kranton (2000) 'Economics and Identity,' *The Quarterly Journal of Economics*, 115(3): 715–53.

—— —— (2005) 'Identity and the Economics of Organizations,' *Journal of Economic Perspectives*, 19: 9–32.

Albert, Stuart and Whetten, David. A. (1985) 'Organizational Identity,' *Research in Organizational Behaviour*, 7: 263–95.

Allen, T. J. (1970) 'Communication Networks in R&D Laboratories,' *R&D Management*, 1(1): 14–21.

—— and Stephen I. Cohen (1969) 'Information Flow in Research and Development Laboratories,' *Administrative Science Quarterly* (March) 14(1): 12–19.

Allison, G. T. (1971) *Essence of Decision: Explaining the Cuban Missile Crisis*. Boston: Little Brown and Co.

Allison, Paul D. (1984) *Event History Analysis: Regression for Longitudinal Event Data*. Beverly Hills: Sage Publications.

—— and J. Scott Long (1987) 'Inter-University Mobility of Academic Scientists,' *American Sociological Review*, 52: 643–52.

Almeida, Paul and Bruce Kogut (1999) 'Localization of Knowledge and the Mobility of Engineers in Regional Networks,' *Management Science*, 47: 905–17.

Altshuler, A., M. Anderson, D. Jones, D. Roos, and J. Womack (1984) *The Future of the Automobile: The Report of MIT's International Automobile Project*. Cambridge: MIT Press.

Amin, Ash and Patrick Cohendet (2004) *Architectures of Knowledge: Firms, Capabilities, and Communities*. New York: Oxford University Press.

Amram, Martha and Nalin Kulatilaka (1999) *Real Options: Managing Strategic Investment in an Uncertain World*. Boston: Harvard Business School Press.

Anderson, Erin and David C. Schmittlein (1984) 'Integration of the Sales Force: An Empirical Examination,' *Rand Journal of Economics* (Autumn) 15: 385–95.

Anderson, Philip and Tushman, Michael L. (1990) 'Technological Discontinuities and Dominant Designs: A Cyclical Model of Technological Change,' *Administrative Science Quarterly*, 35: 604–33.

Angel, David P. (1989) 'The Labor Market for Engineers in the U.S. Semiconductor Industry,' *Economic Geography*, April 65(2): 99–112.

Anton, James J. and Dennis A. Yao (1995) 'Start-Ups, Spinoffs, and Internal Projects,' *Journal of Law and Economics and Organization*, 11: 362–78.

Aoki, Masahiko (1990) 'Toward an Economic Model of the Japanese Firm,' *Journal of Economic Literature*, 28: 1–27.

Appelbaum, E. and Batt, R. (1994) *The New American Workplace*. Ithaca, NY: ILR Press.

Argote, Linda, Sara Beckman, and Dennis Epple (1990) 'The Persistence and Transfer of Learning in Industrial Settings,' *Management Science*, 36: 140–54.

Argyres, Nicholas S. (1999) 'The Impact of Information Technology on Coordination: Evidence from the B-2. Stealth.Bomber,' *Organization Science*, 10(2): 162–80.

Argyris, C. and Schön, D. (1978) *Organizational Learning: A Theory of Action Perspective*. Reading, MA: Addison Wesley.

Armour, Henry and David Teece (1978) 'Organizational Structure and Economic Performance,' *Bell Journal of Economics*, 9: 106–22.

Arrow, Kenneth (1974) *The Limits of Organization*. New York: Norton.

Arthur, W. Brian (1989) 'Competing Technologies, Increasing Returns, and Lock-In by Historical Events,' *The Economic Journal*, (March) 99(394): 116–31.

Athey, S. and S. Stern (1999) 'Information Technology and Training in Emergency Call Centers,' *Proceedings of the Fifty-First Annual Meetings (New York, Jan 3–5, 1999)*. Madison, WI: Industrial Relations Research Association, pp. 53–60.

Axtell, Robert and Joshua Epstein (2004) *Growing Artificial Societies: Social Science from the Bottom Up*. Washington, DC: Brookings Institution/MIT Press.

Axelrod, Robert and Michael D. Cohen (2000) *Harnessing Complexity*. New York: Free Press.

——and William D. Hamilton (1981) 'The Evolution of Cooperation in Biological Systems,' in R. Axelrod (ed.), *The Evolution of Cooperation*. New York: Basic Books, 88–105.

——Will Mitchell, Robert Thomas, D. Scott Bennett, and Erhard Bruderer (1995) 'Coalition Formation in Standard-Setting Alliances,' *Management Science*, 41: 1493–508.

Azoulay, Pierre (2004) 'Capturing Knowledge Within and Across Firm Boundaries: Evidence from Clinical Development', *American Economic Review*, 94: 1591–612.

Babbage, C. (1835) *On the Economy of Machinery and Manufactures*, 4th edn. London: Charles Knight.

——and Martin Campbell-Kelly (1989) *The Works of Charles Babbage: The Difference Engine and Table Making*. ed. Martin Campbell-Kelly. London: William Pickering.

Baillie, Richard T. and Tim Bollerslev (1989) 'Common Stochastic Trends in a System of Exchange Rates,' *Journal of Finance*, 44: 167–80.

Baker, Wayne (1984) 'The Social Structure of a National Securities Market,' *American Journal of Sociology*, 89: 775–811.

Balakrishnan, Srinivasan and Mitchell P. Koza (1988) 'Information Asymmetry, Market Failure and Joint Ventures,' mimeo, UCLA.

Baldwin, Robert E. (1982) 'The Political Economy of Protectionism,' in Jagdish N. Bhagwati (ed.) *Import Competition and Response*. Chicago: University of Chicago Press.

Baldwin, Richard E. (1989) 'Sunk Cost Hysteresis,' NBER Working Paper, No. 2911, March.

—— and Paul Krugman (1989) 'Persistent Trade Effects of Large Exchange Rate Shocks,' *Quarterly Journal of Economics*, 104: 636–54.

Baldwin, Carliss and Kim Clark (1991) 'Capabilities and Capital Investment: New Perspectives on Capital. Budgeting', *Journal of Applied Corporate Finance*, 5: 67–82.

—— —— (1992) 'Modularity and Real Options: An Exploratory. Analysis,' Harvard Business School Working Paper #93-026, October.

—— —— (2000) *Design Rules, Vol. 1: The Power of Modularity.* Cambridge, MA: MIT Press.

Bandura, A. and McDonald, F. J. (1963) 'The Influence of Social Reinforcement and the Behavior of Models in Shaping Children's Moral Judgments,' *Journal of Abnormal and Social Psychology*, 67: 274–81.

—— and Walters, R. (1963) *Social Learning and Personality Development.* New York: Holt, Rinehart & Winston.

Bartlett, F. (1958) *Thinking.* New York: Basic Books.

Bartlett, Chris and Ghoshal Sumantra (1989) *Managing Across Borders: The Transnational Solution.* Boston: Harvard Business School Press.

Barnes and D. Edge (eds.) (1982) *Science in Context: Readings in the Sociology of Science.* Open University Press.

Barney, Jay B. (1986) 'Strategic Factor Markets: Expectations, Luck, and Business Strategy,' *Management Science*, 32: 1231–41.

—— (1991) 'Firm Resources and Sustained Competitive Advantage,' *Journal of Management*, 17(1): 99–120.

Barro, Robert and Rachel McCleary (2003) 'Religion and Economic Growth Across Countries,' *American Sociological Review*, 68: 760–81.

Baum, Joel A., Tony Calabrese, and Brian S. Silverman (2000) 'Don't Go It Alone: Alliance Networks and Startups' Performance in Canadian Biotechnology,' *Strategic Management Journal*, Special Issue (21): 267–94.

Bavelas, A. (1950) 'Communication Patterns in Task Oriented Groups,' *Journal of the Acoustical Society of America*, 22: 271–82.

Becker, G.S. and K. M. Murphy (1992) 'The Division of Labor, Coordination Costs, and Knowledge,' *Quarterly Journal of Economics*, 107: 1137–60.

Bendix, Reinhard (1956) *Work and Authority in Industry.* Berkeley, CA: University of California.

Berg Maxine (1980) *The Machinery Question and the Making of Political Economy, 1815–1848.* Cambridge: Cambridge University Press.

Berger, Peter L. and Thomas Luckmann (1966) *The Social Construction of Reality: A Treatise in the Sociology of Knowledge*, Garden City, NY: Doubleday.

Berners-Lee, Tim and Mark Fischetti (1999) *Weaving the Web: Origins and Future of the World Wide Web.* Britain: Orion Business.

Bies, Robert J., Thomas M. Tripp, and Margaret A. Neale (1993) 'Procedural Fairness and Profit Seeking: The Perceived Legitimacy of Market Exploitation,' *Journal of Behavioral Decision Making* (December) 6: 243–56.

Boltanski, L. (1982) *Les Cadres: La formation d'un groupe social.* Paris: Minuit.

—— and Chiapello, F. (1999) *Le nouvel esprit du capitalisme.* Paris: Gallimard.

Boorman, Scott (1974) 'Island Models for Takeover by a Social Trait Facing a Frequency-Dependent Barrier in a Mandelian Population,' *Proceedings of the National Academy of Sciences*, 71: 2103–7.

Boorman, Scott and Paul Levitt (1980) *The Genetics of Altruism*. New York: Academic Press.

Bowles, S., J. K. Choi, and Hopfensitz, A. (2003) 'The Co-Evolution of Individual Behaviors and Social Institutions,' *Journal of Theoretical Biology* (July) 223(2): 135–47.

Bowman, E. H. (1963) 'Consistency and Optimality in Managerial Decision Making,' *Management Science*, 9: 310–21.

——(1980) 'A Risk/Return Paradox for Strategic Management,' *Sloan Management Review*, 21: 17–31.

——and Gary Moskowitz (1997) 'The Use of Options Analysis in Strategic Decision Making,' Reginald H. Jones Center Working Paper.

Boyer, M. (1998) 'Hybridization and Models of Production: Geography, History and Theory,' in R. Boyer, E. Charron, U. Jürgens, and S. Tolliday (eds.) *Between Imitation and Innovation: the Transfer and Hybridisation of Productive Models in the International Automobile Industry*. Oxford: Oxford University Press.

Boyer, R. (1996) 'The Convergence Hypothesis Revisited: Globalization but Still the Century of Nations?' in S. Berger and R. Dore (eds.) *National Diversity and Global Capitalism*. Ithaca and London: Cornell University Press.

——and Andre Orléans (1992). 'How Do Conventions Evolve?' *Journal of Evolutionary Economics*, 2: 165–77.

Brannen, J., P. Moss, C. Owen, and C. Wale (1998) 'Mothers, Fathers and Employment: Parents and the Labour Market in Britain, 1984–1994' DfEE Research Brief, Research Report No. 10.

Brennan, Michael and Eduardo Schwartz (1978) 'Finite Difference Methods and Jump Processes Arising in the Pricing of Contingent Claims: A Synthesis,' *Journal of Financial and Quantitative Analysis*, September: 461–74.

Brittain, J. W. and J. H. Freeman (1980) 'Organizational Proliferation and Density-Dependent Selection: Organizational Evolution in the Semiconductor Industry', in John Kimberly and Robert Miles (eds.), *The Organizational Life Cycle*. San Francisco: Jassey Bass.

Brooks, F. P. Jr. (1975) *The Mythical Man-Month*. Reading, MA: Addison-Wesley.

Brown, John S. and Paul Duguid (1991) 'Organizational Learning and Communities-of-Practice: Toward a Unified View of Working, Learning, and Innovation,' *Organization Science*, 2:40–57.

Buckley, P. and M. Casson (1986) 'A Theory of Cooperation in International Business,' in F. Contractor and P. Lorange (eds.), *Cooperative Strategies in International Business*. Lexington, MA: Lexington Books.

————(2007) 'Edith Penrose's Theory of the Growth of the Firm and the Strategic Management of Multinational Enterprises,' *Management International Review (MIR)*, 47(2): 151–73.

Burgelman, Robert (1994) 'Fading Memories: A Process Theory of Strategic Business Exit in Dynamic Environments,' *Administrative Science Quarterly*, 39: 24–56.

Burt, Ronald (1992) *Structural Holes: The Social Structure of Competition*. Cambridge, MA: Harvard University Press.

——(1997) 'The Contingent Value of Social Capital', *Administrative Science Quarterly*, 42: 339–65.

——(2000) *The Network Structure of Social Capital*. Chicago: University of Chicago.

Burton, L. and J. Wang (1999) 'How Much Does the US Rely on Immigrant Engineers?' NSF Issue Brief.

Business International (1976) *Operating in a Floating Rate World*. New York: International Corporation.

—— (1989) *Evaluating the Performance of International Operations*. New York: International Corporation.

—— (1990) *Protecting Profits from Market Turmoil: Strategic Financial Risk Managing for the 1990s*. New York: International Corporation.

Cable, John and Manfred J. Dirrheimer (1983) 'Hierarchies and Markets: An Empirical Test of the Multidivisional Hypothesis in West Germany,' *International Journal of Industrial Organization*, 1: 43–62.

Camerer Colin (1981) 'General Conditions for the Success of Bootstrapping Models,' *Organizational Behavior and Human Performance*, 27: 411–22.

—— and Ernst Fehr (2006) 'When Does "Economic Man" Dominate Social Behavior?,' *Science*, 311: 47–52.

—— George Loewenstein, and Drazen Prelec (2005) 'Neuroeconomics: How Neuroscience Can Inform Economics,' *Journal of Economics Literature*, 63: 9–64.

Cantwell, John (1989) *Technological Innovations and Multinational Corporations*. New York: Basil Blackwell.

Cappelli, Peter and Peter D. Sherer (1990) 'Assessing Worker Attitudes Under a Two-Tier Wage Plan,' *Industrial and Labor Relation Review*, 43: 225–44.

Carpenter, Mark, Francis Narin, and Patricia Woolf (1981) 'Citation Rates to Technologically Important Patents,' *World Patent Information*, 3(4): 160–3.

Chandler, Alfred (1962) *Strategy and Structure: Chapters in the History of the Industrial Enterprise*. Cambridge, MA, MIT Press.

—— (1977) *The Visible Hand: The Managerial Revolution in American Business*. Cambridge, MA, Harvard University Press.

—— (1990) *Scale and Scope*. Cambridge: Harvard University Press.

Channon, Derek (1973) *The Strategy and Structure of British Enterprises*. Boston: Division of Research, Harvard Business School Press.

Chomsky, Noam (1980) *Rules and Representation*. New York: Columbia University Press.

Christensen, Kurt H. and Cynthia A. Montgomery (1981) 'Corporate Economic Performance: Diversification Strategy Versus Market Structure,' *Strategic Management Journal*, 2: 327–43.

Clark, K. B. and C. Y. Baldwin (1994) 'Capital Budgeting Systems and Capabilities Investments in U.S. Companies after World War II,' *Business History Review*, 68(1): 73–109.

—— W. Bruce Chew, and Takahiro Fujimoto (1987) 'Product Development in the World Auto Industry,' *Brookings Papers on Economic Activity*, 3: 729–81.

Coase, R. H. (1991) 'Contracts and the Activities of Firms,' *Journal of Law & Economics* (October) 34(2): 451–2.

—— ([1937] 1995) 'The Nature of the Firm,' in S. Estrin and A. Marin (eds.), *Essential Readings in Economics*. New York: St Martin's Press.

Coffee, John C. (1999) 'Privatization and Corporate Governance: The Lessons from Securities Market Failure,' *Journal of Corporation Law*, 25: 1–39.

Cohen, Jonathan D. (2005) 'The Vulcanization of the Human Brain: A Neural Perspective on Interactions Between Cognition and Emotion,' *Journal of Economic Perspectives* (Fall) 19(4): 3–24.

Cohen, Michael D. and Paul Bacdayan (1995) 'Organizational Routines are Stored as Procedural Memory: Evidence from a Laboratory Study,' *Organization Science*, 5: 545–68.

Cohen, Morris and Hau Lee (1989) 'Strategic Analysis of Integrated Production–Distribution Systems: Models and Methods,' *Journal of Operations Research*, 36: 216–28.

——and Huchzermeier Arnd (1991) 'Valuing Manufacturing Flexibility Under Foreign Exchange Uncertainty,' Working Paper, Wharton School, Department of Decision Sciences, University of Pennsylvania.

——Marshall Fisher, and Jaikumar Ramchandran (1989) 'International Manufacturing and Distribution Networks: A Normative Model Framework,' in Kasra Ferdows (ed.), *Managing International Manufacturing*. Netherlands: North-Holland, 67–93.

Cohendet, Patrick, Patrick Llerena, Hubert Stahn, and Gisèle Umbhauer (eds.) (1998) *The Economics of Networks: Interactions and Behaviors*. Springer-Verlag.

Cole, Robert E. (1985) 'The Macropolitics of Organizational Change: A Comparative Analysis of the Spread of Small-Group Activities,' *Administrative Science Quarterly*, 30: 560–85.

Coleman, James (1990) *Foundations of Social Theory*. Cambridge, MA: Harvard University Press.

Collins, Harry M. (1982) *The Tea Set: Tacit Knowledge and Scientific Networks, School of Humanities and Social Sciences*, in B. Barnes and D. Edge (eds.) *Science in Context: Readings in the Sociology of Science*. Milton Keynes: Open University Press.

Contractor, Farok (1981) *International Technology Licensing*. Lexington, MA: Lexington Books.

——(1985) 'A Generalized Theorem for Joint Ventures and Licensing Negotiations,' *Journal of International Business Studies*, 16: 23–50.

Coriat, Benjamin (1991) *Penser à l'envers: Travail et organisation dans l'Enterprise Japonaise*. Paris: Christian Bourgois Editeur.

Cornes, Richard and Todd, Sandler (1996) *The Theory of Externalities, Public Goods and Club Goods*, 2nd edn. New York: Cambridge University Press.

Cox, David R. (1972) 'Regression Models and Life Data,' *J. Royal Statistical Society*, 34(B): 187–202.

——and David, Oakes (1984) *Analysis of Survival Data*. London: Chapman & Hall.

Cox, E. H. (1980) 'The Optimal Number of Response Alternatives for a Scale: A Review,' *Journal of Marketing Research*, 17: 407–22.

Cox, John, Jonathan Ingersoll, and Stephen Ross (1985) 'An Intertemporal General Equilibrium Model of Asset Prices,' *Econometrica*, 53: 363–84.

Crane, Diana (1965) 'Scientists in Major and Minor Universities: A Study of Productivity and Recognition,' *American Sociological Review*, 30: 699–714.

Crawford, Vincent and Hans Haller (1990) 'Learning How to Cooperate: Optimal Play in Repeated Coordination Games,' *Econometrica*, 58: 571–95.

Crémer, Jacques, Luis Garicano, and Andrea Prat (2007) 'Language and the Theory of the Firm,' *Quarterly Journal of Economics* (February) 122(1): 373–407.

Cusumano, Michael (1991) *Japan's Software Factories*. New York: Oxford University Press.

——and Richard W. Selby (1991) *Microsoft Secrets*. New York: Free Press/Simon & Schuster.

————(1995) *Microsoft Secrets: How the World's Most Powerful Software Company Creates Technology, Shapes Markets, and Manages People*, New York: The Free Press.

Cyert, Richard M. and James G. March (1963) *A Behavioral Theory of the Firm*. Englewood Cliffs, NJ: Prentice-Hall.

Dasgupta, P. and P. David (1994) 'Towards a New Economics of Science,' *Research Policy*, 23: 487–521.

Dataquest (1990) 'A Decade of Semiconductor Start-ups,' San Jose, CA: Dataquest.

David, Paul (2000) 'A Tragedy of the Public Knowledge "Commons"? Global Science, Intellectual Property, and the Digital Technology Boomerang,' *mimeo*. Oxford: All Souls College.

Davidson, W. and Donald McFetridge (1984) 'International Technology Transactions and the Theory of the Firm,' *Journal of Industrial Economics*, 32(3): 253–64.

Davies, Howard (1977) 'Technology Transfer Through Commercial Transactions,' *Journal of Industrial Economics*, 26: 161–75.

Daviet, Jean-Jacques (1989) *Une Multinationale à la Française: Saint-Gobain, 1665–1989*. Paris: Fayard.

Dawkins, Richard (1976) *The Selfish Gene*. Oxford: Oxford University Press.

—— (1987) *The Blind Watchmaker*. New York: Basic Books.

Delery, John and Harold D. Doty (1996) 'Modes of Theorizing in Strategic Human Resource Management: Tests of Universalistic, Contingency, and Configurational Performance Predictions,' in Special Research Forum: Human Resource Management and Organizational Performance, *Academy of Management Journal*, 39: 802–35.

De Meza, David and Frederick van der Ploeg (1987) 'Production Flexibility as a Motive for Multinationality,' *Journal of Industrial Economics*, 35: 343–52.

Dempsey, Bert J., Debra Weiss, Paul Jones, and Jane Greenberg (1999), 'A Quantitative Profile of a Community of Open Source Linux Developers,' School of Information and Library Science, University of North Carolina, Chapel Hill. Available at: http://metalab.unc.edu/osrt/develpro.html

DiBona, Chris, Sam Ockman, and Mark Stone (eds.) (1999) *Open Sources: Voices from the Open Source Revolution*. Sebastopol, CA: O'Reilly.

Dierickx, Ingemar and Karel Cool (1989) 'Asset Stock Accumulation and Sustainability of Competitive Advantage,' *Management Science*, 33: 1504–13.

Dijksterhuis, Aps (2005) 'Why are We Social Animals? The High Road to Imitation as Social Glue,' in Susan Hurley and Nick Chater (eds.), *Perspectives on Imitation*, Vol. 2. Cambridge, MA: MIT Press.

DiMaggio, Paul J. and Walter W. Powell (1983) 'The Iron Cage Revisited: Institutional Isomorphism and Collective Rationality in Organizational Fields,' *American Sociological Review*, 48: 147–60.

———— (1991) *The New Institutionalism in Organizational Analysis*. Chicago: University of Chicago Press.

Dixit, Avinash (1989a) 'Entry and Exit Decisions Under Uncertainty,' *Journal of Political Economics*, 97: 620–38.

—— (1989b), 'Hysteresis, Import Penetration, and Exchange Rate Pass-Through,' *Quarterly Journal of Economics*, 104: 205–28.

—— and Robert, Pindyck (1994) *Investment Under Uncertainty*. Princeton: Princeton University Press.

Djelic, Marie-Laure (1998) *Exporting the American Model: The Postwar Transformation of European Business*. Oxford, Oxford University Press.

Doeringer, Peter. B. and Michael J. Piore (1971) *Internal Labor Markets and Manpower Analysis*. Lexington, MA: Heath.

Douglas, Mary (1986) *How Institutions Think*. Syracuse: Syracuse University Press.

Dore, Ronald (1986) *Flexible Rigidities, Industrial Policy and Structural Adjustment in the Japanese Economy, 1970–80*. Stanford, CA: Stanford University Press.

Dornbusch, Rudiger (1976) 'Expectations and Exchange Rate Dynamics,' *Journal of Political Economics*, 84: 1161–76.

—— (1987) 'Exchange Rates and Prices,' *American Economic Review*, 77: 93–106.

Dosi, Giovanni (1982) 'Technological Paradigms and Technological Trajectories: A Suggested Interpretation of the Determinants and Directions of Technical Change,' *Research Policy*, 11: 147–63.

—— and Bruce Kogut (1992) 'National Specificities and the Context of Change—The Coevolution of Organization and Technology,' in B. Kogut (ed.), *Country Competitiveness: Technology and the Organization of Work*. New York: Oxford University Press.

Dougherty, Deborah (1990) 'Interpretative Barriers to Successful Product Innovation in Large Firms', *mimeo*. Philadelphia, PA: Wharton School, University of Pennsylvania.

—— (1995) 'Managing Your Core Incompetencies for Innovation,' *Entrepreneurship, Theory, and Practice*, 19: 113–35.

—— (2007) 'Contingent Organising for Games of Innovation: Diverse Configurations of Core Principles for Innovative Organisational Design,' *International Journal of Innovation Management* (March) 11(1): 115–38.

Doz, Yves (1978) *Managing Manufacturing Rationalization with Multinational Corporations*. Columbia: Journal of World Business.

—— and Amy Shuen (1988) 'From Intent to Outcome: A Process Framework for Partnerships,' working papers, INSEAD.

Dreyfus, Hubert and Stuart Dreyfus (1988) 'Making a Mind versus Modeling the Brain: Artificial Intelligence Back at a Branchpoint,' in Stephen Graubard (ed.), *The Artificial Debate*. Cambridge, MA: MIT Press.

Dumas, Bernard (1988) 'Perishable Capital and Hysteresis in Capital Formation,' Working Paper, Rodney White Center.

Dumez, Hervé and Alain Jeunemaitre (1994) 'Knowledge and Decision. Reflexions on Strategic Management,' mimeo, for Academy of Management Conference, Vancouver.

Duncan, Jérôme L. (1982) 'Impacts of New Entry and Horizontal Joint Ventures on Industrial Rates of Return,' *Review of Economics and Statistics*, 64: 120–5.

Durkheim, Emile ([1893] 1933) *The Division of Labor in Society*. New York: Free Press.

Dutton, Jane E., Janet M., Dukerich and Celia V. Harquail (1994) 'Organizational Images and Member Identification,' *Administrative Science Quarterly*, (June) 39(2): 239–63.

Dyas, Gareth P. and Heinz T. Thanheiser (1976) *The Emerging European Enterprises: Strategy and Structure in French and German Industry*. London: Macmillan.

Efron, Brad (1977) 'The Efficiency of Cox's Likelihood Function for Censored Data,' *Journal of Royal Statistical Society*, series B 34: 187–202.

Eisenhardt, Kathleen M. and Claudia B. Schoonhoven (1990) 'Organizational Growth: Founding Teams Strategy and Environment and Growth Among US Semiconductor Ventures 1978–88,' *Administrative Science Quarterly*, 35(3): 504–29.

Elster, Jon (1978) *Logic and Society: Contradictions and Possible Worlds.* Chichester and New York: John Wiley & Sons.

—— (1983) *Explaining Technical Change—A Case Study in the Philosophy of Science.* Cambridge: Cambridge University Press.

Fagin, Ronald, Joseph Y. Halpern, Yoram Moses, and Moshe Y. Vardi (2003) *Reasoning About Knowledge.* Cambridge, MA: MIT Press.

Fehr, E. and U. Fischbacher (2003) 'The Nature of Human Altruism,' *Nature*, 425(6960): 785–91.

—— —— and Micael Kosfeld (2005) 'Neuroeconomic Foundations of Trust and Social Preference: Initial Evidence,' *AEA Papers and Proceedings*, 346–51.

Ferguson, David and D. Ketchen (1999) 'Organizational Configurations and Performance: The Role of Statistical Power in Extant Research,' *Strategic Management Journal*, 20(4): 385–95.

Fine, Charles and Robert Freund (1990) 'Optimal Investment in Product-Flexible Manufacturing Capacity,' *Management Science*, 36: 449–66.

Finegold, David and David Soskice (1988) 'The Failure of Training in Britain: Analysis and Prescription,' *Oxford Review of Economic Policy*, 4(3): 21–53.

Flaherty, M. Therese (1986) 'Coordinating International Manufacturing and Technology,' in M. E. Porter (ed.), *Competition in Global Industries.* Boston, MA: Harvard Business School Press.

—— and Hiroyuki Itami (1984) 'Finance,' in Daniel I. Okimoto, Takuo Sugano, and Franklin Weinstein (eds.), *Competitive Edge: The Semiconductor Industry in the United States and Japan.* Stanford: Stanford University Press.

Fleck, Ludwik ([1935] 1979) *The Genesis and Development of a Scientific Fact.* Chicago: University of Chicago Press.

Fligstein, Neil (1990) *The Transformation of Corporate Control.* Cambridge, MA: Harvard University Press.

Flood, Eugene and Donald Lessard (1986) 'On the Measurement of Operating Exposure to Exchange Rates: A Conceptual Approach,' *Financial Management*, 32: 25–35.

Florida, Richard and Martin Kenney (1991) 'Transplanted Organizations—The Transfer of Japanese Industrial Organization to the United States,' *American Sociological Review*, 56: 381–98.

Foss, Nicolai Juul (1992) 'Theories of the Firm: Contractual and Competence Perspectives,' *Journal of Evolutionary Economics*, 3: 127–44.

—— (1996a) 'Knowledge-Based Approaches to the Theory of the Firm: Some Critical Comments,' *Organization Science* (September–October) 7(5): 470–6.

—— (1996b) 'More Critical Comments on Knowledge-Based Theories of the Firm,' *Organisation Science*, 7: 519–23.

Frank, Robert (1988) *Passions Within Reason: The Strategic Role of the Emotions*, New York: W. W. Norton & Co.

Franklin B. Weinstein (eds.) (1984) 'Competitive Edge: The Semiconductor Industry in the US and Japan.* Stanford: Stanford University Press, 134–76.

Franko, Lawrence G. (1971) *Joint Venture Survival in Multinational Corporations.* New York: Praeger.

—— (1976) *The European Multinationals.* London: Harper & Row.

Frey, Bruno (2007) 'Awards as Compensation,' *European Management Review*, forthcoming.

—— and Felix Oberholzer-Gee (1997) 'The Cost of Price Incentives: An Empirical Analysis of Motivation Crowdingout,' *American Economic Review*, 87(4): 746–55.

Frey, Bruno and Margit Osterloh (2000) 'Motivation, Knowledge Transfer, and Organizational Forms,' *Organization Science*, 11: 538–50.

Fridenson, Patrick (1997) 'France: The Relatively Slow Development of Big Business in the Twentieth Century,' in A. Chandler, F. Amatori, and T. Hikino (eds.) *Big Business and the Wealth of Nations*. New York: Cambridge University Press, 207–45.

Friedman, Philip, Sanford V. Berg, and Jerome Duncan (1979) 'External vs. Internal Knowledge Acquisition: JV Activity and R&D Intensity,' *Journal of Economics and Business*, 31: 103–10.

Friedman, Wolfgang and George Kalmanoff (1961) *Joint International Business Ventures*. New York: Columbia University Press.

Gallese, Vittorio (2004) 'The Manifold Nature of Interpersonal Relations: The Quest for a Common Mechanism,' in C. Frith and D. M. Wolpert (eds.) *The Neuroscience of Social Interaction: Decoding, Imitating and Influencing the Actions of Others*. Oxford: Oxford University Press, pp. 159–82.

Gerlach, Michael L. (1992) 'The Japanese Corporate Network: A Blockmodel Analysis,' *Administrative Science Quarterly*, 37: 105–39.

Gilfillan, S. (1935) *The Sociology of Intention*. Cambridge, MA: MIT Press.

Girin, Jacques (1990) 'Problèmes du langage dans les organismes,' *L'Individu dans l'organisation: les dimensions oubliées*, ed. Jean-François Chanlat. Quebec, Canada: Les Presses de l'Université Laval.

—— (1995) *Les Agencements organisationnels des savoirs en action*. Contributions de la recherche en gestion, ed. by F. Charue-Duboc. Paris, France: L'Harmattan.

—— (1996) 'Cognition,' *International Encyclopedia of Business and Management*, volume on organization behavior, ed. A. Sorge. London: Routledge.

Gittelman, Michelle (1999) 'Scientists and Networks: A Comparative Study of Cooperation in the French and American Biotechnology Industry', Ph.D. thesis, Wharton School, University of Pennsylvania.

—— and Bruce Kogut (2003) 'Does Good Science Lead to Valuable Knowledge? Biotechnology Firms and the Evolutionary Logic of Citation Patterns,' *Management Science*, 49(4): 366–82.

Glass, Robert L. (1995) *Software Creativity*. Englewood Cliffs, NJ: Prentice Hall.

Gneezy, Uri and Aldo Rustichini (2000) 'Pay Enough or Don't Pay at All,' *Quarterly Journal of Economics*, 115(3): 791–810.

Goleman, D. (2005) *Emotional Intelligence: Why it Can Matter More Than IO*. New York: Bantam Books.

Guth, Werner (1995) 'On Ultimate Bargaining Experiments: A Personal Review,' *Journal of Economic Behavior and Organization*, 27: 329–44.

Gomes-Casseres, Ben (1985) 'Multinational Ownership Strategies,' Unpublished DBA thesis. Boston: Harvard Business School.

—— (1988) 'Evolution of Ownership Strategies of U.S. MNEs,' in *Cooperative Strategies in International Business*, ed. F. Contractor and P. Lorange. Lexington, MA: Lexington Books.

—— (1994) 'Group versus Group: How Alliance Networks Compete,' *Harvard Business Review*, 72: 62–74.

Gorton, Gary and Frank Schmid (1996) 'Universal Banking and the Performance of German Firms,' '*National Bureau of Economic Research*,' NBER Working Paper No. 5453.

Granstrand, Ove and Soren Sjölander (1990) 'Managing Innovation in Multi-Technology Corporations,' *Research Policy*, 19: 35–60.

Gueth, W. (1995) 'On Ultimatum Bargaining Experiments: A Personal Review,' *Journal of Economic Behavior*, 27: 329–44.

Guillen, Mauro (1994) *Models of Management: Work, Authority, and Organization in a Comparative Perspective*. Chicago: University of Chicago Press.

Guiso, Luigi, Paola Sapienza, and Luigi Zingales (2006). 'Does Culture Effect Economic Outcomes?' *Journal of Economic Perspectives*, 20: 23–48.

Gulati, Ranjay (1995) 'Social Structure and Alliance Formation Pattern: A Longitudinal Analysis,' *Administrative Science Quarterly*, 40: 610–52.

—— (1998) 'Alliances and Networks,' *Strategic Management Journal*, 19(4): 293–318.

—— and Paul Lawrence (1999) 'Organizing Vertical Networks: A Design Perspective,' paper presented at the SMJ Special Issue Conference on Strategic Networks.

Güth, Werner, Rolf Schmittberger and Berndt Schwarze (1982) 'An Experimental Analysis of Ultimatum Bargaining,' *Journal of Economic Behavior and Organization*, 3(4): 367–88.

Hacking, Ian (1999) *The Social Construction of What?* Cambridge, MA: Harvard University Press.

Hall, Georges and Robert Johnson (1970) *Transfer of United Aerospace Technology to Japan: The Technology Factor in International Trade*, ed. R. Vernon. New York: Columbia University Press.

Hall, Peter (ed.) (1989) *The Political Power of Economic Ideas: Keynesianism Across Nations*. Princeton: Princeton University Press.

Hall, P. A. and D. Soskice (2001) 'An Introduction to Varieties of Capitalism,' *Varieties of Capitalism: The Institutional Foundations of Comparative Advantage*. Oxford: Oxford University Press.

Hamel, Garry and C. K. Prahalad (1994) 'Competing for the Future: Breakthrough Strategies,' Boston: Harvard Business School Press.

Hamilton, Gary and Nicole Biggart (1988) 'Market Culture and Authority: A Comparative Analysis of Management and Organization in the Far East,' *American Journal of Sociology*, 94: 52–94.

Hampton, James (1997) 'Conceptual Combination,' in K. Lamberts and D. Shanks (eds.), *Knowledge, Concepts, and Categories*. Cambridge: MIT Press: 133–60.

Hannan, Michael and John Freeman (1977) 'The Population Ecology of Organizations,' *American Journal of Sociology*, 82: 929–64.

—— —— (1984) 'Structural Inertia and Organizational Change', *American Sociological Review*, 49: 149–64.

Hansen, Morten (1999) 'The Search–Transfer Problem: The Role of Weak Ties in Sharing Knowledge Across Organization Subunits,' *Administrative Science Quarterly*, 44: 82–111.

—— (2002) 'Knowledge Networks: Explaining Effective Knowledge Sharing in Multiunit Companies,' *Organization Science*, 13: 232–48.

Hardin, Garrett (1968) 'The Tragedy of the Commons,' *Science*, 16: 1243–8.

Harrigan, Kathryn (1985) *Strategies for Joint Ventures*. Lexington, MA: Lexington Books.

—— (1986) *Managing for Joint Venture Success*. Lexington, MA: Lexington Books.

Harvard Business School (1981) *Badger (Belgium) N. V.*, 9(4): 81–127.

—— (1985) *Caterpillar Tractor Co.* Boston: Harvard Business School.

Haryi, Aydin and Gerald McDermott (1998) 'The Network Properties of Corporate Governance and Industrial Restructuring: A Post-Socialist Lesson,' *Industrial and Corporate Change*, 7: 153–93.

Hatchuel, Armand and Benoit Weil (1992) *L'Expert et le système*. Paris, France: Economica.

Haunschild, Pamela and Anne Miner (1997) 'Modes of Interorganizational Imitation: The Effects of Outcome Salience and Uncertainty,' *Administrative Science Quarterly*, 42: 472–500.

Hayek, Friedrich A. (1945) 'The Use of Knowledge in Society,' *American Economic Review*, 35: 519–30.

—— (1952) *The Sensory Order: An Inquiry into the Foundations of Theoretical Psychology*. Chicago: University of Chicago Press.

—— (1962) 'Rules, Perception, and Intelligibility,' *Proceedings of the British Academy*, 48: 321–44.

—— (1988) *The Fatal Conceit: The Errors of Socialism*. Chicago, IL: University of Chicago Press.

Hayes, Robert and Steven Wheelwright (1984) *Restoring Our Competitive Edge-Competing Through Manufacturing*. New York: Wiley and Sons.

Hedlund, Gunnar (1986) 'The Hypermodern MNC: A Heterarchy,' *Human Resource Management*, pp. 9–35.

—— and Dag Rolander (1990) 'Action in Heterarchies: New Approaches to Managing the MNC,' in Christopher A. Bartlett, Yves Doz, and Gunnar Hedlund (eds.), *Managing the Global Firm*. London: Routledge.

—— and Ikujiro Nonaka (1991) *Models of Knowledge Management in the West and Japan*. Stockholm: School of Economics.

Heller, Michael A. and Rebecca S. Eisenberg (1998) 'Can Patents Deter Innovation? The Anticommons in Biomedical Research,' *Science*, 2480: 698–701.

Helper, Susan, John MacDuffie, and Charles Sabel (1998) 'Boundaries of the Firm as a Design Problem,' Reginald H. Jones Center Working Paper Series, the Wharton School, WP98–11.

Henderson, Rebecca (1993) 'Underinvestment and Incompetence as Responses to Radical Innovation: Evidence from the Photolithographic Alignment Equipment Industry,' *The Rand Journal of Economics*, 24: 248–70.

—— and Kim Clark (1990) 'Architectural Innovation: The Reconfiguration of Existing Product Technologies and the Failure of Established Firms,' *Administrative Science Quarterly*, 35: 9–31.

Hennart, Jean-François (1991) 'A Transaction Cost Theory of Equity Joint Ventures,' *Strategic Management Journal*, 37: 483–97.

—— (2006) 'Alliance Research: Less is More,' *Journal of Management Studies*, November 43(7): 1621–8.

Herrigel, Gary (1993) 'Large Firms, Small Firms, and the Governance of Flexible Specialization: The Case of Baden Wurttemberg and Socialized Risk,' *Country Competitiveness*, ed. Brice Kogut. London: MacMillan, 15–35.

Ho, Teck, Colin Camerer, and Juin-Kuan Chong (2004) 'A Cognitive Hierarchy Model of One-Shot Games,' *Quarterly Journal of Economics*, 119: 861–98.

Hodder, James and James Jucker (1985a) 'International Plant Location under Price and Exchange Rate Uncertainty,' *Engineering Costs and Production Economics*, 9: 225–9.

—— —— (1985b) 'A Simple Plant-Location Model for Quantity-Setting Firms Subject to Price Uncertainty,' *European Journal of Operational Research*, 21: 39–46.

Hogarth, Robin M. (1982) *Judgment and Choice*. New York: Wiley.

Holland, John (1992) *Adaptation in Natural and Artificial Systems: An Introductory Analysis with Applications to Biology, Control, and Artificial Intelligence*. Cambridge, MA: MIT Press.

Hollingsworth, Roger and Robert Boyer (eds.) (1997) *Contemporary Capitalism: the Embeddness of Institutions*. Cambridge: Cambridge University Press.

Holzner, Burkart and John Marx (1985) *Knowledge Application: The Knowledge System in Society*. Boston: Allyn and Bacon, Inc.

Huchzermeier, Arnd (1990) 'Global Manufacturing Strategy Planning under Exchange Rate Uncertainty,' Ph.D. thesis, University of Pennsylvania.

Hughes, Thomas (1983) *Networks of Power Electrification in Western Society, 1880–1930*. Baltimore, MD: Johns Hopkins University Press.

Hull, John (1989) *Options, Futures, and Other Derivative Securities*. Englewood Cliffs, NJ: Prentice-Hall.

——(1997) *Options, Futures, and Other Derivatives*, 3rd edn. Upper Saddle River, NJ: Prentice Hall.

Hunter, Larry W. and John J. Lafkas (1998) 'Information Technology, Work Practices, and Wages,' Working Paper: 98-02, Wharton School, Financial Institutions Center, Philadelphia.

Huy, Quy Ngyuen (1999) 'Emotional Capability, Emotional Intelligence, and Radical Change,' *The Academy of Management Review*, 24: 325–45.

Hyde, Alan (1997) '*How Silicon Valley has Eliminated Trade Secrets and Why This is Efficient*, Mimeo. New Brunswick, NJ: Rutgers University.

——(1998) *Silicon Valley's Efficient Abolition of Trade Secrets, Corporate Governance Today*. New York: Columbia Law School.

Hymer, Stephen (1960) 'The International Operations of National Firms,' Ph.D thesis, Massachusetts Institute of Technology, Cambridge, MA.

Ibarra, Herminia (1999). 'Provisional Selves: Experimenting with Image and Identity in Professional Adaptation,' *Administrative Science Quarterly*, 44: 764–91.

Ichniowski Casey and Kathryn Shaw (2003) 'Beyond Incentive Pay: Insiders' Estimates of the Value of Complementariy Human Resource Management Practices,' *Journal of Economic Perspectives*, 17: 155–80.

——————and Giovanni Prennushi (1997) 'The Effects of Human Resource Management Practices on Productivity,' *American Economic Review*, 87: 291–313.

——Thomas Kochan, David Levine, Craig Olson, and Georges Strauss (1996) 'What Works at Work: Overview and Assessment,' *Industrial Relations*, 35: 325–33.

Ittner, Chris (1996) 'Exploratory Evidence on the Behavior of Quality Costs,' *Operations Research*.

——and Bruce Kogut (1995) 'How Control Systems Can Support Organizational Flexibility,' in Edward Bowman and Bruce Kogut (eds.), *Redesigning the Firm*. New York: Oxford University Press.

Jacobs, Jane (1969) *The Economies of Cities*. New York: Random House.

Jacque, Laurent and Peter Lorange (1984) 'The International Control Conundrum: The Case of "Hyperinflationary" Subsidiaries,' *Journal of International Business Studies*, 15: 185–201.

Jacquillat, Bertrand and Bruno H. Solnik (1978) 'Multinationals are Poor Tools for Diversification,' *Journal of Portfolio Management*, 8–12.

Jaffe, Adam B., Manuel Trajtenberg, and Rebecca Henderson (1993) 'Geographic Localization of Knowledge Spillovers as Evidenced by Patent Citations,' *Quarterly Journal of Economics*, 108: 577–98.

Jain, Amit and Bruce Kogut (2006) 'Neutrality, Categories and the Sometimes Optimality of Inertia,' *mimeo*.

Janger, Allen (1980) *Organizations of International Joint Ventures*. New York Conference Board Report, 87.

Janis, Irving L. (1972) *Victims of Groupthink*. Boston: Houghton Mifflin Company.

Janowitz, Morris and Edward A. Shils (1948) 'Cohesion and Disintegration in the Wehrmacht in World War II,' *Public Opinion*, 12: 280–315.

Jenkins, William O. and Julian C. Stanley (1950) 'Partial Reinforcement: A Review and Critique,' *Psychological Bulletin*, 47: 193–234.

Johnson, H. Thomas and Robert Kaplan (1987) *Relevance Lost: The Rise and Fall of Management Accounting*. Boston, MA: Harvard Business School Press.

Joseph, Henrich, Robert Boyd, Samuel Bowles et al. (2001) 'In Search of Homo Economicus: Behavioral Experiments in 15 Small-Scale Societies,' *American Economic Review*, 91(2): 73–8.

Juergens, Ulrich, Katrin Naumann, and Joachim Rupp (2000) 'Shareholder Value in an Adverse Environment: The German Case,' *Economy and Society*, 29: 54–79.

Kadushin, Charles (1995) 'Friendship Among the French Financial Elite,' *American Sociological Review*, 60: 202–21.

Kahneman, Daniel and Dan Lovallo (1993) 'Timid Choices and Bold Forecasts: A Cognitive Perspective on Risk Taking,' *Management Science*, 39: 17–31.

—— Jack L. Knetsch, and Richard H. Thaler (1986) 'Fairness as a Constraint on Profit Seeking: Entitlement in the Market,' *American Economic Review*, 76: 728–41.

Kalbfleisch, John D. and Ross L. Prentice (1980) *The Statistical Analysis of Failure Time Data*. New York: Wiley.

Kant, Immanuel ([1784] 1983) 'Idea for a Universal History with a Cosmopolitan Intent,' *Perpetual Peace and Other Essays*. Indianapolis: Hackett Publishing Company, 29–41.

Kaplan, Sarah and Rebecca Henderson (2005) 'Inertia and Incentives: Bridging Organizational Economics and Organizational Theory,' *Organization Science*, 16: 509–21.

Katz, Daniel and Robert L. Kahn (1966) *The Social Psychology of Organizations*. New York: Wiley.

Katz, Harry (1985) *Shifting Gears: Changing Labor Relations in the U.S. Automobile Industry*. Cambridge, MA: MIT Press.

Katz, Michael L. and Carl Shapiro (1985) 'Network Externalities, Competition, and Compatibility,' *American Economic Review*, 75: 424–40.

Kenney, Martin (2000) *Understanding Silicon Valley: The Anatomy of an Entrepreneurial Region*. Stanford: Stanford University Press.

Kester, Carl W. (1984) 'Today's Options for Tomorrow's Growth,' *Harvard Business Review*, Mar–Apr.

Khanna, T. and Khrishna G. Palepu (1999) 'The Right Way to Restructure Conglomerates in Emerging Markets,' *Harvard Business Review*, Jul–Aug.

—— R. Gulati, and N. Nohria (1998) 'The Dynamics of Learning Alliances: Competition, Cooperation, and Relative Scope,' *Strategic Management Journal*, 19(3): 193–210.

Kieser, Alfred (1989) 'Organizational, Institutional, and Societal Evolution: Medieval Craft Guilds and the Genesis of Formal Organizations,' *Administrative Science Quarterly*, 34: 540–64.

Killing, Peter J. (1982) 'How to Make a Global Joint Venture Work,' *Harvard Business Review*, 60: 120–7.

—— (1983) 'Strategies for Joint Venture Success,' New York: Praeger.

Kim, Dong-Jae and Bruce Kogut (1996) 'Technological Platforms and Diversification,' *Organization Science*, 7(3): 283–301.

Kimberly, J. and R. M. Miles (eds.) (1980) *The Organizational Life Cycle*. San Francisco, CA: Jossey Bass.

Kipping, Matthias (1999) 'American Management Consulting Companies in Western Europe, 1920 to 1990: Products, Reputation, and Relationships,' *Business History Review*, 73: 190–220.

Klir, George J. and Bo Yuan (1995) *Fuzzy Sets and Fuzzy Logic: Theory and Applications*. Upper Saddle River, NJ: Prentice Hall PTR.

Knez, Marc and Colin Camerer (1994) 'Creating Expectational Assets in the Laboratory: Coordination in 'Weakest-Link' Games,' *Strategic Management Journal*, 15: 101–19.

Knight, Frank H. ([1921] 1971) *Risk, Uncertainty, and Profit*. Chicago, IL: University of Chicago.

Kocka, Juergen (1981) *Angestellte im Europaeischen Vergletch: Die Herausbildung angestellter Mittelschichten seit dem spaeten 19ten Jahrhundert*. Goettingen: Vandenhoeck and Ruprecht.

Kogut, Bruce (1983) 'Foreign Direct Investment as a Sequential Process,' in Charles P. Kindelberger and David Audretsch (eds.), *The Multinational Corporations in the 1980s*. Cambridge, MA: MIT Press.

—— (1985) 'Designing Global Strategies: Profiting from Operating Flexibility,' *Sloan Management Review*, 26: 27–38.

—— (1987) 'Competitive Rivalry and the Stability of Joint Ventures,' Working Paper Reginald H. Jones, Wharton School.

—— (1988). 'Joint Ventures: Theoretical and Empirical Perspectives,' *Strategic Management Journal*, 9: 319–32.

—— (1989) 'The Stability of Joint Ventures: Reciprocity and Competitive Rivalry,' *Journal of Industrial Economics*, 38(2): 183–98.

—— (1991b) 'Joint Ventures and the Option to Expand and Acquire,' *Management Science*, 37: 19–33.

—— (1992) 'National Organizing Principles of Work and the Erstwhile Dominance of the American Multinational Corporation,' *Industrial and Corporate Change*, 1: 285–325.

—— (1993) *Country Competitiveness: Technology and the Organizing of Work*. Oxford: Oxford University Press.

—— (1995) 'Notes on the Division of Labor, Ownership Boundaries, and Loyalty,' *Actes du Seminaire Contradictions et Dynamique des Organisations*, Dossier. Paris: Centre de Recherche en Gestion, Ecole Polytechnique.

—— (1996) 'Country Capabilities and the Permeability of Borders', *Strategic Management Journal*, (Summer) 12(4): 33–47.

—— (1997) 'Identity, Procedural Knowledge, and Institutions: Functional and Historical Explanations for Institutional Change,' in F. Naschold, D. Soskice, B. Hancké, and U. Jürgens (eds.), *Ökonomische Leistungsfähigkeit und institutionelle Innovation: Das deutsche Produktions- und Politikregime im internationalen Wettbewerb*. WZB-Jahrbuch.

—— (2000) 'The Network as Knowledge: Generative Rules and the Emergence of Structure,' *Strategic Management Journal*, (March) 21(3): 405.

—— and Dong-Jae Kim (1991) 'Technological Platforms and the Sequence of Entry,' Working Paper, Reginald H. Jones Center, Wharton School.

—— and E. H. Bowman (1995) *Redesigning the Firm*. New York: Oxford University Press.

Kogut, Bruce and Sea Jin Chang (1996) 'Platform Investments and Volatile Exchange Rates: Direct Investment in the U.S. by Japanese Electronic Companies,' *Review of Economics and Statistics*, 78: 221–31.

————(1992) 'Strategic Alliances in the Semiconductor Industry,' Unpublished report to Dataquest, Wharton School, University of Pennsylvania, Philadelphia, PA.

——and Nalin Kulatilaka (1988) 'Multinational Flexibility and the Theory of Foreign Direct Investment,' Working Paper No. 88–10, Reginald H. Jones Center for Management Policy, Strategy and Organization, University of Pennsylvania.

————(1991) 'Multinational Flexibility, Growth Options, and the Theory of Foreign Direct Investment,' Mimeo. Wharton School, University of Pennsylvania.

————(1992) 'What is a Critical Capability?,' Working Paper, Reginald H. Jones Center for Management Policy, Wharton School, University of Pennsylvania.

————(1994) 'Operating Flexibility, Global Manufacturing, and the Option Value of Multinationality,' *Management Science*, 40: 123–39.

————(1994) 'Options Thinking and Platform Investments: Investing in Opportunity,' *California Management Review*, Summer, 36: 4.

————(2001) 'Capabilities as Real Options,' *Organization Science*, 12: 744–58.

——and David Parkinson (1998) 'Adoption of the Multidivisional Structure: Analyzing History from the Start,' *Industrial and Corporate Change*, 7: 249–73.

——and Harbir Singh (1988) 'The Effect of National Culture on the Choice of Entry Mode,' *Journal of International Business Studies*, 19: 411–432.

——and Gordon Walker (1999) 'The Small World of Firm Ownership in Germany: Social Capital and Structural Holes in Large Firm Acquisitions—1993–1997,' Working paper, Reginald H. Jones Center, Wharton School, University of Pennsylvania.

————(2001) 'Small Worlds and the Durability of National Systems: Owners and Acquisitions in Germany,' *American Sociological Review*, 66: 317–35.

——and Udo Zander (1990) 'The Imitation and Transfer of New Technologies,' *mimeo*.

————(1992) 'Knowledge of the Firm, Combinative Capabilities, and the Replication of Technology,' *Organization Science*, 3: 383–97.

————(1994) 'Knowledge of the Firm and the Evolutionary Theory of the Multinational Enterprise,' *Journal of International Business Studies*, 24: 625–45.

————(1996) 'What Firms Do? Coordination, Identity, and Learning,' *Organization Science*, 7: 502–14.

————(2003) 'A Memoir and Reflection: Knowledge and an Evolutionary Theory of the Multinational Firm 10 Years Later,' *Journal of International Business Studies*, 34: 505–15.

————and Done Jae Kim (1996) 'Cooperation and Entry Induction as a Function of Technological Rivalry,' *Research Policy*, 24: 77–95.

——John Paul MacDuffie, and Charles Ragin (1999) 'Prototypes and Fuzzy Work Practices: Assigning Causal Credit for Performance,' Working Paper, Reginald H. Jones Center for Management Policy, University of Pennsylvania.

——Pietro Urso, and Gordon Walker (2007) 'The Emergent Properties of a New Financial Market: American Venture Capital Syndication from 1960 to 2005,' *Management Science*, forthcoming.

Kosko, Bart (1993) *Fuzzy Thinking: The New Science of Fuzzy Logic*. New York: Hyperion.

Krafcik, John (1988) 'Triumph of the Lean Production System,' *Sloan Management Review*, 29: 41–52.

Kreps, D.M. (1990) 'Corporate Culture and Economic Theory,' in James Alt and Kenneth Shepsle (eds.) *Perspectives on Positive Political Economy*. Cambridge: Cambridge University Press.

Krugman, Paul and Marcus Miller (eds.) (1992) *Exchange Rate Targets and Currency Bands*. Cambridge: Cambridge University Press.

Kuan, Jennifer (2000) 'Open Source Software as Consumer Integration into Production,' Working Paper, Berkeley.

Kuhn, Thomas (1962) *The Structure of Scientific Revolution*. Chicago, IL: University of Chicago Press.

Kulatilaka, Nalin (1987) 'The Value of Flexibility,' Working Paper, MIT-EL 86–014, MIT Energy Laboratory, Cambridge, MA.

—— (1988) 'The Value of Real Options,' Unpublished manuscript, Boston University, Boston.

—— and Bruce Kogut (1990) 'Direct Investment, Hysteresis, and Real Exchange Rate Volatility,' Mimeo, Wharton School, University of Pennsylvania.

—— and Alan Marcus (1988) 'A General Formulation of Corporate Operating Options,' *Research in Finance*, 183–200.

——— —— (1991) 'The Use and Misuse of Options and Futures in Hedging Foreign Project Risk,' Proceedings of the Financial Engineering and Risk Management Conference.

—— and S. Marks (1988) 'The Strategic Value of Flexibility: Reducing the Ability to Compromise,' *American Economic Review*, 78: 574–80.

—— and Enrico Perotti (1988) 'Strategic Growth Options,' *Management Science*, 44(8): 1021–31.

Kunreuther, Howard (1969) 'Extensions of Bowman's Theory on Managerial Decision-Making,' *Management Science*, 16: B415–439.

La Porta, Rafael, Florencio Lopez-de-Silanes, Andrei Shleifer, and Robert W. Vishny (1997) 'Legal Determinants of External,' *Finance*, 52: 1131–50.

Lakhani, Karim and Eric von Hippel (2000) 'How Open Source Software Works: "Free" User-to-user Assistance,' Working Paper No. 4117, MIT Sloan School of Management, Cambridge, MA.

Lakoff, George (1973) 'Hedges: A Study in Meaning Criteria and the Logic of Fuzzy Concepts,' *Journal of Philosophical Logic*, 2: 458–508.

—— (1987) *Women, Fire, and Dangerous Things What Categories Reveal about the Mind*. Chicago, IL: University of Chicago Press.

Lambert Richard, David Larcker, and Robert Verrecchia (1991) 'Portfolio Considerations in Valuing Executive Compensation,' *Journal of Accounting Research*, 29: 129–49.

Lave, Jean and Etienne Wenger (1991) '*Situated Learning: Legitimate Peripheral Participation*. Cambridge: Cambridge University Press.

Lazarsfeld, P.F. (1937) 'Some Remarks on the Typological Procedures in Social Research,' *Zeitschrift fur Sozialforschung*, 6: 119–39.

Leach, J. Chris (1994) 'Good and Bad Variance in Valuing Production and Technological Expenditure Programs or Are Real Options Really Options?' Mimeo. Wharton School, University of Pennsylvania.

Lee, Chong-Moon, William Miller, Marguerite Gong Hancock, and Henry Rowen (2000) *The Silicon Valley Edge: A Habitat for Innovation and Entrepreneurship*. Stanford: Stanford University Press.

Leonard-Barton, Dorothy (1988) 'Implementation as Mutual Adaptation of Technology and Organization,' *Research Policy*, 17: 251–67.

Lepper, Mark R. and David Greene (eds.) (1978) *The Hidden Costs of Reward: New Perspectives of the Psychology of Human Motivation*. Hillsdale, NJ: L. Erlbaum Associates.

Lerner, Josh (1995) 'Patenting in the Shadow of Competitors,' *Journal of Law and Economics*, 38(2): 463–95.

—— and Jean Tirole (2000) 'The Simple Economics of Open Source,' NBER Working Paper 7600.

—— —— (2002) 'Some Simple Economics of Open Source,' *Journal of Industrial Economics*, 46: 125–56.

Leslie, Stuart and Robert Kargan (1996) 'Selling Silicon Valley: Frederick Terman's model for regional advantage,' *Business History Review*, 70: 435–72.

Lessard, Donald and Peter Lorange (1977) 'Currency Changes and Management Control: Resolving the Centralization-Decentralization Dilemma,' *Accounting Review*, 7: 628–37.

—— and David Sharp (1984) 'Measuring the Performance of Operations Subject to Fluctuating Exchange Rates,' *Midland Corporate Finance Journal*, 2.

Lessig, Lawrence (1999) *Code and Other Laws of Cyberspace*. New York: Basic Books.

Levin Richard, Alvin Klevorick, Richard Nelson, and Sidney Winter (1987) 'Appropriating the Returns from Industrial Research and Development,' *Brookings Papers on Economic Activity*, 3: 783–820.

Levine, David (1993) 'What do Wages Buy?' *Administrative Science Quarterly*, 38: 462–83.

Levine, Ross (1997) 'Financial Development and Economic Growth: Views and Agenda,' *Journal of Economic Literature*, 35: 688–726.

Levinthal, Daniel (1997) 'Adaptation on Rugged Landscapes,' *Management Science*, 43: 934–50.

Levy, Steven (1984) *Hackers: Heroes of the Computer Revolution*. New York: Dell.

Lieberman, Marvin (1989) 'The Learning Curve, Technology Barriers to Entry, and Competitive Survival in the Chemical Processing Industries,' *Strategic Management Journal*, 10: 431–47.

Liker, Jeffrey, Mark Fruin, and Paul Adler (1999) *Remade in America: Transplanting and Transforming Japanese Management Systems*. New York: Oxford University Press.

Lincoln, James (1985) 'Work Organization and Workforce Commitment: A Study of Plants and Employees in the U.S. and Japan,' *American Sociological Review*, 50: 738–60.

—— (1993) 'Comparison of Japanese and US Organizational Structures,' in B. Kogut (ed.), *Country Competitiveness: Technology and the Organizing of Work*. New York: Oxford University Press.

Lippman, Stan and Richard Rumelt (1982) 'Uncertain Imitability: An Analysis of Interfirm Differences in Efficiency under Competition,' *Bell Journal of Economics*, 13: 418–38.

Lipparini, Andrea and Alessandro Lomi (1996) 'Relational Structures and Strategies in Industrial Districts: An Empirical Study of Interorganizational Relations in the Modena Biomedical Industry,' Mimeo. University of Bologna.

Lorenzoni, Gianni and Charles Baden-Fuller (1993) 'Creating a Strategic Center to Manage a Web of Partners,' *California Management Review*, 3: 146–63.

Lyles, Marjorie A. (1988) 'Learning Among Joint Venture Firms,' *Management International Review*, 28: 85–97.

McDonald, Robert and Dan Siegel (1984) 'Option Pricing When the Underlying Asset Earns a Below-Equilibrium Rate of Return: A Note,' *Journal of Finance*, March: 261–5.

———— (1986) 'The Value of Waiting to Invest,' *Quarterly Journal of Economics*, 101: 707–27.

MacDuffie, John Paul (1995) 'Human Resource Bundles and Manufacturing Performance: Organizational Logic and Flexible Production Systems in the World Auto Industry,' *Industrial and Labor Relations Review*, 48: 197–221.

—— (1996) 'International Trends in Work Organization in the Auto Industry: National-Level vs. Company-Level Perspectives,' in Kirsten Wever and Lowell Turner (eds.), *The Comparative Political Economy of Industrial Relations*. Madison, WI: Industrial Relations Research Association, 71–113.

—— (1997) 'The Road to "Root Cause": Shop-Floor Problem-Solving at Three Auto Assembly Plants,' *Management Science*, 43: 479–502.

McKelvey, Bill (1983) *Organizational Systematics: Taxonomy, Evolution, Classification*. Berkeley: University of California.

—— and Howard Aldrich (1983) 'Populations, Natural Selection and Applied Organizational Science,' *Administrative Science Quarterly*, 20: 509–25.

McKenna, Chris (1999) 'Economics of Knowledge: A Theory of Management Consulting,' Mimeo, ESSEC.

Mackenzie, Donald and Graham Spinardi (1995) 'Tacit Knowledge, Weapons Design, and the Uninvention of Nuclear Weapons,' *American Journal of Sociology*, 101: 44–99.

Majd, Saman and Robert Pindyck (1987) 'Time to Build, Option Value, and Investment Decisions,' *Journal of Financial Economics*, 18: 7–27.

Manière, Philippe (1999) *Marx à la Corbeille: Quand les actionnaires font la révolution*. Paris: Stock.

Mansfield, Edwin (1985) 'How Rapidly Does New Industrial Technology Leak Out?' *Journal of Industrial Economics*, 35: 217–23.

—— (1988) 'Industrial R&D in Japan and the United States: A Comparative Study,' *The American Economic Review* 78(2): 223–8. (Papers and Proceedings of the One-Hundredth Annual Meeting of the American Economic Association, May).

—— Mark Schwartz, and Samuel Wagner (1981) 'Imitation Costs and Patents: An Empirical Study,' *Economic Journal* (December) 91(364): 907–18.

March, James (1991) 'Exploration and Exploitation in Organizational Learning,' *Organization Science*, 2: 71–87.

—— and Herbert Simon (1958) *Organizations*. New York: John Wiley.

Marshall, Alfred (1920) *Industry and Trade*. London: Macmillan.

Marston, Richard (1989) 'Pricing to Market in Japanese Manufacturing,' *Journal of International Economics*, 29: 217–36.

Mason, Scot and Robert, Merton (1985) 'The Role of Contingent Claims Analysis in Corporate Finance,' in E. Altman and M. Subrahmanyam (eds.), *Recent Advances in Corporate Finance*. New York: Irwin.

Matsushita, Electric Industrial (MEI) (1987) *European Institute of Business Administration (INSEAD)*. Boston: Harvard Business School.

Mazzoleni, Roberto and R. R. Nelson (1998) 'Economic Theories about the Benefits and Costs of Patents,' *Journal of Economic Issues*, 32(4): 1031–52.

Mead, W. (1967) 'Competitive Significance of Joint Ventures,' *Antitrust Bulletin*, 12: 819–51.

Merges, Robert (1999a), 'Who Owns the Charles Bridge? Intellectual Property and Competition in the Software Industry,' Working Paper, University of California, Berkeley.

—— (1999b), 'Institutions for Intellectual Property Transactions: The Case of Patent Pools,' Working Paper, University of California, Berkeley.

Merton, Robert (1949) '*Social Theory and Social Structure: Toward the Codification of Theory and Research*. Glencoe, IL: Free Press.

—— (1973) 'Theory of Rational Option Pricing,' *Bell Journal of Economics and Management Science*, 41–83.

—— (1976) 'Option Pricing When Underlying Stock Returns are Discontinuous,' *Journal of Financial Economics*, Jan./March, 3: 125–44.

—— (1990) 'On the Mathematics and Economics Assumptions of Continuous-time Models,' *Continuous Time Finance*. Cambridge, MA: Basil Blackwell, 57–96.

Meyer, John, J. Boli, G. M. Thomas, and F. O. Ramirez (1997), 'World Society and the Nation-State,' *American Journal of Sociology*, 103: 144–81.

Miles, Raymond and Charles Snow (1978) '*Organizational Strategy, Structure and Process*. New York: McGraw-Hill.

Milgram, Stanley (1974) *Obedience to Authority: An Experimental View*. New York: Harper & Row.

Milgrom, P. and J. Roberts (1990) 'The Economics of Modern Manufacturing: Technology, Strategy and Organization', *American Economic Review*, 80: 511–23.

Miller, George (1956) 'The Magical Number Seven, Plus or Minus Two,' *The Psychological Review*, 63: 81–97.

Miller, D. (1996) 'Configurations Revisited,' *Strategic Management Journal*, 17: 505–12.

Minsky, Marvin (1985) '*The Society of Mind*. New York: Simon & Schuster.

Mintzberg, Henry (1973) '*The Nature of Management Work*. New York: Harper & Row.

—— (1990) 'Strategy Formulation: Schools of Thought,' in J. Fredrickson (ed.), *Perspectives on Strategic Management*. New York: Harper Business.

Mitchell, W. (1989) 'Whether and When? Probability and Timing of Incumbent's Entry into Emerging Industrial Subfields,' *Administrative Science Quarterly*, 34: 208.

Mitchell, G. R. and W. F. Hamilton (1988) 'Managing R&D as a Strategic Option,' *Research-Technology*, 31: 15–22.

Mockus, A., Fielding, R. T., and Herbsleb, J. (2000) 'A Case Study of Open Source Software Development: The Apache Server,' Proceedings of the 22nd International Conference on Software Engineering, pp. 263–72.

Monteverde, K. and D. Teece (1982) 'Supplier Switching Costs and Vertical Integration in the Automobile Industry,' *Bell Journal of Economics*, 13: 206–13.

Moore, Gordon E. (1986) '*Entrepreneurship and Innovation: The Electronic Industry*,' ed. by R. Landau and N. Rosenberg. Washington, DC: Positive Sum Strategy, National Academy Press.

Moutet, Aimée (1992) 'La Rationalisation Industrielle dans l'économie Française au XXeme siècle,' Etude sur les rapports entre changements d'organisation technique et problèmes sociaux (1900–1939), thèse de doctorat d'Etat.

Myers, Stewart (1977) 'Determinants of Corporate Borrowing,' *Journal of Financial Economics*, 5: 147–76.

—— (1984) 'Finance Theory and Financial Strategy', *Interfaces*, 14: 126–37.

Narin, Francis, Elliot Noma, and Ross Perry (1987) 'Patents as Indicators of Technological Strength,' *Research Policy*, 16: 143–55.

Nee, Victor (1992) 'Organizational Dynamics of Market Transition: Hybrid Forms, Property Rights and Mixed Economy in China,' *Administrative Science Quarterly*, 37: 1–27.

Nelson, Richard (1956) 'A Theory of the Low-Level Equilibrium Trap in Underdeveloped Economies,' *American Economic Review*, 46: 894–908.

—— (1993) *National Innovation Systems: A Comparative Analysis*. New York: Oxford University Press.

—— and S. Winter (1982a) 'The Role of Knowledge in R & D Efficiency,' *Quarterly Journal of Economics*, 96: 453–70.

—— —— (1982b) *An Evolutionary Theory of Economic Change*. Cambridge: Belknap Press.

Nickerson, Jackson and Todd Zenger (2006) 'Envy, Comparison Costs, and the Economic Theory of the Firm,' March 20, 2006. Available at: http://ssrn.com/abstract=898873

Nohria, N. and C. Garcia-Pont (1991) 'Global Strategic Linkages and Industry Structure,' *Strategic Management Journal* (Summer Special Issue), 12: 105–24.

Nooteboom, Bart (1999) 'Learning, Innovation and Industrial Organization,' *Cambridge Journal of Economics*, 23: 127–50.

North, Douglass (1990) *Institutions, Institutional Change, and Economic Performance*. New York: Cambridge University Press.

—— and Robert Thomas (1973) *The Rise of the Western World: A New Economic History*. Cambridge: Cambridge University Press.

Novick, M. and G. Lewis (1967) 'Coefficient Alpha and the Reliability of Composite Measurements,' *Psychometrica*, 32: 1–13.

Nunnally, Jum (1978) '*Psychometric Theory*, 2nd edn. New York: McGraw Hill.

Ochsner, Kevin and Matthew Lieberman (2001) 'The Emergence of Social Cognitive Neuroscience,' *American Psychologist*, 56: 717–34.

Ohmae, Kenichi (1982) '*The Mind of the Strategist: The Art of Japanese Business*'. New York: McGraw-Hill.

Ordover, J. A. and R. D. Willig (1985) 'Antitrust for High-Technology Industries: Assessing Research Joint Ventures and Mergers,' *Journal of Law and Economics*, 28: 311–43.

Ortmann, Andreas and Gerd Gigerenzer (1997) 'Reasoning in Economics and Psychology: Why Social Context Matters,' *Journal of Institutional and Theoretical Economics*, 153: 700–10.

Osterloh, Margit and Bruno S. Frey (2000) 'Motivation, Knowledge Transfer, and Organizational Forms,' *Organization Science* (September/October) 11(5): 538.

Ostrom, Elinor (1990) '*Governing the Commons: The Evolution of Institutions for Collective Action*. Cambridge: Cambridge University Press.

—— J. Walker, and R. Gardner (1992) 'Covenants With and Without a Sword: Self-governance Is Possible,' *American Political Science Review*, 86(2): 404–17.

Ouchi, William G. *Theory Z: How American Business Can Meet the Japanese Challenge*. Reading, MA: Addison-Wesley.

Pack, Howard and Larry E. Westphal (1986) 'Industrial Strategy and Technological Change: Theory vs. Reality,' *Journal of Development Economics*, 22: 87–128.

Padgett, John and Chris Ansell (1993) 'Robust Action and the Rise of the Medici, 1400–1434,' *American Journal of Sociology*, 98: 1259–1319.

Padioleau, Jean (1981) *Quand la France s'enferre*. Paris: Presses Universitaire de France.

Palmer, Donald and X. Zhou (1993) 'Late Adoption of the Multidivisional Form by large U.S. Corporations: Institutional, Political and Economic Accounts,' *Administrative Science Quarterly*, 38: 100–31.

—— Devereaux J., and M. Powers (1987) 'The Economics and Politics of Structure: The Multi-divisional Form and the Large US Corporations,' *Administration Science Quarterly*, 32: 25–48.

Papert, Seymour (1979) 'Computers and Learning,' in M. Dertouzos and J. Moses (eds.), *The Computer Age: A Twenty-Year View*. Cambridge, MA: MIT Press.

Parker, Mike (1985) *Inside the Circle: A Union Guide to QWL*. Boston: South End Press.

Pate, J. L (1969) 'Joint Venture Activity, 1960–1968,' *Economic Review*, Federal Research Bank of Cleveland, pp. 16–23.

Pavitt, Keith (1985) 'Technology Transfer Among the Industrially Advanced Countries An Overview,' in Nathan Rosenberg and Claudio Frischtak (eds.), *International Technology Transfer Concepts, Measures, and Comparisons*. New York: Praeger.

Penrose, Edith ([1959] 1995) *The Theory of the Growth of the Firm*. Oxford: Oxford University Press.

Pfeffer, Jeffrey (1998) '*The Human Equation: Building Profits by Putting People First*. Boston: HBS Press.

—— and N. Langton (1993) 'The Effect of Wage Dispersion on Satisfaction, Productivity, and Working Collaboratively: Evidence from College and University Faculty,' *Administrative Science Quarterly*, 38: 382–407.

—— and P. Nowak (1976) 'Joint Ventures and Interorganizational Interdependence,' *Administrative Science Quarterly*, 21: 315–39.

Phelps, E. A., K. J. O'Conner, W. A. Cunningham et al. (2000) 'Performance on Indirect Measures of Race Evaluation Predicts Amygdala Activation,' *Journal of Cognitive Neuroscience*, 12(5): 729–38.

Piaget, Jean (1948) '*The Moral Judgment of the Child*. Glencoe, IL: Free Press.

Pil, Frits and J.P. MacDuffie (1996) 'The Adoption of High-Involvement Work Practices,' *Industrial Relations*, 35: 423–55.

Pindyck, Robert (1988) 'Irreversible Commitment, Capacity Choice, and the Value of the Firm,' *American Economic Review*, 78: 967–85.

—— (1991) 'Irreversibility, Uncertainty and Investment,' *Journal of Economic Literature*, 29: 1110–48.

Piore, Michael (1985) 'Introduction,' in P. Doeringer and M. Piore (eds.), *Internal Labor Markets and Manpower Analysis*. New York: M. E. Sharpe Inc.

—— (1995) *Beyond Individualism*. Cambridge, MA: Harvard University Press.

Piore, M. J. and C. F. Sabel (1984) *The Second Industrial Divide: Possibilities for Prosperity*. New York: Basic Books.

Podolny, Joel and Toby Stuart (1995) 'A Role-Based Ecology of Technological Change,' *American Journal of Sociology*, 100: 1224–60.

—— and Andrea Shepherd (1996) 'When are Technological Spillovers Local? Patent Citation Patterns in the Semiconductor Industry?' Working Paper, Stanford University, Stanford, CA.

Polanyi Michael (1966) *The Tacit Dimension*. New York: Anchor Day Books.

Ponssard, Jean-Pierre (ed.) (2000) *Montée en Puissance des Fonds d'investissemeet étrangers et impacts sur la gestion des enterprises industrielles*. Paris: Digitip, CPCI Etude FIE.

Porter, Michael (1980) *Competitive Strategy: Techniques for Analyzing Industries and Competitors*. New York: Free Press.

Postrel, S. (2002) 'Islands of Shared Knowledge: Specialization and Mutual Understanding in Problem-Solving Teams,' *Organization Science*, 13(3): 303–20.

Powell, William (1990) 'Neither Market nor Hierarchy: Network Forms of Organization,' *Research in Organizational Behavior*, 12: 295–336.

—— K. Koput, and L. Smith-Doerr (1996) 'Interoganizational Collaboration and the Locus of Innovation: Networks of Learning in Biotechnology,' *Administrative Science Quarterly*, 41: 116–45.

Prahalad, C. K. and Yves Doz (1987) *The Multinational Mission*. New York: Free Press.

—— and Gary Hamel (1990) 'The Core Competence of the Corporation,' *Harvard Business Review*, May–June. 79–91.

Prais, S.J (1976) *The Evolution of Giant Firms in Britain: A Study of the Growth of Concentration in Manufacturing Industry in Britain, 1909–70*. New York: Cambridge University Press.

Priem, Richard and John Butler (2001a) 'Is the Resource-Based 'View' a Useful Perspective for Strategic Management Research?' *Academy of Management Review*, 26: 22–40.

—— —— (2001b) 'Tautology in the Resource-Based View and the Implications of Externally Determined Ressource Value: Further Comments,' *Academy of Management Review*, 26: 57–66.

Pringle, John W. (1951) 'On the Parallel Between Learning and Evolution,' *Behavior*, 3: 175–215.

Raff, Daniel (1988) 'Wage Determination Theory and the Five-dollar Day at Ford,' *Journal of Economic History*, 48: 387–99.

—— and Timothy Bresnahan (1997) 'Plant Shutdown Behavior During the Great Depression and the Structure of the American Motor Vehicle Industry,' *Journal of Economic History*.

Ragin, Charles C. (1987) '*The Comparative Method Moving Beyond Qualitative and Quantitative Strategies*. Berkeley: University of California, Berkeley.

—— (2000) '*Fuzzy-Set Social Science*. Chicago: University of Chicago Press.

Rao, Rukmini and Linda Argote (1995) 'Collective Learning and Forgetting: The Effects of Turnover and Group Structure,' Mimeo.

—— —— (2005) 'Organizational Learning and Forgetting: The Effects of Turnover and Structure,' *European Management Review*, 3: 77–85.

Rapoport, Anatol (1957) 'Contributions to the Theory of Random and Biased Nets,' *Bulletin of Mathematical Biophysics*, 19: 257–77.

Raymond, Eric S. (1998) '*The Cathedral and the Bazaar*. Available at: http://www.tuxedo.org/~esr/writings/cathedral-bazaar/

Reber, Arthur (1993) *Implicit Learning and Tacit Knowledge: An Essay on the Cognitive Unconscious*. New York: Oxford University Press.

Reed, Richard and Robert DeFillippi (1990) 'Causal Ambiguity, Barriers to Imitation, and Sustainable Competitive Advantage,' *Academy of Management Review*, 15(1): 88–102.

Reynolds, J. I. (1984) 'The Pinched Shoe Effect on International Joint Ventures,' *Columbia Journal of World Business*, 19: 23–9.

Richeson, J. A., A. A. Baird, H. L. Gordon et al. (2003) 'An fMRI Investigation of the Impact of Interracial Contact on Executive Function,' *Nature Neuroscience*, 6(12): 1323–8.

Rizzolatti, Giacomo, Leonardo Fogassi, and Vittorio Galese (2006) 'Mirrors of the Mind,' *Scientific American*, 295(5): 54–61.

Rivkin, Jan (2000) 'Imitation of Complex Strategies,' *Management Science*, 46(6): 824–45.

Rob, Rafael and Peter Zemsky (2002) 'Social Capital, Corporate Culture, and Incentive Intensity,' *Rand Journal of Economics*, 22: 243–57.

Roberts, John (2004) *The Modern Firm: Organizational Design for Performance and Growth*. Oxford: Oxford University Press.

Rogers, Everett M. (1980) *Communication Networks: Toward a New Paradigm for Research*. New York: Free Press.

—— (1983) *The Diffusion of Innovations*, 3rd edn. New York: Free Press.

—— and Judith Larsen (1984) *Silicon Valley Fever*. New York: Basic Books.

Rosch, Eleanor (1978) 'Principles of Categorization,' in Eleanor Rosch and B. B. Lloyd (eds.), *Cognition and Categorization*. Hillsdale, NJ: Lawrence Erlbaum Associates.

Rosenberg, Nathan (1976) *Perspectives on Technology*. Cambridge: Cambridge University Press.

—— (1987) *Learning By Using: Inside the Black Box*. Cambridge: Cambridge University Press.

—— (1994) 'How the Developed-Countries Became Rich,' *DAEDALUS* (Fall) 123(4): 127–40.

Roth, Alvin and Françoise Schoumaker (1983) 'Expectations and Reputations in Bargaining,' *American Economic Review*, 73: 362–72.

Rousseau, Denise M. and Sandra L. Robinson (1994) 'Violating the Social Contract: Not the Exception but the Norm,' *Journal of Organizational Behavior*, 3: 245–59.

Rowley, Timothy, David Behrens, and D. Krackhardt (2000) 'Redundant Governance Structures: An Analysis of Structural and Relational Embeddedness in the Steel and Semiconductor Industries,' *Strategic Management Journal* (Special Issue), 21: 369–86.

Rukmini, Devadas Rao and Linda Argote (2006) 'Organizational Learning and Forgetting: The Effects of Turnover and Structure,' *European Management Review*, 3: 77–85.

Rumelt, Richard P. (1974) '*Strategy, Structure and Economic Performance*. Boston: Graduate School of Business, Harvard University.

—— (1984) 'Towards a Strategic Theory of the Firm,' in Robert Boyden Lamb (ed.), *Competitive Strategic Management*. Englewood Cliffs, NJ: Prentice-Hall, Inc.

Ryle, Gilbert (1949) *The Concept of Mind*. London: Hutchinson.

Sabel, Charles (1996) 'Learning by Monitoring: The Institutions of Economic Development,' in N. Smelser and R. Swedberg (eds.), *The Handbook of Economic Sociology*. Princeton: Princeton University Press, 137–65.

Sacks, Oliver (1985) *The Man Who Mistook his Wife for a Hat and Other Clinical Tales*. New York: Summit Books.

Sanfey Alan G., James K. Rilling, Jessica A. Aronson, Leigh E. Nystrom, and Jonathan D. Cohen (2003) 'The Neural Basis of Economic Decision-Making in the Ultimatum Game,' *Science*, 300: 1755–8.

Sassen, Saskia (1998) *Globalization and its Discontents*. New York: New Press.

Saxenian, Anna Lee (1994) *Regional Advantage: Culture and Competition in Silicon Valley and Route 128*. Cambridge, MA: Harvard University Press.

—— (1999) *Silicon Valley's New Immigrant Entrepreneurs*. San Francisco: Public Policy Institute of California.

Schaede, Ulrike (1995) 'The "Old Boy" Network and Government-Business Relationships in Japan,' *Journal of Japanese Studies*, 21: 293–317.

Schein, Edgar (1956) 'The Chinese Indoctrinational Program for Prisoners of War: A Study of Attempted "Brainwashing"', *Journal for the Study of Interpersonal Processes*, 19: 149–72.

Schelling, Thomas (1960) *The Strategy of Conflict*. Cambridge, MA: Harvard University Press.

Scherer, F. M. (1965) 'Firm Size, Market Structure, Opportunity, and the Output of Patented Inventions, *American Economic Review* (December) 55(5): 1097.

—— (1967) 'Research and Development Resource Allocation under Rivalry,' *Quarterly Journal of Economics*, 81: 359–94.

Schmookler, Jacob (1966) *Invention and Economic Growth*. Cambridges, MA: Harvard University Press.

Schonberger, Richard J. (1982) *Japanese Manufacturing Techniques: Nine Hidden Lessons in Simplicity*. New York: The Free Press.

Schumpeter, Joseph ([1911] 1934) *The Theory of Economic Development*. Cambridge, MA: Harvard University Press.

—— (1942) *Capitalism, Socialism, and Democracy*. New York: Harper & Brothers.

Scott, A.J. (1993) *Technopolis: High-Technology Industry and Regional Development in Southern California*. California: University of California Press.

Searle, John (1995) *The Construction of Social Reality*. New York: The Free Press.

Selznick, Philip (1957) *Leadership in Administration: A Sociological Interpretation*. Evanston, IL: Row, Peterson.

Sengenberger, Werner (1992) 'Lean Production: The Way of Working and Producing in the Future?' Paper given at the Labour in a Changing World Economy Forum, International Institute for Labour Studies, International Labour Organization.

Servan-Schreiber, Jean-Jacques (1967) *Le Défi americain*. Paris: Denoël.

Shan, Weijian (1988) 'An Analysis of Organizational Strategies by Enterpreneurial High-Technology Firms,' working paper, Sol C. Sinder Enterpreneurial Center, Wharton School, University of Pennsylvania.

Shang, Jen and Rachel Croson (2006) 'Field Experiments in Charitable Contribution: The Impact of Social Influence on the Voluntary Provision of Public Goods. *mimeo*. Wharton, University of Pennsylvania.

Shannon, C.E. and W. Weaver (1949) *The Mathematical Theory of Communication*. Urbana: University of Illinois Press.

Sharp, David (1987) 'Control Systems and Decision-making in Multinational Firms: Price Management Under Floating Exchange Rates,' Ph.D. Thesis, Massachusetts Institute of Technology, Cambridge, MA.

Shepherd, William (1976) *Public Enterprise: Economic Analysis of Theory and Practice*. Lexington, MA: Lexington Books.

Shonfield, Andrew (1965) *Modern Capitalism: the Changing Balance of Public and Private Power*. New York: Oxford University Press.

—— (1969) *Modern Capitalism: The Changing Balance of Public and Private Power*. Oxford: Oxford University Press.

Siggelkow, Nicolaj (2001) 'Change in the Presence of Fit: The Rise, the Fall, and the Renaissance of Liz Claiborne,' *Academy of Management Journal*, 44(4): 838–57.

Simon, Herbert A. (1957) *Models of Man: Social and Rational; Mathematical Essays on Rational Human Behavior in a Social Setting*. New York: Wiley.

Simons, T. and P. Ingram (1997) 'Organization and Ideology: Kibbutzim and Hired Labor, 1951–1965,' *Administrative Science Quarterly*, 42: 784–813.

—— ([1962] 1979) 'The Architecture of Complexity,' *The Sciences of the Artificial*. Cambridge, MA: MIT Press.

—— (1992) *The Sciences of the Artificial*. Cambridge: MIT Press.

Singer, T., S. J. Kiebel, J. S. Winston, R. J. Dolan, and C. D. Frith (2004) 'Brain Responses to the Acquired Moral Status of Faces,' *Neuron*, 41: 653–62.

Singley, Mark and John Anderson (1989) *The Transfer of Cognitive Skill*. Cambridge, MA: Harvard Press.

Skocpol, Theda (1979) *States and Social Revolutions: A Comparative Analysis of France, Russia, and China*. New York: Cambridge University Press.

Smith, Adam (1965) *The Wealth of Nations*. New York: Modern Library.

Soskice, David (1990) 'Wage Determination: The Changing Role of Institutions in Advanced Industrialized Countries,' *Oxford Review of Economic Policy*, 6: 36–61.

Spender, J. C. (1989) *Industry Recipes: The Nature and Sources of Managerial Judgement*. Oxford: Basil Blackwell.

Squire, Larry (1987) *Memory and the Brain*. New York: Oxford University Press.

Starbuck, William (1992) 'Learning by Knowledge-Intensive Firms,' *Journal of Management Studies*, 29: 713–40.

Stark, David (1996) 'Recombinant Property in East European Capitalism,' *American Journal of Sociology*, 101: 993–1027.

—— and László Bruszt (1998) *Postsocialist Pathways: Transforming Politics and Property in East Central Europe*. Cambridge: Cambridge University Press.

Steinbrunner John (1974) *The Cybernetic' Theory of Decision*. Princeton, NJ: Princeton University Press.

Stewart, George (1983) 'A Proposal for Measuring International Performance,' *Midland Corporate Finance Journal*, 1: 56–71.

Stigler, Georges (1951) 'The Division of Labor is Limited by the Extent of the Market,' *Journal of Political Economy*, June: 185–93.

Stobaugh, Robert (1988) *Innovation and Competition*. Cambridge: MA: Harvard Business School Press.

Stuart, Leslie and Robert Kargon (1996) 'Selling Silicon Valley: Frederick Terman's Model for Regional Advantage,' *Business History Review*, 70: 435–72.

Stuart, Toby, Ha Hoang, and Ralph C. Hybels (1999) 'Interorganizational Endorsements and the Performance of Entrepreneurial Ventures,' *Administrative Science Quarterly*, 44: 315–49.

Stuckey, John. A. (1983) *Vertical Integration and Joint Ventures in the Aluminum Industry.* Cambridge, MA: Harvard University Press.

Suzuki, Yoshitaka (1991) *Japanese Management Structures,* 1920–80. New York: St. Martin's Press.

Szulanski, Gabriel (1995a) 'Appropriating Rents from Existing Knowledge: Intra-Firm Transfer of Best Practice,' Ph.D. thesis, INSEAD, UMI Number 9600790.

—— (1995b) 'Unpacking Stickiness: An Empirical Investigation of the Barriers to Transfer Best Practice Inside the Firm,' Academy of Management Best Paper proceedings.

—— (1997) 'Exploring Internal Stickiness Impediments to the Transfer of Best Practice Within the Firm,' *Strategic Management Journal* (Summer) 17: 27–43.

Tajfel, Henri, M. Billig, R. Bundy, and C. Flament (1971) 'Social Categorization and Intergroup Behavior,' *European Journal of Social Psychology*, 2: 149–78.

Tal, Simons and Paul Ingram (1997) 'Organization and Ideology: Kibbutzim and Hired Labor, 1951–1965,' *Administrative Science Quarterly*, 42: 784–814.

Taylor, Donald and Vaishna Jaggi (1974) 'Ethnocentrism and Causal Attribution in a South Indian Context,' *Journal of Cross-Cultural Psychology*, 5: 162–71.

Teece, David (1977) 'Technology Transfer by Multinational Firms,' *Economic Journal*, 87: 242–61.

—— (1980) 'Economies of Scope and the Scope of an Enterprise,' *Journal of Economic Behavior and Organization*, 1: 223–47.

—— (1981a) 'Internal Organization and Economic Performance: An Empirical Analysis of the Profitability of Principal Firms,' *Journal of Industrial Economics*, 30: 173–99.

—— (1981b) 'The Market for Know-How and the Efficient International Transfer of Technology,' *The Annals of the American Academy of Political and Social Science*, 458: 81–96.

—— (1982) 'Towards an Economic Theory of the Multiproduct Firm,' *Journal of Economic Behavior and Organization*, 3: 39–63.

—— (1987) 'Profiting from Technological Innovation: Implications for Integration, Collaboration, Licensing and Public Policy,' in D. Teece (ed.), *The Competitive Challenge-Strategies for Industrial Innovation and Renewal*, Cambridge, MA: Ballinger, 185–220.

—— Richard Rumelt, Giovani Dosi, and Sid Winter (1994) 'Understanding Corporate Coherence: Theory and Evidence,' *Journal of Economic Behavior and Organization*, 23: 1–30.

—— Gary Pisano, and Amy Shuen (1997) 'Dynamic Capabilities and Strategic Management,' *Strategic Management Journal*, 18: 509–34.

Thompson, Peter and Melanie Fox-Kean (2005). 'Patent Citations and the Geography of Knowledge Spillovers: A Reassessment,' *American Economic Review*, 95: 450–60.

Tidd, Joe, John Bessant, and Keith Pavitt (2001) *Managing Innovation: Integrating Technological, Market and Organizational Change*, 2nd edn. New York: Wiley.

Tilly, Charles (1984) *Big Structures, Large Processes, Huge Comparisons*. New York: Russell Sage Foundation.

—— (1998) *Durable Inequality*. Berkeley: University of California Press.

Titmuss, Richard M. (1971) *The Gift Relationship: From Human Blood to Social Policy*. New York: Pantheon.

Topkis, Donald (1999) *Complementarities and Supermodularity*. Princeton, NJ: Princeton University Press.

Trajtenberg, Manuel (1990) 'A Penny for Your Quotes', *Rand Journal of Economy*, 21: 172–87.

Tushman, Michael (1977) 'Special Boundary Roles in the Innovation Process,' *Administrative Science Quarterly*, 22: 587–605.

—— and Philip Anderson (1986) 'Technological Discontinuities and Organizational Environments,' *Administrative Science Quarterly*, 31: 439–65.

Tversky, Amos and Daniel Kahneman (1971) 'Belief in the Law of Small Numbers,' *Psychological Bulletin*, 2: 105–10.

—— —— (1982) 'Evidential Impact of Base Rates,' in D. Kahneman, P. Slovic, and A.Tversky (eds.), *Judgement under Uncertainty: Heuristics and Biases*. Cambridge: Cambridge University Press.

Tyre, Marcie (1991) 'Managing the Introduction of New Process Technology International Differences in a Multi-Plant Network,' *Research Policy*, 20: 57–76.

Useem, Michael (1996a) 'Corporate Restructuring and the Restructured World of Senior Management,' in P. Osterman (ed.), *Broken Ladders: Managerial Careers in the New Economy*. New York: Oxford. 23–54.

—— (1996b) *Investor Capitalism: How Money Managers are Changing the Face of Corporate America*. New York: Basic Books.

Usher, Abbot (1971) 'Technical Change and Capital Formation,' in Nathan Rosenberg (ed.), *The Economics of Technological Change*. Harmondsworth: Penguin.

Uzzi, Brian (1996), 'The Sources and Consequences of Embeddedness for the Economic Performance of Organizations: The Network Effect,' *American Sociological Review*, 61: 674–98.

Van Maanen, John and Stephen Barley (1984) 'Occupational Communities: Cultural and Control in Organizations,' *Research in Organizational Behavior*, 6: 287–365.

Vernon, Raymond (1983) 'Organizational and Institutional Responses to International Risk,' in R. Herring (ed.), *Managing International Risk*. New York: Cambridge University Press.

Vickers, John Stuart (1985) 'Pre-emptive Patenting, Joint Ventures, and the Persistence of Oligopoly,' *International Journal of Industrial Organization*, 3: 261–73.

Von Hippel, Eric (1988) *The Sources of Innovation*. New York: Oxford University Press.

Wagner, Richard K. and Robert J. Sternberg (1987) 'Tacit Knowledge in Managerial Success', *Journal of Business and Psychology*, 1: 301–12.

Walker, Gordon (1998) 'Strategy and Network Formation,' in J. Baum and H. Rao (eds.), *Advances in Strategic Management*. Greenwich, CT: JAI Press, pp. 149–65.

—— and Douglas Weber (1984) 'A Transaction Cost Approach to Make or Buy Decisions,' *Administrative Science Quarterly*, 29: 373–91.

—— Bruce Kogut, and Weijian Shan (1997) 'Social Capital, Structural Holes and the Formation of an Industry Network,' *Organization Science*, 8: 109–25.

Wallmark, Torsten and Douglas McQueen (1986) *100 viktiga suenska innovationer under tiden 1945–1980*. Lund, Sweden: Studentlitteratur.

Wasserman, Stanley and Katherine Faust (1994) *Social Network Analysis: Methods and Applications*. New York: Cambridge University Press.

Watts, Duncan and Steven Strogatz (1998) 'Collective Dynamics of "Small-world" Networks,' *Science*, 393: 440–2.

Weber, Max ([1922] 1968) *Economy and Society*, ed. G. Ruth and C. Wittich. Berkeley, CA: University of California Press.

Weber, Roberto A. (2006) 'Managing Growth to Achieve Efficient Coordination in Large Groups,' *American Economic Review*, 96(1): 114–26.

Weick, Karl and Karlene Roberts (1993) 'Collective Mind in Organizations: Heedful Interrelating on Flight Decks,' *Administrative Science Quarterly*, 38: 357–81.

Weil, Thierry (2000) *'Why and How European Companies Reach out to the Silicon Valley*, No. 25. Paris: Institut Français des Relations Internationales.

Wells, Louis T. and John Stopford (1972) *Managing the Multinational Enterprise*. New York: Basic Books.

Wernerfelt, Birger (1984) 'A Resource-Based View of the Firm,' *Strategic Management Journal*, 5: 171–80.

—— and Aneel Karnani (1987) 'Competitive Strategy under Uncertainty,' *Strategic Management Journal*, 8: 187–94.

Westney, D. E. (1987) *Imitation and Innovation: The Transfer of Western Organizational Patterns to Meiji Japan*. Cambridge, MA: Harvard University Press.

Westney, Eleanor (1993) 'Country Patterns in R&D Organization: The United States and Japan,' in Bruce Kogut (ed.), *Country Competitiveness: Technology and the Organizing of Work*. New York: Oxford University Press, 36–53.

Westphal, Larry, Linsy Kim, and Carl Johan Dahlman (1985) 'Reflections on the Republic of Korea's Acquisition of Technological Capability,' in Nathan Rosenberg and Claudio Frischtak (eds.), *International Technology Transfer*. New York: Praeger.

White, Harrison (1963) *An Anatomy of Kinship*. Prentice-Hall, Englewood Cliffs, NJ.

—— (1970) *Chains of Opportunity: System Models of Mobility in Organizations*. Cambridge, MA: Harvard University Press.

—— (1992) *Identity and Control: A Structural Theory of Social Action*. Princeton, NJ: Princeton University Press.

Whittington, Richard and Michael Mayer (2000) The European Corporation', *Strategy, Structure, and Social Science*. Oxford: Oxford University Press.

Whyte, William H. (1956) *The Organization Man*. New York: Simon & Schuster.

Williamson, Oliver, E. (1975) *Markets and Hierarchies: Analysis and Antitrust Implications*. Basic Books, New York.

—— (1981) 'The Economics of Organization: The Transaction Cost Approach,' *American Journal of Sociology*, 87: 548–77.

—— (1985) *The Economic Institutions of Capitalism*. New York: Free Press.

Windolf, Paul (2001) *Corporate Networks in Europe and the United States*. New York: Cambridge University Press.

Winter, Sidney (1987) 'Knowledge and Competence as Strategic Assets,' in D. Teece (ed.) *The Competitive Challenge—Strategies for Industrial Innovation and Renewal*. Cambridge, MA: Ballinger.

Wolf, B.M. and S. Globerman (1992) 'Strategic Alliances in the Automotive Industry: Motives and Implications,' Working Paper No. 62, Ontario Centre for International Business.

Womack, James, Daniel T. Jones, and Daniel Roos (1990) The *Machine That Changed the World*. New York: Rawson Associates.

Yergin, Daniel and Joseph Stanislaw (1998) *The Commanding Heights*. New York: Simon & Schuster.

Yourdon, Edward (1996) *Rise and Resurrection of the American Programmer*. Upper Saddle River, NJ: Prentice Hall.

Zadeh, Lotfi A. (1972) 'A Fuzzy Set Interpretation of Linguistics Hedges,' *Journal of Cybernetics*, 2: 4–34.

Zaheer, Akbar and Srilata Zaheer (1997) 'Catching the Wave: Alertness, Responsiveness, and Market Influence in Global Electronic Networks,' *Management Science*, 43: 1493–509.

Zander, Udo (1991) *Exploiting a Technological Edge-Voluntary and Involuntary Dissemination of Technology*. Stockholm, Sweden: IIB.

—— and Bruce Kogut (1995) 'Knowledge and the Speed of the Transfer and Imitation of Organizational Capabilities: An Empirical Test,' *Organization Science*, 6: 76–92.

Zak, Paul, Robert Kurzban, and William Matzner (2005) 'Oxytocin is Associated with Human Trustworthiness,' *Hormones and Behavior*, 48: 522–7.

Zeitlin, Jonathan and Gary Herrigel (eds.) (2000) *Americanization and its Limits*. Oxford: Oxford University Press.

Zelitzer, Viviana (1978) 'Human Values and the Market: The Case of Life Insurance and Death in19th-Century America,' *American Journal of Sociology*, 84: 591–610.

Ziman, John (1978) *Reliable Knowledge*. Cambridge: Cambridge University Press.

Zucker, Lynne and Michael Darby (1995) 'Present at the Revolution: Transformation of Technical Identity for a Large Incumbent Pharmaceutical Firm After the Biotechnology Breakthrough,' NBER Working Paper 5243, Cambridge, MA.

—— —— and Marilynn Brewer (1994) 'Intellectual Capital and the Birth of US Biotechnology Enterprises,' NBER Working Paper No. 4653, Cambridge, MA.

Zuckerman, Ezra W. (1999) 'The Categorical Imperative: Securities Analysts and the Illegitimacy Discount,' *The American Journal of Sociology*, 104: 1398–438.

☐ INDEX

Note: page numbers in *italic* refer to tables.